WELLINGTON'S OPERATIONS IN THE PENINSULA

MAP OF SPAIN & PORTUGAL to illustrate the CAMPAIGNS OF 1808 ETC.

A. K. JOHNSTON, F.R.G.S.

To face title-page of Captain Butler's "Wellington's Operations in the Peninsula."—(Vol. I.)

Wellington's Operations in the Peninsula

1808–1814

By
Captain Lewis Butler
Late King's Royal Rifle Corps

WITH SKETCH MAPS

IN TWO VOLUMES

VOLUME ONE

The Naval & Military Press Ltd

published in association with

**FIREPOWER
The Royal Artillery Museum**
Woolwich

Published by
The Naval & Military Press Ltd
Unit 10 Ridgewood Industrial Park,
Uckfield, East Sussex,
TN22 5QE England
Tel: +44 (0) 1825 749494
Fax: +44 (0) 1825 765701
www.naval-military-press.com

in association with

FIREPOWER
The Royal Artillery Museum, Woolwich
www.firepower.org.uk

In reprinting in facsimile from the original, any imperfections are inevitably reproduced and the quality may fall short of modern type and cartographic standards.

Printed and bound by Antony Rowe Ltd, Eastbourne

Preface

ALTHOUGH many apologies are required on behalf of the writer, none should be necessary for the repetition of the story of the most successful campaigns ever waged by the British Army.

This work is intended only to give a sketch of the operations in the Peninsula to those who have not leisure to study Napier's incomparable classic, and to furnish certain points of military detail which are either omitted or, at all events, not prominently brought forward by him. It is hoped that it may be found of some use to the military student, and not uninteresting to the general reader.

Although great care has been taken in the various estimates of the numerical strength of the opposing forces, it is difficult to arrive at anything more than an approximation of numbers. The difficulty is increased by the British custom of counting only sabres and bayonets, whereas other nations include in their reckoning officers, sergeants, drummers, artillerymen, &c., and the consequence is that numerical inferiority is often attributed to Wellington's army when he was in reality superior in numbers. For purposes of comparison, in order to make the British reckoning correspond with the

French, $\frac{1}{8}$ has been added to the known numbers of Wellington's sabres, bayonets, and artillerymen, and $\frac{1}{5}$ or $\frac{1}{6}$ to the number of sabres and bayonets only.

It is impossible to answer for the correct spelling of names of places. Almost every town or river in Spain and Portugal seems capable of being spelt in half a dozen different ways.

I beg to express my acknowledgments to Lieutenant-Colonel W. H. James, for the use of his unpublished *précis*, and to Mr. Eden Phillpotts, for a variety of kind services.

LEWIS BUTLER.

July 18, 1904.

Contents

	PAGE
PREFACE	V

PART I

CHAPTER I

Introductory 1

CHAPTER II

State of Europe—Napoleon's views on Portugal—Treaty of Fontainebleau—Junot occupies Lisbon—Affairs in Spain—Abdication of King Charles—Marshal Murat enters Madrid—Joseph Bonaparte declared King—The Spaniards rise against the French—Theatre of War—Forces available on either side—Operations of Marshal Moncey in Valencia and of General Dupont in Andalusia—Capitulation of Baylen—Joseph Bonaparte evacuates Madrid—Operations in Catalonia and Aragon—Operations of Bessières on the line of communications—His victory at Rio Seco . . 14

CHAPTER III

A deputation from the Asturias appeals to England—England eagerly responds—Her lack of forethought and statesmanship—Description of the geography of the Peninsula . 41

CONTENTS

CHAPTER IV

Sir Arthur Wellesley appointed to command a British force in the Peninsula—Choice of lines of operation—Wellesley lands in Mondego Bay and advances upon Lisbon—Fight at Roriça—Battle of Vimeiro—Arrival of Sir H. Dalrymple—Convention of Cintra 46

CHAPTER V

Views of Napoleon on the situation—Assembly of his troops—He arrives in Spain—Forces the Somosierra—Enters Madrid 75

CHAPTER VI

The British army assembled under Sir H. Dalrymple—Sir J. Moore appointed to command a force in Spain—He crosses the Portuguese frontier—His difficulties—Hears of the fall of Madrid—Forms his junction with Sir D. Baird—Advances against the enemy's line of communications—Attacked by Napoleon—Retreats—Battle of Corunna—Moore's death—Comments 92

PART II

CHAPTER VII

State of the French forces—Siege and capture of Saragossa—Soult invades Portugal—Captures Oporto—Operations of Victor 131

CHAPTER VIII

Sir J. Cradock takes command in Portugal—Is superseded by Sir A. Wellesley—State of the British forces—Wellesley advances on Oporto—Passage of the Douro—Soult driven from Portugal—Misconduct of British soldiers—Quarrel between Soult and Ney 143

CONTENTS

CHAPTER IX

Wellesley marches southward and takes post at Abrantes—Remarks on his troops, staff, and departmental arrangements—Observations of General Foy—Movements of the army—Wellesley advances against Victor—Battle of Talavera—Wellesley retires across the Tagus . . 177

CHAPTER X

Operations in Catalonia—Siege of Gerona—Wellington rebukes the Spaniards—Battle of Ocana—Victor invests Cadiz by land—Operations in Catalonia 224

CHAPTER XI

Wellington restores discipline—State of affairs in Spain—Wellington leaves the Guadiana—Posts two Divisions at Abrantes and the remainder on the Mondego . . 237

PART III

CHAPTER XII

Problem of the defence of Portugal—Measures adopted . . 252

CHAPTER XIII

Measures adopted for the defence of Portugal (*continued*)—Preparation of the Lines of Torres Vedras—Crauford commands the Light Division—Fall of Ciudad Rodrigo—Fight on the Coa 259

CHAPTER XIV

Wellington's force—Correspondence thereon with the Home Government—French "Army of Portugal"—Other French forces—Fall of Almeida—Wellington retreats—Battle of Busaco—Wellington continues his retreat on Torres Vedras 281

CONTENTS

CHAPTER XV

Occupation of the Lines of Torres Vedras . . . 309

CHAPTER XVI

Masséna retires—Takes up a position about Santarem . . 326

CHAPTER XVII

Soult advances in order to co-operate with Masséna—Captures Olivenza—Defeats Mendizabel on the Gebora—Masséna's difficulties—Retreats—Pursued by Wellington—Sufferings of both armies—Fall of Badajoz—Masséna continues his retreat 331

CHAPTER XVIII

Fight at Sabugal—Masséna evacuates Portugal—Wellington's cares 360

CHAPTER XIX

Affairs in the south—Battle of Barossa—Fall of Campo Mayor—Recaptured by Beresford, who then advances to the Guadiana—Crosses the river 372

PART IV

THE FRONTIER FORTRESSES

CHAPTER XX

Difficulties of the rival Commanders—Advance of Masséna—Battle of Fuentes d'Onoro—Retreat of the French—Escape of Brennier from Almeida—Masséna superseded by Marmont 387

CHAPTER XXI

Beresford besieges Badajoz—Battle of Albuera—Hill relieves Beresford 406

List of Sketch Maps

GENERAL MAP OF SPAIN AND PORTUGAL . *Facing title page*

THE BATTLE OF VIMEIRO 73

SIR A. WELLESLEY'S MARCH TO VIMEIRO . *Facing* 74

THE BATTLE OF CORUNNA 125

OPERATIONS IN PORTUGAL, MARCH–MAY, 1809 . *Facing* 176

THE BATTLE OF TALAVERA 201

WELLESLEY'S ROUTE TO TALAVERA . . *Facing* 220

THE BATTLE OF BUSACO 303

THE LINES OF TORRES VEDRAS 319

DEFENCE OF PORTUGAL, 1810–11 . . *Facing* 362

THE MARCH TO BAROSSA, MARCH, 1811 . . . 381

THE COUNTRY ABOUT FUENTES D'ONORO . . *Facing* 400

THE BATTLE OF ALBUERA . . . . „ 414

PART I

CHAPTER I

INTRODUCTORY

IN order to appreciate the principles governing the action of British statesmen in their dealings with Spain and Portugal, and the keen anxiety with which, since the beginning of the eighteenth century, they have watched all attempts of French intrusion into, or interference with, those countries, it is necessary to have a clear, general idea of the strategic position of the Iberian Peninsula with reference to other European States, and more particularly those of France and England.

For this purpose one cannot do better than quote the words of the great American writer, Captain Mahan: "Spain," * he says, "under good government has, and at that crisis (1793) still more had, a military situation singularly fitted to give her weight in the councils of Europe. Compact and symmetrical in shape, with an extensive seaboard not deficient in good harbours, her physical conformation and remoteness from the rest of the Continent combined to indicate that her true strength was to be found in a powerful navy, for which also her past colonial system imperiously called. Her maritime

* "Influence of the Sea Power upon the French Revolution," vol. i. p. 80.

advantages were indeed diminished by the jog which Portugal takes out of her territory and coast-line, and by the loss of Gibraltar. Lisbon, in the hands of an enemy, interposes between the arsenals of Ferrol and Cadiz, as Gibraltar does between the latter and Cartagena. But there was great compensation in the extent of her territory, in her peninsular formation, and in the difficult character of her only Continental frontier, the Pyrenees. Her position is defensively very strong; and whenever events make France the centre of European interest as they did in 1793, and as the genius of that extraordinary country continually tends to make her, the external action of Spain becomes doubly interesting. So far as natural advantages go, her military situation at the opening of the French Revolution may be defined by saying that she controlled the Mediterranean, and baffled the flank and rear of France by land. Despite Gibraltar, her action was to determine whether the British navy should or should not enter the Mediterranean; whether the wheat of Barbary and Sicily should reach the hungry people of Southern France; whether the French fleet should have Toulon; whether the French army could advance against the Germans and Piedmont, feeling secure as to the country behind it, then seething with revolt. The political condition of Italy divided, like Germany, into many petty States, not unlike Germany in having no powerful centre around which to gather, left to Spain, potentially, the control of the Mediterranean."

Of the two peoples inhabiting the Peninsula, Portugal at the period of the French Revolution had, for a century and a half, been the traditional ally of Great Britain. Spain, on the other hand, had for a much longer period been uniformly hostile to England, and usually closely connected with France. The execution of Louis XVI., however, completely altered the relations existing between the two countries. The Spanish Bourbons viewing with feelings of horror the revolutionary excesses, of which their relative had been the victim, gave vent to their feelings in no uncertain manner; and early in March, 1793, by a declaration of war, added Spain to the number of European Powers, already coalesced against France. Some fighting ensued on either extremity of the Pyrenees, and strange to say the Spanish armies at first gained an advantage and penetrated into French territory as far as St. Jean Pied de Port on the west, and Perpignan on the east. During the same year Spanish troops also took part with the British in the defence of Toulon, but behaved extremely badly, and gave the British Government a warning as to their military capacity which ought not to have remained disregarded at the crisis of 1808.* A curious instance of the arrogance so often and so conspicuously shown at the later period was given on this occasion by the appointment, without reference to the British, of a Spanish Admiral as Commander-in-Chief of the whole allied armies!

By a treaty signed at Aranjuez on the 25th of May, the British Government had rashly engaged not to make peace with France until they had obtained full restitution for the Spaniards "of all places, towns, and territories

* "The whole body of Spanish troops, full 6,000, are worse than useless. It is impossible to describe them. There never were beheld such wretches to the eye; and as for soldiers, they carry their muskets on the right or left shoulder, as it happens, and always run away, officers and men together. The Spaniards, however, claiming an equality with us at Toulon, and one of their admirals having been appointed, by the King of Spain, Commander-in-Chief of *all* the combined forces, they will not listen to any orders or any advice given by (General) O'Hara. These people are necessarily entrusted with very important posts, and the first time a serious attempt is made upon them I fear the worst is certain" ("Life and Letters of Sir Gilbert Elliot," vol. ii. p. 191).

which belonged to them at the commencement of the war, and which the enemy may have taken during its continuance." But the energy of our Spanish ally quickly evaporated. General Dugommier, after the recapture of Toulon, reorganised the French army of the Eastern Pyrenees, attacked the Spaniards in their position at Ceret, and drove them in headlong rout under the walls of the fortress of Figueras, April 30, 1794. At the other extremity of the Pyrenees, the French forces forced the heights of San Marcial, carried the entrenched camp on the Bidassoa, on the 24th July, and, following up with vigour their successes, captured the fortress of San Sebastian. By the middle of September, Spain, exhausted by the struggle, sought terms of peace, but her proposals were considered so monstrous, that the Republican Government returned no answer; except to order Dugommier to carry the position at Figueras. In the consequent assault that officer was killed. Perignon —at a later date Marshal of France—assumed the command, followed up the attack, carried the enemy's lines and captured the fortress of Figueras, November 24th. Rosas was abandoned by the Spaniards on the 7th of the following January, and winter terminated the campaign.

Meanwhile, on the western side of the Pyrenees, the Spanish chiefs had, after the fall of San Sebastian, endeavoured to excite insurrection among the people of Biscay, but with no other result than to encourage the Republicans to erect a guillotine, and do their best to imitate therewith the exploits of their compatriots at home. Their ranks thinned by disease—30,000 men are said to have died from the effects of want and exhaustion—the French troops were in no condition to pursue their successes, and indeed were laid open to the possibility of a decisive counter-stroke. Nothing, however, of the kind took place, and the Republicans, recruited at length from the interior of France, were enabled to resume the offensive in October, and to inflict a severe defeat upon their opponents in the valley of Roncesvalles. The Spaniards were now heartily sick of the war, and throughout the winter of 1794-95, negotiations for peace passed to and fro. Nothing at first came of them, but the severity of the frost having choked the graveyards and hospitals of the French, the latter, reduced from 60,000 to 25,000 effectives, were in no condition to resume hostilities on the approach of spring. At length, in June, they took the field, and early in the following month, General Moncey—well known in Spain at a later date—forced the passage of the Deva, and broke the centre of the Spanish line, driving the wings in different directions, and pursuing the left to the boundary of old Castille, with a loss of 7,000 men. But by this time the apparently interminable negotiations had come to an end, and the treaty of Bâle, signed on the 22nd of July, 1795, concluded the war.

Peace being thus restored, the relations between France and Spain soon became intimate, and on the 19th of August, 1796, by the treaty of St. Ildefonso an offensive and defensive alliance was concluded between them. By the terms of this instrument, they "mutually guaranteed to each other their dominions both in the Old and the New World, and engaged to assist each other, in case of attack, with 24,000 land troops, thirty ships of the line, and six frigates" (Alison, "Hist. of Europe," chap. xxi. p. 73). From an alliance with France, to a declaration of war with Great Britain was but a step, for which Spanish jealousy of our naval power and colonial empire had long been preparing. It actually took place early in October of the same year, in the form of a manifesto, reciting a long series of grievances, real or imaginary, a great number of which had occurred during the period that Spain and England were in alliance, and none of which afforded any pretext for the horrors of war. The manifesto was replied to by Mr. Canning in a long-winded document, which, if shorn of three-fourths of its contents, might have been impressive.

"The alliance of Spain and Holland with France," observes Mahan,* "much increased the difficulties of Great Britain by throwing open their colonial ports to French privateers. The extensive sea coasts of Cuba and Haiti became alive with them. In 1807 it was estimated that there were from two to three hundred depending upon those two islands and unfitted from their size to go far from them." In spite, however, of this disadvantage, the first-fruits of the declaration of war were the loss to Spain of the large West Indian island of Trinidad, which, together with four ships of the line, was captured by General Abercromby in February, 1797. At almost exactly the same time a still heavier misfortune awaited Spain in Europe. Admiral Sir John Jervis, cruising with fifteen sail of the line in the neighbourhood of Cape St. Vincent, encountered and decisively defeated a Spanish fleet almost double in number, destroying by his victory the last shred of prestige attaching to the naval power of Spain.

Minorca was captured by Sir Charles Stuart in 1798, but after this event the war to some extent languished. Spain was no more than an appanage of France, and so little was the Court actuated by feelings of hostility to England, that, in 1799, the Spanish Prime Minister, feeling that a delay in the payment of the army and other public servants might bring on a revolution, which would give France the excuse of invading Spain in the guise of

* "Influence of the Sea Power upon the French Revolution," vol. i. p. 120.

IN THE PENINSULA

popular deliverers from tyranny, applied to Jervis now Lord St. Vincent—to send a frigate to South America in order to bring to Spain in safety the remittances of specie sent annually from the Colonies to the mother country!

In the year 1800 an expedition was despatched from England under command of Lieut.-General Sir James Pulteney, against Ferrol, an important point from its harbour and naval establishment. The regiments embarked comprised the 1st, 9th (three battalions), 13th, 27th (two battalions), 52nd, 54th (two battalions), and 79th. They were reinforced by the 23rd, 31st, 63rd, and 2nd Bn. 52nd from the Île Houat, making a grand total of 13,663 men. The troops were landed and the opposing Spaniards driven into the town, but Pulteney, deeming the place too strong to be captured by a *coup de main*, re-embarked his men and sailed away amid the jeers of the ship's crews. The decision was nevertheless almost certainly a correct one. Sailors are not always the best judges of what can or cannot be effected on land. And Sir John Moore, who reconnoitred the place in 1804, confirmed Pulteney's view. The convoy then sailed in hopes of striking a blow against Vigo, but finding that port also too strong to be attacked, Pulteney abandoned the enterprise and made for Gibraltar, where he formed a junction with another fleet from Minorca, containing 10,000 men under Sir Ralph Abercromby. Reinforcements raised the number of the troops to 23,000 men, and Sir Ralph prepared to carry out the secret instructions of his Government by an attack upon Cadiz, off which port the fleet anchored on the 4th of October. Yellow fever was raging in the town, the daily mortality exceeded 200 persons, and now it transpired that the winds prevalent at that season of the year rendered disembarkation uncertain, and subsequent communication with the fleet more than doubtful. When questioned on these matters by Abercromby, Lord Keith, the British admiral, equivocated; but on being pressed, he finally acknowledged the real facts of the case; whereupon Sir Ralph, very rightly, took upon himself the responsibility of abandoning the enterprise. Keith had not been straightforward in the matter, but the principal blame must rest with the British Government which, with its customary lack of forethought, had not taken the trouble to consider whither the landing of so large a force could, with reasonable probability, be effected; had provided no special appliances, such as boats of light draught for the service; and had selected the most dangerous season of the year for the operation. Abercromby then sailed for Egypt, while Pulteney, with that portion of the troops—nearly half of the Army—which had been enlisted for service in Europe only, returned to Lisbon, to visit the Portuguese, whose fortunes it is now time to review.

During the campaign of 1793 Portuguese troops had co-operated with the Spaniards in the Pyrenees, but in the subsequent treaty of peace between France and Spain Portugal did not participate. In 1796, after the conclusion of the alliance between the two first-named Powers, Portugal had reason to believe that her independence was threatened by the confederates; and Great Britain accordingly directed Sir John Jervis to cruise at the mouth of the Tagus in case of an attack upon Lisbon. A military force, consisting of the 12th Light Dragoons, 600 strong, the 1st, 50th, and 51st regiments from Corsica (each 600), with seven foreign battalions (4,324), and a few artillerymen, 6,828 in all, was despatched to Portugal under Lieut.-General Sir Charles Stuart, and being joined in January, 1797, by the 18th Royal Irish Regiment, formed a welcome reinforcement to the Portuguese army. Yet the Government at Lisbon had made no preparations for the comfort of its allies, who consequently suffered unnecessary hardships. In December, 1799, General Bonaparte, as First Consul, assumed supreme power in France. His first act was to make a proposition for peace with England. The sincerity of Bonaparte in making the proposal has been called in question, but, sincere or not, the arrogant letter which he received in reply from Lord Grenville was nothing less than a gratuitous insult, and only served to give a diplomatic victory to the enemy by justifying the Consul in the eyes of Europe. Thenceforward, the war was conducted on business-like principles, and the chief object of Bonaparte being to seize from England the command of the Mediterranean, and with that end to exclude England from Portuguese ports, the peril to Portugal, hitherto rather imaginary, became acute. In October, 1800, by the terms of a secret treaty between France and Spain, it was determined to compel the Court of Lisbon to separate itself from the alliance of Great Britain and cede, till the conclusion of general peace, a fourth of its territory to the French and Spanish forces. In pursuance of this treaty a Corps of Observation was formed at Bordeaux, and by degrees posted in the neighbourhood of Bayonne. Early in the following year Spain declared war, whereupon Portugal begged from England the assistance of 25,000 men, offering as at a later date to give her the command of her forces. England, however, who had frittered away her forces in a variety of useless enterprises, and whose principal remaining force was engaged in Egypt, felt herself unable to give the aid requested, and contented herself with sending a few regiments and a loan of £300,000.

Spain was at this period occupied by three political parties, each to some extent friendly and to some extent averse to a French alliance. The first, consisting of the King (Charles IV.), the Queen, and her favourite, one Emanuel Godoy, formerly a private soldier in the Royal Guard, who at the conclusion of the late war with France had received the title of Prince of the Peace, wielded the executive power, swayed alternately by dread of their northern neighbour and fear of their countrymen. The nobles of Spain, a haughty, overbearing, but, generally speaking, incapable set of grandees, mainly actuated by jealousy of Godoy, and ready to take the side of the French in hopes of thereby getting rid of the Prince, formed the second party; while the third was made up of the peasantry, who, wild, impulsive, ignorant, yet more truly patriotic than either the sovereign or the nobility, feared and hated the French, but cherished a hope that the diffusion of the principles of political liberty, so loudly boasted by the latter, might under Bonaparte's influence do something to relieve them from the tyranny of the governing classes.

It was partly the secret dislike felt by all classes towards the French Republic that animated Godoy in his request already mentioned, for the services of a British frigate, in 1799, and the same feeling now prompted him to come to a clandestine understanding with Portugal, the consequence of which was that when, in the month of May 1801, a Spanish army of 30,000 men entered Portugal, it met with no resistance, and in a fortnight's time preliminaries of peace were signed at Abrantes. By the terms of the Treaty the ports of Portugal were closed to English trade, but of actual territory the outlying town of Olivenza only was ceded to Spain. General Bonaparte was not, however, a person to be trifled with by any one, least of all by a despised Spaniard. He refused to ratify the treaty, and his Army of Observation, which had already reached Ciudad Rodrigo from

IN THE PENINSULA 11

Bayonne in support of the Spanish troops, was promptly marched into Portugal to threaten the capital. Shrewdly suspecting the Spanish Court of duplicity, the First Consul sent to Godoy a message in unmistakeable terms to the effect that the first sign of open enmity would be the signal for the deposition of the King. Resistance on the part of either Peninsular power was futile; Portugal, deserted by England, purchased peace at the cost of its possessions in Guiana and a war indemnity of £800,000, while Spain was compelled to cede to France the Island of Trinidad; a concession apparent rather than real, for the island was in the hands of the British, but of value to France as a makeweight in the negotiations for the peace with England that was evidently not far distant. Peace actually came under the Treaty of Amiens in March, 1802, but proved merely a suspension of hostilities. On its rupture, May 16, 1803, Bonaparte demanded from Spain the fulfilment of the treaty of St. Ildefonso. To carry out its provisions in their entirety would have involved an instant declaration of war on the part of England against Spain, and the First Consul consequently found it equally advantageous to allow the stipulated naval and military force to be commuted for an annual tribute of £2,880,000; while Portugal, as the price of peace, was forced to promise £640,000 a year to France. Great Britain, recognising the fact that Spain was no longer a free agent, hesitated to commence hostilities on what were perfectly adequate grounds; but the subsequent acts of the Spanish Court proved more than suspicious, and the British Minister at Madrid, finding his remonstrances against the continuous preparation of armaments ineffectual, quitted the capital in accordance with instructions from home on the 10th of November, 1804. Up to this point the conduct of the British Government was abundantly justified; but although the

12   WELLINGTON'S OPERATIONS

fact was unknown as yet at Madrid, an event had occurred which, in appearance at least, put England to some extent in the wrong. The chief source of Spanish wealth was the annual remittance of silver from the South American Colonies, to which allusion has already been made. The British ministers were perfectly well aware that the bullion on arrival would be at once transmitted to France. It was determined to intercept the treasure and hold it on behalf of Spain. On the 5th of October, 1804, four English frigates fell in with the four ships conveying the silver. The Spanish commander very properly refused to submit to detention. A conflict ensued. One of the Spanish ships blew up. The other three were captured, with bullion to the value of £2,000,000 on board. Justification for the proceeding may be fairly pleaded on the grounds just mentioned, but it was more than unfortunate that the British squadron engaged was not of such strength as to make all idea of resistance clearly impossible. On hearing of the capture of the treasure ships the Spanish Court, not unnaturally, refused to listen to any explanations, and declared war with England December 12, 1804.

A great victory was thus scored to French diplomacy, but ere long the Spanish people had cause to rue bitterly the side they had taken. On the 21st of October, 1805, the combined fleets of the Allies were destroyed at Trafalgar. In the following year Napoleon, now Emperor, opened negotiations for a general peace. Not only was Spain, however, refused a representative in the proceedings, but Napoleon even offered her possession, the Balearic Islands, as a compensation to the King of Naples for Sicily. The negotiations proved futile, but the Emperor's schemes having come to the knowledge of the Spanish Court, the deepest indignation was aroused. The fact that a French corps was also observed to be concentrat-

IN THE PENINSULA 13

ing at Bayonne added to the general discontent; advantage was taken of Napoleon's Prussian war, and on the 4th of October proclamations were issued by Godoy calling out the militia and summoning recruits to fill up the vacancies of the army in view of a war which would "soon be called for by the common good." The enemy was not named, but it was obvious against whom the proclamation was directed. The moment was ill chosen. On the very day when news of Godoy's manifesto reached Napoleon, Prussia had been prostrated at Jena. The Proclamation was hastily withdrawn by the Spanish Court, and in reply to his inquiries Napoleon was informed that it had been directed against an expected descent by the Moors. The Emperor pretended to believe the story, but in the most practical manner obtained hostages for the good behaviour of Spain by demanding the aid of a Spanish corps of 15,000 men under the Marquis de Romana, which, when granted, he despatched forthwith to Holstein to be out of harm's way. Napoleon had, in point of fact, been made aware by intercepted despatches of the intention of Spain to join the European Powers against France, and the knowledge made him once more revolve in his mind the advisability of dethroning the reigning Power of the Peninsula—a project the permission of which by Russia was subsequently embodied in the secret articles of the Treaty of Tilsit, signed July, 1807. Charles IV. and Godoy, playing a double game, fell between two stools, and the incident affords an excellent example of the fact that a person wishing to be a knave had better first take care that he is not a fool, and that if he is a fool he had better not try to be a knave.

CHAPTER II

State of Europe—Napoleon's views on Portugal—Treaty of Fontainebleau—Junot occupies Lisbon—Affairs in Spain—Abdication of King Charles—Marshal Murat enters Madrid—Joseph Bonaparte declared king—The Spaniards rise against the French—Theatre of war—Forces available on either side—Operations of Marshal Moncey in Valencia, and of General Dupont in Andalusia—Capitulation of Baylen—Joseph Bonaparte evacuates Madrid—Operations in Catalonia and Aragon—Operations of Bessières on the line of communications—Victory of Rio Seco.

THE Treaty of Tilsit, signed in July, 1807, left Napoleon free to carry out his designs against England. Russia, Austria, Prussia, those arrogant army-millionaires of the present day, were compelled to follow humbly the French Emperor's triumphal car and to join in the hostile combination against Great Britain in whom alone they could hope for emancipation from their thraldom. Spain and Portugal had, as we have seen, already sided—nominally at least—against her. Holland and Italy were nothing more than provinces of France; while of the other European States, Denmark had long been passively, and from force of circumstances was now actively, hostile to England; and Sweden, hitherto our faithful ally, found it eventually impossible to hold aloof from the coalition. Sicily, it is true, was occupied by our troops amid the enthusiasm of its inhabitants; but Queen Caroline, the master-spirit of the Court—accurately described by Napoleon as the basest of her sex—was only awaiting her opportunity to betray the British to the enemy: an opportunity which the infatuation of Sir William Drummond, our envoy, seemed likely to afford, and which indeed the sagacity of our general officers on the spot alone prevented. Thus Britain was left alone to bear the brunt of the approaching conflict: a conflict which her ministers, far from avoiding, accepted with a lightness of heart, the result rather of lack of foresight and boastful ignorance than of the unassuming confidence prescient of future victory.

The immediate object of Napoleon was to combine against England the navies of all the European Powers, including those of Denmark and Portugal. This arrangement formed one of the secret Articles of the Treaty of Tilsit. Hardly, however, had the Treaty been signed than the British Government — possibly through the treachery of Talleyrand — got wind of the scheme, pounced down upon Denmark, seized her battleships, and conveyed those of Portugal far out of the Emperor's reach. The possession of these two fleets secured England, at all events for a long time to come, from all danger of invasion; and Napoleon was consequently obliged to fall back upon his Continental System in hopes of forcing England into submission by excluding her goods from all European ports and thus ensuring her commercial ruin.

For the perfecting of the Continental System, the co-operation of Portugal was indispensable. That of Spain had already been secured; but many circumstances about this time served to turn Napoleon's attention to the affairs of the Peninsula. Primary among these was the danger of having a secret foe in his rear, in the event of circumstances again calling him into Germany—a danger which the proclamation of Godoy already mentioned, had shown to be a very real one. It was, however, necessary to handle the subject with the greatest delicacy, and his first movements were calculated to allay the suspicions of Spain by inducing her to act in concert with himself, for the promotion of his more immediate designs against Portugal.

"Portugal," observed Napoleon, "is nothing more than a province of England." In the sense in which he made it the remark was just. Her policy was largely dictated by England; her harbours were open to British vessels; her commerce was upheld by British merchants. As early as the spring (at all events) of 1806, the partition of Portugal had been decided on. A French force, termed "the Army of the Gironde," had been assembled at Bayonne, for the invasion of Portugal. The British Government, fully aware of the fact, sent General Simcoe and Lord Rosslyn to warn the Portuguese Court. The latter affected to disbelieve the information. The Jena campaign called away the Army of the Gironde, and for the time being the danger passed away. On the conclusion of the Treaty of Tilsit, Napoleon reverted at once to, and—under the title of the Treaty of Fontainebleau—confirmed his project of the preceding year. The provisions of the treaty which were kept secret were as follows:—The House of Bragança to be expelled. The kingdom to be divided into three portions: of which one, the Entre Minho e Duero, was to be given to the King of Etruria in exchange for the kingdom of which he had been dispossessed. The southern provinces of the Alemtejo and Algarves were to form a principality for Godoy, and the remainder of Portugal to be held by France until a general peace, when it was to be exchanged against British colonial conquests.

In order to carry out the provisions of this treaty it was agreed that France should employ 3,000 Cavalry and 25,000 Infantry; Spain an equal amount of Cavalry,

24,000 Infantry, and 30 guns. The French contingent was, however, to act in one mass, while of the Spanish, only the guns, Cavalry, and 8,000 of the Infantry were to march, in conjunction with their ally, on Lisbon. Of the remainder, 10,000 men were to invade the Entre Minho and 6,000 the Algarves.

In pursuance of the compact, the Corps of Observation in the Gironde, commanded by General Junot, entered Spain on the 19th of October, 1807, joined the Spanish Division at Alcantara, and crossed the boundary of Portugal on the 21st November. "Thence," says General Thiébault, Chief of Junot's Staff, "the march was terrible. General Caraffa's Spanish Division lost 1,700 or 1,800 men from hunger or fatigue; drowning in torrents or falling down precipices. After this Abrantes seemed to us like a haven of refuge. I need not again relate the details of our arrival, or the exhaustion of our men, who had been marching night and day through inaccessible gorges, living on acorns and honey. I preserved a moral courage which occasionally deserted General Junot. At Sobreira Formosa, for example, not having strength to reach the hovel intended for him, he flung himself into the one marked as my quarters, only got upstairs with our support, and on reaching the room in which the staircase ended, flung himself on a pallet, and there passed the rest of a terrible night. . . . Junot took possession of Lisbon, of the army that was there, and of the entire kingdom without having at hand a single trooper, a single gun, or a cartridge that would burn, with nothing save the 1,500 Grenadiers remaining from the four battalions of his advance guard. Fagged out, unwashed, ghastly objects, the Grenadiers had no longer strength to march even to the sound of the drum. . . . The rest of the army dropped in at intervals of one or two days in still worse condition, some even falling down dead at the gates."

It was on the 30th of November that this "remnant of an army" entered Lisbon. The Royal Family had already fled. Embarked under British escort, their ships were even at this moment clearing the mouth of the Tagus *en route* for Brazil. Junot thereupon took over the government of Portugal thus deserted by its sovereign; but, swift as had been his march, he had arrived too late to attain the chief object of his master. Under the auspices of Admiral Sir Sydney Smith, commanding the British squadron off the Tagus, the Portuguese fleet, consisting of eight ships of the line and three frigates, had already been withdrawn, and was out of reach of the French. But the property of the British merchants was confiscated, the Tricolour was hoisted, and the whole country—not the central provinces only—was by degrees administered in the name of the French Emperor. Junot, through his Chief of the Staff, now set himself to consolidate his forces and strengthen his position. He had met with no resistance on his march, but the Portuguese soon began to show a spirit of insurrection, and, among other precautionary measures, the French commander despatched 9,000 of the Portuguese troops to Bayonne. Many died *en route* and many others deserted, but about 5,000 were incorporated in Napoleon's armies, and part served against their country during the ensuing war.

Meantime affairs in Spain had been rapidly approaching a crisis. The proclamation of the Prince of the Peace already noted had warned Napoleon that his alliance with Spain by no means secured him from her attack, and among the secret articles of the Treaty of Tilsit, to which he had already procured the Czar's assent, was one for the overthrow of the Spanish as well as the Portuguese dynasty. The stipulation seems to have been drawn up rather as a measure of precaution in case of need than as an irrevocable decision, and for several months afterwards the Emperor appears to have thought it in accordance with the best practical policy to retain Charles IV. on the throne of Spain, provided that he could obtain adequate safeguards against any act of treachery on the part of his ally. Events forced his hand. The King's favourite, Godoy, although destitute neither of moral courage nor administrative capacity, was the best hated man in the kingdom. Some of his most praiseworthy reforms had been directed against the clergy, and in that priest-ridden country such measures, however necessary, would be certain to encounter a howl of indignation. The nobility also were terribly jealous of his influence with the King and Queen; and Ferdinand, their eldest son, in consonance with the traditions of royal families, sided strongly against his parents. Both father and son appealed to Napoleon, and the immediate result was the Treaty of Fontainebleau already mentioned, while Ferdinand's advances were disregarded. Into the domestic quarrel between father and son the Emperor resolutely declined to be drawn. As to the future of Spain, he does not seem to have yet taken any determination; but the course of events gradually led him to feel the impossibility of maintaining Charles on the throne, with an adequate guarantee against Spain proving a snake in the grass in the event of another continental war; and as he could not be sovereign of Spain himself the need arose of making one of his brothers king, relying on the support of the people as opposed to that of the nobles, and earning the gratitude and loyalty of the former by the establishment of a liberal constitution. The greatest caution was, however, necessary.

Under the provisions of the Treaty of Fontainebleau an Army of Reserve was formed at Bayonne. In December it was marched into Spain, organised in two

Army Corps, each of about 20,000 men, commanded respectively by General Dupont and Marshal Moncey. By the strict terms of the treaty this army, intended as a support to Junot, was not to be moved across the frontier without the consent of the King of Spain. No such consent appears to have been received, but, on the other hand, no protest was made, and it is not unfair to infer that the advance was made with the tacit approval of the king and his minister. "Receive the French well; they are our friends," was the answer of Godoy to the officials of the northern provinces, who asked for instructions.

The intrigues of Ferdinand against his father resulted in the trial of his confidants. They were acquitted in January, 1808, but by this time Napoleon had thoroughly convinced himself of the worthlessness of both father and son, and had determined to solve the difficulty by the annexation of the Spanish provinces north of the Ebro. By stratagem the French troops got possession of the important fortress of Pampeluna. A third Corps —unauthorised by the Convention—under General Duhesme, consisting of 1,600 Cavalry, 11,000 Infantry and 18 guns, crossed the eastern spurs of the Pyrenees early in February, 1808, and by treachery made themselves masters of Barcelona and Figueras. Early in March, St. Sebastian was given up to the French in accordance with orders from the Prince of the Peace, who felt that it was now too late to resist; and the four most important fortresses of Northern Spain being now in his hands, Napoleon proposed the cession of the above-named provinces in exchange for Portugal. Godoy actually consented, but recalled his despatch and advised Charles IV. to quit Spain and embark for America. The preparations for the king's departure however raised a tumult among the populace at Aranjuez and Madrid.

IN THE PENINSULA

The traces of the royal carriage were cut, Godoy was seized, and hardly rescued alive from the infuriated mob. On the 19th of March, Charles abdicated, and Ferdinand was proclaimed king amid the enthusiasm of the people. Meanwhile Marshal Murat had been appointed Commander-in-Chief of the French forces in Spain. On his arrival on the 10th inst. he had crossed the frontier and was proceeding southwards in conjunction with Dupont and Moncey. In spite of the trickery by which they had got possession of the Spanish fortresses, the French were received everywhere with open arms by the people whose resentment up to the present time was entirely directed against the Prince of the Peace. At the time of Charles's abdication Murat was near Madrid. On the 23rd of March, exceeding his instructions, he entered the capital. Next day Ferdinand arrived from Aranjuez, but was not recognised as monarch by the French commander who rightly gauged the Emperor's feelings on the subject. On receiving the news of the king's abdication, Napoleon had offered the throne to his brother Louis. When the news of the riots arrived ten days later the Emperor grasped in a moment the critical nature of affairs and hesitated. "I fear," said he, in a letter to Murat dated the 29th of March, "that you are deceiving me as to the real situation of Spain, and that you are deceiving yourself also. The events of the 19th of March have singularly complicated our affairs; I am in the greatest perplexity. Never suppose you are engaged with a disarmed nation, and that you have only to show yourself to ensure the submission of Spain. . . . You have to deal with a virgin people; they have already the courage and they will soon have all the enthusiasm which you meet among men who are not worn out by political passions."

"The aristocracy and clergy are masters of Spain; if

they become seriously alarmed for their privileges and their existence they will raise an unending war. At present I have many partisans among them; if I show myself as a conqueror I shall soon cease to have any. The Prince of the Peace is detested because they accuse him of having given up Spain to France: that is the cry which led to the usurpation of Ferdinand; but for it the popular party would have been the least formidable. The Prince of the Asturias has none of the qualities essential for the chief of a nation; that want however will not prevent them, in order to oppose us, from making him a hero. I have no wish to use violence to that family; it is never expedient to render oneself odious and to inflame hatred. Spain has about 100,000 men in arms; less would suffice to sustain an internal war; scattered over several points they might succeed in effecting the total overthrow of the Monarchy. . . . The persons who see the monstrous state of the government in its true light are a small minority; the great majority profit by its abuses. Consistently with the interests of my Empire I can do infinite good to Spain. What are the best means of attaining that object? . . . It is difficult to re-establish Charles IV. His rule and that of his favourite have become so unpopular they could not stand three months. Ferdinand again is the enemy of France; it is because he is so that they have put him on the throne. To keep him there would be to assist those factions who for twenty-five years have wished the subjugation of France. . . . I think we should precipitate nothing, and take counsel for future events. I do not approve of your taking possession so precipitately as you have done of Madrid; you should have kept the army ten leagues from the capital. Your entry into Madrid, by exciting the alarm of the Spaniards has powerfully supported Ferdinand. . . . I have not fixed upon a course.

Impress upon the nobles and clergy, that if France is obliged to interfere in the affairs of Spain, their privileges will be respected. Say to the magistrates and citizens and to the enlightened persons that Spain . . . has need of institutions which will preserve it from the pressure of feudality, and protect and encourage industry. . . . Let the French army avoid any encounter with the Spanish army or with any detached bodies; not a cartridge should be burned on either side. Always keep the army some days' march distant from the Spanish corps. If war breaks out all is lost." *

Immediately after assuming the crown, Ferdinand set out for Burgos to have an interview with the Emperor. Hitherto no open violence had been shown towards the French. A few of the stragglers of Junot's army are said to have been assassinated in the previous year, but generally speaking the troops had been received if not with enthusiasm, at all events with a certain good humour not unmingled with contempt at the youth and physical debility of the French soldiers, who for the most part consisted of raw and undisciplined conscripts. The attempted flight of Charles to America appears to have been the primary cause of an altered demeanour, which was still further accentuated by the publication of a protest from Charles to the effect that his abdication had been only made under compulsion, and by the suppression of Ferdinand's name on all public documents. Gloomy brows and gathering crowds testified to the approach of the storm. On the 23rd of April a riot broke out at Toledo, and the Spaniards for the first time came

---

* It should be stated that this letter is not conclusively proved to be genuine. It never reached Murat, and no draft of it was ever found. Méneval gives the reasons pro and con, but sums up decidedly in its favour. Thiers agrees. Others are convinced that it was written only at St. Helena.

into collision with the French troops. Nine days later, on the occasion of the attempted departure from Madrid of Don Antonio and Don Francis, the last members of the Royal Family, the popular fury burst forth. Every Frenchman found in the streets was massacred. Murat with two battalions, the only infantry immediately available, marched through the city to quell the tumult, and was received with grape shot. Messengers were sent in hot haste to the camps nearest to the capital for assistance. The cavalry of the Imperial Guard and a division of Dragoons from Buen Retiro arrived at a gallop. Galled by a fire from the neighbouring houses, every window of which was occupied by sharpshooters, the squadron advanced through the streets and sent the mob flying in all directions. Napier states that no Spanish soldiers took part in the riot. Marbot, who was present, avers that thousands of them were engaged. Under the circumstances the French must be said to have behaved with conspicuous moderation. Only 120 Spaniards lost their lives in the affray, inclusive of forty men who suffered by military execution after tranquillity had been restored, while of the French upwards of 500 were killed.

It is now time to return to Ferdinand, whom we left travelling to meet the Emperor. On reaching Burgos and finding that Napoleon had not yet arrived, he went on to Vittoria, and thence, not unwillingly yet under some compulsion, for he was now surrounded by Napoleon's officers, to Bayonne, where he arrived about the 20th of April. His father had preceded him by a few hours, and had been received with honours due to royalty. Ferdinand was treated with civility by the Emperor, and offered the kingdom of Etruria, but informed that he could not be recognised as King of Spain. He refused to resign his pretensions, and for some days negotiations

IN THE PENINSULA 25

were carried on between himself, Charles, and the Emperor. On the 5th of May an aide-de-camp arrived in hot haste with the news of the Madrid riot. The Emperor hesitated no longer. The negotiations at once came to an end. Charles, endowed with a large pension, gladly relinquished his throne a second time, not only for himself but also for his heirs; and even bequeathed it absolutely to Napoleon—as if a kingdom were a personal property to be transferred at the will of the owner like a Stock Exchange security! Ferdinand, personally menaced by his parents, and horrified at the news of the bloodshed, also resigned; and both he and Charles forthwith despatched proclamations to Madrid exhorting the Spaniards to look on the Emperor as their best friend and to acquiesce quietly in his arrangements for the future government of the kingdom. By a stipulation—the only one of importance—in his Deed of Abdication, Charles had secured the promise of Napoleon that the integrity of the kingdom should be preserved. The idea of annexing the northern provinces to France was consequently shelved, if not abandoned; but Napoleon had, as already stated, for a long time past revolved the project of placing a member of his own family upon the throne of Spain. Circumstances had now brought the idea into the sphere of practical politics, and his ultimate choice fell upon his brother Joseph, at present King of Naples. Hence, under the new scheme, in the event of matters running smoothly, not merely the north but the whole of Spain would be nothing more than a dependency of France; and the Continental system, his most powerful weapon against England, would be carried out in its entirety.

Napoleon's policy has over and over again been described by writers as "dark" and "tortuous," and in truth it is not in all respects to be defended; yet the view of Napier that the Emperor was forced on by a rapid succession of unforeseen circumstances would seem to be pretty correct. The time had not so long passed since France had been encircled by European armies, and his patriotism compelled Napoleon to do all in his power to secure his country from invasion in the future. On the northern and western frontiers his preparations were complete. It only remained to organise matters on a sound basis in the south. That he enormously miscalculated the strength of popular feeling in Spain must of course be admitted; and also that he might have attained his object (as indeed he himself owned at a later date) by acceding to Ferdinand's wishes and allowing him to remain on the throne as his puppet. Yet it cannot be denied that he offered the Spaniards a really good government, such a one as they never had before or since. What he could not understand was that a community may prefer the tyranny and oppression in which it has been brought up, to the benefits of a government, however good, to which it is unaccustomed.

The example of Madrid was quickly followed throughout almost the whole land. It was in vain that the Council of Castille, and the governing Junta, declared that their choice of a monarch had fallen upon Joseph Bonaparte. It was to no purpose that the selection was confirmed and Napoleon's Constitution accepted by an assembly of the notables of Spain at Bayonne in the middle of June. Riots broke out in all parts of the kingdom, and as the clergy and populace were actuated less by patriotism than by a sense of disappointed vengeance upon Godoy, anarchy reigned supreme. Under the cloak of patriotism private revenge was gratified on every side. Murder was rampant. Many of the purest patriots were foully slain; others feeling that under the circumstances their duty to their country would be so best performed, ranged themselves on the side of Napoleon, preparing to avail themselves of the constitutional government which he offered.

War with France was now a recognised fact throughout the Peninsula; and though Napoleon in common with Murat had for a moment cherished the idea that the repression of the Madrid riot would put an end to all disturbance, and that the people would quickly appreciate and fall in with his measures of reform, he very soon realised his error and set himself in earnest to cope with the new state of affairs.

Unable for political reasons to enter Spain in person, the Emperor directed the military operations, so far as he was able, from Bayonne. Murat returned to France in the month of June, and General Savary took his place as King Joseph's lieutenant. Savary's position was a difficult one; his talents were not of the highest order, and though his appointment gave him precedence, the very fact that Marshals such as Moncey and Bessières received military orders from an officer junior to themselves did not in all probability conduce either to harmony or to the advancement of the Emperor's interests.

The Spanish regular forces amounted at this period to about 80,000 men. Of these 15,000, as already noted, were in Holstein under Romana, and consequently were not at present available. Twenty-seven thousand were in Portugal, the remainder in various garrisons, principally in Andalusia. Eleven thousand Swiss aided the regular troops, and there were in addition 30,000 militiamen.

Exclusive of 30,000 men, under Junot in Portugal, the French forces in the Peninsula numbered 70,000 effectives ready to take the field; a heterogeneous mass of which the purely French element—with the exception of a few regiments of the Imperial Guard—consisted almost entirely of the latest levy of conscripts, nominally soldiers, in reality undrilled and undisciplined plough-boys. "This fact," observes Napier, "goes far to explain the otherwise incomprehensible checks which the invaders met with in the early stages of the war."

Each province of Spain had its separate Junta or form of government, tariff of customs, &c., and Galicia, the Asturias, and Biscay had certain additional privileges which rendered them still more independent of any central authority. The newly-formed Junta of Seville arrogated to itself the title of the supreme government of Spain and was recognised as such by England, but had no more real claim to it than any of the other Juntas, beyond that which the wealth and position of Andalusia afforded.

Madrid, governed by the Central Council of Castille, was for the moment the pivot of military operations. "There are," says Napier, "four principal roads leading from Spain into France. First, a royal causeway passing the frontier at Irun runs over San Sebastian, and thence through a wild country, full of dangerous defiles to the Ebro; it crosses that river by a stone bridge at Miranda, goes to Burgos, and then turning short to the left, is carried over the Douro at Aranda; it surmounts the Carpentarios by the Somosierra Pass, and then descends upon the capital.

"Second, an inferior road penetrating by St. Jean Pied de Port, Pampeluna and Tafalla; it crosses the Ebro at Tudela and enters the basin of Madrid by the eastern range of the Sierra de Guadalaxera, where the declination of the mountains presents a less rugged barrier than the snowy summits of the northern and western parts of the chain.

"Third, a road not practicable for guns, threads the Pyrenees by Jaca, passes the Ebro at Saragossa, and uniting with the second, crosses the Guadalaxara ridge.

"The fourth is the great road from Perpignan by Figueras, Gerona, Barcelona, Cervera, Lerida, and Saragossa to Madrid."

The first object of Napoleon was to secure the line of communications between Paris and Madrid, and for that purpose the strategical points along the royal causeway were occupied in force by Marshal Bessières, who on Moncey's advance southward in March, had been pushed forward from Bayonne to Burgos with an Army Corps of 23,000 men. On the eastern coast Duhesme's Corps was augmented to 22,000 after the capture of Barcelona. It is hardly necessary to say that on the preservation of these lines of communication and more particularly on that between Bayonne and Burgos, depended the safety of the whole French army in the Peninsula.

Next in importance was the need of occupying the town of Saragossa—"a capital of a province uniting two great roads, and containing one of the great Spanish arsenals. An army could thence operate by either bank of the Ebro, interrupt the communication between the eastern and western Pyrenees, and block three of the four great roads to Madrid."

After securing these points, the province of Andalusia would become the point of interest, as containing pretty nearly 30,000 Spanish regular troops, including the Corps of Solano, which during the year previous had occupied the Alemtejo in co-operation with Junot, another of veteran troops under General Castanos, and the garrisons of Grenada, Cadiz, etc. This latter town contained a large arsenal, and was in easy communication with the British at Gibraltar. "Seville contained a cannon foundry, and as its Junta assumed the title of the

Government of Spain, it became an object of political importance to the Emperor to crush it. Andalusia was consequently an appreciable factor in the general situation as forming a base for the operations of regular troops in contra-distinction to the insurrectionary efforts chiefly of the peasantry in other parts of the country; but such operations would require careful preparation, hence the danger to the French from Andalusia was not immediately pressing."*

Unfortunately Savary failed to grasp the relative importance of these three points, and Napoleon's orders, not being carried out in their entirety, failed to attain their end.

The forces of the French were disposed as follows:—

1. Corps of the Western Pyrenees.

Marshal Bessières commanding.

				Present under Arms.	Guns.
1st Division: General Mouton	1st Brigade	General	Reynaud	3,000	6
	2nd ,,	,,	Rey	2,100	6
2nd Division: General Merle	1st ,,	,,	D'Armagnac	1,800	16
	2nd ,,	,,	Gaulois	1,800	
	3rd ,,	,,	Sabathier	2,800	
	4th ,,	,,	Ducos	2,000	
Guard	1 ,,			1,900	6
Cavalry Division				1,950	
			Total	17,350	34
Garrison of San Sebastian		,,	Thouvenot	1,000	
,, Burgos				600	
Flying Column, Burgos		,,	Bonet	1,500	2
,, Aranda				1,000	4
,, Vittoria		,,	Monthion	1,600	2
		Grand total of Bessières' Corps		23,050	42

* This is Napier's opinion, and, looking at the French position from the defensive point of view, and in the light of subsequent

IN THE PENINSULA

The duty of this corps was to guard the road between the frontier and Madrid, a distance of about 300 miles; to occupy the fortresses of San Sebastian and Burgos, Biscay, and the mountains of Santander, and to take the offensive in Galicia and the Asturias.

For the performance of special duties, the following troops were placed under command of Bessières:—Garrison of Burgos, 600 men; of San Sebastian, 1,000; and three movable columns: 1. Under General Bonet, 1,500 men, including a squadron of cavalry and two guns, to maintain order in the town and environs of Burgos. 2. Also under Bonet's orders, 1,000 men and 4 guns, to guard the line of communications as far as the mountains in front of Aranda. 3. Under General Monthieu, which occupied Vittoria with 1,700 men and 2 guns.

2. THE ARMY OF ARAGON,

commanded by General Verdier, was made up in the first instance of a detachment from Bessières' Corps. Its duty was the occupation of Navarre, with a garrison in Pampeluna, and the prosecution of the siege of Saragossa. On the capture of that town Bessières was to be reinforced by 2,000 men from this army, and movable columns were to patrol the passes of the Pyrenees.

The Corps was made up of a Cavalry Brigade 1,100 strong, and 4 brigades of Infantry, mustering in all 9,500 men. Navarre was occupied by a flying column of about 1,400 men, and Pampeluna garrisoned by a depôt 800 strong. Thus the whole Army Corps mustered about 13,000 men, of which 10,600 under Verdier's immediate command were directed upon Saragossa.

events, would seem to be sound. Napoleon, however, writing so to speak on the offensive, and desirous of crushing the regular troops of Spain, continually impressed upon Savary the superior importance of the operations in Andalusia to those in Aragon.

3. THE ARMY OF CATALONIA.

General Duhesme commanding.

1st Division, General Chabran.   2nd Division, General Lechi.

Comprising 1,600 Cavalry, 11,000 Infantry, and 18 guns.

This Corps (based upon Barcelona, the largest city of Spain, and defended by two fortresses) was charged with the duty of maintaining order in Catalonia, and was supported by a Division, estimated by Napoleon at 9,000 men, commanded by General Reille, operating along the sea-coast from Perpignan.

Besides the above named, there were the Corps of Moncey and Dupont, each consisting of three divisions, and making up (inclusive of about 2,000 men available from Madrid) a combined total of approximately 8,000 Cavalry, 40,000 Infantry, and 80 guns available for offensive operations in the south and south-west of Spain, which were forthwith begun, three divisions being however retained at Madrid by Savary, to strengthen Bessières or act as reserves.

On the breaking out of the insurrectionary movement throughout the country, Marshal Moncey, with 10,000 men, was directed upon Cuenca, a central position whence he could either move to the left, and separate the Valencian insurgents—a formidable body of 30,000 men provided with artillery—from those of Aragon, or by marching to his right intercept the junction of the roads leading from Valencia and Cartagena upon Madrid. Hearing, on arrival at Cuenca, of the enemy's strength and intention to march to the relief of Saragossa—now attacked by Verdier—the Marshal determined on the former course, and seeing prudence in audacity, left a detachment in Cuenca, and with 8,000 men advanced to

IN THE PENINSULA

the attack of Valencia, expecting the co operation of a Division of Duhesme's Corps, which the Emperor had, in such a contingency, placed at his disposal. Defeating with heavy loss the Spanish bodies who ventured to oppose him, Moncey reached Valencia on the 27th of June. Of the expected division from Catalonia no news was, however, received, and, having failed to take the city by a *coup de main*, Moncey fell back upon Quarte. Here he heard of the approach of a force from Murcia under the Spanish Captain-General Serbelloni, whereupon the Marshal marched rapidly to the Zucar river, caught the Spaniards on both banks, forced the passage of the river, pursued the enemy, defeated him a second time, and entered Almanza. Thence he returned to San Clemente, where he awaited the Division of his corps which had been retained at Madrid. Savary had, however, sent it off on a fool's errand to Raquena on the Cuenca road, whence it returned sickly and exhausted. Moncey then prepared to resume the offensive, but Savary, with little tact, recalled one of his divisions, and Moncey, finding himself obliged to abandon his enterprise, and offended at his treatment by a junior officer, retired to Madrid, " having," as Napier observes, " warred without cessation for a month, forced two of the strongest mountain passes, crossed several difficult rivers, and even penetrated to the suburbs of Valencia ; . . . defeated his opponents in five actions, killed and wounded a number equal in amount to his whole force, and made a circuit of 300 miles through a hostile populous country, without any serious loss, without any desertions from the Spanish battalions incorporated with his own, and what was of more importance, having these battalions increased by desertions from the enemy. The real objects had been attained ; the plan of relieving Saragossa was frustrated, the organisation of an efficient Spanish force retarded."

Meanwhile matters of importance were taking place in Andalusia. Dupont, starting from Madrid about the middle of May with a Brigade of Cavalry, 3 Brigades of Infantry, and 18 guns, reached Andujar on the 2nd of June. Here he received startling intelligence. A supreme Junta was established at Seville; the whole country was in arms; a Division of Junot's Corps, which was to have co-operated from the side of Portugal, was returning to Lisbon. Although alarmed, Dupont pushed on to Cordoba, scattering the enemy *en route* and spreading terror as far as Seville. Previous to this, Solano, murdered by the mob, had shared the fate of so many general officers. Castanos was now Captain-General; an immediate advance on the part of the French was expected; and the Spanish Commander believed that his sole resource lay in a retreat to Cadiz, where, by means of an entrenched camp and the possible support of a British contingent, he might hope to hold his own. Pressed on, however, by the populace and encouraged by the attitude of Dupont—who, alarmed at the general situation, failed to follow up his victory and, after waiting ten days at Cordoba for reinforcements, began a retreat upon Andujar—Castanos resumed the offensive, but in the feeblest manner imaginable, and in fact did little more than watch the French from a respectful distance. The gallant patriots had, however, not been idle, but during Dupont's stay at Cordoba had attacked his hospital at Andujar and had murdered every defenceless person that they could lay hands on! Early in July, General Vedel with one of the two remaining Divisions of the Army Corps which had hitherto been retained in reserve by Savary at Madrid, forced the passes of the Morena and came down to Baylen, 16 miles west of Andujar. He was shortly followed by a third Division under General Gobert. By this time the Spanish forces had

IN THE PENINSULA

been augmented to about 50,000 men, of which 27,000 were regular troops furnished with a powerful artillery. Castanos had made an appeal to the English General, Spencer, who was cruising off Cadiz with 5,000 men. Spencer declined. The circumstances were, however, peculiar; each of the three countries, France, Spain, and England, being at war with the other two, a sort of triangular duel was going on; but what influenced Spencer in his refusal was the fact that he knew that the British force in the Peninsula was about to be largely increased, and feeling it his duty therefore to seek no personal advantage, he would not do more than disembark his Division at Xerez and await events. But his assistance, as it turned out, was not required. On the 10th of July Castanos attacked the bridge of Andujar in force, while two of his Divisions, commanded by General Reding, a Swiss, forced the passage of the Guadalquiver 18 miles higher up at Menjibar, driving Gobert's Division before him. On hearing of this disaster, Dupont, who had been joined by Vedel, sent that officer back to Baylen on the high road to Madrid, with a view to securing his retreat; but Vedel, misunderstanding the orders, which appear to have been vaguely given, followed Gobert's Division to Carolina. Reding, with 20,000 men, then interposed between him and Dupont. On the night of the 18th the latter retired from Andujar and attacked Reding next morning, but failing to carry his position at Baylen, hoisted the white flag and proposed an armistice. Shortly afterwards Vedel, returning from Carolina, attacked, and was in the act of defeating Reding, when an order arrived from Dupont to cease firing. On the 20th two general officers were sent to Castanos, who was dawdling at Andujar, to demand a convention. At this moment an intercepted letter from Savary to Dupont recalling the latter to Madrid was brought to the Spanish headquarters. The surrender not only of Dupont but also of Vedel was then demanded and immediately acceded to; and Vedel, who had retired with his own and Gobert's Divisions to Carolina, actually came back and laid down his arms! Nor did the matter end there, for a French Staff officer with a Spanish escort went round and brought in as prisoners the detachments of Dupont's Corps left to guard his line of communications up to a distance of 120 miles from the field of battle! One officer, Major St. Eglise, alone refused to obey the disgraceful order, and made the best of his way back to Madrid, for which conduct he was made a colonel by the Emperor. The terms of capitulation, by which the French troops were to be sent to France, were shamefully broken, and the prisoners left to die of cold and hunger on the desert island of Cabrera. It is perhaps unnecessary to observe that the British Government, which, woefully destitute of all chivalrous feeling, treated its own prisoners of war with the utmost brutality, did nothing to compel its Spanish ally to observe the terms of the capitulation.*

On the 23rd of July the news of the surrender at Baylen reached Madrid. Three days previously Joseph Bonaparte had entered the capital as King; on the 30th he crossed the Somosierra in headlong flight.

While these events were passing in the south, Duhesme had been conducting operations in Catalonia with no very decisive result. He was badly served by his subordinates and the country was extremely difficult. One of his Divisions was beaten, and another, which had been

* The life of the prisoners at the Isle of Cabrera, their self-imposed rules and regulations, their courts of justice, the gaiety which never deserted them amid their inconceivable misery, and found vent in improvised theatrical entertainments, &c., are well described in a work recently reprinted, called "The Memoirs of a French Sergeant."

IN THE PENINSULA 37

sent to co-operate with Marshal Moncey, had consequently to be recalled. Two futile attacks were made upon Gerona, and Duhesme found himself eventually compelled to confine himself to the outskirts of Barcelona.

In Aragon a force of less than 5,000 men under Lefèbre Desnouettes, detached by Bessières, attacked and as nearly as possible captured Saragossa by a *coup de main* on the 16th of June. As with the British on a subsequent occasion at Bergen op Zoom, so here it happened with the French that in the full tide of success their troops dispersed for plunder; whereupon the Spaniards, recovering from their panic, rallied and drove the enemy out of the town. Verdier then arrived with 7,000 men and took command. The circumstances of the case were compared by Napoleon with those of Whitelocke's attack on Buenos Ayres the year previous. Fifty thousand inhabitants garrisoned every convent, defended every house. Nevertheless in an assault on the 4th of August, Verdier was within an ace of capturing the city. A few days later, a letter from King Joseph directed him, in view of the catastrophe at Baylen, to raise the siege and retire to Logrono.

Meantime, the position of Marshal Bessières, guarding, as we have seen, the main line of communications between France and Madrid, had been a source of considerable anxiety to the Emperor. Hardly had he taken up his quarters at Burgos during the first days of June than he found himself surrounded by revolt. Aided, however, by Frere's Division of Moncey's Corps, he rapidly stamped out the insurrection in a series of actions at Logrono, Torquemada, Segovia, and Cabeçon, and occupied Santander on the sea-coast. But a more formidable enemy soon approached. Twenty-five thousand men well equipped with artillery—the nucleus of which was furnished by Taranco's Division which had invaded the north of Portugal in conjunction with Junot—and commanded by General Blake, formed a junction at Benevente with 10,000 men under Cuesta, Captain-General of Leon and Old Castille. The danger was pressing. Segovia, a crucial point on the line of communication, had been left unoccupied. Gobert and Vedel had been sent to reinforce Dupont; Frere had been despatched to Requeña. Yet, to use Napoleon's expression, "A check given to Dupont would have a slight effect; but a wound received by Bessières would give the army a locked jaw. Not an inhabitant of Madrid, not a peasant of the valleys, that does not feel the affairs of Spain are involved in the affairs of Bessières." Realising at length the imminence of the danger, Savary recalled Frere from Requeña; Vedel, Gobert, and Dupont from Andalusia.

To meet the coming attack, Marshal Bessières concentrated every available man and horse at Palencia, mustering a Division of Light Cavalry, two Divisions and a Brigade of Infantry, having a total strength of 15,000 men and 30 guns. Several courses were open to the enemy, any of which would have caused annoyance and embarrassment to the French. Cuesta, like the Khalifa at Omdurman, selected the one most calculated to ensure to himself crushing defeat. Leaving 10,000 men at Benevente, he marched into the flat country with 26,000 regular troops, 18,000 armed peasants, and about 30 guns to try the effect of a pitched battle. Bessières at once advanced to meet him; struck the Spaniards on the 14th of July at Medina de Rio Seco and drove them headlong from the field with the loss of 7,000 men and 18 guns. The French, whose casualties had been trifling, entered Benevente on the 16th, and captured vast quantities of arms and stores recently arrived from England. On the

IN THE PENINSULA

29th they entered Leon, and were marching thence against Galicia when news arrived of the Capitulation of Baylen, whereupon Bessières, realising the crisis, retired and took up a defensive position at Mayorga, abandoning his ultimate object of lending a helping hand to Junot in Portugal. So far as the people of the Peninsula were concerned, his retreat was most fortunately timed. Junot was left isolated at the very moment when a British army was landing in Mondego Bay.

The state of affairs in Spain not unnaturally caused Napoleon the greatest discontent. Apart from the disgraceful surrender at Baylen, the retreat of Moncey from San Clemente to Madrid called forth a sharp rebuke from the Emperor. Savary was leniently dealt with; his cleverness was eulogised and his deficiencies attributed to the fact that he had not as yet acquired the habit of commanding-in-chief. The retirement of Verdier from Saragossa was considered premature, but the greatest error of all is to be found in the fact that King Joseph, on hearing of the Baylen disaster, not only failed to redeem the honour of the French by assuming the offensive with the troops available, amounting to 25,000 men and 80 guns, but actually retreated behind the Ebro, and by so doing destroyed the Emperor's arrangements for confining each province to its own insurrection, and isolating it from its neighbours.

These, then, were the consequences of the Capitulation of Baylen: the loss of 25,000 men; the nullification of Bessières' victory; Moncey prevented resuming the offensive for which he was now ready; the siege of Saragossa raised; Madrid abandoned, and the prestige of the French arms destroyed. Yet in the moment of his extreme anger, Napoleon's generosity and sense of justice prevailed. The former services of the General Officers who had now so greatly disgraced themselves, were borne in mind; the lives of Dupont and his colleagues, which would inevitably have been forfeited by sentence of a court-martial, were spared; and one at least of them, Vedel, took advantage of the opportunity to show his gratitude and redeem his character before the fall of the Empire.

CHAPTER III

A deputation from the Asturias appeals to England—England eagerly responds—Her lack of forethought and statesmanship —Description of the geography of the Peninsula.

AT the period of which we are speaking, Great Britain was, and—with one short interlude—for many years had been, at war with France; she did not quite know why; she expected to emerge from the struggle victorious; she did not quite know how. During the preceding years her troops had for the most part been frittered away either under the mismanagement of an incompetent commander of royal birth, or on inane projects in every quarter of the globe. Successes had, it is true, been occasionally gained —notably that in Egypt by Sir Ralph Abercrombie and General Hutchinson—and in a variety of conflicts the British soldier had again and again proved his undeniable fighting power, yet disasters had lowered our military reputation, not only abroad, but at home, and it became a kind of axiom, more particularly about the Court, that the Hessian and every other species of the riff-raff of Germany was unquestionably superior to the Englishman in every soldier-like quality. That the latter could hope to encounter with anything more than a transient success the legions of France on equal terms, would have been considered by many people a madman's dream.

The chief motive animating the British Government

appears to have been a personal hatred of Napoleon and a dread of the democratic principles which he represented. Among the people at large the unexpected resistance of the Spaniards excited the greatest interest. The arrival, during the first week in June, 1808, of a deputation from the Asturias invoking the assistance of England, raised the general enthusiasm to fever-point. Shortly afterwards a similar message arrived from the Bishop of Oporto as representing the insurrection which had by this time spread to Portugal. A theatre on which a British Army could distinguish itself seemed at last to have been found, and the most sanguine hopes, based upon the most shallow foundation, prevailed among all classes. The indolence and degeneracy of the Spaniards, the intriguing duplicity of the Portuguese, and the feeble nature of the insurrection, on the one hand, and the enormous strength, moral and physical, of Napoleon and his armies, on the other, were alike disregarded. Every statement of a Spaniard, however ridiculous, was accepted as a gospel truth, while no calumny against the French, however gross, could be too great for the credulity of the hearer. For the British public is totally devoid of the judicial faculty and of the power of impartial discrimination. Of the laws of evidence it is profoundly ignorant, and gives credit only to what falls in with its preconceived ideas.

The fact that Spain and Britain were now at war did not affect the conduct of the Ministry in the slightest degree. "They seemed," observes Napier, "by their precipitate measures, to be more afraid of losing the assistance of the Spaniards than prepared to take the lead in a contest which could only be supported by the power and riches of Great Britain. Instead of a statesman with rank and capacity to establish the influence of England by judicious counsels and applications of succour, a number of obscure and inexperienced men were sent to

IN THE PENINSULA 43

various parts of the Peninsula and were empowered to distribute money and supplies at discretion. Instead of carefully sifting the information obtained from such agents, and consulting distinguished military and naval officers in the arrangement of a comprehensive plan which might be supported vigorously, the ministers formed crude projects, parcelled out their forces in small expeditions without any definite object, altered their plans with every idle report, and altered their commanders as lightly as their plans. Disregarding all prudent considerations, and entering into formal relations with every knot of Spanish politicians assuming the title of a supreme Junta, the government dealt with unsparing hands enormous supplies at the demand of those self-elected authorities. They made no conditions, took no security for the succours being justly applied, and with affected earnestness renounced the right of interfering with the Spanish internal arrangements, when the ablest Spaniards expected and desired such interference to repress folly and violence. England was entitled in policy and justice to direct the Spanish councils. Spain solicited her aid in a common cause, and a generous, vigorous interference was necessary to save that cause from a few ignorant, conceited men accidentally invested with authority. Numerous and ill-chosen military agents also produced infinite mischief. Selected principally because they spoke Spanish, few of them had any knowledge of war beyond regimental duty, and there was no controlling authority; each did what seemed good to him. The Spanish Generals willingly received men whose inexperience was a recommendation, and whose friendship could advance their consequence. Their flattering, confidential politeness diverted the attention of the agents from the true objects of their mission, they looked not to the efficiency of the Armies, but adopted the inflated language and extravagant opinions of the chiefs, and by their reports raised erroneous notions as to the relative situations of the contending forces. Some exceptions there were, but the Ministers were better pleased with the sanguine than the cautious, and made their own wishes the measure of their judgment. Accordingly enthusiasm, numbers, courage, and talent were gratuitously found for every occasion, and money, arms, and clothing were demanded incessantly and supplied with profusion. The arms, however, were generally left in their cases to rot or fall into the hands of the enemy, and sometimes they were sold to foreign merchants. The clothing seldom reached the soldier's back; the money, always misapplied, was sometimes embezzled by those who received it for the nation; more often employed to forward the private views of the Juntas, to the detriment of public affairs, and it is a fact that from the beginning to the end of the war, an English musket was rarely to be seen in the hands of a Spanish soldier." "There is," says the same author, with fine irony, "a way of conferring a favour which seems like accepting one, and this secret being discovered by the English Cabinet, the Spaniards soon demanded as a right what they had at first solicited as a boon."

The population of Spain at the period of which we are speaking, amounted to about 11,000,000; that of Portugal to about 1,200,000 souls. As regards the configuration of the Peninsula, "the land," observes Hamley ("Operations of War," part v. ch. i.), "rises from the coast towards the centre, and the line of the watershed traverses the country, from south-west in Andalusia to the north, where it merges in the western extremity of the Pyrenees. From this spinal ridge ribs of mountain ranges extend east and west. Between these run the great streams thrown off by the watershed, mostly to the westward.

"A French army entering Spain would therefore find its path crossed by barriers of mountains and rivers, which when mastered would become successive lines of defence against an enemy coming from the south. But they would form obstacles of a different character if an enemy should operate from Portugal in the direction of their length; and this was a mainly important feature in the Peninsula War. . . . As for Spain, we find that the Pyrenees form a barrier between it and France, forbidding the supply of large armies, except by roads which lie between the extremities of the mountains, and the coast on each side; that the great rivers, far from marking the lines of the great roads (which in other countries so frequently lie along the banks) flow in broken, rocky channels difficult of access; that the cultivated districts are few and small as compared with the extent of the country; that the frontier of Portugal is so rigid as to admit of only two roads by which Lisbon can be reached from Madrid, and we shall then comprehend the situation of the French armies in Spain, how dependent they were on the one great road on each side of the Pyrenees, how disjointed was their front when it faced towards Portugal, how difficult it was to subsist on the resources of the country, and how perilous to draw together the scattered parts of the army, separated by rugged defiles which were held by guerillas."

CHAPTER IV

Sir A. Wellesley appointed to command a British force in the Peninsula—Choice of Lines of Operation—Wellesley lands in Mondego Bay and advances on Lisbon—Fight at Roriça—Battle of Vimeiro—Arrival of Sir H. Dalrymple—Convention of Cintra.

THE deputation from the Asturias arrived in England on June 6, 1808. The Cabinet lost no time in making up its mind to employ a military force in the Peninsula. On the 14th a letter from H.R.H. the Commander-in-Chief appointed Lieutenant-General Sir Arthur Wellesley—at that time Chief Secretary for Ireland—who had just been promoted to the rank of Lieutenant-General, to the command of the only body of troops immediately available for active service. The letter ran as follows :—

"HORSE GUARDS, *June* 14, 1808.

" SIR,—His Majesty having been graciously pleased to appoint you to the command of a detachment of his army, to be employed on a particular service, I have to desire that you will be pleased to take the earliest opportunity to assume the command of this force and to carry into effect such instructions as you may receive from H.M.'s Ministers. . . . The Staff appointed to this force is composed as follows: Major-General Spencer, Major-General Hill,

Major-General Ferguson, Brigadier-Generals Nightingall, Fane, and Catlin Crauford. . . . On all subjects relative to your command, you will be pleased to correspond with me, and you will regularly communicate to me all military transactions in which you may be engaged, reporting to me all vacancies that may occur in the troops under your command. You will transmit monthly returns of the troops under your command to the Secretary at War and to the Adjutant-General for my information : and you will strictly adhere to H.M.'s Regulations, in regard to the pay, clothing, and appointments of the troops; and your special attention must necessarily be directed to their discipline, and to the interior economy of the different Corps, which is so essential, not only to the comfort of the soldier but to the promotion of his health under every change of climate to which he may be exposed. . . . It is particularly desirable that the officer at the head of the Quartermaster-General's Staff should be directed to keep a journal descriptive of the movements of the troops and occurrences in which they are engaged; as also that he should take and collect plans of the harbours, positions, or fortified places in which the troops may be, for the purpose of being transmitted to me and lodged in the military depôt. In all points where any question or doubt may arise, and in which you may be desirous of receiving further and more specific instructions, you will always find me ready to pay the earliest attention to your representations.

"I am, &c.,
(Signed) "FREDERICK,
"*Commander-in-Chief.*
"Lieutenant-General Sir Arthur Wellesley, K.B."

For the selection of a strategical line of operations in

48 WELLINGTON'S OPERATIONS

the Peninsula several alternative courses presented themselves. Among them were the following :—

1. To operate from the east coast based upon Barcelona. "Barcelona," observes Napier, "with its immense population, great riches, good harbour and strong forts, might be called the key of the South of France. . . . The proximity of Sicily where a large British army was kept in a state of constant preparation, made it more than probable an English force would reach Barcelona to establish a war at the threshold of France. Napoleon . . . well knew that thirty or forty thousand British troops occupying an intrenched camp in front of Barcelona, supported by a powerful fleet and having reserved depôts in Sicily and the Spanish islands might have been so wielded as to give ample occupation to 150,000 French. Protected by such an army, the Spanish levies might have been organised and instructed; their actual numbers could have been masked, increased, or diminished; the fleet would have been ready to co-operate, and the South of France whence the provisions of the enemy must have been drawn, would have been exposed to descents and the inconvenience of actual hostilities." It was for these reasons that the Emperor had so promptly seized Barcelona. An attack from the sea would now be consequently a hazardous process : the voyage from England, for the transport of reinforcements, stores, &c., would be double the length of that to the mouth of the Tagus, and, finally, it must be noted that since the Royal Road was the principal communication with France, operations from the eastern coast could not ensure the decisive effect which might be looked for from an advance from the north or west.

2. To make Cadiz the base of operations and advance thence against Madrid. This was a favourite project of the Ministry, was well thought of by Sir John Moore,

IN THE PENINSULA 49

and warmly advised by General Spencer on the ground that the presence of an English army would give strength not only to the forces of Castanos, but to the Junta of Seville, which had constituted itself the central government of Spain. "From Carolina (in the Morena) to Madrid is," says Napier, "only ten marches, and posted at the former, the allied army could have protected Lisbon as well as Seville, because a forward movement would force the French to concentrate round the Spanish capital. Andalusia would thus have become the principal object of the invaders; but the allied armies, holding the passes of the Morena, having left their flank protected by Estremadura and Portugal, and their right by Murcia and Valencia; having rich provinces and large cities behind them, a free communication with the sea, and abundance of ports, could have fought a fair field for Spain." But although from the purely military point of view this was the correct line of advance, it was made out of the question by the conduct of the Spaniards who refused us admission to Cadiz.

3. To occupy Portugal and, after expelling Junot, operate by the valley either of the Tagus or Douro; the former, leading directly on Madrid and bringing the army into conjunction with the Spanish levies of the south; the latter, menacing the enemy's direct line of communication with France and compelling him to "form front to a flank" in order to meet the attack.

4. To land in Galicia or the Asturias and move eastward on a line parallel to the sea-coast, supported by the fleet. The difficulties of the rugged coast and mountainous country were, however, enormous hindrances in the way of such an advance; while the flank of the invading army would be exposed to an attack from the side of Burgos.

5. To assail the neck of the French communications

by landing in the neighbourhood of Fuenterrabia and cutting the enemy from his base at Bayonne. But although such an operation if practicable would have enormously increased the difficulties of the French, and, under certain conditions, might well have had decisive effect, the hour for it had not yet arrived. The fortresses of San Sebastian and Pampeluna were in the hands of the French, and it was that fact which probably led to the abandonment of the idea, if entertained, for although subsequent information showed that the French on either side of the Pyrenees were strong enough to crush any force that could have been landed, the numbers of the enemy were enormously underrated in England at this period.

In regard to the selection of a theatre of war or indeed the carrying out of military operations in any form, the views of the Government were, however, singularly vague and undecided. "Spencer," says Napier (bk. ii. ch. 3), "supposed to be at Gibraltar was directed to repair to Cadiz and await Sir Arthur's orders; the latter was permitted to sail under the impression that Spencer was actually subject to his command, while other instructions empowered Spencer at his own discretion to commence operations in the south without reference to Sir A. Wellesley's proceedings. Admiral Purvis, who after Lord Collingwood's arrival, had no separate command, was authorised to undertake any enterprise in that quarter and even to control the operations of Sir Arthur by calling for the aid of his troops, that General being enjoined to pay all due obedience to such requisition. Yet Sir Arthur himself was informed that the accounts from Cadiz were bad; that no disposition to move either there or in the neighbourhood of Gibraltar was visible, and that the Cabinet was unwilling that he should go southward while the spirit of exertion appeared to reside more in the northward. Admiral Sir C. Cotton was informed that Wellesley was to co-operate with him in a descent at the mouth of the Tagus; but Sir Arthur himself had no definite instructions given for his own operations, although his instructions pointed to Portugal. Thus, in fact, no officer, naval or military, knew exactly what his powers were with the exception of Purvis; who being only second in command for his own service, was really authorised to control all the operations of the land forces, provided he directed them to that quarter which had been declared unfavourable for any operations at all."

"To occupy Cadiz was a favourite project with the Cabinet. Neither Spencer's unsuccessful attempt to gain admittance nor the representations of Sir Hew, who had ground to believe that the attempt would bring down the army of Castanos to oppose it by force, had any weight with the Ministers. They did not see that in a political view such a measure pressed as a preliminary would give a handle for misrepresentation; and that in a military view, the burden of Cadiz would clog operations in Portugal. Adopting all projects and weighing none, they displayed the most incredible confusion of ideas; for the plan of sending 10,000 men to Seville was said to be in pursuance of a promise made by Sir H. Dalrymple to the Junta, whereas the despatch of that General quoted as authority for this promise of help, contained nothing of the kind, and was written before any Junta existed!"

"But at this period, personal enmity to Napoleon and violent party prejudices, had so disturbed the judgments of men relative to that monarch, that any information speaking of strength or success for him was regarded with suspicion. The Ministers . . . became the dupes of their own practices, listening with complacency to all those tales of mutiny among his troops, disaffection of his generals and insurrections in France, which the cunning or folly of their agents transmitted to them. Hence sprung such projects as the one above. The whole English force disposable was not much above 30,000 men, and was distributed off Cadiz, off the coast of Portugal, on the eastern parts of England and in the Channel. The French in the Peninsula were about 120,000 men, and they possessed all the Portuguese and most of the Spanish fortresses. The English Army had no reserve, no fixed plan; it was to be divided and act upon a double line of operations. The French had a strong reserve at Bayonne, the Grand French Army of 40,000 veterans was untouched, and ready to succour the troops in the Peninsula if they required it.

"Happily this visionary plan was in no particular followed by the generals entrusted with its execution. The catastrophe of Baylen marred the great combinations of the French emperor, fortune drew the scattered divisions of the English Army together, and the decisive vigour of Sir Arthur Wellesley sweeping away all those cobweb projects, obtained all the success the bad arrangements of the Ministers would permit."

On the 12th of July, a day memorable in English history, Sir Arthur Wellesley sailed with the following troops from Cork Harbour :—

	Officers	N.C.O's and Men.
20th Light Dragoons	13	368
Royal Artillery	14	408
Royal Engineers	6	12
5th Regiment	46	1061
9th "	39	1022
36th "	43	660
38th "	47	1032
40th "	47	993
45th "	34	560
60th (5th Battalion)	33	1006
71st Highland	38	946
91st "	40	978
95th (2nd Battalion) 4 Companies	19	427
Total	419	9,478

IN THE PENINSULA 53

A veteran battalion, intended for garrison duty at Gibraltar, accompanied the convoy; which also conveyed 5 nine-pounder, 6 six-pounder, and 22 three-pounder guns and 15 howitzers; as well as a large quantity of pikes and small arms for the Spanish insurgents. Sir Arthur on board a fast-sailing frigate soon outstripped the fleet and landed at Corunna, where the citizens demanded arms and money, but declined the aid of his troops, in spite of the fact that the battle of Rio Seco had been lost only the week before and, that Galicia was at the mercy of Bessières. Wellesley then re-embarked and landed at Oporto where he received an utterly false account of the state of affairs, being given to understand that 10,000 Portuguese troops were under arms, and that the whole force of the enemy did not exceed 15,000 men.

At the latter end of 1807 a force of five or six thousand * men had, as we have seen, been despatched from England under command of Major-General Spencer, primarily to capture the Spanish colony of Ceuta, but with a kind of roving commission to attack any foe whom he might chance to encounter. He had chiefly spent the interval in sailing about between Cadiz and Lisbon. At this moment Wellesley received from him a letter stating that the French force in Portugal amounted to 20,500 men— an estimate still below the mark, but much more accurate than that of the Bishop of Oporto, and urging a disem-

* Royal Artillery	...	...	...	66	Rank and File.
6th Regiment	...	...	...	966	,,
29th ,,	...	...	...	810	,,
32nd ,,	...	...	...	921	,,
50th ,,	...	...	...	957	,,
82nd ,,	...	...	...	945	,,
Staff Corps	...	...	...	48	,,
			Total	4,718	,,

barkation in Andalusia. Sir Arthur discredited Spencer's estimate, declined the proposal, and determined to land in Portugal with a view to the expulsion of Junot and his corps. An attack on the mouth of the Tagus had been urged by the home government, but the general soon ascertained from Sir Charles Cotton, the British Admiral, that such an operation would be fraught with extreme hazard on account of the bar in the river, and the strength of the protecting forts. Another landing place had consequently to be sought. "It was difficult to find a place," says Napier. "The coast from the Minho to the Tagus, save at a few points is rugged and dangerous. . . . With the slightest breeze from the seaboard, a terrible surf breaks along the whole coast; and when the south wind which usually prevails from August to the winter months, blows, a more dangerous shore is not to be found in any part of the world."

Eventually the choice fell upon Lavaos, a village on the left bank of the Mondego river, a spot ill-adapted to the purpose, but the best available under the circumstances. Previous to disembarkation the following instructions were issued—"29th July, 1808. . . . The Infantry will be directed to be landed from the transports in the roads, and to be rowed in the boats up the river, and landed on the south bank of it: General Fane's Brigade first; then General Ferguson's; then General Crauford's. . . . The men will land with three days' bread and two days' meat cooked. The C.O. R.A. is to land the three brigades of artillery each with half the usual proportion of ammunition, the forge cart, etc. He will also land 500,000 rounds of musket ammunition for the use of the troops, for which carriage will be provided.

"Each soldier will have with him three good flints.

"Besides the bread above directed to be landed with

IN THE PENINSULA

the soldiers, three days' bread to be packed up in bags containing 100 lbs. each on board each of the transports, for the number of soldiers who shall be disembarked from it.

"Three days' oats to be landed with each horse."

Next day, the 30th, a letter from the Secretary of State brought what could not fail to be a keen disappointment to Sir Arthur. It had been decided to increase the expeditionary force by the addition of the corps, recently returned from Sweden, under Sir John Moore, K.B., about 12,000 strong, consisting of a regiment of Cavalry, 11 battalions of Infantry and 42 guns; by two Brigades under Generals Anstruther and Acland, and by the 18th Hussars. The whole force employed—including Wellesley's troops—would then amount to about 35,000 men with 66 guns. It was to be commanded by Lieut.-Gen. Sir Hew Dalrymple with Sir Harry Burrard as second in command. The army was to be organised in five Divisions, and Wellesley, hitherto commander of the force, would become the junior General of Division; the others being Lieut.-Gens. Sir John Moore, the Hon. John Hope, Mackenzie Fraser, and Lord Paget. Brigadier-General H. Clinton was appointed Acting-Adjutant-General, and Lieut.-Col. G. Murray Acting-Quartermaster General.

The fact of his supersession did not however affect Wellesley's plans. Having ascertained that Loison's Division of Junot's army was at a distance, and that his landing could not be opposed in force, he resolved not to cancel the orders which he had issued; but wrote to give Sir Harry Burrard, who was almost momentarily expected, every information; and to suggest that Sir John Moore's Corps would do well to land in Mondego Bay and march thence upon Santarem—about 60 miles distant—with a view to cutting off the retreat of the enemy should he attempt to make it either by the north of the Tagus and Almeida or south of that river by Elvas.

The disembarkation, begun on August 1st, was not completed until the 5th, when, in the very nick of time, General Spencer with 5,000 men—the 6th, 29th, 32nd, 50th, and 82nd Regiments and a Battery of R. A.—arrived at the mouth of the river, not in obedience to any instructions—for Wellesley's letter had not reached him —but having started on his own initiative from Cadiz on hearing of the proposed descent on Portugal.

The troops were forthwith brigaded as follows:—

1st Brigade	Major-Gen. Hill		5th, 9th, 38th Regts.
2nd ,,	,,	Ferguson	36th, 40th, 71st ,,
3rd ,,	Brigd.- ,,	Nightingall	29th and 82nd ,,
4th ,,	,, ,,	Bowes	6th and 32nd ,,
5th ,,	,, ,,	Catlin Crauford	45th, 50th, 91st ,,
6th or Light Brigade	,, ,,	Hon. H. Fane	5th Batt. 60th and (4 Coys.) 95th Rifles.

General Spencer, as second in command, was not put in charge of any special body of troops.

For parade purposes the 1st Brigade was ordered to take the right of the line; the 2nd, the left; the 3rd, the right centre; the 5th, the centre; the 4th, the left centre. The Light Brigade was drawn up on one of the flanks, according to circumstances, but on the march always formed the advance guard.

Orders were issued that regiments in line were to be formed in two ranks instead of three, as had hitherto been the custom, the result being a great increase of fire-power.

The Artillery under command of Lieut.-Col. Robe, R.A.—exclusive of Spencer's battery, which was left behind for want of horses—comprised 6 nine-pounders, 12 six-pounders, and 4 howitzers, the guns being drawn

IN THE PENINSULA

either by horses cast from Dragoon regiments, or by cart horses bought in Ireland at £12 apiece. A half-battery was attached to each Brigade, and a howitzer to the 1st, 2nd, 5th, and Light Brigades.

Of the Cavalry, only 180 troopers were mounted. Preparations were made for an immediate advance. Arrangements were made for the conveyance of 17 days' bread and 5 days' meat. The scale of rations was fixed at 1 lb. of bread or biscuit and 1 lb. of meat per man. On the issue of salt meat, ¼ pint of spirits or 1 pint of wine was allowed. Six women per each company of 100 men were allowed to accompany the column. Each woman received a half and each child a quarter ration. It was a standing order that whenever troops were ordered to march they were to receive one day's meat, which was to be immediately cooked, and carried by the men on the following day.

The scale of forage for horses was laid down at 10 lbs. hay and 10 lbs. oats: otherwise 14 lbs. Indian corn or barley and 10 lbs. of straw.

Requisitions were only to be made by order of a general, or officer commanding a brigade or detachment; and proper receipts were in all cases to be given for goods supplied.

In regard to ammunition, the Infantry soldiers carried 60 rounds per man. Five hundred thousand additional rounds were carried on the R.A. carts, and 180,000 rounds on mules—2,000 per mule.

"Sir Arthur's plan," says Napier, "embraced three principal objects:—

"1st. To hold on by the coast for ship supplies, thus avoiding a drain of men to protect magazines on shore and covering the landing of reinforcements from England." (To this may be added a still more pressing reason, viz., the fact that Portugal was known to be very short of bread supplies. Indian corn was the staple food, but there was little remaining, and at this time of year the streams were so low that the mills were unable to grind it.)

"2nd. To keep the troops in mass to strike an important blow.

"3rd. To strike that blow as near Lisbon as possible and bring the affairs of Portugal to a crisis."

The landing of Spencer's force was completed on the 8th, and at 3 a.m. on August 9th the advance guard—made up of 50 Dragoons and the Light Brigade—quitting Lavaos a day's march ahead of the main body, started on the road for Lisbon. On the 10th it reached Leiria, 24 miles distant, unopposed. On that day Wellesley heard of King Joseph's flight from Madrid, and felt assured that for the present he was safe from any attack on the part of Bessières. Leaving Leiria on the 13th, the army, marching in two columns—the 2nd and 4th Brigades by Batalha, the remainder by the direct road—reached Calvario that day, Alcobaça on the 14th, and arrived on the next at Caldas. The army, as already stated, had marched from Lavaos with 17 days' bread—of which enough for 4 days was carried in the men's havresacks—salt meat for 5 days, and spirits for 10 days. Nearly 3 days' bread had been received from the port of Nazareth on the 14th, so that, 6 days' bread having been consumed, the army had enough for 14 days in hand. Wine could be bought along the line of march, and by the terms of a contract it had been arranged that 3 days' fresh meat should always be in camp.

Meanwhile, General Junot had been engaged in strengthening his positions about Lisbon and in consolidating the French power in Portugal. On the breaking out of the Spanish insurrection in May the position of Junot became one of considerable difficulty.

The example of the Spaniards was quickly followed in
Portugal. Tarranco's Division at Oporto arrested its
French commander. Solano had already quitted the
Alemtejo. Caraffe's Division at Lisbon—6,000 strong—
became a growing menace to the French. Vigorous
measures were necessary. Five thousand men of the
Division were cleverly disarmed and put on board the
hulks in the Tagus; the remainder escaped. Flying
columns scoured the country, and the insurgents in arms
were speedily crushed. The appearance of General
Spencer at the mouth of the Tagus early in July
created an alarm which died away on the return of
that officer to Cadiz. The respite was only temporary.
News arrived of Dupont's surrender at Baylen and the
flight of the King from Madrid. Matters were evidently
going from bad to worse. The approach of vessels conveying two British battalions—one from Madeira, the
other from Gibraltar—added fuel to the excitement of
the populace of Lisbon, already furious at the robberies
of the French troops, and eager to turn upon and rend
the national enemy at the earliest opportunity. In order
to hold the inhabitants in check, it became necessary to
occupy the forts with a garrison of about 7,000 men, a
force altogether out of proportion to the whole strength
of Junot's army. At the same time the Spanish General
Galuzzo was threatening the Alemtejo from the side of
Estramadura. To crown everything came news on
August 2nd of the British landing at the mouth of the
Mondego.

Junot's Corps contained at this period about 28,000
men, of which, however, garrisons—apart from that of
Lisbon—absorbed 5,000. Of the remainder, not many
more than 15,000 were available to make head against
the English. A strong division under General Loison
was immediately directed to march from Estremos to

Abrantes. General de Laborde was despatched on the
6th from Lisbon to Leiria with orders to retard
Wellesley's advance and gain time for the concentration
of the French army. In pursuance of these orders,
de Laborde on the 9th was at Candeiros; Loison at
Abrantes. Next day, the former finding himself anticipated at Leiria by the British, who had thus interposed
between him and Loison, seeing no position suitable for
defence at Batalha, and divining the road nearest the sea
to be that on which Wellesley was most likely to advance,
retired southward by Alcobaça and Obidos, and on the
14th took up a position at Roriça, whence he sent a
detachment to his right in hopes of communicating with
Loison.

On this day Sir Arthur was at Alcobaça. Short as was
the time which had elapsed since he had set foot in the
country, it was enough to imbue him with the utmost
distrust of Spanish and Portuguese statements and
promises. He now had his first practical experience of
their value. General Freire, commanding a Portuguese
Division 6,000 strong, had met him on landing with the
loudest protestations of support and the most sanguine
assurances of success. The combined forces had marched
together as far as Leiria, but on the approach of the
French the courage of the Portuguese general seemed
quickly to evaporate. At Calvario on the 13th Sir
Arthur had received a letter from him expressing his
intention of operating on a separate line along the
Tagus. Remonstrance and appeal to his honour were
alike unavailing. The utmost that Freire could be
induced to do was to allow 260 of his Cavalry and 1,400
of his Infantry to accompany his ally under command of
Colonel Trant, a British officer.

On the 15th the Light Brigade came into contact with
the French picquets at Obidos, drove them in, was in

IN THE PENINSULA 61

turn repulsed by the supports, and the first British shot was thus fired in the Peninsular War. Next day De Laborde was discovered at Roriça, three miles distant, strongly posted on high ground commanding the valley through which ran the road to Lisbon. His force consisted of about 5,000 men (including 500 cavalry) and 6 guns, and was thus outnumbered by nearly three to one. Support was, however, at hand. Loison, who had been at Thomar on the 11th, finding himself cut off from his colleague, had retired southward, and was now near Cercal, about fourteen miles distant from De Laborde. The latter, therefore, relying on his own ability and the strength of his position, determined to hold his ground.

At 7 a.m. on the 17th August the British troops issued forth in three columns from Obidos. In the centre Sir Arthur, with the Brigades of Hill, Crauford, and Nightingall, 350 British and Portuguese Cavalry, 400 Portuguese Light Infantry, and 12 guns, moved directly against the village of Roriça. On his right Trant, with 50 Portuguese Dragoons and 1,000 Infantry, threatened the enemy's left. On the other flank Ferguson, with 40 troopers, the 2nd and 4th Brigades, 250 Riflemen, and 6 guns, moved along a line of heights parallel to the main road with the double object of turning De Laborde's right and intercepting the approach of Loison. The Light Brigade covered the advance of Ferguson on the left as well as that of Wellesley in the centre. The encircling movement was well executed, but De Laborde, thus menaced on both flanks, had no intention of losing his line of retreat. Waiting till the last moment, he retired in excellent order for a mile, then took up a second position on the Columbeira height, a strongly marked ridge falling steeply to the front and only to be approached by three or four difficult passes. It was intended that Trant and Ferguson, with Fane, should turn the position as before and that the centre should be held back pending the completion of the enveloping movement. These orders were unfortunately not properly executed. Fane's Brigade was already in touch with the enemy's right. Ferguson, instead of turning his flank, wheeled too soon and moved directly against his right. Whether with a view to supporting the riflemen or that he expected little resistance, Wellesley allowed Nightingall to join in the action without waiting for the full effect of the turning movements. The 9th Regiment, with the 29th from Hill's Brigade, in its impatience to come to close quarters, assailed the front instead of the left of the French. One might be describing one of the earlier actions in the Boer War. The ascent was steep, the ground broken by rocks and copses. On reaching the summit the 29th, leading the advance, was met by a vigorous counter attack and forced below the brow of the hill with heavy loss. Once more the two regiments gained the height; a second time the French dashed at them. "I never saw such desperate fighting," wrote Wellesley next day. The nature of the ground prevented the aid of the supporting regiments. At length the 5th, which had maintained the true direction, came up on the right of the 29th and outflanked De Laborde's left. About the same time Ferguson, retrieving his initial error, had, in pursuance of his orders, got in rear of the enemy's right and severed his line of communication with Loison, whereupon the French commander abandoned the Columbeira height and retired by alternate wings, covered by his cavalry, to the Zambugeiro ridge, three-quarters of a mile in rear. Here he again attempted to make a stand, his flanks being protected by deep ravines, but the British were not to be denied; the position became untenable, and De Laborde fell back, still disputing the ground, to the Quinta de Bugagliera, having furnished a

IN THE PENINSULA 63

most admirable illustration of the duties of a retarding force in the face of overwhelming numbers. The firing ceased about four o'clock, and about the same time the approach of a patrol was observed from Loison's Division. The main body of that General was, however, still five miles distant, beyond Bombarral, and in the night De Laborde, who had lost 600 men and 3 guns, retreated through the pass of Runa to Montechique, nearly thirty miles south of Roriça. Although Wellesley's plan of attack had not been carried out in its entirety, the action served to inspire his troops with confidence in themselves and their commander. The British loss amounted to 70 killed, 335 wounded, and 74 missing, casualties which but for the impetuosity of the troops should have been reduced by two-thirds. Sir Arthur had intended to march next day to Torres Vedras, but on hearing of the arrival off the coast of the Brigades under Acland and Anstruther, he halted at Lourinham, and on the 19th occupied the heights and village of Vimeiro, as the most suitable spot for covering their disembarkation in Maceira Bay.

A slight change was now made in the organisation of the army. With a view to the better distribution of the light troops, a company of the 60th Rifles was attached to each of the Brigades, while, to fill their place in the Light Brigade, the 50th Regiment was transferred to it from the 5th.

Anstruther landed on the evening of the 19th, and Acland next day. The Brigade of the former comprised the 2nd Battalion 9th (675 R. and F.), the 2nd Battalion 43rd (861), the 2nd Battalion 52nd (585), and the 97th (769); that of the latter the 2nd, 20th, and 2 companies 95th Rifles, with 2 companies and 6 guns R.A. The Riflemen were transferred to the Light Brigade. Anstruther's and Acland's were numbered respectively the 7th and 8th Brigades.

Orders were then issued for an advance at 4.30 a.m. on the morrow to the heights of Mafra, whereby Lisbon would be almost reached and the enemy's position on the mountains south of Torres Vedras turned. But on the evening of the 20th Sir Harry Burrard arrived in Maceira Roads. Wellesley at once waited on him and stated his projects. Sir Harry, however, thought them too bold, and not only forbade the movement proposed for Sir John Moore upon Santarem, but ordered Wellesley's force to halt in its present position pending Sir John's arrival. Wellesley then went on shore again, while Sir Harry slept on board the *Brazen*.

Meanwhile, on the 15th, two days before the fight at Roriça, Junot, who had been detained at Lisbon, partly awaiting General Kellermann, who was engaged in suppressing disorder beyond the Tagus, partly on account of the increasing unrest in the city and by the alarm caused by the arrival of the two British regiments at the mouth of the river, marched *viâ* Villa Franca, effected a junction with Loison at Alcoentre, and returned to join De Laborde at Torres Vedras. Upwards of 7,000 men were, however, left to keep down the populace in the capital, and Junot's whole force when concentrated at Torres Vedras—organised in three Divisions of Infantry (De Laborde, Loison, and Kellermann) and one of Cavalry (Margeron), with 23 light guns—fell short of 14,000 men. Preceded by his Cavalry, which harassed the British camp and concealed his movements, Junot marched during the night of the 20th, cleared the defile of Torres Vedras, and at 9 a.m. found himself in the presence of the British army posted about the village of Vimeiro on a ridge behind the Lourinham road, with its back to the sea, from which its centre was about a mile distant. Observing that the left of the position—which, indeed, had been taken up rather with a view to covering the landing of the new arrivals than for purposes of defence—was practically unguarded and liable to be outflanked, but unaware of the fact that Wellesley had been reinforced by Acland and Anstruther with an additional battery, whose arrival had raised his fighting strength to 20,000 men, Junot, instead of taking the precaution to make a proper reconnaissance, boldly resolved to fall upon the British left and centre and drive them into the sea. With this object Brennier's Brigade of De Laborde's Division, supported shortly afterwards by that of Solignac from the Division of Loison, was pushed forward through broken and wooded ground to turn the British left; while De Laborde and Loison each with the remaining Brigade of his Division hurled themselves against the front.

Wellesley had been to some extent caught napping. His mind was set on resuming the offensive; the possibility of being himself attacked seems hardly to have occurred to him. About midnight he had been warned of the enemy's approach. He did not, however, credit the news, for, writing to the Secretary of State at 6 a.m. on the 21st, he stated Junot to be about Torres Vedras, nine miles distant.

Six of his Brigades were drawn up on a ridge on the left bank of the Maceira stream. Those of Fane and Anstruther, with 6 guns, occupied an advanced hill on the right bank in front of the village of Vimeiro, a hill commanded, however, from the left rear by a narrow line of heights, separated by the Maceira from, but otherwise forming a continuation of, the ridge on which the remaining six Brigades had been posted. Along the foot of these heights ran a ravine, and beyond it the ground was so wooded and broken that the movements of each army were unseen by its opponents. Owing to the scarcity of water this part of the position was, as noticed by Junot, guarded originally by only one regiment, but on the first approach of the French Sir Arthur had quickly divined that the attack would be made upon his advanced Brigades and the left of his position. Leaving Hill to guard the right, he had consequently moved the other five Brigades—*i.e.*, the 2nd, 3rd, 4th, 5th, and 8th, under the immediate command of Ferguson—unperceived by the enemy across the stream on to the further line of heights to form front against Brennier and Solignac.

Long before these troops could take up their new position De Laborde and Loison with General Kellermann in reserve had begun the action in the centre. Their prospects of success were hardly encouraging, for to the eyes of the French the British troops appeared to be " established on an isolated mamelon commanding all approaches, and itself commanded in rear and on the flanks by heights showing a double range of steep escarpments. These were garnished with two lines of troops and a double row of batteries of heavy calibre forming four lines of fire independently of the mamelon " (Thiébault's Memoirs).

Against the Brigades of Fane and Anstruther thus strongly posted, De Laborde and Loison hurled themselves with their remaining two Brigades of Infantry formed in half battalion columns. Loison's attack upon the right of our position held by Anstruther proved little more than a demonstration and was easily repulsed by the 52nd and 97th. De Laborde's assault upon Fane was a much more serious affair. The riflemen thrown out as skirmishers were driven in after a vigorous resistance, disputing every inch of ground ; but Fane, in pursuance of a discretionary power given him by Wellesley, called up Colonel Robe with the reserve battery of Artillery, which poured in a terrible fire upon the enemy's front; while that of Acland who, hurrying up to support Ferguson and the Brigades moving to the extreme left of our position, happened to be passing at the moment and promptly unlimbered, struck him in flank. In vain the French columns, torn with grapeshot, pressed gallantly forward. On reaching the summit of the ridge they were met by a terrific volley by the 50th Regiment under Colonel Walker, charged in flank with the bayonet, and driven to the bottom of the hill in confusion. Observing the crisis, Kellermann brought up a Brigade of his Reserve Division on De Laborde's right, and attempted to pass Fane's left with a view to penetrating into the village of Vimeiro. The manœuvre was a clever one. It would have cut the British centre from its left and might easily have been successful, for Fane had no spare troops with whom to oppose it. But at the critical moment Anstruther, who had held the 43rd in reserve, despatched it to the threatened point. A desperate conflict ensued. One wing of the regiment, occupying an advanced post, was overpowered by numbers: the other, holding a churchyard in rear, stood firm. Kellermann's veteran grenadiers, their ranks torn with grapeshot from both flanks, wavered. The 43rd seized the occasion; dashed forward with the bayonet, and drove them back in "irrecoverable confusion"; but the loss of the regiment—120 men—gave evidence of the severity and critical nature of the struggle.

Then Colonel Taylor, issuing forth with his single squadron from the valley in rear of Vimeiro, fell upon the crowded fugitives and was cutting down many, when, with the swoop of a hawk, General Margeron charged down at the head of a Cavalry Brigade, cut Taylor and his Dragoons to pieces, and with the assistance of Kellermann's remaining Brigade covered the retreat of his comrades, leaving, however, seven guns in the hands of the victors.

Hardly had the attacks on the centre been repelled

than the contest broke out on the extreme left of the British position, a mile and a half distant. Among the rocks and watercourses of the broken and wooded ground Brennier's Brigade had wandered about until pulled up short by the ravine running along the foot of the heights already mentioned; but on his right, Solignac, turning the obstacle, scaled the height and wheeled to the left expecting to enfilade the British line and take its centre in reverse. But by this time Ferguson had reached his new position, and Solignac, instead of debouching on to an open space, found himself in presence of three Brigades of infantry formed in two lines at right angles to the main position, fronting north, having their left flank and rear guarded by Crauford's Brigade and Trant's Portuguese posted on a parallel ridge. He had little time to retrieve his error. Ferguson, with the leading Brigade, dashed at him with the bayonet and drove him, horse, foot, and artillery, over the brow of the ridge with the loss of six guns. Ferguson continued to advance, pressing the French in their retreat into the valley across which ran the road leading northward to Lourinham. As the ground widened Nightingall's Brigade prolonged the line. Bowes and Acland followed in support. Crauford and Trant, with his Portuguese advancing along a parallel road on the left, threatened to encircle the enemy as he retired.

On approaching the village of Pereganza events took an unexpected turn. Brennier, who had at length surmounted the various obstacles in his path and found a way across the ravine, appearing suddenly, fell upon the 71st and 82nd, and retook the captured guns. Supported by the 36th and 40th, the regiments quickly rallied, repelled the attack, recaptured the guns once more and made Brennier prisoner. The French columns retired in disorder. Solignac was cut off from his friends and in imminent danger of being surrounded by Ferguson and

IN THE PENINSULA 69

Crauford. Sir Arthur Wellesley saw a grand opportunity to strike a decisive blow. Unfortunately he was no longer in command. Sir Harry Burrard had landed, and though with great self-abnegation he had hitherto not interfered, it was impossible for a junior officer to initiate a new movement of such importance without his consent. Sir Arthur, therefore, pointed out that the direction taken in their retreat by De Laborde and Loison left Hill's Brigade nearer Torres Vedras than themselves, and begged Sir Harry to move with Hill, Anstruther, and Fane upon Torres Vedras, with a view to turning the formidable position of Montechique and cutting the enemy from Lisbon. At the same time Wellesley proposed to take the rest of the force himself, and pursue the French across the Baragueda mountains on to the Tagus. It was only midday. Half the army had not fired a shot and was quite fresh. But Burrard had not been on shore long enough to be able to realise the exact state of affairs. He considered that enough had been done, and not only stopped the proposed advance, but went so far as to order Ferguson—now nearly three miles distant—to halt in his victorious career. The victory was thus rendered incomplete and a great opportunity missed. To Sir Arthur the sense of disappointment must have been of the keenest. Had Burrard not refused his consent Junot's army must, in Wellesley's opinion, have been driven into a corner, and, in spite of our lack of cavalry, could hardly have escaped destruction.

Junot himself made no effort to retrieve the day, but drove off in a carriage. De Laborde therefore took command of the French centre in its retreat, while Thiébault, the Chief of the Staff, galloped to the right and with great promptitude carried off the Brigades of Solignac and Brennier. Being, in consequence of Burrard's order, unmolested, he quickly reunited them to the main body, and by a circuitous route regained the road to Torres Vedras.

All said and done, a good deal had been achieved. Wellesley had given proof of his unrivalled capacity to deal with the varying phases of a battle and snatch victory from impending defeat. The French had felt the weight of the British arms, and had been no less surprised than demoralised. The loss on our side amounted to 135 officers and men killed, 585 wounded and missing, one sixth of whom belonged to the 43rd alone. That of the enemy—including Generals Solignac wounded and Brennier prisoner—exceeded 2,000 men. Thirteen guns were left in our hands. Junot had committed glaring errors during the short campaign. His faulty and imperfect concentration; his lack of vigour in meeting the danger caused by the insurgent populace of Lisbon, and the advance of Wellesley; his failure to reconnoitre the British position at Vimeiro; his elementary blunder in breaking up his Divisions instead of keeping them intact; his tactics during the action and his culpable supineness after it, afford evidence of such incapacity that General Thiébault, his Chief of the Staff, considers Junot to have then shown the beginning of that mental aberration which terminated five years later in his self-destruction.

On the day after the battle, Sir Hew Dalrymple, arriving from Gibraltar, landed, and in his turn superseded Sir H. Burrard. Moore, with his reinforcement, was already in Maceira Bay, and on learning the state of affairs Sir Hew resolved on an immediate advance. Just at that moment, however, General Kellermann appeared with a flag of truce. On his initiative negotiations were begun which a few days later resulted in the Convention of Cintra—so called—pursuant to the terms of which the French army of 25,747 men and 30 guns evacuated Por-

tugal by the end of September and was conveyed back by
sea to France. Although exception may be taken to
some matters of detail, yet as to the general policy of this
measure, under the circumstances, there can be no doubt
whatever. The observations made on the subject at the
time by Sir Arthur Wellesley are absolutely conclusive:
1st. That a kingdom would be liberated with its fortresses and arsenals. 2nd. That the Spanish army of
Estremadura would be reinforced by five or six thousand
Spanish soldiers, who were prisoners on board the ships
in the Tagus. 3rd. That valuable lives, which would
undoubtedly be sacrificed in a protracted campaign, in
the event of the French retiring across the Tagus, would
be saved. And Napier (bk. ii. ch. 6), going into detail,
remarks that "although parts of the convention were
objectionable in point of form, parts imprudently worded,
taken as a whole it was fraught with prudence. Sup-
posing Sir Arthur, unimpeded by Sir H. Burrard, had
pursued his own plan; that Junot, cut from Lisbon and
the half of his forces, had been driven upon the Upper
Tagus. He was still master of flying to Almeida or
Elvas; and the thousand men in Santarem could have
joined him on either line. Then the advantages of a
convention would have been appreciated. The army,
exclusive of Moore's Division, had neither provisions, nor
means of transporting provisions, for more than ten
days; the fleet was the only solid resource, but a gale
from any point between south and north-west would
have driven the ships away or cast them on a lee shore.
It was therefore indispensable to secure the mouth of the
Tagus for the safety of the fleet; and this could only be
done by occupying Cascares, Bugio, and St. Julian's, the
last of which would alone have required ten days' open
trenches and a battering train which must have been
dragged by men over the mountains, for the artillery

horses were scarcely able to draw the field guns, and no country animals were to be found. In the meantime the French troops in Lisbon, upon the heights of Almada, and in the men-of-war, retiring tranquilly through the Alemtejo, would then have united with Junot; or if he fell back upon Almeida, they could have retired upon Elvas and La Lippe . . . and here it may be observed that even after the arrival of Moore, only 25,000 British infantry were fit for duty.

"Let it be supposed that the forts were taken, the English fleet in the river, the resources of Lisbon organised, the battering guns and ammunition necessary for the siege of Elvas transported to Abrantes by water. Seventy miles of land remained to traverse, and then three months of arduous operations in the sickly season of the most pestilent of situations, would have been the certain consequences of any attempt to reduce that fortress. Did the difficulty end there? Almeida remained, and in the then state of the roads of Portugal, taking into consideration only the known and foreseen obstacles, it is certain that six months more would have been wasted before the country could have been entirely freed from the invaders; but long before that period Napoleon's eagles would have soared over Lisbon again. The conclusion is inevitable. The Convention was a great and solid advantage for the allies, a blunder on the part of the French."

Napoleon's dry remark that the English had sent their Generals before a Council of War and had thus saved him the pain of punishing an old friend, indicates pretty clearly the opinion of that authority. Yet the British public, ever ready to express a loud opinion on matters that it knows nothing about—and its ignorance on military subjects was no less astounding at that period than at the present day—burst into a torrent of fury, before it

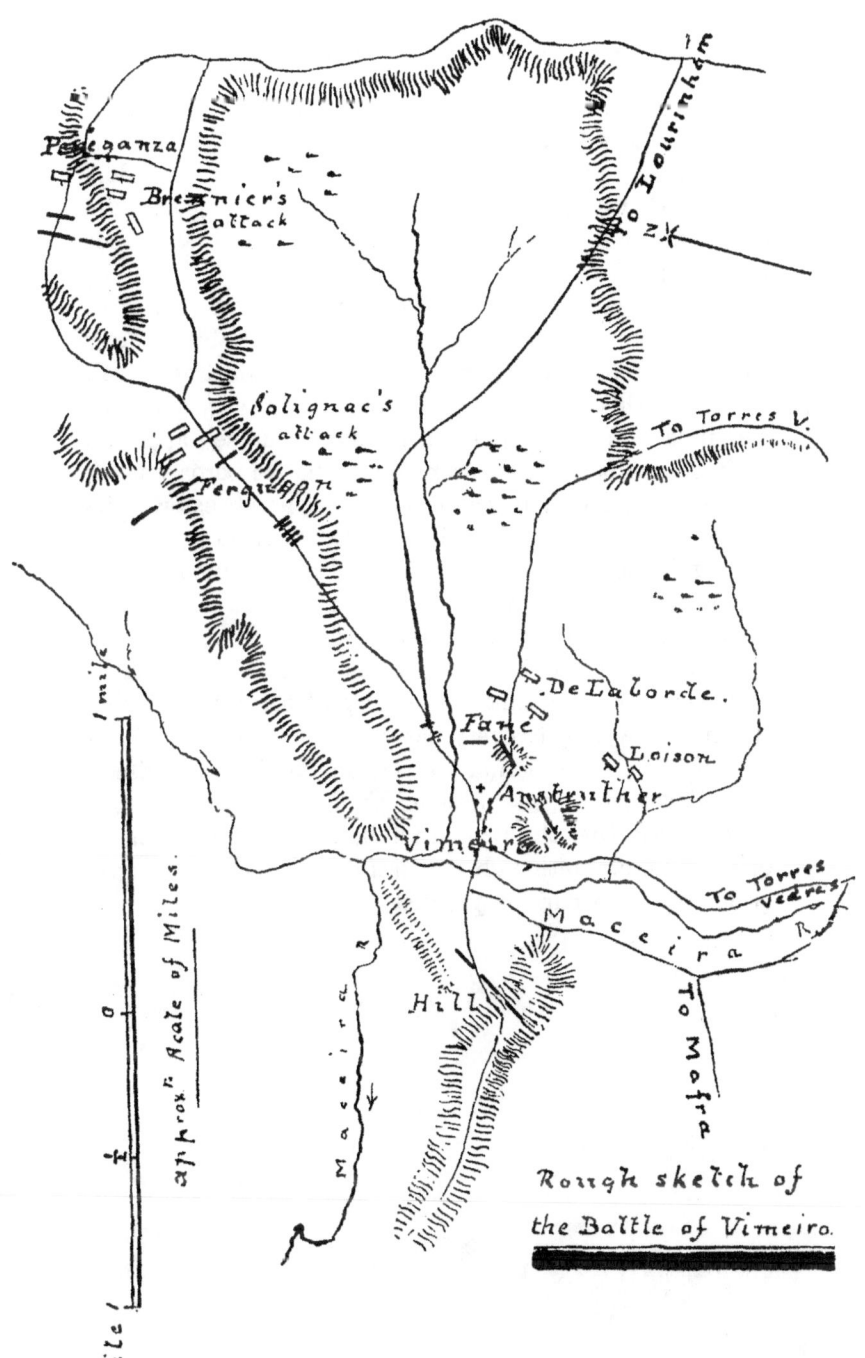

was even aware of the stipulations of the Convention. The ministers bowed before the storm, and Wellesley, Dalrymple, and Burrard in turn went home, " to abide," in Napier's words, " the fury of the most outrageous and disgraceful public clamour ever excited by the falsehoods of venal political writers."

It is a characteristic of Englishmen never to tire of extolling our own magnanimity; but invariably to deny that virtue to our adversaries. In our dealings with Napoleon this feature is more than usually prominent. Yet it is difficult at times to reconcile our self-applause with actual fact. At this moment the Emperor was, as was natural, deeply incensed at the Baylen disaster. His mortification was redoubled at the Convention of Cintra, the significance of which he grasped in a moment. But even in Napoleon's first outburst of anger, it was not justice but mercy which asserted her claims; and the trial of Dupont and his colleagues was deferred until public opinion had time to recall past services and give the utmost weight to every plea of their defence. In the case of the Convention of Cintra, the Emperor dismissed the subject in a contemptuous phrase. It is no exaggeration to say that the British public thirsted for the blood of its generals, although successful. Truly our boasted patriotism is a curious product.

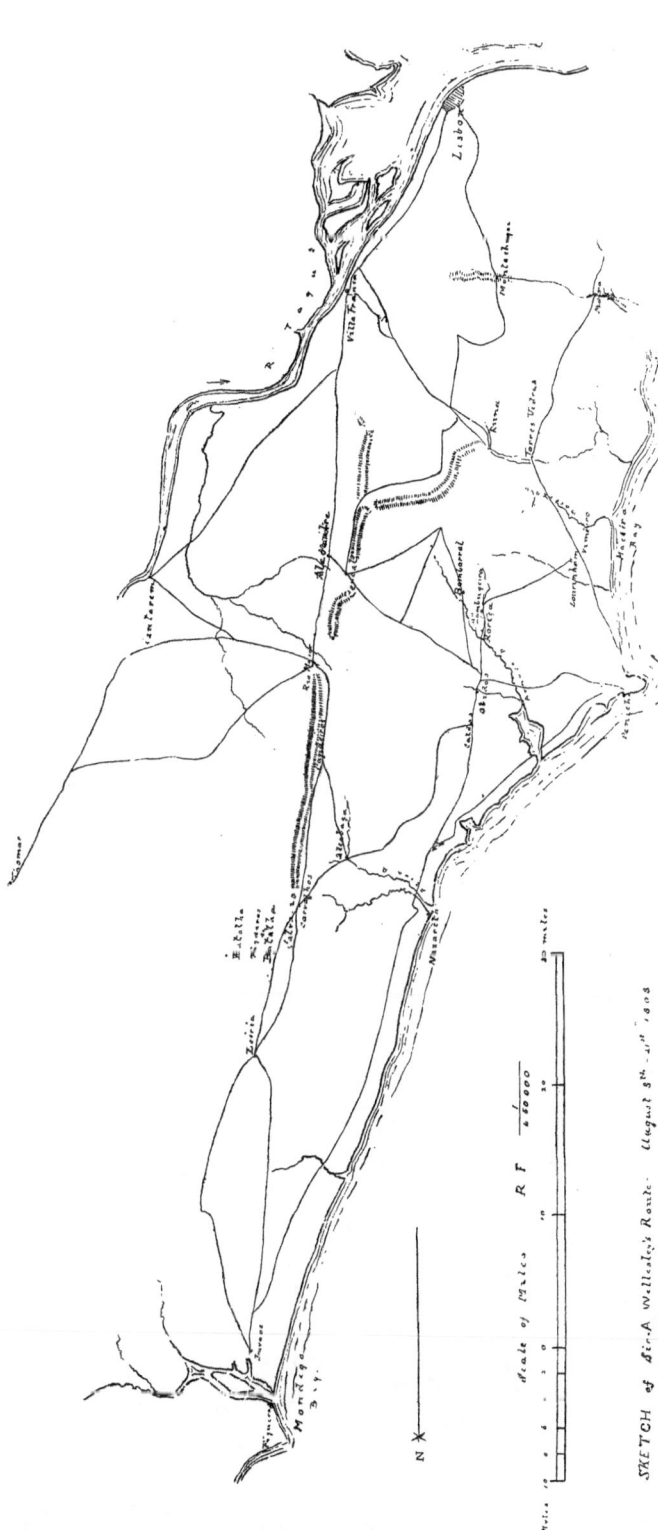

CHAPTER V

View of Napoleon on the situation—Assembly of his troops—He arrives in Spain—Forces the Somosierra—Enters Madrid.

WE have seen that on hearing of the Baylen disaster, the "intrusive monarch," Joseph Bonaparte, at once abandoned Madrid and, neglecting other lines of defence, retired across the Ebro and took up a position at Aranda on the further bank. His movements illustrate the fable of lions led by a deer, for the resources at his disposal were ample for the purpose of holding the Spaniards in check; ample even for redeeming the stain cast upon the honour of the French arms by Dupont's surrender. Marshal Jourdan acted as his Chief of the Staff. Bessières and Moncey were Corps Commanders of enterprise and ability. The fiery Ney had just arrived. Without drawing either upon his garrisons or the troops guarding the lines of communication, 50,000 men were available. Joseph, however, devoid of military genius and panic stricken, had little idea of doing more than just hold his own. Calling in Verdier from the siege of Saragossa and abandoning Tudela, the king posted his left under Moncey at Milagro in the angle formed by the junction of the Arga and Ebro. The centre under Ney occupied the line of the Ebro from Miranda to Logrono. Bessières on the extreme right held Bilbao and thence reached out a hand to Ney. Trevino was selected as the position for a defensive action.

To judge by these dispositions it might have been supposed that the Spanish armies were approaching from all sides in overwhelming numbers, but in point of fact "guided by the caprice of the generals they moved in various directions without a fixed object and without concert." "It was a month after the capitulation of Dupont before Castanos entered the capital at the head of 70,000 men," there forming a junction with the Murcian levies. A body of 16,000 men had a few days previously occupied Saragossa on the retirement of the French. Thus at the end of August, at a time when Napoleon observed, and observed truly, that the whole of the Spanish forces were not capable of resisting 25,000 Frenchmen concentrated in a good position, Joseph with twice that number had surrendered the initiative and had allowed himself to be cooped up and intimidated by disjointed masses of the enemy not exceeding in the aggregate 35,000 men.

The Emperor, needless to say, was profoundly discontented with his brother's conduct. Writing from St. Cloud on the 30th of August, he commented strongly on the abandonment of Tudela, an important point protecting the line of communication with Pampeluna, and provided with a stone bridge over the Ebro which enabled the garrison to resume the offensive towards Saragossa; and the occupation of Milagro, a position devoid of strategical importance and liable to be turned from Tudela. "The position of Burgos," he went on to say, "is equally important as being a centre of communication. Thence parties, not only of cavalry, but also of from two to five thousand infantry in columns, can push forward patrols of Hussars in all directions within a radius of two days' march and, making themselves per-

IN THE PENINSULA 77

fectly acquainted with everything that is going on, can inform Headquarters; so that if the enemy approaches Burgos in force, the different Divisions will have time to concentrate in support and give battle or mislead the enemy and retreat with the view of appearing elsewhere." Then, with indignation at the slur on the prestige of the Army: "Does not a Corps of twelve or fifteen thousand men take up twenty positions a day on the mere orders of an Adjutant-General; and would not our troops be reduced to the condition of a mob, if obliged to take up the selected positions for battle a fortnight beforehand? Bessières' Corps should be at Miranda or Briviesca, but to take up a shameful and cramped position like Trevino, instead of an honourable and menacing one at Burgos, at a time when the enemy is at Madrid, the position of the army of Galicia is unknown, and the rebels are suspected of being able to employ part of their force against Portugal, is tantamount to telling the enemy that he has nothing to fear, and can make his dispositions without risk of disturbance. . . . In conclusion, the position of Burgos should be guarded, troops should be under arms every day at 3 o'clock in the morning and reconnaissances made in all directions at 1 a.m. Intelligence should then be received within a radius of 12 or 15 miles, in order to enable you to act according to circumstances. This is the first time that it has happened to an army to abandon the initiative in order to take up bad defensive positions, and to appear to select battlefields when the distance of the enemy, the thousand and one different combinations which may occur, leave no probability of foreseeing whether the battle will take place at Tudela, between Tudela and Pampeluna, between Soria and the Ebro, or between Burgos and Miranda. The position of Burgos, held in force and on the offensive, menaces Palencia, Valladolid, Aranda, and even Madrid. . . . At a distance of 1,000 miles, and without a 'State' of the army, it is impossible to dictate exactly what ought to be done, but one may say that unless prevented by a superior force, Burgos and Tudela should be occupied. . . . Marshal Bessières, with the whole of his Corps, reinforced by the Light Cavalry, must be encamped in the wood near Burgos, holding the citadel in force, with his hospitals, depôts, and impedimenta behind the Ebro. . . . Moncey's Corps must be at Miranda and Briviesca, with his hospitals and baggage in rear of Vittoria, his troops under arms every day before sunrise and constantly reconnoitring the enemy in the direction of Soria, &c. You must not lose sight of the fact that as the Corps of Bessières and Moncey ought to be reunited, you must link yourself as little as possible with Logrono, and in fact look on General Lefébre's force as a detachment under separate instructions and with a line of communication of its own with Pampeluna. To wish to hold Tudela as a continuous part of the line would involve too great an extension. . . . The reconnaissances which will be made daily from the side of Soria, Burgos, upon Palencia, and from Aranda can be arranged so as to make three points of intersection every day and gain three reports from persons arrested, who will be treated well and released after giving the information desired. In this way, you will see the enemy approaching, you will be able to concentrate your force, harass his marches, and fall upon his flanks at the very moment that he is projecting an offensive movement."

Joseph, however, had no spark of his military genius, and, being unable to appreciate his instructions, failed to reoccupy Tudela, but contented himself with moving his right and centre across the Ebro.

"On the 18th of September," says Napier ("Peninsular War," bk. iii. ch. 5), "the French forces were disposed as follows:—

		Under Arms.	
Right Wing	Marshal Bessières	15,595	Three Infantry Divisions. In front of Pancorbo, at Briviesca, Santa Maria and Cuba. Light Cavalry behind Burgos
Centre ...	Marshal Ney... ...	13,756	Logrono, Nalda, and Najera
Left Wing	Marshal Moncey ...	16,636	Milagro, Lodosa, Caparosa and Alfara
Reserve of the King Imperial Guard ...	General Saligny ... General Dorsenne	5,413 2,423	Miranda, Haro, and Puentelara
Garrisons...		6,004	Pampeluna (under Moncey's command)
,, ...	General Monthieu	1,500	Bilbao
,, ...	General La Grange	6,979	Composed of small garrisons and movable columns, guarding the communications of Biscay, Alava, and Guipuscoa
General Reserve	General Drouet ...	1,984. Movable columns ...	Bayonne,and watching the valleys of the Pyrenees opening into Navarre
		20,005. Stationary	

" Total, 90,289 present under arms, exclusive of the troops in Catalonia, and when the communications were secured, the fortresses garrisoned, and the fort of Pancorbo armed, there remained above 50,000 sabres and bayonets disposable on a line of battle from Bilbao to Alfaro."

By this time the Spanish forces had been considerably augmented, and, to oppose the French, were divided into

three principal masses, denominated the Armies of the
Right, Centre and Left.

Of these the first, otherwise called the Army of
Aragon, was commanded by Count Palafox. Organised
in two Divisions under Generals St. Marc and O'Neil, it
contained 500 Cavalry, 17,500 Infantry, and 24 guns;
and was posted between Saragossa and Sanguessa.

The Army of the Centre, under General Castanos, contained the three Divisions of La Pena, Llamas and Caro,
making up 1,300 Cavalry, 26,000 Infantry, with 36 guns,
and occupied Borja, Taranzona and Agreda.

The Army of the Left, commanded by General Blake,
composed of Galicians, comprised 100 Cavalry, 30,000
Infantry, and 26 guns. It was preparing to operate from
Reynosa at the source of the Ebro.

Thus the whole Spanish force immediately available
did not exceed 75,400 Cavalry and Infantry with 86 guns;
it was under no central command, but, operating on
exterior lines, occupied a space of 200 miles, from Reynosa
to Saragossa; and was unable to concentrate more than
40,000 men at any given point.

There were, in addition, 12,000 Castilians at Segovia;
13,000 Estremadurans under the Condé de Belvidere at
Talavera; 14,000 Andalusians in La Mancha, and
nominally 18,000 Asturians at Llanes.

A forward movement, with the object of expelling the
French from Spain, was loudly talked of on all sides.
" *Vox et preterea nihil.*" The Junta of Seville, intent on
everything but patriotism, forbade Castanos to advance
beyond Madrid, and denied him even the supplies
necessary for the subsistence of his army. Every kind
of ridiculous project was, however, propounded. Some
feeble and ill-combined movements at length took place.
Blake received a rough check at Zornoza on the
31st of October; but Napoleon, distrustful of his brother's

capacity, had by this time ordered him to remain strictly on the defensive, and at the head of a mighty army was on his way to assume command in person. He had secured the combination of all the Great Powers of Europe against England, yet had failed in his projects for getting possession of the Danish and Portuguese fleets. Appreciating, after the Baylen disaster and the Convention of Cintra, the enormous efforts necessary to pacify Spain and re-conquer Portugal in face of the power, arms, and gold of England; and suspicious of the attitude of Austria, Napoleon, backed up by Russia with whom he had concluded an offensive and defensive alliance, proceeded to make pacific overtures to the British Government. His sincerity has been called in question, but the careful study of his correspondence gives abundant evidence of his constant desire for peace, provided that it could be concluded on an honourable basis and with the prospect of permanence. Canning, the Foreign Secretary, unfortunately replied in the tone of personal insult habitual to his department in its communications with the Emperor, and the negotiations were in consequence broken off. Had they been brought to a successful issue, the prowess of our troops and of their great leader in the Peninsula, would probably have remained unknown. But misery, bloodshed and ruin to an extent absolutely incalculable would have been saved, and the progress of civilisation accelerated in proportion.

On the 3rd November Napoleon arrived at Bayonne. His columns, consisting chiefly of the 1st, 5th, and 6th Army Corps of the Grand Army, veteran troops drawn from Germany and Poland, had for the most part preceded him. Two hundred thousand men were pouring along the Royal Road between Bayonne and Miranda. Forty thousand were threading the passes of the Western Pyrenees to reinforce the troops in Catalonia. But in

82 WELLINGTON'S OPERATIONS

spite of these large drafts the outworks of the Empire were by no means left unguarded. For the occupation of Germany and Poland, Marshal Davoust was left in command of the remainder of "The Grand Army," now called the Army of the Rhine. It comprised three Divisions of Heavy and three Brigades of Light Cavalry, four Divisions of Infantry (under St. Hilaire, Morand, Gudin, and Friant), posted respectively at Stettin, Magdeburg, Hanover and Halle; with Oudinot's Corps in reserve; making up nearly 100,000 men and 192 guns, exclusive of the Divisions of Boudet and Molitor, newly arrived from Italy, who were ordered to Frankfort on the Main, and those of Legrand and Carra St. Cyr at Wurtzburg.

Bernadotte, with two Divisions, was given the government of the Hanseatic towns, and, inclusive of auxiliary troops, Napoleon calculated on having 260,000 men beyond the Rhine.

In Italy, under the Viceroy, Prince Eugene, were the Divisions of Seras, Broussier, Grenier, Barbou, Lemarois and Lamarque. Marmont had 16 Battalions in Dalmatia. Four others were in Corfu and six in Naples. Inclusive of Italians, &c., the Emperor reckoned on having 150,000 men beyond the Alps.

For the march through France of the vast reinforcements, elaborate preparations were necessary to save the country from being devoured as by a swarm of locusts. Enormous supplies of every kind were collected at the frontier towns. At Bayonne, orders were given to form a siege train consisting of 24 howitzers; 12 6-inch guns; 8 8-inch mortars; with 500 rounds per gun. A million rations of biscuit were to be continually kept in store there, with three to four million rations of flour; of which 30,000 rations could be cooked in a day. A thousand

IN THE PENINSULA 83

bullocks were to be herded, and vast supplies of clothing stored. At Perpignan and Bellegarde were collected 2,000,000 cartridges, 6,000 muskets, 10,000 cannon balls, &c.

On the 10th of October, 1808, the general state of the French army in or *en route* for Spain was as set out in the table on the following page. The 5th and 8th Corps had not as yet crossed the frontier. The number of guns is not given. It was probably about 600. 19,371 Artillery, 38,954 Cavalry, and 189,509 Infantry soldiers were "present under arms."

On the 8th of November the Emperor, accompanied by Marshals Soult and Lannes, quitted Bayonne and reached Vittoria the same evening. On his arrival the myth of Spanish prowess was quickly dissipated. On the 10th, Soult, who had been placed in command of the 2nd Army Corps *vice* Bessières transferred to the command of the Heavy Cavalry, struck the Condé de Belvidere at Gamonal, a little to the south of Burgos, captured 20 of his 30 guns, killed 2,500 of his men—the picked troops of Spain—dispersed the remainder and occupied Burgos. On the next day Victor, with the 1st Corps, routed the armies of Blake and Romana at Espinosa. Within two days the centre and left of the whole Spanish line were thus irretrievably broken.*

The French Cavalry now overran Leon and Castile without resistance. By these victories the line of communication with France had been secured; and Burgos became the pivot of operations in place of Vittoria. The

* Romana's troops had a curious experience. They had been sent to join Napoleon in 1807, *vide* p. 13, had been quartered in Holstein, whence the British Admiral Keats had embarked them in August for their native country. Hardly had they landed when they were called upon to fight at Espinosa. The greater part were taken prisoners and incorporated once more in the French Army. No less than 4,000 of them were captured by the Russians in 1812, and sent back again to Spain in British ships.

84 WELLINGTON'S OPERATIONS

Corps.	Commander.	Present under Arms.		Detached.		Hospital.	Prisoners.	Effective.		
		Men.	Horses.	Men.	Horses.	Men.	Men.	Men.	Cavalry Horses.	Artillery Horses.
1	Marshal Victor	28,797	5,615	2,201	219	2,939		33,937	3,329	2,501
2	,, Bessières	20,093	3,219	7,394	1,199	5,536	30	33,054	3,616	802
3	,, Moncey	18,867	3,186	11,082	2,472	7,522	219	37,690	4,537	821
4	,, Lefébvre	22,859	2,410	955	40	2,170		25,984	1,791	659
5	,, Mortier	24,552	3,833	188	6	1,971	2	26,713	1,805	2,084
6	,, Ney	29,568	4,304	3,381	257	5,051	33	38,033	2,465	2,096
7	General St. Cyr	35,657	2,247	1,302	198	4,948	1,200	42,107	4,045	1,404
8	,, Junot	19,059	2,247	2,137	1	3,528	1,006	25,730	1,776	472
	Reserve	34,924	23,604	3,533	733	3,553	392	42,382	21,225	3,112
	1st Hussars and 27th Chasseurs	1,424	1,463	256	208	74		1,754	1,675	
	Artillery and Engineers on the march from Germany	3,446	958	107				3,446		958
	Movable columns for defence of the French frontier	8,588	477	107		146	19	8,860	268	209
	Total ...	247,884	56,670	32,643	5,333	37,438	1,901	319,690	46,822	15,068

(Napier, vol. i. app. 28).

IN THE PENINSULA 85

next point was to destroy the armies of the Right and Centre under Castanos and Palafox. The 2nd Army Corps, supported by the 1st, was left to protect the right flank of the French. The 6th had been pushed forward to Aranda on the Douro. It was now ordered to ascend the river and operate on the left flank of Castanos at Calahora, while Lannes with the 3rd Corps and two other Divisions moved up the left bank of the Ebro to attack him in front. In pursuance of these orders Ney marched on the 19th, and, reaching Soria on the 21st, intercepted the Spanish line of retreat upon Madrid. Castanos then retired down the Ebro, and with 45,000 men and 50 guns, took up a position, his right resting on Tudela, his left on Taranzona, 10 miles distant. Here, on the morning of the 23rd, he was attacked by Lannes in command of 35,000 men and 60 guns. The result was as usual. After three hours the Spaniards were driven from their positions with the loss of 9,000 men and 30 guns, their flight being accelerated by the appearance of Ney's Cavalry from Soria. Fifteen thousand took refuge in Saragossa. The rest of the army was taken or dispersed, with the exception of two Divisions which were rallied by Castanos at Calatayud. But for an erroneous direction taken by Ney, these should have shared the fate of their comrades. As it was, they evaded the 6th Corps and marched on Madrid. Five thousand men—a miserable remnant—reached Guadalajara on the 2nd of December, but on approaching the capital found it already in the hands of the French, and retired upon Cuenca.

Meanwhile Napoleon in person had established his headquarters on the 23rd of November at Aranda, on the Duero. He had heard of the advance of a British force under Sir John Moore to Salamanca, but his information was to the effect that it was now retiring again on Portugal. Believing himself secure therefore from danger in that direction, on the 28th he marched with the 1st Corps, the Guard and the Reserve upon Madrid; covering his right flank with the 4th Corps which was directed to move by Palencia, Valladolid, and Segovia. On the 30th, the enemy, 12,000 strong with 16 guns, was discovered by the advance guard in a strong position holding the passes of the Somosierra. The only means of approach was by a road ascending by a zigzag in a narrow gorge, and cut by a succession of torrents. The beds of the latter were now dry, but the bridges over them had been broken. Batteries posted in tiers one above the other, commanded every portion of the road liable to enfilade. Infantry supported the guns on either side of the ravine.* The first battery was covered by an epaulement and placed behind two of the broken bridges. Under a heavy fire and with great loss, the French sappers succeeded in bridging the gaps with planks and beams. The advance guard was composed of a Cavalry Division, a Battery, a Brigade of Infantry, and a Cavalry Brigade of the Imperial Guard. At daybreak on the 1st of December three Battalions of Infantry attacked the Spanish right, and the same number their left. A third column, supported by the guns, attempted to advance up the gorge in the centre, but was repulsed. The moment was critical and time precious. When regular means failed it was just possible that an unexpected coup might succeed; the rather that the defenders of the pass were the runaways from Gamonal. The Emperor ordered the Chasseurs of the Guard to charge the batteries. No wider front could be used than column of fours. The Chasseurs advanced at a gallop, their attack partly covered by the fog which hung about the mountains. The concentrated fire of the enemy struck the leading sections to the ground. The first squadron recoiled. Unfortunately

* " Souvenirs du Colonel de Gonneville."

IN THE PENINSULA 87

the proper squadron intervals had not been kept, and for want of space it was unable to rally. The whole regiment then fell back in great disorder. Undismayed by the failure, Napoleon called up the Polish Lancers of the Guard. General Montbrun was placed at their head. Advancing up the gorge, the Lancers, like the Chasseurs, were checked by the enemy's fire. This time the intervals had been preserved. The leading squadron rallied, dashed forward and carried the battery. The strongest points of the position had yet to be taken. But the infantry were gaining ground, and the Spaniards, disheartened and dismayed by the gallant feat of arms, abandoned the whole mountain and fled in disorder, hotly pursued by the Lancers to Buitrago. A part, however, under their commander General St. Juan, not only held together but broke through the French and made good their retreat to Sepulveda and Segovia, possibly in hopes of meeting the British army believed to be approaching from Salamanca. Turned, however, by the Cavalry of the French 4th Corps, they crossed the Guadarama mountains and reached Talavera, where, Spaniard-like they terminated their evolutions by the murder of their General.

In the meantime the French armies had pressed forward. Lefébre, with the 4th Corps, was approaching the capital from Segovia; Ney, with the 6th, from Guadalajara. On the 2nd of December Napoleon was at the gates of Madrid.

"The energy and rapidity of the French Emperor," observes Napier, in reviewing the course of this short campaign, "demands careful attention. His operations were . . . a series of skilful and scientific movements worthy of so great a general and politician. His force was immense and the Spaniards but contemptible soldiers, yet he never neglected the lessons of experience, nor deviated from the strictest rules of art. With astonishing activity, and, when we consider the state of his political relations on the Continent, with astonishing boldness, he collected ample means to attain his object. Deceiving his enemies with regard to his numbers, position, and intentions, choosing his time with admirable judgment, he broke through the weak part of their line and seized Burgos, a central point, which enabled him to envelope and destroy the left wing of the Spaniards before their right could hear of his attack, the latter being itself turned by the same movement and exposed to a like fate. His first position enabled him to menace the capital, keep the English army in check, and cover the formation of those magazines and stores which were necessary to render Burgos the base and pivot of further operations.*

"Napoleon's forces were numerous enough to have attacked Castanos and Palafox while Blake was being pursued by the 1st and 4th Corps, but trusting nothing to chance, he waited for twelve days until the position of the English army was ascertained, the strength of the northern provinces quite broken, and a secure place of arms established. Then, leaving the 2nd Corps to cover his communications, and sending the 4th Corps into the flat country to coast, as it were, the heads of the English columns and turn the passes of the Carpenterio mountains, he caused the Spanish right wing to be destroyed, and approached the capital when no vestige of a national army was left, when he had good reason to think the English in full retreat, when the whole of his Corps were close at hand, and consequently when the greatest moral

---

* One object in keeping his numbers concealed was no doubt to encourage the Spaniards to offer battle, the result of which was certain. What he dreaded was a guerilla warfare. Conf. Lord Wolseley's action before and during the battle of Tel-el-Kebir under somewhat similar circumstances.

effect could be produced and the greatest physical power concentrated at the same time to take advantage of it. Napoleon's dispositions were indeed surprisingly skilful, for . . . it is certain that even reverses in battle could neither have checked the Emperor nor helped the Spaniards.

"If Soult had been beaten at Gamonal, Napoleon was at hand to support the 2nd Corps, and the 6th Corps would have fallen upon the flank and rear of the Spaniards.

"If the 1st Corps had been defeated at Espinosa, the 2nd and 4th Corps and the Emperor's troops would have taken Blake in flank and rear.

"If Lannes had been defeated at Tudela he could have fallen back on Pampeluna; the 5th and 8th Corps were marching to support him, and the 6th Corps would have taken the Spaniards in flank.

"If the Emperor had been repulsed at the Somosierra, the 6th Corps would have turned that position by Guadalaxara, and the 4th Corps by Guadarama.

"If Moore had retreated on Portugal, the 4th Corps was nearer to Lisbon than he was; and if he had overthrown Soult, the 5th and 8th Corps were ready to sustain that Marshal, while Napoleon, with 50,000 men, was prepared to cut the British line of retreat into Galicia. No possible event could have divided the Emperor's forces, and he constantly preserved a central position which enabled him to unite his masses in sufficient time to repair any momentary disorder."

Inside the walls of Madrid the populace breathed fury and defiance; the streets were cut and barricaded; the walls loopholed; but the Government had fled to Badajoz. Mob rule was supreme and devoted its energies rather to rapine and murder than to the organisation of a reasonable plan of defence. A summons to surrender was rejected with scorn. During the night General Senarmont with 36 guns breached the walls of the Retiro, a large work commanding the town, which in the early morning of the 3rd was stormed by Villatte's Division of the 1st Army Corps. Negotiations were then resumed. Napoleon, wishing to avoid the horrors of a storm, ordered the firing to cease. The Spanish regular troops, 6,000 men with 16 guns, under the Marquis de Castellar, took the opportunity to evacuate the city, which had not been completely invested; a deputation, of whom the minister Morla formed one, came out to treat with the Emperor. Napoleon addressed Morla in terms which must have made that worthy writhe with shame at the perfidy of his conduct towards Dupont's army, but gave the citizens till 6 a.m. the next morning to make up their minds. There could no longer be any question of effective resistance; the chances had been wasted and the time gone by. Within the period of grace Madrid, a prey to internal dissensions, civil anarchy and treason, surrendered at discretion. An assembly of the principal personages waited on the Emperor to beg for King Joseph's return. In his reply Napoleon expressed at length the principles on which he intended Spain to be governed. He abolished feudal rights and gave free scope to industry of every kind. He promised to reorganise the Courts of Justice and make them efficient. He limited the number of monks, but encouraged "the most useful and interesting of the clergy—the parish priests." He abolished the Inquisition, remarking that the proper function of the clergy is to guide the conscience, but not to exercise any corporal jurisdiction over citizens; and suppressed the rights usurped by the nobles during the civil wars. He declared a general amnesty from which ten persons only were excepted. "The present generation," he observed in conclusion, "may differ in opinions; too many passions have been excited; but your descendants will bless me as the regenerator of the nation; they will mark my sojourn among you as memorable days, and from those days they will date the prosperity of Spain."

Within two days the citizens were pursuing their ordinary avocations and amusements as if nothing had happened, and not only was the capital tranquil, but the outlying provinces of Castile and Leon readily submitted to the requisitions made by parties of cavalry numbering as few as ten or twelve troopers. No Spanish army existed in the field. Saragossa alone held out, but was about to be invested by the 3rd Corps, supported by the 5th. The 2nd Corps, reinforced by the Divisions of the 8th—which was shortly afterwards broken up as an independent unit—was preparing to advance into Galicia; the 1st from Toledo into Andalusia; while with the 4th, 6th, the Guard, and the Reserve the Emperor intended to move upon Lisbon, driving before him the British army, the only organised force still in the field.

From this state of security Napoleon was suddenly aroused by the startling intelligence that the British troops, far from retiring, had abandoned their line of retreat to Lisbon, had resumed the offensive, and were now threatening the vital point of his communications with France. The Emperor's measures for the defeat of his new antagonists were decided on in an instant. The 5th Corps was halted on its road to Saragossa. The 4th Corps, whose advance guard had reached Merida, and was threatening Badajoz, was halted and called up to Placentia. The 2nd Corps, in the event of being attacked, was directed to fall back a day's march. The 6th Corps and Imperial Guard, under his own immediate command, were put in motion for Benavente to intercept the bold assailant.

CHAPTER VI

The British Army assembled under Sir H. Dalrymple—Sir J. Moore appointed to command a force in Spain—He crosses the Portuguese frontier—His difficulties—Hears of the capture of Madrid—Forms his junction with Sir D. Baird—Advances against the enemy's line of communications — Attacked by Napoleon — Retreats—Battle of Corunna—Moore's death—Comments.

IT has already been seen that Sir Arthur Wellesley had hardly sailed from Cork in July, 1808, when the British Government decided to largely increase the strength of the expeditionary force by the addition of several bodies of troops, including one of 12,000 men under Sir John Moore, who had just returned home from a ridiculous and abortive errand in Sweden. Moore was senior to Wellesley, and his prestige and attainments appeared to mark him as fitted for the command-in-chief. But he was not altogether a *persona grata* to the Ministers. Lord Seaton tells us that Sir John was " one of those determined and independent characters who act and speak what they think best without paying the least regard to the opinions of persons of interest or in power." The command was consequently given to Sir Hew Dalrymple, and Moore was placed on the Staff as a General of Division only. The army thus assembled in Portugal (including two Battalions which arrived from Madeira under Major-General Beresford) consisted of two British and one regiment of K.G.L. Cavalry, 28

British and 6 K.G.L. Battalions of Infantry; in all, a force of about 35,000 men with 66 guns.

After the conclusion of the Convention of Cintra, matters did not run quite harmoniously in the British army. It was only in accordance with human nature that Wellesley should feel nettled at his supersession; and disappointed at losing the fruits of his victory. He was junior to all the other Lieutenant-Generals. He did not get on well with Sir Hew Dalrymple, disapproved of his actions and gave vent to his annoyance with some freedom in his private letters to Lord Castlereagh and others. Yet in the light of subsequent events it would seem that part at least of his criticisms were based on insufficient information and that Sir Hew in general grasped the situation, both military and political, correctly. On the 20th of September Sir Arthur returned to England to resume the duties of the Irish Office. Dalrymple was now making preparations for an advance into Spain by way of Badajoz or Almeida, but was shortly afterwards recalled home to answer for his conduct in regard to the Convention of Cintra. The command then fell once more to Sir Harry Burrard.

Prior to his departure Sir Arthur had, in reply to a question, given Lord Castlereagh his views regarding the state of the Peninsula and the mode in which military operations ought to be carried on there by a British force.* Fifteen thousand men, he said, should be sent to strengthen Castanos on the Ebro; five thousand should remain to hold Portugal; and the remainder, say ten thousand men, aided by a similar force from England and based upon the port either of Gijon or St. Ander, should operate in conjunction with Blake's army upon the right flank of the French by way of Leon or Reynosa with the object of confining the enemy to the

* Sir A. Wellesley to Lord Castlereagh, 5th of September, 1808.

line of the Ebro, and of compelling him eventually to retire into France. It was, no doubt, partly in pursuance of these suggestions that on the 6th of October Sir H. Burrard received a despatch dated September 25th from Lord Castlereagh, informing him that it had been decided to employ a British force of 40,000 men in the north of Spain. Of this force 12,000 men, under Lieut.-General Sir David Baird, were to be despatched immediately from England and disembarked at Corunna—St. Ander being rightly considered a point too near the enemy, and the navigation off the coast of the Asturias too precarious at this time of year—the remainder to be furnished from the army in Portugal, and to form a junction with Baird's Division either by sea at Corunna or by land in Leon or Galicia. The precise plan of operations to be concerted later with the Spanish Generals. In deference to public opinion and the wishes of the King the command of this army was vested in Sir John Moore; but Sir John was directed to place himself and his force under any Spaniard who might be appointed Commander-in-Chief!

Wellesley's letter had been written under a complete misapprehension of the strength of the French army in Spain, which he estimated at only 40,000 men. Nor had he made allowance for the enormous reinforcements which the Emperor could bring into the field, and which were in fact now threading the passes of the Pyrenees. In other respects also circumstances had changed, and what at the date of the letter would have been at best of very doubtful prudence, had by this time become a foolhardy adventure. One error was, however, avoided by the British Government. The suggestion to divide the army and send half to Castanos was ignored.

A memorandum of the Duke of York, Commander-in-Chief shows that he realised the position of affairs. The

IN THE PENINSULA 95

Spanish armies, he observed, were scattered over a large extent of country and therefore weak. The French were concentrated. The Spaniards might well be beaten before the British could arrive; and in view therefore of the risk of having to meet the French unaided it was necessary that Moore's force should be made up to 60,000 men. He proceeded to point out how this could be done:—

MEMORANDUM OF H.R.H. THE DUKE OF YORK.

	Cavalry.	Infantry.
"At present in Portugal	1,640	29,806 (84 Batts.)
Under orders to embark	3,410	11,419
Total	5,050	41,225

"Of this force the 20th Dragoons and 8 Battalions should remain in Portugal. The disposable force would then be:

	Cavalry.	Infantry.
From Portugal	1,313	23,575
Under orders	3,200	11,419
Force to be drawn from Italy		8,000
To this may be added four Regiments of Cavalry and the two Brigades of Guards	2,560	2,434
Total	7,073	45,418

There are in addition four Battalions of Infantry which can be spared; which, together with the Artillery attached to the force, make up a grand total of 60,000 Rank and File."

But no attention was paid to the Duke's views. "The Ministers' plans," observes Napier (bk. iii. ch. 3), "were equally vast and inconsiderate." The General was not referred to any person with whom he could communicate at all, much less concert a plan of operations. He was unacquainted with the views of the Spanish Government and was alike uninformed of the numbers, composition and situation of the armies with

96 WELLINGTON'S OPERATIONS

which he was to act, and those with which he was to contend. His own genius and £25,000 in the military chest constituted his resources for a campaign which was to lead him far from the coast and all its means of supply. He was to unite his forces by a winter march of 300 miles; another 300 were to be passed before he crossed the Ebro; he was to concert a plan of operations with generals, jealous, quarrelsome and independent; their positions extended from the northern sea-coast to Saragossa, their men insubordinate, differing in customs, discipline, language and religion from the English and despising all foreigners; and all this was to be accomplished in time to defeat an enemy already in the field, accustomed to great movements, and conducted by the most rapid and decided of men; " who, it may be added, had the exclusive control of the resources of a large empire.

The difficulties to be surmounted in order to enable the British army to take the field at all, were enormous. The General had no means of transport and no money to buy it with. His army and commissariat staff were inexperienced. He was encumbered with a crowd of soldiers' wives and children who, according to custom, would accompany his march. Roads in Portugal were almost non-existent and the rainy season was at hand. Odd as it seems, it was impossible to procure reliable information of the enemy. With the indomitable energy of his nature Sir John Moore set to work, however, to overcome countless obstacles in his path; and Sir Harry Burrard, disregarding any feeling of soreness at his own virtual supersession, aided his colleague to the best of his ability. Still Moore, a remarkably clear-sighted man—a fact which has earned for one whose principal characteristics were serenity and firmness of mind, the epithets from the ignorant and unreflecting of "desponding and vacillating"—could not but appreciate the facts of the case;

and in letters to Lord Castlereagh dated October 9th, after assuring him that nothing on his part would be wanting to secure success, the General gives fair warning that although the march would be begun within 48 hours, yet it was impossible to say when he would be able to cross the Portuguese frontier, since the question depended upon a knowledge, as yet unacquired, of the country; upon arrangements for the equipment of the army which was at present non-existent; upon formation of magazines, &c., &c. No delay, however, occurred in forwarding the regiments to the frontier. It was important to get out of Portugal before the rainy season, now at hand. Within five days of the receipt of Lord Castlereagh's letter, the leading troops were on the march. Agents were sent to Madrid and elsewhere to make contracts and procure money; for with incredible folly the British Ministers had deluged the Spaniards with gold and had left their own army destitute. It was found impossible to procure adequate transport. Consequently no reserves of ammunition could be taken. The supply of medical comforts was of the most scanty nature. Personal baggage was cut down to a minimum.

It was now stated that the roads north of the Tagus were impracticable for artillery. Junot had, it is true, brought his guns over them the year previous, but the carriages had been broken to pieces. On the other hand it was found impossible to supply the whole army should it take the southern line through Estremadura. Hence with great reluctance Moore was compelled to divide his force. General Hope, with the Cavalry Brigade, five Batteries of Artillery and a Brigade of Infantry, was directed to move by Elvas, Talavera, the Escurial and Arevalo to Salamanca, which had been fixed on as the point of concentration of the whole army.

Of the Infantry under Moore's personal command, two Brigades moved upon Almeida by Elvas and Alcantara, two by Coimbra and three by Abrantes, accompanied by Wilmot's Battery, for Moore wished to test the roads for himself, and the Battery did eventually reach Almeida, although only after inconceivable exertions. On the 26th of October Sir John started from Lisbon. On the 8th of November he reached Almeida, where he found all the Brigades concentrated; for General Anstruther had unfortunately halted the regiments instead of sending them on to Salamanca. The discipline of the troops was good, but they had suffered considerably on the march from the terrific rain. " On the day on which we marched into Guarda," says an officer present, " the 5th Regiment lost five, and the 28th two men, who actually perished on the road in consequence of heavy rain which incessantly fell during the whole day. A person who has never been out of England can hardly imagine its violence . . . . large globular drops pouring down vertically and descending in such rapid succession as to give the appearance rather of a torrent than a shower . . . . exposed to such rain we marched many miles to gain the top of the hill upon which stands Guarda." . . . . " The regiments were lodged in large convents, situated in the immediate suburbs, which had been prepared for our reception. Immense fires were soon lit : rations were delivered as soon as possible, and the glad tidings of a double allowance of rum loudly rang throughout the holy aisles."

A number of "military agents"—mostly officers who had served in South America, and from their experience at Buenos Ayres in 1807 had acquired exaggerated notions of Spanish bravery and resolution — were scattered through the provinces of Spain. Their reports in general reflected the extravagant language of the

Spaniards, and Moore very properly recalled them to their duty. Harm had, however, already been done. They had been allowed to report directly to the British Government and their statements were implicitly believed. By the Spanish Government also, Moore was officially informed that Burgos would make the best point of concentration, with Madrid and Valladolid as magazines; that he might expect the armies under Blake and Romana to be 60,000 to 70,000 strong, and to cover his advance into Spain; without taking into account the Spanish armies of the Right and Centre who were reckoned at as many more. The British Commander very soon learned to place information of this kind at its proper value, and to rely upon his own judgment rather than on the statements of other persons, however high in office.

On the 10th of November the advance guard of the British Army crossed the Spanish frontier, and on the 13th entered Salamanca. On the 23rd, the rear of Moore's Corps, which from the want of transport was compelled to march by detachments, had closed up. But his difficulties by no means diminished. The Spaniards proved to be absolutely apathetic. Supplies were not forthcoming. The accounts from Sir David Baird were bad. He had arrived at Corunna on the 13th of October, but had not been allowed by the local authorities to land until the 21st. He had been sent off from England destitute of money. On the other hand, an interrupted despatch from the governor of Bayonne to Marshal Jourdan showed that reinforcements for the French Army to the extent of over 70,000 men might be expected to enter Spain by the middle of November. Major-General Lord William Bentinck had been sent on a special mission to Madrid, and quickly convinced himself of the ridiculous over-confidence and unreliability of the Spaniards.

Writing to him on the 13th of November, Sir John remarked, "I am sorry to say, from Sir David Baird I hear nothing but complaints of the Junta of Corunna, who afford him no assistance. They promise everything but give nothing, and after waiting day after day for carts his Commissary was at last obliged to contract for them at an exorbitant price. This is a sort of conduct quite intolerable to troops that the Spanish Government have asked for, and whose advance they are daily pressing. . . . If the Spaniards expect the advance of the British Army, they must pay more attention to its wants. Proper officers must be sent to me, vested with full powers to call out the resources of the country where they are wanted and without delay. . . . The advance will depend on the aid and activity of the authorities of the country; if they are slow it is impossible for me to be quick. . . . At Ciudad Rodrigo I received a letter from the Condé de Belvedere from Burgos, dated the 9th, stating that he expected to be attacked by superior numbers, and begging that I would hasten to his assistance. I wrote to him that I had been marching for some time with all the haste I could; but that if he was to be attacked so soon it was impossible for me to render him any assistance. . . . Though Castanos and Blake know that a British force is marching from different parts in order to unite, they have marched away from the point of assembly, and have left us exposed to be attacked and interrupted before our junction. . . ."

The overthrow of Blake and de Belvedere on the 10th of November left him exposed to the attack of the 2nd and 4th Corps; and on the 15th, two days after his arrival at Salamanca, Sir John Moore received news that a French force had occupied Valladolid, only three marches distant. Not more than three Brigades had yet come up and the whole of the column could not be expected for another ten days. The junction of Baird and Hope was more than doubtful. The Spaniards had utterly failed to cover his advance, as promised, and his army was liable to be beaten in detail. Yet Valladolid had been one of the places prescribed by the Spanish Government for the formation of his magazines! Happily the enemy's force merely proved to be a Cavalry Brigade with two guns; but the singular fact was that in spite of their alleged enthusiasm, the French advance was viewed without the slightest consternation by the country people, and that patrols of ten or twelve French troopers traversed the country in all directions and collected supplies without encountering the slightest resistance. "I had no conception," writes Moore, "of the weakness of the Spanish armies, the apparent apathy of the people and the selfish imbecility of the Government. . . . There seems to be neither an army, generals, nor a government."

On the 28th came news of the defeat of the remaining Spanish Army at Tudela, and the position of the British forces became more than critical. Baird had been delayed in every possible way by the Spanish authorities at Corunna. He had been despatched from England without money, and though 2,000,000 dollars were sent after him the difficulties of supply and transport were so great that he could only advance in small detachments. The head of his column was now at Astorga; the rear would not be closed up before the 4th of December, and the distance from Astorga to Salamanca was not much less than 150 miles. The 4th French Corps under Lefébre was already threatening Moore's line of retreat on Lisbon. The 2nd, under Soult, who had succeeded Bessières, was free to crush Baird. Sir John judged rightly that his troops had not been sent into Spain to encounter the whole French Army. Of the entire strength of that army he was not indeed aware; but, in spite of Spanish assertions to the contrary, he knew very well that it exceeded by many times that of his own. The armies of his allies had all been crushed : there was no spirit of resistance among the people. Under these circumstances he felt that he had no alternative but to retire his own column upon Portugal, Baird's upon Corunna, whence it could subsequently join him by sea. Orders to that effect were sent to Sir David, but he was directed to show a bold front for a few days in order to facilitate the junction of General Hope with his Commander. Hope had been making slow progress. Compelled by want of money and supplies to march in six detachments at intervals of as many days, he at length reached Talavera about the 25th of November. A visit thence to Madrid convinced him that the Government was utterly unreliable and he determined to follow his own counsel. Moving by Naval Carneiro and the Escurial, he crossed the Guadarama Mountains on the 28th, and reached Espinar. Here he heard of the Spanish disasters at Tudela and the Somosierra, and, headed off as he was by Lefébre's Cavalry, his chances of reaching Salamanca appeared little short of desperate. Knowing, however, how essential it was to Sir John Moore that he should be joined by his Artillery and reserve ammunition, Hope, in place of falling back, marched without loss of an hour on Avila, covering his flank movement with his Cavalry Brigade. At Avila he crossed the mountains to Peneranda. Here he was again threatened, though unwittingly, by Lefébre's Corps which, as already mentioned, had been directed to move by Palencia, Valladolid and Olmedo on Segovia, and whose main body was still at Olmedo. Hope drew up his Cavalry and Infantry in line of battle, but directed his guns and park, without halting, upon Alba de Tormes. Lefébre

IN THE PENINSULA   103

was, however, unaware of the prize which lay within his grasp. Finding himself unmolested, Hope followed in due course with the rear guard, and on the 5th of December had the satisfaction of seeing his bold operations crowned with complete success by bringing his whole force without loss into Salamanca.

Moore's resolution to retreat filled the Spanish authorities with alarm, and every effort was made by misrepresentation of facts to induce him to reconsider his determination. Mr. Hookham Frere, British Minister at Madrid, who was nothing more than the dupe of men, partly blind and partly treacherous, joined in the clamour, and, in place of supporting the British Commander, exposed his own unbounded ignorance of the situation and set himself to write insulting letters to Moore and disseminate absurdly false information. To this Sir John gave no heed; but just at this moment, from various quarters, intelligence reached him to the effect that the citizens of Madrid had flown to arms and were resolved to die in defence of their capital. In reality Madrid had capitulated on the 4th of December, after the faintest show of resistance, but the fact was not known to Moore till the 9th; and in the meantime the Junta of Toledo had written to say that it would never submit. Saragossa also was once more bidding defiance to the enemy. The spirit of patriotic resistance appeared to be spreading. With brilliant conception Moore resolved to take advantage of it by throwing himself across the line of the enemy's communications, hoping thus to relieve the pressure on Madrid and Saragossa, while giving time for the southern provinces to organise their forces against the invader. Had he, in the first instance, been in time to oppose the French on the Ebro, it was his intention, if overpowered, to retire through Madrid upon the Morena and Andalusia. But the strategical situation was now utterly changed, and, as matters stood, he resolved to abandon his communications with Portugal and form magazines upon a new line of retreat for the whole of his force on Corunna. Baird, who had retired as far as Villa Franca, was recalled to take part in the new operation. Romana, who was at the head of about 5,000 half-armed peasants, informed Moore, with the true spirit of Spanish exaggeration, that he would co-operate with 20,000 men. The gleam of sunshine was but momentary. On the 9th came news of the surrender of Madrid, and Moore found that, in spite of all its boasting, it had held out for only one day. Toledo followed suit; but there still remained the hope of drawing the enemy from the southern provinces, and, with the chivalrous wish to attract the mass of the enemy's forces upon the British army and thus give his allies every chance of organising their forces even at the imminent risk of being himself overwhelmed by numbers, Sir John was resolute to pursue his strategy.

In anticipation of Baird's arrival the British army was now organised as follows:—

       Lieut.-Gen. Sir J. Moore, K.B., Commander-in-Chief.
       Major J. Colborne, 20th Regt., Military Secretary.
       Brig.-Gen. Clinton, Adjutant-General.
       Lieut.-Col. G. Murray, Quartermaster-General.

Cavalry Division.
Lieut.-Gen. Lord Paget.

1st Brigade. 18th Hussars; 3rd Light Dragoons, K.G.L. Brig.-Gen. Hon. C. Stewart.
2nd Brigade. 7th, 10th, and 15th Hussars. Brig.-Gen. Slade.
2 Batteries R.H.A.

Reserve Artillery.
Colonel Harding.

5 Batteries R.A.

IN THE PENINSULA

1st Infantry Division.

Lieut.-Gen. Sir David Baird, K.B.

1st Brigade. 1st and 3rd Batts., 1st Guards. Major-Gen. Warde.
2nd ,, 1st, 26th, and 81st Regts. Major-Gen. Manningham.
3rd ,, 4th, 42nd, and 50th Regts. Major-Gen. Lord W. Bentinck.
1 Battery R.A.

2nd Infantry Division.

Lieut.-Gen. Hon. John Hope.

4th Brigade. 51st, 59th, and 76th Regts. Major-Gen. Leith.
5th ,, 2nd, 5th, 14th, and 32nd Regts. Major-Gen. Hill.
6th ,, 36th, 71st, and 92nd Regts. Brig.-Gen. Catlin Crauford.
1 Battery R.A.

3rd Infantry Division.

Lieut.-Gen. McKenzie Fraser.

7th Brigade. 6th, 9th, 23rd, and 2nd Batt. 43rd. Major-Gen. Beresford.
8th Brigade. 36th, 79th, and 82nd. Brig.-Gen. Hon. H. Fane.
1 Battery R.A.

Reserve Division.

Major-Gen. Hon. Edward Paget.

9th Brigade. 20th and 1st Batt. 22nd. Brig.-Gen. Anstruther.
10th ,, 28th, 91st, and 1st Batt. 95th Rifles. Brig.-Gen. Disney.
1 Battery R.A.
1st Flank Brigade. 1st Batt. 43rd, 2nd Batt. 52nd, and 2nd Batt. 95th Brig.-Gen. R. Crauford.
2nd Flank Brigade. 1st and 2nd Light Batts., K.G.L. Brig.-Gen. Baron C. Alten.

The combined force was reckoned by Lord Castlereagh at something above 41,000 men, but between paper strength and reality a wide discrepancy must always exist. Leith's Brigade had been left behind at Lugo and Astorga to guard the line of communications. A few days later the Adjutant-General's "State" showed 4,035 men in hospital, 1,687 on detachment; and, inclusive of officers, the effective strength of the army seems never to have exceeded 25,000 men with 66 guns—a small force to be pitted against the enormous armies of

the French. The men were inexperienced and had little
cohesion, though the material was good. Twelve additional battalions remained to guard Portugal. Of these,
one, the Buffs, was left by Sir John Moore to garrison
Almeida; and the 5th Battalion 60th, who began the
march into Spain, had to be sent back to Portugal.
In accordance with the vicious system of the day, this
regiment had been filled up with men formerly belonging
to Junot's Corps, who at the time of the Convention had
been induced, in defiance of good faith, to enlist in the
British army. These men, on approaching their old
comrades, deserted in large numbers.

Sir John Moore, the Commander-in-Chief, deservedly
bore the highest reputation. In fact, to use an expression rather common a few years ago, he was looked upon
by many as "our only General." His experience began
in America. He distinguished himself in Holland. In
Egypt he had been Abercrombie's right hand; and,
though he had not been under fire since 1801, Moore
had had the command of the British army in Sicily,
where his military duties were complicated by a peculiarly
difficult political position, which he successfully met by
the exercise of unceasing tact and discrimination. His
brilliant strategy, his resolution, and the way in which
he handled his troops during the present brief campaign,
stamp him as a master of the art of war, and elicited the
praise of Napoleon; but Moore's best claim to admiration
lies perhaps in his unrivalled power of instructing the
men and officers under his command, and in the number
of his pupils who afterwards attained distinction. In
person he was tall and handsome. The expression of his
countenance, once seen, was never to be forgotten. In
character he was the soul of honour. He had all the
qualities of a successful general, but an unfortunate fate
attended him, and he never went into action without

being hit. At this period Sir John was forty-seven years of age.

Of the general officers under his command, Sir David Baird had seen a great deal of service—in India, Egypt, the Cape of Good Hope, &c. He had indeed more than once held an independent command, but he showed no talent during this campaign.

Sir John Hope had been Adjutant-General under Abercrombie in Egypt. He was a man of great military capacity, which would no doubt have had greater scope in the future, had he not unfortunately been senior to Wellington as a general officer. When the latter was made a Field Marshal in 1813, Hope at once volunteered to serve under him, and commanded an Army Corps during the rest of the war with distinction. He died comparatively young.

Mackenzie Fraser was personally most popular, but not a great soldier. He had commanded the unfortunate expedition to Egypt in 1807. Under Moore he showed no ability.

Edward Paget, brother to Lord Paget, had commanded the 28th Regiment with distinction in Egypt in 1801. His conduct during the present campaign gave evidence of very considerable military talent which an unlucky fate gave him but little opportunity of subsequently displaying. He twice joined Wellington's army, and on each occasion was rendered *hors de combat* within a very few days—the first time by a wound, the second by being taken prisoner. In India, at a later date, he quelled a mutiny of the native troops by his determined resolution.

Paget's Division had originally been intended for Sir Arthur Wellesley, but the latter, when on the point of sailing from England, was summoned before the Court of Enquiry directed to investigate the circumstances connected with the Convention of Cintra.

108 WELLINGTON'S OPERATIONS

Lord Paget had given proofs of his ability to command Cavalry at the Helder in 1799. He greatly added to his laurels under Moore, but appeared to more advantage during the advance than in the retreat. Being senior to Wellington he was debarred from earning further distinction in the Peninsula, but commanded a Division in Walcheren and the Cavalry Corps at Waterloo.

On the 11th of December Sir John Moore put the force under his own immediate command in motion on the road leading to Valladolid, covering his advance with Edward Paget's Division and the Cavalry. Next day Charles Stewart surprised a picquet of the enemy at Rueda and took nearly the whole prisoners. On the 13th, Headquarters were at Alaejos. Information of the enemy was hard to get; nothing would induce the Spaniards to furnish it, and Frere's reports were too ridiculous for words. On the 14th, however, an intercepted despatch from Berthier, the French Chief of the Staff, to Soult cleared up the situation. The 8th (Junot's) Corps was on the march for Burgos; the 4th (Lefébre's) was close to Talavera de la Reyna. Madrid was perfectly tranquil. Soult was enjoined to move on Valladolid and Zamora from the Carrion river with a view to reducing the province of Leon north of the Douro; and, with that object, to push on as rapidly as possible, if satisfied that the British Army had, as the Emperor expected, retired on Portugal. This information showed Moore that Lefébre was already nearer Lisbon than he himself was, and that Burgos was too strong to be attacked. A dash at Soult on the Carrion was still feasible. Consequently, the British Commander, avoiding Valladolid and swinging his columns round to the left, moved directly through Toro and Tordesillas on Villepando, with a view to forming an immediate junction with Baird, the head

IN THE PENINSULA 109

of whose column was now at Benevente, and whose march would be menaced in the event of an advance by Soult. On the 18th, Headquarters were at Castro Nuevo. The Cavalry Division, beautifully handled by Lord Paget, covered the march, and in a succession of brilliantly successful actions gained for its commander the opportunity of displaying his consummate skill as a leader of cavalry. The occasion lasted hardly longer than a fortnight, but those few golden days were worth almost a lifetime, and bitterly must Paget have lamented the cruel fate which, through family interest, gave him seniority to Lord Wellington and deprived him of the command of the Cavalry during the subsequent years of the Peninsular War—a deprivation for which three days of the Waterloo campaign could be no compensation. We have had in our service from time to time an officer whose scanty opportunities have but enabled him to give promise of what he might do on a larger scale. Lucans and Cardigans we have had by the score, but—curiously enough for a nation so devoted to field sports—in order to find a General of Cavalry, we have, with the possible exception of Paget, to look back as far as Oliver Cromwell.

The weather was now bitter: the ground covered with snow, and fuel scanty. The marches were long, but the discipline of the troops left nothing to be desired. On the 20th of December the columns of Moore and Baird were concentrated at Mayorga, with the Cavalry Division pushed forward to within three leagues of Sahagun. The Marquis de Romana promised to co-operate from the town of Leon, but his statements as to the numbers and equipment of his force were so mythical, that he neither did, nor was expected by Moore to do, anything except make an obstruction. Meanwhile, on the 16th, Soult, for the first time, had become aware of the British Army. Of his Divisions, one, under Bonet, was on the Deva, 60 miles north of the town of Carrion, covering Santander; while Mermet's was at Carrion, and Merlé's at Saldana. Franceschi's Cavalry Brigade was retiring from Valladolid, Debelle's was at Sahagun. Bonet was too far off to be recalled, and the French Marshal could at first concentrate only 12,000 men on the Carrion. At once he ordered up every available man from Burgos, and about the 21st, was reinforced from that town by General Lorge with a Brigade of Dragoons (1,300 sabres). On that day Debelle was attacked and defeated with great loss by Lord Paget at the head of the 15th Hussars, and Sahagun was immediately occupied by the British Headquarters. On the 22nd and 23rd Moore was compelled to halt. His reserve supplies had not come up, and the men's shoes were already worn out. Soult, fearing to be cut off from Palencia, called in Merlé to Carrion, and sent an urgent summons to the 8th Corps, which had been broken up into Divisions and placed under his orders. The Division of De Laborde was already at Palencia; Heudelet and Loison were two days' march further back.

On the evening of the 23rd the British troops were under orders to move on Carrion, with the intention of attacking at daybreak. Edward Paget's Division had actually started, when information reached the Commander-in-Chief to the effect that Napoleon was in full march from Madrid to intercept his retreat. On the 21st the Emperor had had intelligence of Moore's advance. His resolve was instantly taken. By the next day, at the head of over 50,000 men and 120 guns, made up of Bessières' Reserve Cavalry, the Imperial Guard, the 6th and two Divisions of the 1st Corps, he was marching on Valladolid. In crossing the Guadarama mountains snowstorms so terrific were encountered that men and horses were hurled over the precipices. The sufferings on that terrible march were almost more than human fortitude could endure. No one in the world but Napoleon could have induced his troops to proceed; but to that extraordinary man nothing could be impossible. Lapisse's Division broke out into almost open mutiny, the soldiers inciting one another to shoot the Emperor, who, riding within earshot, took not the smallest notice of their frenzy, which was in a moment forgotten on reaching comfortable cantonments at the bottom of the mountains. On the 24th the French army was at Villacastrin, fifty miles from Madrid. Snow had by this time given place to rain, and in rain men always march well. On the 26th, the Emperor with the 1st Corps and the Guards was at Tordesillas, seventy miles further on; while Ney, with the 6th Corps, had reached Rio Seco. Orders were despatched to Soult. Should the English advance, he was to retire and draw them on; should they retreat, he was to pursue them closely. The net was being tightly drawn. Success seemed almost assured; but in spite of this superhuman effort, Moore had already eluded its meshes and was safely across the Esla. On hearing of the Emperor's approach the General had lost no time in sending his baggage to the rear. Hope, with his own Division and Fraser's, followed on the 24th by way of Mayorga. Baird approached the Esla at Valencia. On Christmas Day, Moore with Paget and the two Light Brigades, followed Hope; the retirement of the whole being covered by Lord Paget and the Cavalry. Baird and Moore crossed the Esla on the 26th, the one at Valencia, the other at Castro Gonzalo, but with some difficulty; Moore being already in contact with the scouts of the Imperial Guard, which cut off part of the baggage, while their main body intercepted the Cavalry Division which had been occupied in retarding Soult. In a bold charge with two squadrons of the 10th Hussars Lord Paget broke through the enemy, crossed the bridge after Moore,

112 WELLINGTON'S OPERATIONS

and reached Benevente, four miles distant. By the evening of the 27th the whole army was behind the Esla with the exception of Crauford's Brigade, which remained on the left bank to protect the fatigue parties engaged in the destruction of the bridge, and for 36 hours kept the rapidly-increasing numbers of the enemy at bay. The solid masonry baffled all effort, and it was not until the night of the 28th that two arches were prepared for demolition. Crauford then passed over and the bridge was blown up. The line of the Esla was, however, untenable. Benevente was evacuated on the 28th, and next day Baird, Hope and Fraser met at Astorga. Edward Paget, Crauford, and the Cavalry Division formed the rearguard, still holding on to the Esla. Early on the 29th, General Lefébre Desnouettes with a Brigade—600 strong—of the Chasseurs and Mamelukes of the Guard, approached the left bank, and seeing only the British videttes on the further side, forded the river and attacked them. Believing his assailants to be the advance guard of a strong force, Lord Paget directed the Infantry to retire upon Astorga. Charles Stewart supported the picquets with his Brigade, but the French, getting the best of the running fight, had driven him back nearly as far as Benevente, when Lord Paget, suddenly bringing out the 10th from behind some buildings, charged with such effect as to hurl the French back into the Esla with the loss of 125 men killed and wounded and 70 prisoners, among them being Lefébre Desnouettes himself, who, like many of his men, was only saved by the victors from a watery grave. The French re-formed on the opposite bank, and were preparing to renew the contest when two guns opening with shrapnel drove them once more to the rear just as Napoleon in person appeared upon the scene of action.

This was the last cavalry action of importance during

IN THE PENINSULA 113

the campaign, but so well had the Cavalry Division acquitted itself that within the last fortnight it had taken nearly 600 prisoners. Its own losses from all causes had been about 80. In the evening Lord Paget retired upon Baneza. The main body of the 1st French Corps was now at Valderas; the 6th at Villaton. Soult was marching on Astorga by Mancilla. The British army was by no means out of danger. Romana failed to defend the bridge at Mancilla, and Soult entered Leon next day without opposition; but by this time rain had rendered the fords of the Esla impassable. On the 30th Bessières, having repaired the bridge at Castro Gonzalo, marched towards La Baneza, and Napoleon, with relentless energy, pushed on next day to Astorga from Benevente, a distance of 35 miles. His Infantry halted perforce at La Baneza, ten miles short of Astorga; for the exertions were beyond human endurance. "All the bridges," says Baron de Marbot who was present, " had been broken by the English. Our men were five or six times compelled to strip, place their arms and clothes on their heads and go naked through the icy water of the streams. It is painful to relate that I saw three veteran Grenadiers of the Guard, unable to march any further and unwilling to fall to the rear at the risk of being tortured and massacred by the peasants, blow out their brains with their own muskets." At nightfall the Emperor reached Astorga, but so slender was his escort that had Lord Paget, who was close at hand, been aware of it, one cannot doubt that Napoleon would have been in imminent peril of becoming his prisoner. An encounter did in fact take place of a singular kind, for the Brigade of Rioult d'Aveney was watering its horses at a brook close to Astorga when a large party of British Hussars came down to the further bank for the same purpose. Each side was in watering order without arms, and at a later period of the war

VOL. I.   9

would probably have finished its occupation in the most friendly manner. At this period French and English did not know each other so well, and in mutual alarm both parties mounted and galloped away. The result of this adventure was that the officer in command of the British patrols, instead of taking the trouble to verify the facts of the case, reported that the enemy was advancing in force. The retreat was in consequence unnecessarily accelerated; and Edward Paget's Division, which had halted at Cambarros, six miles from Astorga, was compelled to make a forced march through the night to Bembibre. On the 1st of January, 1809, Napoleon halted at Astorga to close up his army and give it a sorely needed day's rest. Ten thousand Cavalry, 70,000 Infantry, and 200 guns were now concentrated; but in spite of his supreme effort the coup had failed, and the British army had escaped the toils. No one knew better than the Emperor how to finish a campaign at a single blow; and so critical was the state of affairs in general that had he in the present case succeeded, the destruction of the only available British force would in all probability have formed the turning point of the war. Yet so little was the peril realised at home that Canning the Minister shortly afterwards eulogised Frere, whose advice if taken would infallibly have led to the loss of the entire army, while he grossly slandered the memory of Moore, by whose firmness and ability alone not only was a catastrophe avoided but the whole Peninsula saved.*

News of hostilities impending on the part of Austria

---

* A pitiable incident occurred while Napoleon was at Astorga. "Cries," says Marbot, "were heard from a large barn. The door was opened and it was found to contain 1,000 to 1,200 English women and children who, exhausted by the long march of the previous days through mud and streams, were unable to keep up with the army and had taken refuge in this place. For forty-eight hours they had lived on raw barley."

IN THE PENINSULA 115

now recalled Napoleon to France. Marshal Soult was entrusted with the further pursuit of the English. His immediate command comprised four Divisions of Cavalry (4,200 sabres), and three of Infantry (21,000 bayonets), with 54 guns. Ney with two Divisions of the 6th Corps—16,000 men and 37 guns—was in support. The Divisions of Heudelet and Loison — formerly of Junot's Corps—were hurrying up from the rear, and thus "nearly 60,000 men with 91 guns were upon the track of the English army."

Meanwhile Sir John Moore had been continuing his retreat under an accumulation of difficulties. Romana had promised to defend the bridge over the Esla at Mancilla. He lost it at the first attack and, instead of retiring as arranged into the Asturias, fled with his rabble to Astorga where he was found by the British troops on their arrival, blocking up the line of march and causing every possible confusion with the assistance of the local authorities. Large stores had been collected here, but distribution was impossible, and the greater part had to be destroyed or abandoned. Disputes arose and—as if Moore had not difficulties enough already—Romana now pestered the General to resume offensive operations on a plan "in comparison with which the visions of Don Quixote were wisdom."

At the advance of the Quarter-Master-General the Light Brigades under Crauford and Alten were detached on the 31st of December, and directed to march by Orense to Vigo. On the same day Hope and Fraser reached Villa Franca; and Baird, Bembibre. They were followed next morning, as already stated, by the rearguard. The discipline of the troops had become relaxed at the outset of the retreat. Edward Paget by his own personal influence, supported by drum-head Courts martial, assembled almost under the fire of the enemy, and the resolute use of the lash, kept his Division in some order. Crauford did the same with the Light Brigade until it was detached from the main body. Baird's Division—with the exception of the Brigade of Guards—was in a disgraceful state. An officer of Paget's Division thus describes his experiences on entering the town. "Bembibre exhibited all the appearance of a place lately stormed and pillaged. Every door and window was broken; every lock and fastening forced. Rivers of wine ran through the houses and into the streets, where lay fantastic groups of soldiers, women, children, runaway Spaniards and muleteers, all apparently inanimate except when here or there a leg or an arm was seen to move, while the wine oozing from their lips and nostrils seemed the effect of gunshot wounds. . . . We had proceeded but a short distance when the enemy's horsemen nearly approached the place, and then it was that the apparently lifeless stragglers, whom no exertions of ours were sufficient to rouse from their torpor, startled at the immediate approach of danger, found the partial use of their limbs. The road instantly became thronged with them; they reeled, staggered, and threw down their arms." * At Villa Franca, and indeed everywhere else, Sir John Moore made the most vigorous efforts to quell the disorders, which cut him—the finest trainer of men, morally and physically, that the army has ever seen—to the heart. "The enemy," he indignantly exclaimed in addressing one regiment, "have taken or cut in pieces many hundred British cowards — for none but unprincipled cowards would get drunk in presence, nay, in the very sight of the enemies of their country; and sooner than survive the disgrace of such infamous conduct I hope the first cannon ball fired by the enemy may take me in the head.

* "A Boy in the Peninsular War," page 49.

And you, -th, are not what you used to be, you are not the regiment who to a man fought by my side in Egypt. If you were, no earthly temptation could for an instant seduce one of you away from your colours!" Moore's reproaches, whether published in orders or delivered personally, did not fail to have at any rate a temporary effect, for the British soldier, although weak and thoughtless, is eminently susceptible to an appeal to his better feelings; but many of the Generals were not entirely loyal to their Chief: the fact of the retreat caused bitter disappointment, and there were frequent cases of gross neglect of duty among the regimental officers.

After the detachment of the Light Brigades the British army still counted about 20,000 officers and men fit for duty; but Franceschi's Cavalry was turning its right flank by the valley of the Syl, and the enemy in front were reinforced too rapidly to allow of a permanent halt. Moore determined to continue his retreat to Vigo and embark his troops for Portugal. The Cavalry, useless in the mountainous country now being entered, gave up the post of honour to Edward Paget's Division, which fought a smart rearguard action on the 3rd of January at the bridge of Calcabellos, during the course of which the French General Colbert was killed. Marching through the night Paget reached Herrerias, eighteen miles distant, next morning. Baird was then at Nogales; Hope and Fraser near Lugo. At Herrerias, Sir John, as usual with the rearguard, received reports which induced him to substitute Corunna for Vigo as his point of retreat. By this time the main body was well ahead of the enemy, and Moore sent orders to concentrate the army for battle at Lugo. It was high time to make a stand. The hardships of the march, enhanced by the terrific cold and rain, had crowded the roads with stragglers. The sufferings of the women, patiently endured, are beyond description. It is even stated that the wives and children of our soldiers, unable to go any further, were found sitting at the roadside by the Spanish peasants, and by them—the persons on whose account our poor people were enduring this terrible misery—stripped of their clothes and left to be frozen to death. If this be true one need go no further to find the cause of the animosity shown afterwards by our troops towards the Spaniards.

The severities inseparable from a winter campaign would seem to have been at times needlessly aggravated. The troop horses were being shot by scores. For want of shoes their feet were in a terrible state. Herrerias was composed almost entirely of blacksmiths' shops —the name signifies a forge—yet after quitting it Cavalry regiments were destitute of nails, and it is difficult to avoid the conclusion that the officers had been guilty of most culpable neglect. But the Staff and Departmental officers were equally to blame. Owing to gross neglect on the part of Baird, Fraser's Division was not halted at Lugo, and was consequently compelled, after a long and toilsome march, to retrace its steps thither. Through the carelessness of a paymaster a large amount of specie had to be abandoned. At Villa Franca the rearguard found waggons full of Spanish clothing and shoes abandoned, and piles of meat being destroyed, yet was not allowed to take what it wanted for its own use. All that the men could do was to stick their bayonets into a few of the joints and carry them thus to the end of the march, when they were found most acceptable. It is, however, only fair to remember that in a retreat it is impossible to provide for every contingency. Waggons are liable to break down at any moment. Orders are given that stores are not to be allowed to fall into the enemy's hands, and as the persons entrusted with the execution of the order are not always in a position to know how far distant the enemy may be, it is difficult for them to decide whether a part may be saved or whether the immediate destruction of the whole is imperative. It is noteworthy that at the end of this particularly long and harassing march many men, forgetting their fatigue, walked back three miles to recover the shoes and brought back a large quantity, in which they drove a brisk trade, payment being accepted in promissory notes payable at Corunna, or on the distribution of cash!

On January 5th the French Cavalry skirmished all day with our rearguard, which by this time presented a nondescript appearance, the men being clothed chiefly in Spanish costumes, and consequently mistaken no doubt by the enemy for Romana's stragglers. The passage of the bridge over the Mino at Constantino—a ticklish business—was skilfully effected under the personal supervision of Sir John Moore. Next day Paget reached Lugo, in front of which town the main body of the army, its discipline and morale largely restored by the prospect of a fight, was drawn up in order of battle. The strength of the force was still about 20,000, with 40 guns, for Moore had been joined by three battalions—the 51st, 59th, and 76th—which had originally been left by Baird to guard the line of communications, and were formed into a Brigade under Major-General Leith. Soult, with a view to ascertaining the strength of his opponent, skirmished with the outposts. But although slightly superior in numbers, he had no intention of playing his enemy's game by fighting a battle in which he must infallibly lose many lives and could gain no advantage that would not equally be his by waiting. On the other hand it was impossible for Moore to assume the offensive. He was not aware of Napoleon's departure, but in the face of an enemy who within two days could bring up overwhelming numbers, any permanent recovery of the ground lost was out of the question ; and in any case it was the paramount strategical object of the British commander to allure the French into the remotest corner of Spain and gain time for the southern provinces to organise resistance. There was only enough ammunition for one battle, food for only one day; and the position occupied, although strong in itself, could be turned by way of Orense. There was no alternative but to resume the retreat. On the night of the 8th Moore withdrew from his position, covered as usual by the Reserve Division under Edward Paget. A terrible storm of rain and sleet washed away the heaps of straw which had been placed to mark the road in the darkness. Paget alone maintained the true direction. The other Divisions lost their way. Baird most imprudently allowed his men to take shelter in houses, and could not get them out again. Paget was obliged to halt all night to enable the other Divisions to regain the road and get ahead. Having been under arms for twenty-four hours, the Army at length, says Napier, " arrived at Betanzos in a state very discreditable to its discipline." The rearguard took up a position three miles short of the town. During this disastrous march more men had fallen out of the ranks than during the whole of the previous part of the campaign. On the 10th the Army halted, and was rejoined by about 1,500 stragglers who had rallied under command of a medical officer's batmân—engaged in saving his master's panniers—and had beaten off the French Cavalry.

On this day supplies had been sent out from Corunna, and the troops, for the first time for many a day, enjoyed a good meal. One more march brought the Army to Corunna. The Divisions, marching for the first time together, were personally commanded by Sir John

Moore, the result being that order and regularity were restored. The rearguard halted at El Burgo. It was determined to destroy the bridge over the Mero river. Excepting at Castro Ganzalo, the Royal Engineers had hitherto been unsuccessful in their attempts at demolition. Nettled perhaps by a few candid criticisms on their past failures, they were determined to make no mistake now, and enacted such a terrible explosion that it was only by the mercy of Providence that two companies of Infantry posted to cover the workmen were not blown into the air at the same time. Paget's duty in command of the rearguard was now at an end. For twelve days his Division had covered the retreat. During this time it " traversed 80 miles in two marches, passed several nights under arms in the snow of the mountains, was seven times engaged, and now took the outposts, having fewer men missing from the ranks, including those who had fallen in battle, than any other Division in the Army." * Deplorable indeed was the fate—like that of his brother, although under different circumstances—which, except for a few days, deprived the Army of the services of an officer of Edward Paget's calibre during the remainder of the war.

On his arrival at Corunna a terrible disappointment awaited the British commander. The transports were not yet in sight. He employed the interval in re-organising his troops, in issuing new muskets which were found in the arsenal (having been sent from England for the use of the Spaniards), and in destroying the enormous powder magazine with its 4,000 barrels. During the evening of the 14th the transports arrived. The Cavalry, sick men, baggage, and 50 guns were embarked. On this day General Anstruther died of exhaustion from the effects of the retreat.

* Napier, bk. iv. ch. 5.

Meanwhile, on the 12th Soult had concentrated his army, which had suffered pretty nearly as much as the British. On the 14th, having repaired the bridge, he crossed the Mero; next day he was reinforced by De Laborde's Division. A good position, running from the sea-coast south-west of Corunna to the village of El Burgo, had been perforce abandoned by Moore as being too extensive for his force, now reduced to about 16,000 of all ranks. It was occupied—though not to its full extent—by Soult; and it not only commanded within cannon-shot the opposite hills nearer Corunna on which the British troops were posted, but enfiladed their right. Merlé's Division occupied the centre of the French line, flanked on the right by De Laborde, who reached down to the Mero, and on the left by Mermet. An isolated hill on Mermet's left was crowned by eleven heavy guns. The dismounted Dragoons of La Houssaye and Lorge, and Franceschi's Light Cavalry, prolonged the line along another range of heights somewhat in advance.

The morning of January 16th wore away. Ney, obstinate and intractable towards his commander, was still in rear. Apart, however, from the Corps of that officer, Soult had concentrated 20,000 men supported by a numerous Artillery; yet he still appeared to hesitate. In the event of the day passing without an attack, it was the intention of the British Commander to embark his Infantry Divisions at night. With this object the Reserve had actually started for the harbour when at 2 p.m. news came that the French Marshal was forming his troops into columns of attack. Paget instantly retraced his steps. Sir John Moore galloped up from Corunna. The British line stood to arms, and the battle began.

Sir Charles Napier—the third of our quartette of great nineteenth-century generals—at that time a Major com-

IN THE PENINSULA 123

manding the 50th Regiment, graphically describes the scene as follows :—" Suddenly I heard a gallop of horses, and turning, saw Moore. He came at speed, and pulled up so sharp and close he seemed to have alighted from the air, man and horse looking at the approaching foe with an intentness that seemed to concentrate all feeling in their eyes. The sudden stop of the animal, a cream-coloured one with black tail and mane, had cast the latter streaming forward, its ears were pushed out like horns, whilst its eyes flashed fire, and it snorted away with expanded nostrils. My first thought was, ' It will be away like the wind '; but then I looked at the rider, and the horse was forgotten. Thrown on its haunches, the animal came sliding and dashing the dirt up with its fore feet, thus bending the General forward almost to its neck; but his head was thrown back, and his look more keenly piercing than I ever before saw it. He glanced to the right and left, and then fixed his eyes intently on the enemy's advancing column, at the same time grasping the reins with both of his hands and pressing the horse firmly with his knees ; his body thus seemed to deal with the animal while his mind was intent on the enemy, and his aspect was one of searching intenseness beyond the power of words to describe. For a while he looked, and then galloped to the left without saying a word." Truly a theme for the sculptor ; yet the gratitude of his countrymen has raised no statue to his memory in England.

The dispositions of Moore showed him to be as great a master of tactics as of strategy. Taking advantage of the fact that his men had just been re-armed with new firelocks and provided with new ammunition, and that their fire would in consequence be far more effective than that of the enemy, he occupied his main position—2,000 yards in length—with only two Divisions, Baird's on the right, Hope's on the left reaching down to the Mero. Each Division had two Brigades deployed, and the third in rear of its outer flank. A Rifle Battalion of Paget's Division, occupying a knoll three-quarters of a mile to the right rear of Baird, made head against the French Dragoons, being connected by another Battalion (extended along the low ground) with the main body of the Division, which was drawn up in rear of the centre. Still further behind, Fraser guarded the approaches to the town of Corunna, but was held in readiness to meet any contingency that might present itself in the development of Soult's attack. All the field guns except nine had been embarked. Thus with two of his four Infantry Divisions Moore contained Soult, holding the other two in hand for a counter attack, and giving an admirable illustration of the art of compensating by tactical skill for inferiority of position and numbers.

To the right front of Sir David Baird, at a distance of about 300 yards, lay the village of Elvina, occupied only by a line of outposts. In front of the right and centre of the enemy's position were the villages of Palavia and Portosa. Elsewhere the ground between the two armies was broken by stone walls. The enemy advanced in three columns of attack. Mermet assailed the British right; Merlé the centre; De Laborde the left. The contour of the hill brought Baird nearest the French, and he accordingly first sustained the brunt of the attack. Elvina was captured, and Mermet, pursuing his advantage, threatened to outflank and roll up the right of our line. Moore only waited to ascertain that Soult had shown his hand, and had nothing further in reserve. Then, bringing up Paget, he fiercely attacked Mermet with the bayonet, and drove him back in confusion. Meanwhile, on our centre and extreme left Hope had been assailed by De Laborde and Merlé, but held his ground.

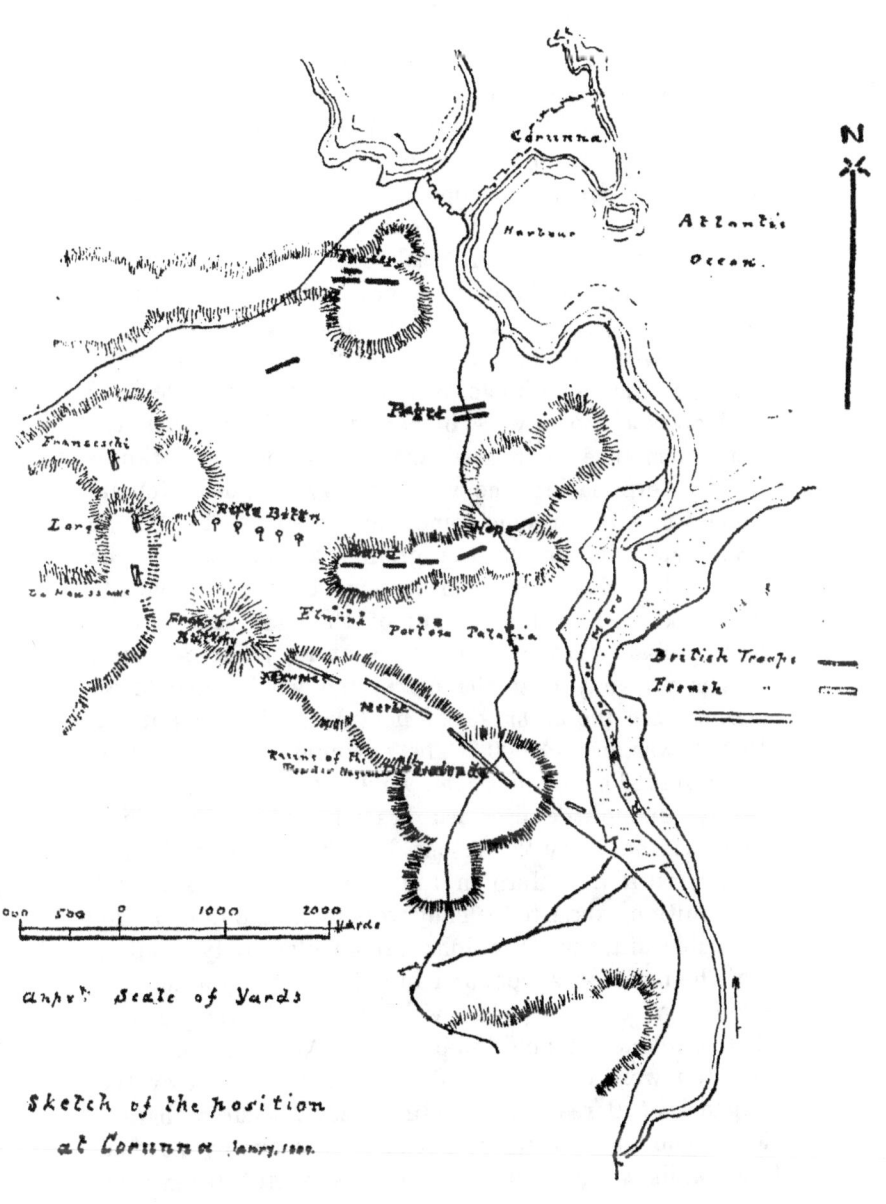

Fierce fighting, however, continued at Elvina, which was taken and retaken alternately. Baird fell grievously hurt. Moore in person restored the fight. Then he too was struck to the ground, mortally wounded. By some mistake Fraser failed to support Paget, and thus, to some extent, stopped the latter from pursuing his victorious advance; yet, on the left flank, Hope, who had repelled his assailants without any great difficulty, assumed the offensive, and captured the village of Palavia. The French, with the defile of the hastily repaired El Burgo bridge as their sole line of retreat, and even that menaced by Hope's advance, were in parlous condition, when the non-appearance of Fraser and the shades of darkness rapidly terminating the winter's day, decided General Hope—now in supreme command—to sound the "Cease fire," and bivouac on the ground already won. The British loss does not seem to have been ever officially published. From the nature of the case the returns were probably never accurately sent in. The estimate, 800, is probably near the mark, and would include all absent from the embarkation next day. The loss of the French was about 3,000. The new muskets and ammunition served out to our men would naturally prove most deadly among the crowded masses of the attacking columns, but Soult's troops had been driven into a corner, with the Mero in full flood behind them and ammunition exhausted. They were fortunate in escaping a terrible disaster. Sir John Moore lived only to know that the battle was won, and breathed his last at sunset. At 10 p.m. the army was withdrawn, and the picquets alone remained to hold the position. At 5 a.m. next day they too were called in, and the troops, covered by the Brigades of Beresford and Hill, effected their embarkation. The inhabitants of Corunna chivalrously manned their walls to gain time for the rearguard to get on

board. The intention had always been to bring the
Army down by sea to Lisbon, but it was in no condition to take the field again without new clothing and
equipment. Accordingly, on the 18th the convoy sailed
for England. Ill-fortune attended the Army to the very
last. A terrible gale arose. Some of the ships were
driven out of their course, others were wrecked, and
hundreds of men who had survived the perils and hardships of the campaign found a watery grave within sight
of English shores.

The losses of the Army, due to all causes, from start
to finish of the campaign, amounted to 4,000, of whom
800 stragglers effected their escape to Portugal. Six
3-pounder guns which had been brought from Corunna
to Villa Franca without orders, were abandoned there.
The nine guns used at the battle of Corunna were spiked
and thrown into the sea.

Thus ended the campaign. The British public, horrified at the haggard and toil-worn appearance of the
troops on landing, disappointed at the result of the
expedition which it had been led to believe would
infallibly end in the expulsion of the French from
Spain, and ignorant on whom the blame lay, lavished
abuse upon the dead General. The Ministry, with the
usual cowardice of politicians, bowed to the storm, and
Canning, in his anxiety to shield his friend Hookham
Frere, seems to have hesitated at nothing in the way of
misstatement and calumny.

Nevertheless, the result of the campaign afforded many
useful lessons, prominent among which was the evidence
of the utter incapacity of the Government to direct, or
even to appreciate the elements of, military operations.
The British force was far too small to gain decisive
success. Equally apparent was the fallacy of depending
in any degree for success upon Spanish promises or

patriotism. But, in point of fact, the direct consequences of Sir John Moore's strategy were of the most important character. Napoleon was arrested in mid career; his projected campaign in the southern provinces thwarted. Saragossa was given a breathing time. Opportunities, although sadly neglected, were afforded to the relics of Castanos' Army, under the Duc d'Infantado, to offer that town substantial relief; and the men of Andalusia had the chance of reorganising their forces. Portugal was saved from invasion; and, lastly, the French Army was severely repulsed in a pitched battle.

One may perhaps speculate on the course of events had Moore been intercepted on the Esla, and one can hardly doubt that he would have signalised the occasion by some brilliant illustration of the art of war. Possibly he would have cut his way through between Ney and Napoleon with a view to eluding or defeating the 4th Corps and making good his retreat into Andalusia. At the same time it must be admitted that with Lefébre in his front and the Emperor thundering on his rear, the case, although not desperate, would at any rate have been most gravely critical.

Moore's retreat through Galicia has been criticised as unduly rapid. But his critics have entirely failed to appreciate the situation, whether viewed from the point of view of strategy or tactics. Many defensive positions, it is true, presented themselves in the line of retreat, but they were every one liable to be turned in flank. On the other hand, the inferiority of his army in point of numbers, its lack of clothing and equipment, its pecuniary destitution, not only forbade the General to resume the offensive permanently, but made it essential to transport the troops as quickly as possible, either to England or Portugal, to be refitted. Wellington, speaking deliberately many years later, saw no error in the conduct of the cam-

IN THE PENINSULA 129

paign; and Napoleon observed that Moore's talents and firmness alone saved the army from destruction. In fine, Moore's strategy was brilliant, his retreat ably conducted, and his battle a masterpiece of resource. If any one doubts this last assertion let him compare the execution of the opposing commanders, and consider the probable result of the action had they changed places.

The biassed censure of contemporary politicians may be disregarded. But it is curious that modern writers, imbued with the theory of the infallibility of a Tory Government and noticing that Sir John was generously defended by many Whigs, have in consequence assumed, erroneously, that his political views coincided with those of the Whig party, and consider that supposed fact to be a justification of the conduct of the Ministry. They set aside the arguments of Sir W. Napier in favour of Moore as "special pleading," forgetting that the views of Napier were shared by every one competent to form an opinion on military matters. But after the evidence of Wellington and Napoleon it is needless to call less distinguished authorities.

A noble epitaph on the fallen General was written by the Duke of York, Commander-in-Chief. "The life of Sir John Moore was spent among his troops." Disregarding the popular outcry, the Duke held him up in a General Order as an example to the Army. But Moore's special distinction is that of being the great military instructor of the day. His pupils—Colborne, Hardinge, the Napiers, and many others—were the best field officers, and the regiments which he had trained were the best battalions in Wellington's army. It is hardly too much to say that it was the instruction of Moore which made it possible for Wellington to gain his victories.

Sir John was buried as a soldier on the rampart of Corunna. Both friend and foe raised a monument to his memory. Spanish poetical imagination weaves bright legends around the tomb of the great English hero. Vast treasures are said by the peasants to lie buried there; and they say truly, for his loss has never been replaced in the British Army.

IN THE PENINSULA 131

PART II

CHAPTER VII

State of the French Forces—Siege and capture of Saragossa—Soult invades Portugal—Captures Oporto—Operations of Victor

AFTER the fall of Madrid, Napoleon gave its citizens another opportunity to accept or reject his brother. Voting by parishes, 28,600 men demanded Joseph as their sovereign, and were supported not only by the public bodies of the capital, but by the deputies from Valladolid, Leon, Astorga, &c., &c. Joseph was consequently permitted to resume the crown.

The composition of that part of the French Army available for operations on the offensive was at this time very much as follows; but changes were being constantly made, and the numbers can only be taken as approximations (*vide* Napoleon's Correspondence, November 8 and December 22, 1808):—

1st ARMY CORPS.
Marshal Victor, Duc de Bellune.

			Men.	Guns.
1st Division.	Gen. Villatte		5,000	
2nd „	„ Ruffin		6,000	40
3rd „	„ Leval		3,000	8
4th „	„ Lapisse		7,000	(detached)
	55th Regiment		3,000	

132 WELLINGTON'S OPERATIONS

			Men.	Guns.
Cavalry Div.	Gen. Latour Maubourg		3,000	6
	26th Chasseurs		300	
	Dutch Light Cavalry		300	

Total (excluding Lapisse detached): 3,600 Cavalry, 17,000 Infantry, and 54 guns.

2ND ARMY CORPS.
Marshal Soult, Duc de Dalmatie.

		Brigadiers.		Men.	Guns.
1st Division.	Gen. Merle	{ Lefébre { Gaulois	86th and 4th Batt. 119th Regts.	6,000	12
2nd „	„	Bonet,	118th, 119th, and 120th Regts.	4,500	12
3rd „	„	Mermet, Foy		7,000	
*{ 4th „	„	De Laborde		9,000	
*{ 5th „	„	Loison	2nd, 4th, 15th Regts.	5,000	
*{ 6th „	„	Heudelet		6,000	
2½ Cavalry Divs.	„	„ La Houssaye Lorge „ Franceschi		7,500	15

Total: 7,500 Cavalry, 37,500 Infantry, and 51 guns.

* These Divisions had been transferred temporarily from the 8th Army Corps, which was broken up. At a later date it was reorganised.

3RD ARMY CORPS.
General Junot, Duc d'Abrantes.

		Brigadiers.		Men.	Guns.
1st Div.	Gen. Mathieu	{ Buget { Habert	44th, 79th Regts.	7,000	10
2nd „	„ Musnier	{ Brun { Razout	114th, 115th; 1st of the Vistula; Westphalian Batt.	5,500	10
3rd „	„ Morlot	Augereau	116th, 117th, 1 Irish and 1 Prussian Batt.	4,000	10
4th „	„ Grandjean	{ Laval { Rostollant	122nd; 1 Reserve Batt; 5th Lt. Infy., 1 Supplementary Batt.	5,000	10
Cavalry Div.	Gen. Wathier			1,600	6

Total: 1,600 Cavalry, 21,500 Infantry, and 46 guns.

4TH ARMY CORPS.
Marshal Lefébre, Duc de Dantzig.

			Men.	Guns.
1st Div. Gen. Sebastiani	28th, 32nd, 58th, 75th Regts.		6,000	12
2nd ,, ,, Valence	3 Polish Regts.		4,000	12
3rd ,,	Dutch Brigade, Westphalian Brigade		6,000	12
Cavalry Div. Gen. Lasalle	10th, 22nd Chasseurs; 9th Dragoons		1,300	6
,, ,, ,, Milhaud	Dragoons		2,000	6
,, Brigade	5th Dragoons (700), Westphalian Light Horse (800)		1,500	

Total, 4,800 Cavalry, 16,000 Infantry, and 48 guns.

5TH ARMY CORPS.
Marshal Mortier, Duc de Trevise.

1st Division. General Suchet
2nd ,, ,, Gazan
Total: 19,000 men, ? guns.

6TH ARMY CORPS.
Marshal Ney, Duc d'Elchingen.

1st Division. General Marchand
2nd ,, ,, Dessolles
3rd ,, ,, ?
4th ,, ,, Maucune   Polish Regiments
Total: 2,200 Cavalry, 27,000 Infantry, 3,000 Artillery, 55–60 guns.

7TH ARMY CORPS.
General Gouvion St. Cyr.

1st Division. General Chabran
2nd ,, ,, Souham
3rd ,, ,, Lechi
4th ,, ,, Pino
5th ,, ,, Chabot
Total: 42,000 men, ? guns.

RESERVE.

6 Battalions Fusiliers, Imperial Guard
5 ,, Grenadiers and Chasseurs ditto   14,000 Infantry
King of Spain's Guard
4 Divisions of Dragoons
Cavalry and Poles of the Guard   18,000 Cavalry
Artillery   2,000 Artillery; 60 guns

The 1st Army Corps, with the exception of Lapisse's Division and a Cavalry Brigade detached at Salamanca, was in La Mancha. The 2nd was at Corunna. The 3rd and 5th besieged Saragossa. The 4th, shortly afterwards commanded by General Sebastiani, which had defeated Galluzzo's army at Almaraz on the 24th of December and had been checked by Moore's advance in its march on Portugal, remained in the neighbourhood of Plasencia and the valley of the Tagus. The 6th Corps held Galicia; the 7th occupied Catalonia. Bessières' Heavy Cavalry Corps was broken up and its Divisions distributed among the various Army Corps.

The Imperial Guard and Kellermann's Cavalry guarded the lines of communication, which were further secured by the fortresses of Burgos, Pampeluna, and St. Sebastian. Infantry Divisions also occupied Santander, Bilbao, and Vittoria. Bayonne formed the base of operations. Between Bayonne and Burgos, Napier states, were 11 military stations; between Burgos and Madrid, on the direct road, 8; on that by Valladolid, 11. Between Valladolid and Saragossa was a chain of 15 forts; between Valladolid and Santander one of 8; and between Valladolid and Villa Franca were 9. The northern provinces were made the seats of military governments, designed to maintain order and repress petty insurrections. The nominal strength of the French armies amounted on January 15, 1809, to 324,000 men and 52,000 horses. Of the former, 58,000 were in hospital. Garrisons, depôts, &c., &c., absorbed 25,000. Fifty thousand men guarded the lines of communication; 192,000 were available for offensive operations.*

The first blow was struck by Victor. Castanos' beaten army, now commanded by the Duc d'Infantado and

---

* These numbers were diminished in the middle of February by 40,000 men taken for the Austrian war.

recruited up to 20,000 men, advanced early in January, 1809, against Toledo. Victor marched against him, routed his army at Ucles, and drove him into the Sierra Morena. D'Infantado was then succeeded by Cartoajal, who took post on the Upper Guadiana and opened up communication with Galluzzo's army under command of General Cuesta, which, on the retirement of Sebastiani, reoccupied the line of the Tagus about Almaraz.

Meanwhile the 3rd and 5th Corps had been busily engaged. The battle of Tudela threw Saragossa open to the French, but a slackness in following up the victory enabled the citizens to recover from their alarm, close the gates and man the walls. On the 24th of December, 1808, the town was invested by Junot and Mortier. On the 22nd of January, 1809, Lannes—an excellent soldier —who had been ill, assumed command of the two Corps. The outworks were stormed but the defence was continued from house to house; and the roofs being fireproof, every church, convent, or other building became a fortress. A series of mining operations enabled the assailants gradually to gain ground. The inhabitants seeking refuge from the incessant bombardment among the vaults and cellars, contracted a pestilence and died at the rate of four or five hundred a day. No attempt was made to relieve the place. At length human nature could hold out no longer, and on the 20th of February Saragossa surrendered. Thus terminated a memorable siege in which, however, after giving every credit to the obstinacy of the defence, the honours of the contest undoubtedly belong to Lannes, who with 35,000 men hemmed in and vanquished a garrison of 50,000. The siege ended, Junot returned to France; and Suchet, taking command of the 3rd Corps, established his headquarters in Aragon. Mortier, with the 5th Corps, occupied both banks of the Ebro, and opened up communication with General St. Cyr, who had been conducting operations in Catalonia with great ability, capturing Rosas and holding Barcelona. In April, Mortier was called to a new sphere of work in Castile. It was, however, for a campaign in the west and south that Napoleon had planned his greatest combinations. Foreseeing the embarkation of Moore's Army, his intention was that Soult should then wheel to the left and invade Portugal with the co-operation of Victor, whose Corps for that purpose was to change places with that of Sebastiani. Then, on the fall of Lisbon, Victor was to advance into Andalusia, assisted by a Division of Soult's Army Corps from the side of the Alemtejo, and capture Cadiz.

On the embarkation of the British, Corunna and Ferrol readily submitted to the French; and an order dated January 21st from Berthier, Chief of the Emperor's Staff, directed Soult to march with two and a half Divisions of Cavalry under Lorge, La Houssaye, and Franceschi, and four Divisions of Infantry commanded respectively by Merlé, Mermet, De Laborde, and Heudelet, followed by that of Loison, upon Oporto and Lisbon. "It is supposed," continued the despatch, "that you cannot be at Oporto before the 5th of February; at Lisbon before the 16th. Thus, when you are near Lisbon, the Army Corps of the Duke of Belluno, composed of his own three Divisions, of Leval's Division, and of ten or twelve regiments of Cavalry, forming a body of 30,000 men, will be at Merida, to make a strong diversion in your favour; and he can push the head of a column upon Lisbon if you find any great obstacles to your entrance, which it is however presumed will not be the case. General Lapisse's Division of Infantry, at this moment in Salamanca, and General Maupetit's Cavalry Brigade, will, on your arrival at Oporto, receive orders to march upon Ciudad Rodrigo and Abrantes, where this Division will again be under the command of the Duke of Belluno, who will send it instructions to join him at Merida: I tell you this in order that you may know of Lapisse's march on your left flank as far as Abrantes. Such are the last orders I am charged to give you in the name of the Emperor: you will have to report to the King and receive his orders for your subsequent operations."

At the time when this order was despatched Napoleon had quitted Valladolid for France. Possibly therefore the time calculations were not his own, but Berthier's. In any case they were framed on the idea that Soult would meet little resistance either from the English or the Portuguese; and they were quickly falsified by events. In the campaign against Moore the French army had had the same hardships as the British and had suffered equally. Twelve thousand men were actually in hospital. Detachments were required for the line of communications as well as for garrisons of Corunna and Ferrol. The whole force needed rest. No time was, however, lost. Headquarters were established at St. Jago de Campostella; and on the 1st of February the Army, consisting of 4,000 Cavalry, 19,000 Infantry and 58 guns, was put in motion for Portugal. Ney remained to hold Galicia, and had no difficulty in doing so, for the Galicians preferred the French to the English.

It was, however, impossible to make the progress hoped for by the Emperor. On the 15th of February—the day prior to that on which Napoleon thought Soult might possibly reach Lisbon—the Marshal was only at Tuy on the Minho. He attempted to cross the river near the mouth at Campo Santo. Being repulsed, he marched forty miles up-stream to Orense and seized the bridge. In the mountainous country in which he was now compelled to operate, all superfluous impedimenta doubled the difficulties of the advance. Thirty-six guns and a vast quantity of carriages were consequently sent back to Tuy, which was occupied by a garrison of 500 men, together with stragglers, sick men, and detachments coming down from St. Jago. The preliminary arrangements and the concentration of his Corps occupied some days. It was not until the 4th of March that he put his troops in motion. Franceschi's Cavalry covered the advance. La Houssaye protected the left flank. The line of advance was by the valley of the Tamega, a confluent of the Douro. Romana, and Silveira, a Portuguese General, were known to be guarding the road, each with about 8,000 men. A charge of Franceschi's Cavalry slew 1,200 and dispersed the remainder of the Spanish advance guard at Monterey, whereupon Romana fled eastward, leaving Silveira to his fate. Soult's movements were deliberate, for he had cut himself adrift from his base and was carrying his field hospitals, stores, &c., with him. Chaves was taken on the 12th of March and a hospital established therein. Thence, the French Marshal quitting the line of the Tamega marched by Ruivaens on Braga; came upon the main body of the Portuguese which had just murdered its general, Bernadim Freire; put it to flight, fought his way to Oporto and captured it on the 28th of March. But the failure at Campo Santo had cost him five weeks, and, as will be seen in the sequel, proved fatal to his campaign. By the exercise of tact and moderation Soult had been doing everything in his power—not without success—to reconcile the people to French rule and alleviate the horrors of war, and the country in his rear was in consequence comparatively tranquil; but the ferocity of the Portuguese at Oporto towards their prisoners, their resistance under impossible circum-

IN THE PENINSULA 139

stances, and the internal anarchy which prevailed, combined to signalise the capture of the town by terrible scenes of horror and bloodshed. Ten thousand soldiers and inhabitants are said to have perished, a large proportion of whom were drowned in their attempt to escape across the Douro.

A Division was now sent to open up communications with Tuy, and another to oppose Silveira who, after Romana's defeat, had at first retired along the Tamega, had then returned and captured Chaves, and was now advancing down the Douro from Amarante to attack Soult. Both Divisions were successful. Tuy was relieved, Silveira defeated and driven first across the Tamega and then over the Douro about the 5th of May. At the same time Franceschi, with a Brigade of Cavalry and one of Infantry, was sent across the Douro to get intelligence of Lapisse, whose movements were unknown, but who should by this time have been near Abrantes. In point of fact, however, that officer, disregarding his instructions, had marched independently on the 6th of April to join Victor on the Tagus, and his duty of protecting Soult's left flank and forming a connecting link between the 1st and 2nd Army Corps was therefore unfulfilled.

Soult's Army Corps was now reduced by 2,500 men, exclusive of the garrisons of the various posts. He could hear nothing either of Lapisse or Victor. A strong British force was assembling in Beira. It was obvious that he lacked strength to attempt unaided the capture of Lisbon, 200 miles distant. The only alternatives remaining to him were either to halt upon the ground which he had won, or to regain communication with the French Headquarters by retiring through Amarante and Braganza. Internal discontent and disloyalty among many of his officers added to his difficulties. There was an idea abroad that he aspired to the throne of Portugal independently of Napoleon. Men like Ney, devoted to the Emperor, were furious at his suspected treason; others, representing the republican element which still strongly pervaded the Army, opposed him on the precisely opposite ground of his fidelity to the Emperor; for these entertained and continued to entertain until a much later date, the hope of curtailing Napoleon's power, or indeed of restoring a commonwealth under the presidency of General Gouvion St. Cyr. The real facts seem to have been that Soult, finding himself in a tight corner, cut off as he was from France on the one side and from Victor on the other, took advantage of the unpopularity of the House of Braganza to gain over to him the party opposed to the nominally reigning dynasty, who were ready to welcome one of Napoleon's family as their sovereign. His policy proved successful, for the outrages hitherto committed on his stragglers, &c., by the peasantry, ceased towards the end of April.

We must now return to Victor. After his defeat of the Duc d'Infantado at Ucles, Napoleon had, as already stated, directed him to exchange places with the 4th Corps and co-operate with the 2nd, in the invasion first of Portugal, afterwards of Andalusia. The Army Corps of Sebastiani and Victor—the one at Toledo, the other on the right bank of the Tagus—were closely connected with each other by good roads and easily supported by the troops at Madrid. They were, in fact, acting upon interior lines, whereas the armies of Cartoajal and Cuesta, separated by the impassable Sierra de Guadaloupe, had no direct communication, and were not in a position to act in unison. The latter also were in point of numbers greatly inferior to the French, the two armies between them mustering only 31,000 men, while Victor and

Sebastiani had 35,000, exclusive of the Reserves at
Madrid. The Emperor's orders to Victor were to push
on and be at Merida by the middle of February, in the
expectation that Soult would be about that time at
Lisbon. The latter had, as we have seen, been delayed
by a variety of circumstances—the battle of Corunna, the
repulse at the mouth of the Minho, &c. There seems,
however, to have been no reason for Victor to fail in
carrying out his orders, but his capacity was not great,
and he overrated the strength of the enemy. Thus it
was not until the 15th of March that, in response to
reiterated instructions, he crossed the Tagus at Talavera
and Arzobispo, drove Cuesta from the banks and across
the Guadiana, routed him at Medellin on the 28th and
occupied Merida. Further than this he refused to go,
although joined by Lapisse on the 19th of April. Cuesta,
who in spite of his defeat was given command of Cartoajal's army in addition to his own, then occupied
Monasterio with a view to covering Seville, reorganised
his forces at leisure, and by the end of the month had
assembled 6,000 Cavalry and 25,000 Infantry.

The general result of these operations must have been
a great disappointment to Napoleon. The grand combination by which the 2nd Corps had been expected to
sweep through Portugal, supported by Lapisse on the
Zezere and Tagus, and Victor from Estremadura—the
line of advance of each force being so arranged as to
place it in easy communication with each other and with
the base of operations—had, through force of circumstances and the jealousy or incapacity of Lapisse and
Victor, utterly failed. The second part of the plan,
namely, the invasion of Andalusia, had consequently to
be abandoned. The absence of Napoleon marred the
whole plan of campaign. Ney had been quarrelling with
Soult and failed to support him from Galicia. Victor was

stubborn or incapable. Of the three Marshals, Soult was the only one of extended capacity.

Again and again during the Peninsular War we find the same forces actively at work, nullifying the Emperor's combinations, however carefully thought out, however scientifically planned. It will in due course be seen that the failure of the operations just considered gave to the British a point of vantage from which they were never driven, and thus led directly to Napoleon's loss of Spain and ultimate downfall.

CHAPTER VIII

Sir J. Cradock takes command in Portugal—Is superseded by Sir A. Wellesley—State of the British forces—Wellesley advances on Oporto—Passage of the Douro—Soult driven from Portugal—Misconduct of British soldiers—Quarrel between Soult and Ney.

ON the recall to England of Sir Hew Dalrymple, the command of the British troops in the Peninsula had, as we have seen, devolved upon Sir Harry Burrard, who, on the appointment of Sir John Moore to lead the army destined to act in Spain, gave that officer every possible assistance in organising his commissariat and transport. But during the month of November Burrard was also recalled to England to appear before the court ordered to inquire into the circumstances of the Convention of Cintra; for the fact that no officer of the necessary standing remained to fill his very responsible and important position weighed little with the Government, whose first object in life, as has been the case on many subsequent occasions, was to pander to the clamour of the mob, and without hesitation to sacrifice thereto public servants on active service, however competent and honourable.

Major-General Mackenzie then assumed command of the force left in Portugal, and held it until the arrival, early in December, of Lieutenant-General Sir John Cradock, K.B., an officer who had gained some distinction as one of Abercrombie's Brigadiers in Egypt.

144 WELLINGTON'S OPERATIONS

Cradock's position was one of considerable difficulty. The Portuguese regency established by Dalrymple failed to show any capacity for government. Military preparations were neglected. Their army was nominally 20,000 strong, but not 10,000 stand of arms existed in the country. Civil anarchy reigned supreme, and the handful of British troops were required rather to keep down the turbulent populace of Oporto and Lisbon than for purposes of warfare with the common enemy. From his own Government the General had had no instructions, for, although he had taken the precaution of putting on paper a series of questions as to his duties and procedure, he had been referred in every case to Mr. Villiers, a political agent—like Frere, a selection of Canning, and, like Frere, a person of the most slender capacity for everything except petty intrigue. Yet to this enterprising young individual Cradock was ordered to defer on every point connected with military as well as civil administration.

The British force at this moment in Portugal consisted of two Squadrons of the 20th Light Dragoons, ten English and four German battalions with 30 guns, of which six only were horsed. The reinforcement of Moore was Cradock's first object, and was carried out regardless of personal considerations. Five battalions were sent to join him. Of the remainder, one garrisoned Almeida, another Elvas. Three British and four German battalions occupied the neighbourhood of Lisbon, which city was thronged with a crowd of soldiers' wives, children, and other non-combatants whose embarkation in case of need would prove a matter of supreme difficulty. Despatches from Moore arriving at the end of the year 1808 exposed the perils of the situation, which were rapidly enhanced by the approach of the 4th French Army Corps along the

IN THE PENINSULA 145

valley of the Tagus. Yet, as if for the very purpose of multiplying the General's cares, it was at this moment—when he had not a single battalion either to spare from the defence of Lisbon or ready to take the field—that the light-hearted Hookham Frere wrote to urge him to undertake a campaign in Andalusia. The approach of Lefébre compelled the recall of two of the battalions which had been sent to reinforce Moore. The British troops were then concentrated round Lisbon. Even the elements were hostile; for seventeen days the wind stopped any vessel leaving the Tagus. But by the end of the year the effect of Moore's advance began to be felt, and the menacing 4th Corps was halted and recalled to Placentia. The pressure was thus relieved, and the arrival of the 14th Light Dragoons on the 22nd of December had made a welcome addition to the mounted troops. Communication with Sir John Moore was, however, completely broken off. Although, exclusive of garrisons, Cradock had not 5,000 men ready for service, Frere was urging him to operate on the Tagus; Villiers, to send troops by sea to Vigo; and Canning from home was inculcating a dispersion of the forces between Portugal and Andalusia. "Minister and Agent alike," says Napier (bk. vi. ch. 2), "followed his own views without reference to any fixed principle; the Generals were the only persons not empowered to arrange military operations." About this time, too, the old project of occupying Cadiz was revived, and with that object 5,000 men—Coldstream and 3rd Guards, 87th and 88th Regiments, and 2 companies R.A.—under Lieutenant-General Sherbrooke, were despatched from England. Before their arrival, however, Cradock, against his own judgment, had sent Mackenzie to Cadiz with 4,000 troops. But the Spaniards refused him permission to enter the town. The affair thus ended in a fiasco.

The versatile Frere then wished Mackenzie to sail for Taragona in Catalonia. Happily he was stopped by a storm, and at the critical moment an order came from Sir John Cradock recalling both him and Sherbrooke to Lisbon. But had it not been for Soult's unexpected repulse at the mouth of the Minho these officers would have returned to the Tagus too late to save Lisbon.

At this period the British Government was only anxious for an excuse to abandon Portugal. In accordance with his instructions Cradock made every preparation to embark, but like a good soldier determined to hold on to the country till the last moment. He was reinforced by the two battalions which had failed to reach Moore, and by a crowd of stragglers from Moore's army, who, together with convalescents from that army who had been left in hospital, were organised in two "Battalions of Detachments." In February a great step was taken by the Portuguese Government, which offered the command of its troops to a British officer, with the rank of Marshal. The selection fell upon Major-General Beresford, who arrived at Lisbon early in March, and set to work at once to organise and discipline his command. He was by degrees supported by a large number of British officers, who were given a step of local rank in the British and a second step in the Portuguese service. Thus Captains in H.M.'s army became Lieutenant-Colonels in the Portuguese. The system proved effective, as has more recently been the case in Egypt, and the Portuguese forces eventually attained a high degree of efficiency. The arrival of Sherbrooke and Mackenzie at Lisbon on the 12th of March raised Cradock's numbers to 14,000 men. His previous weakness and, strange to say, the active hostility of the populace had compelled him to take up a position at the mouth of the Tagus as the best means

IN THE PENINSULA

of securing his embarkation in the last resort. To such an extent had the insults and aggressiveness of the mob reached that Sir John was obliged to place guns in battery on the main streets of Lisbon. The reinforcements enabled him to take up a more advanced position on the Tagus three miles from the capital. Ten or twelve thousand troops of the Portuguese army were at the same time assembled by Beresford in the province of Beira; while Colonel Trant, a British officer, collected an irregular force on the Vouga, twelve miles south of Oporto; and Colonel Wilson with a similar body watched Lapisse on the Agueda. Matters had in this way greatly brightened; but had Napoleon's orders been carried out, and had Soult not been repulsed at the Minho—a repulse entailing a delay of five weeks in the capture of Oporto— the defence of Portugal would have been impossible. Soult's accidental failure—for the chances were twenty to one that the peasantry, in place of defending the passage, would have fled in all directions—forms an additional instance to the many enumerated by Napier of the singular good fortune attending us at this period, which made up for the utter want of forethought and foresight on the part of our Government.

Sir John Cradock, quietly ignoring the wild schemes on the one hand of Hookham Frere, and on the other of the Bishop of Oporto, who was urging him to march to the relief of that city, awaited in his camp the reinforcements now known to be on their way from Cork, and utilised the time by untiring efforts to procure transport for his troops and field equipment for active service. A new crisis intervened. Soult stormed Oporto. Victor, having defeated Cuesta at Medellin, approached Badajoz. The enemy's advance evoked a wild outburst of civil anarchy and military insubordination among the Portuguese. It appeared not improbable that our arms might have to be used in self-defence against our allies. But just then, at the beginning of April, Major-General Hill, with 5,000 men (7th, 30th, 48th, 53rd, 66th, and 83rd Regiments) and 300 Artillery horses, landed at Lisbon; whereupon Sir John Cradock, having established magazines at Peniche, Santarem and Abrantes, advanced to Leiria, rather with a view to helping Beresford to maintain order among his troops than for the purpose of initiating offensive operations against Soult.

His force was organised as follows:—

Commander-in-Chief, Lieutenant-General Sir John Cradock, K.B.
Major-General Sherbrooke, 2nd in command.

Cavalry	800	rank and file.
First Line: 5 Brigades of Infantry	10,418	,, ,,
Second Line: 3 ,, ,,	3,810	,, ,,
Reserve: 1 Brigade	1,858	,, ,,
Total	16,886	

Meanwhile the Ministers in England had been drifting along without any fixed line of policy. At one moment they wanted only an excuse to abandon Portugal; at another, they sent Cradock reinforcements. Then they had recourse to that meanest of all expedients which an opportunist Government so often embraces in times of difficulty. During the critical period from the middle of January to the end of February they left their General without any instructions whatever. At last it occurred to them to consult Sir Arthur Wellesley. That officer in reply furnished a masterly memorandum in the following terms:—

"MEMORANDUM ON THE DEFENCE OF PORTUGAL.
"LONDON, 7th *March*, 1809.

"I have always been of opinion that Portugal might be defended, whatever might be the result of the contest in Spain; and that in the meantime the measures adopted for the defence of Portugal would be highly useful to the Spaniards in their contest with the French.

"My notion was that the Portuguese military establishments, upon the footing of 40,000 Militia and 30,000 regular troops, ought to be revived; and that, in addition to these troops, his Majesty ought to employ an army in Portugal amounting to about 20,000 British troops, including about 4,000 Cavalry. My opinion was, that even if Spain should have been conquered, the French would not have been able to overrun Portugal with a smaller force than 100,000 men; and that as long as the contest should continue in Spain, this force, if it could be put in a state of activity, would be highly useful to the Spaniards, and might eventually have decided the contest.

"It is obvious, however, that the military establishments of Portugal could not be revived without very extensive pecuniary assistance and political support from this country; and the only mode in which it appeared to be safe or even practicable to give this assistance and support, or to interfere at all in a military way in the concerns of Portugal, was to trust the King's Ambassador at Lisbon to give or withhold such sums as he might think necessary for the support of military establishments only, and to instruct him to see that the revenues of Portugal, whatever they might be, were in the first instance applied to the same objects. By the operation of these powers and instructions, it is probable that he would have a complete control over the measures of the Portuguese Government; and we might have expected by this time to have in the field an efficient Portuguese army.

"As it was not possible, however, to adopt these measures at that time, and as the attention of the

Government has necessarily been drawn to other objects, it is probable that the military establishments of Portugal have made but little progress; and in considering the extent of the British force required for the defence of that country, and the other measures to be adopted, the small extent of the Portuguese force, and the probability of an early attack by the enemy, must be considered on the one hand; and on the other, the continuance of the contest in Spain, and the probability that a very large French force will not be disposable in a very short period of time for the attack upon Portugal.

"I would still recommend the adoption of the political measures above suggested, with a view to the revival of the military establishments in Portugal. It is probable that the expense of these measures will not in this year exceed a million sterling. But if they should succeed, and the contest should continue in Spain and in Portugal, the benefit which will accrue from them will be more than adequate to the expense incurred.

"The British force employed in Portugal should in this view of the question not be less than 30,000 men, of which number 4,000 or 5,000 should be Cavalry, and there should be a large body of Artillery.

"The extent of force in Cavalry and Artillery above required, is because the Portuguese military establishments must necessarily be deficient in these two branches; and British or German Cavalry and Artillery must be employed with the Portuguese Infantry.

"The whole of the Army in Portugal, Portuguese as well as British, should be placed under the command of British officers. The Staff of the Army, the commissariat in particular, must be British, and these departments must be extensive in proportion to the strength of the whole Army which will act in Portugal, to the number of detached posts which it will be necessary to occupy, and

IN THE PENINSULA 151

in a view to the difficulties of providing and distributing supplies in that country. In regard to the detail of these measures, I recommend that the British Army in Portugal should be reinforced as soon as possible with some companies of British Riflemen, with 3,000 British or German Cavalry; that the complement of ordnance with that Army should be made thirty pieces of cannon, of which two Brigades of 9-pounders; that these pieces of ordnance should be completely horsed; that twenty pieces of brass (12-pounders) ordnance upon travelling carriages should be sent to Portugal, with a view to the occupation of certain positions in the country; that a Corps of Engineers for an army of 60,000 men should be sent there, and a Corps of Artillery for 60 pieces of cannon.

"I understand that the British Army now in Portugal consists of 20,000 men, including Cavalry. It should be made up 20,000 Infantry at least, as soon as possible, by additions of Riflemen and other good Infantry, which by this time may have been refitted after the campaign in Spain.

"The reinforcements may follow as the troops shall recover from their fatigues.

"The first measures to be adopted are to complete the Army in Portugal with its Cavalry and Artillery, and to horse the ordnance as it ought to be. As soon as this shall be done the General and Staff Officers should go out; as it may be depended upon that as soon as the newspapers shall have announced the departure of officers for Portugal, the French armies in Spain will receive orders to make their movements towards Portugal, so as to anticipate our measures for its defence. We ought, therefore, to have everything on the spot, or nearly so, before any alarm is created at home respecting our intentions.

"Besides the articles above enumerated, 30,000 stands

of arms, clothing, and shoes, for the Portuguese Army, should be sent to Lisbon as soon as possible.

"ARTHUR WELLESLEY."

The result of this Memorandum—which no doubt carried the more weight that it was written by a member of the Government—was to inspire Lord Castlereagh and his colleagues with new courage. Hill was forthwith despatched from Cork with 5,000 men; and arguing, logically enough, that the person who stated opinions was the proper one to carry them into effect, the Ministers decided to supersede Sir John Cradock and to appoint Sir Arthur Wellesley in his place. Wellesley, in the spirit of a gentleman, urged consideration for Cradock's feelings; and eventually it was decided that Sir Arthur should go out to Lisbon: that if he found Sir John engaged in active operations he should serve under him, but that if, on the contrary, no special course had been adopted, he should assume command.

Sir Arthur Wellesley arrived at Lisbon on the 22nd of April, 1809, and finding that Cradock was not actively engaged, but was remaining on the defensive at Leiria in expectation of Soult's advance from Oporto or Victor's from Merida, he considered that the circumstances justified him in taking command. Sir John then went to Gibraltar. He was not a Moore or a Wellington, but he had done well in a time and under circumstances of exceptional difficulty; had equipped the army for active service; his measures had all been approved by his Government, and his supersession, although amply justified in the public interest by the result, was hard on him personally.

The problem to be solved by the new Commander was that which had already confronted his predecessor: viz., the comparative importance of operating against Soult or

IN THE PENINSULA

Victor. As already mentioned, the two Corps were no longer connected by Lapisse; and the position of the British army, on interior lines—strengthened by the possession of Abrantes on the Tagus and the frontier fortresses of Elvas and Badajoz, Ciudad Rodrigo, and Almeida—enabled Wellesley to move at will against either Marshal. Taking Lisbon as the pivot of operations, the strategic position appeared to point to a dash at Victor. Including Lapisse's Division, Victor had about 33,000 men under arms. The road to him was the easier; his defeat would have the greater effect, and the aid of Cuesta could be ensured. On the other hand, combined operations with the Spanish General would require time and trouble to concert—how much of both Wellesley subsequently learned by bitter experience. Victor was eighteen marches distant from Lisbon, whereas Soult was only eight from Leira, and in possession, not only of rich cattle-breeding provinces, but of the second city in the kingdom, the recovery of which good policy appeared to demand. These considerations determined the British Commander to march on Oporto, leaving Major-General Mackenzie with 9,000 Portuguese and 6,000 British troops to hold the right bank of the Tagus between Abrantes and Santarem—with an advanced post at Alcantara—and act as a retarding force should Victor advance; thus gaining time for the return of Wellesley from the north to his assistance.

Two regiments of Heavy Dragoons and the 24th Regiment landed in Portugal a day or two after Wellesley, whose army was, at the beginning of May, distributed as follows. (N.B.—The initials K.G.L. refer to the King's German Legion, composed of Hanoverians who had enlisted in the British Army, on the occupation of their country by the French in 1803.) :—

Name of Corps.	Quarters.	State.			
		Fit for Duty.	Sick.	On Command.	Total.
3rd Dragoon Guards	Belem	645	10		655
4th Dragoons	,,	659	13		672
14th Light Dragoons	Coimbra	578	22	71	671
16th ,, ,,	Santarem	639	12	20	671
20th ,, ,,	Coimbra	215	1	66	282
3rd ,, ,, K.G.L.	,,	73		50	123
Artillery, British	Leiria	477	77	353	907
,, German	,,	310	44	126	480
Royal Engineers	,,	25	1		26
Royal Waggon Train	Lisbon	91	49	90	230
1st Batt. Coldstream Guards	Coimbra	1097	90	2	1189
1st. Batt. 3rd Guards	,,	1135	74	3	1212
,, ,, 3rd Regt.	Pombal	682	10	113	805
2nd ,, 7th Fusiliers	,,	535	38		573
,, ,, 9th Regt.	Leiria	406	153	5	564
1st ,, ,, ,, (detachment)	,,	113	51		164
2nd Batt. 24th Regt.	Lisbon	700	26	3	729
3rd ,, 27th ,,	Ourem	658	134	2	794
1st ,, 29th ,,	Condeixa	552	72	6	630
2nd ,, 30th ,,	Lisbon	496	38	99	633
,, ,, 31st ,,	Ourem	680	97	4	781
,, ,, 40th ,, (detachment)	,,	27			27
1st Batt. 45th ,,	,,	615	125	27	767
2nd Batt. 48th ,,	Coimbra	661	54		715
,, ,, 53rd ,,	Condeixa	645	46	3	694
5th ,, 60th Rifles	Coimbra	559	56	4	619
2nd ,, 66th Regt.	,,	619	34	9	662
,, ,, 83rd ,,	Leiria	801	48	7	856
,, ,, 87th ,,	Coimbra	612	88	1	701
1st ,, 88th ,,	,,	550	143	28	721
,, ,, 97th ,,	Pombal	523	63	17	603
1st ,, Detachments	Coimbra	740	137	44	921
2nd ,, ,,	Pombal	741	200	14	955
1st & 2nd Lt. Batts. K.G.L.	,,	103	37	4	144
1st Line Batt. K.G.L.	,,	609	83	11	703
2nd ,, ,, ,,	,,	744	51	8	803
5th ,, ,, ,,	,,	658	106	11	775
7th ,, ,, ,,	,,	653	60	9	722
Independent Garrison Company	Santarem	26	15	7	48
Total of Rank and File	...	20,652	2,358	1,217	24,272

IN THE PENINSULA 155

PORTUGUESE ARMY.

Major General. }
Local Rank, Lieutenant-General. } William Beresford, commanding.
Portuguese Rank, Marshal. }
   Colonel D'Urban, Quartermaster-General.
3 Squadrons of Cavalry, at Condeixa for Coimbra. 460 men.
4 Batteries Portuguese Artillery. Coimbra. (17 guns : 3 howitzers.)

Infantry.

4th Caçadores	Coimbra.	580 Rank and File.
Grenadier Battalion	,,	580 ,,
10th Regiment	,,	1,383 ,,
16th ,,	,,	1,048 ,,
2nd ,, On march from Espinhal to Lamego		1,039 ,,
14th ,, ,, ,, ,,		1,189 ,,

Total : 460 Cavalry, 5,919 Infantry, and 20 guns.

Under General Bacellar.

3rd Caçadores	Viseu.	573 Rank and File.
6th ,,	,,	541 ,,
9th Regiment	,,	566 ,,
11th ,,	,,	1,412 ,,
2 Squadrons of Cavalry	,,	290 ,,
10 guns.		

Advanced posts at Pedro de Sal.
Total : 290 Cavalry, 3,092 Infantry, and 10 guns.

Under Colonel Trant on the Vouga.

2 Squadrons (150 rank and file), 1,500 Militia, and 10 guns.
Grand total : 900 Cavalry, 10,411 Infantry, and 40 guns.

In addition to the force above named which was about to take part in the advance upon Oporto about 9,000 Portuguese—regular troops and Militia—were with Mackenzie on the Tagus.

Colonel R. Wilson, with about 2,000 of the "Lusitanian Legion"—an irregular body in all senses of the word—was at Almeida.

The Portuguese General Silveira was on the Upper Douro with 8,000 Militiamen who had been driven from Amarante by Loison.

156 WELLINGTON'S OPERATIONS

Perhaps 10,000 of the Militia and "Ordenanzas" Local Militia) were in garrison in Elvas and other places. For the approaching campaign the Staff and organisation of Wellesley's army was as follows:—

COMMANDER-IN-CHIEF.

Lieut.-General the Hon. Sir Arthur Wellesley, K.B.
(Marshal-General of the Portuguese Army).

Military Secretary — Lieut.-Col. Bathurst, 60th Rifles.

Aides-de-Camp
- Captain the Hon. F. Stanhope, 1st Guards.
- „ Lord Fitzroy Somerset, 43rd Regt.
- „ Henry Bouverie, Coldstream Guards.
- „ G. Canning, 3rd Guards.

Adjutant-General — Brigdr.-General the Hon. Charles Stewart.

Assistant Adjutant-Generals
- Lieut.-Col. Darrock, 36th Regt.
- „ Lord Aylmer, Coldstream Guards.
- „ Hinuber, 68th Regt.
- „ J. Elley, Royal Horse Guards.
- Major F. S. Tidy, 14th Regt.
- „ Williamson, 30th Regt.
- „ Berkeley, 35th Regt.
- „ Campbell, 70th Regt.

Deputy-Assistant Adjutant-Generals
- Captain W. Cotton, 3rd Guards.
- „ J. Elliot, 48th Regt.
- „ C. Dashwood, 3rd Guards.
- „ F. Cockburn, 60th Rifles.
- „ V. Graham, 26th Regt.
- „ H. Mellish, 87th Regt.
- Lieut. G. During, K.G.L.

Quartermaster-Gen. — Colonel George Murray.

Assistant Quartermaster-Generals
- Lieut.-Col. W. Delancey, Staff Corps.
- „ J. Bathurst, 60th Rifles.
- „ R. Bourke, Staff Corps.
- Major G. de Blaquière.
- „ A. Northey.

Deputy-Assistant Quartermaster-Generals
{
Captain Sutton, 97th Regt.
" A. Langton, 61st Regt.
" D. Kelly, 27th Regt.
" J. Haverfield, 48th Regt.
" G. Scovell, 57th Regt.
" R. Waller, 103rd Regt.
" W. Beresford, 8th Garrison Batt.
}

Lieut.-Generals on the Staff, Sherbrooke, Payne, Hon. E. Paget.
Commanding Royal Artillery, Brigdr.-General Howarth.
" " Engineers, Lieut.-Colonel Wood.
Colonel on the Staff   Colonel Donkin.
Commanding Portuguese   Major-General (Local Lieut.-
Forces   General; Portuguese rank, Marshal) Beresford.

MEDICAL DEPARTMENT.

Inspector of Hospitals   -   A. Thompson.
Deputy-Inspector of Hospitals   —. Bolton.
3 Physicians.
8 Staff Surgeons.
2 Apothecaries, 1 Acting ditto, 1 Deputy Purveyor,
24 Hospital Mates.

COMMISSARIAT DEPARTMENT.

Commissary-General   J. Murray.
Deputy Commissary-General   C. Dalrymple.
3 Acting Deputy Commissary-Generals, 10 Assistant Commissaries,
20 Acting Assistant Commissaries.

ORGANISATION OF COMBATANT FORCES.

Cavalry.

Lieut.-General Payne, Commanding.

1st Brigade.

Brigadr.-General the Hon. H. Fane.

3rd Dragoon Guards } 1,314 Sabres.
4th Dragoons

2nd Brigade.

Major-General Cotton.

14th Light Dragoons }
16th " " } 1,432 Sabres.
20th " "

Royal and German Artillery (30 Guns).
Brigdr.-General Howarth, Commanding.

Infantry Brigades.

Brigade of Guards (2,292 Rank and File).
Brigdr.-General H. F. Campbell.
Coldstream; 3rd Guards; 1 Company 60th Rifles.

1st Brigade (2,022 Rank and File).
Major-General Hill.
3rd; 48th; 66th; 1 Company 60th Rifles.

2nd Brigade (2,653 Rank and File).
Major-General MacKenzie.
24th; 27th; 31st; 45th.

3rd Brigade (1,771 Rank and File).
Major-General Tilson.
60th (5 Companies); 87th; 88th; 1st Portuguese Grenadiers.

4th Brigade (1,674 Rank and File).
Brigadr.-General Sontag.
97th; 2nd Battalion Detachments; 1 Company 60th;
2nd Battalion 16th Portuguese Regiment.

5th Brigade (1,590 Rank and File).
Brigadr.-General A. Campbell.
7th; 53rd; 1 Company 60th; 1st Battalion 10th Portuguese
Regiment.

6th Brigade (1,702 Rank and File).
Brigadr.-General R. Stewart.
29th; 1st Battalion Detachments; 1st Battalion 16th
Portuguese Regiment.

7th Brigade (1,617 Rank and File).
Brigdr.-General Cameron.
9th; 83rd; 1 Company 60th; 2nd Battalion 10th
Portuguese Regiment.

King's German Legion.
Major-General J. Murray, Commanding.

IN THE PENINSULA

1st *Brigade* (1,262 Rank and File).
Brigdr.-General Langwerth.
1st and 7th Battalions K.G.L.

2nd *Brigade* (1,402 Rank and File).
Brigdr.-General Drieberg.
2nd and 5th Battalions K.G.L.

The numbers of the rank and file are based on the returns of the men actually at headquarters and fit for duty on May 1st. The Companies of the 60th are taken at 60 Riflemen, and the Portuguese Battalions at 350 rank and file, which was about their effective strength at the time.

The Infantry Brigades stood in line of battle from right to left as follows :—Guards, 1st, 3rd, 5th, 7th, 6th, 4th, 2nd Brigades, K.G.L. 1st and 2nd Brigades.

The 30th Regiment was left in garrison at Lisbon, as were also the detachments of the 3rd K.G.L. Hussars, 1st Battalion 9th, and 1st and 2nd Battalions Light Infantry K.G.L.

The 23rd Light Dragoons and 1st Hussars K.G.L. had not yet disembarked. Two Batteries R.A., other than those specified were not yet horsed. The 40th Regiment was at Seville.

The 20th Light Dragoons, the 2nd Battalion 9th, the 5th Battalion 60th, the 97th and the 45th were the only regiments of Wellesley's present army that had fought under him at Vimeiro.

The combined Anglo-Portuguese force nominally available for service comprised about 66,000 men and officers, with 70 guns; but the Portuguese troops were badly officered and equipped, and at this period in general unreliable. The regiments brigaded with the British troops did not much exceed 300 men actually present on parade.

There was every reason to hope for a successful advance against Soult. The wave of the French invasion appeared to have spent itself; and the personal renown of the British Commander was so bright that the blaze of national insurrection immediately burst forth from the Tagus to the Tamega. The conspiracy against Soult, already alluded to, had also reached such a height that French officers were in the British lines with information as to the Marshal's position, numbers, and lines of retreat, and suggestions for seizing him. From these traitors Sir Arthur seems to have gleaned some useful intelligence; but he took very good care to give none in return, and flatly refused to allow his operations to be influenced in the slightest degree by their schemes. A few days later, but not until the British Army was on the Douro, the plot was discovered. Its ramifications had extended far and wide among Soult's officers, and he believed indeed that the whole of the Divisional Generals who had come to him from Junot's Corps were involved in it.

Preparatory to the advance the following General Orders were published:—

"COIMBRA, 3rd *May*, 1809.

"2. Upon all occasions, when the Army will march, it will be in one or more columns, on one or different roads, with a view to take up a position, or by separate battalions, brigades, or larger divisions, with a view to occupy certain cantonments. In the first case the reserve artillery and stores, drawn or carried by horses or mules, are to follow the troops; then the baggage of regiments, and individuals of each column, is to follow, arranged in the order in which the corps or individual will stand in the columns; and lastly, the artillery and commissariat stores on carts, drawn by bullocks.

"3. In the other cases, when battalions or larger divisions are to take up cantonments, the baggage of each division going to a separate cantonment, is to follow that division, and is to be arranged in the order in which each corps or individual will stand in the order of march of the division to which he may belong.

"4. On all occasions the leaders of columns, whether composed of the whole army or of smaller divisions, will halt once in every hour and a half for five minutes, to allow the men to fall out; and commanding officers of companies will be held responsible if any man falls out of the ranks at any time during the march, excepting during these halts, or is absent from his company at the end of it, upon any occasion excepting sickness and consequently inability to keep up. . . .

"6. When circumstances will oblige battalions in rear of any column to halt, the head of such column must not be halted without the special orders of the officer commanding the column, who will judge of the necessity of halting, according to the length of the interval which will thereby be occasioned in his column, the necessity there is that the column should be well closed up, and the probability that from the nature of the impediments of the road, the head of the column will soon be halted, and give time to the rear to close up. . . .

"18. General Orders will be issued at the Adjutant-General's office at 10 o'clock precisely every morning. The officers in the department and Majors of Brigade to be responsible that the Adjutants have them by 12."

"COIMBRA, 4th May, 1809.

"3. The light infantry companies belonging to, and the riflemen attached to each brigade of infantry, are to be formed together, on the left of the brigade, under command of a field officer or captain of light infantry of the brigade, to be fixed upon by the officer who commands it. Upon all occasions in which the brigade may be formed in line, or in column, when the brigade will be formed for the purpose of opposing an enemy, the light infantry companies and riflemen will be, of course, in the front, flanks, or rear, according to the circumstances of the ground, and the nature of the operation to be performed. On all other occasions the light infantry companies are to be considered as attached to their battalions, with which they are to be quartered or encamped, and solely under the command of the commanding officer of the battalion to which they belong."

"COIMBRA, 5th May, 1809.

"2. Whenever an order is given for the troops to march on the following day, the Commissaries attached to those troops are to issue to them one day's meat, which is to be cooked on that night for the following day so that the troops, on their arrival at their new ground, having carried their provisions for the day, will be sure to have them."

"COIMBRA, 6th May, 1809.

"9. The Portuguese troops attached to the British brigades are to be victualled by the Assistant-Commissary of brigades to which they are attached, and are to receive each man 1½ lb. of bread, or 1 lb. of biscuit, and ½ lb. of meat per diem. Cavalry the same as the British cavalry. . . .

"11. The Commander of the Forces recommends the companies of the 5th Battalion of the 60th Regiment to the particular care and attention of the general officers commanding the brigades of infantry to which they are attached. They will find them to be most useful, active, and brave troops in the field, and that they will add essentially to the strength of their brigades."

Mackenzie was directed to remain on the Tagus with Fane's Cavalry Brigade, the 2nd Infantry Brigade, a

IN THE PENINSULA 163

battery Royal Artillery, and the following Portuguese troops:—Five squadrons of Cavalry, the 4th and 13th Regiments of Infantry, a battalion of each of the 1st, 3rd, and 15th Regiments, three battalions of Caçadores or Light Infantry, 800 Yagers, three regiments of Militia and 20 guns, forming a Division under General Hamilton. Mackenzie's instructions were to retard the enemy in the event of Victor invading Portugal, and to fall back as gradually as possible upon Lisbon.

The 40th Regiment was ordered up from Seville, where it had been uselessly detained by Hookham Frere; and the co-operation of Cuesta, at the present time on the Guadiana with 36,000 men, was to be expected.

Having given orders for the formation of a depôt at Coimbra, with supplies for 30,000 men and 5,000 horses for six days, Sir Arthur on the 7th of May began his advance thence upon Oporto. Meat and forage for three days, bread for six, accompanied the column. Cotton's Cavalry Brigade led the way; the remainder of the advance guard consisting of a Division under General Paget, made up of the 6th Brigade, the two Brigades K.G.L., and two batteries of Artillery. Sherbrooke's Division, comprising the Guards, the 4th and 5th Brigades, with a battery Royal Artillery, followed. The 1st and 7th Brigades and a battery under General Hill moved on Aveiro.

The Cavalry Brigade and the three Divisions made up a total of about 18,000 of all ranks, with 24 guns.

Beresford, with about 6,000 Portuguese and 30 guns, and the 3rd British Brigade moved simultaneously on Lamego, which Wellesley hoped he would reach on the 10th or 11th. The news of the loss of the bridge over the Tamega at Amarante precluded any great hope of cutting off the French retreat, and as the Portuguese regiments were but half trained and unreliable, Beresford was directed not even to take possession of Villa Real unless he could be certain of holding it with the force under his command for at least three or four days.

Franceschi, supported by Mermet's Division at Grijon, was himself at Albergaria Nova, eight miles behind the Vouga, with a Brigade of Cavalry, a regiment of Infantry, and six guns. His outpost duty was inefficiently performed, and he had no idea of Wellesley's approach. On the morning of the 10th of May Hill, at Ovar, had turned his right flank, and but for an accident Franceschi's retreat would have been intercepted. He then retired upon Mermet, and on the following evening, after a rearguard action, the two generals fell back on Oporto, fifteen miles distant, crossed the Douro, and destroyed the bridge of boats; while Beresford simultaneously drove Loison from the Upper Douro to the Tamega.

On hearing of the British advance Soult resolved to carry out the retreat on Bragança which he had already been contemplating. Amarante was the key to his position, and Loison was consequently directed to hold on to the bridge at any cost. Mermet was directed on Vallongo. The bridge of boats over the Douro was broken, and all barges and other vessels conveyed across to the right bank. Franceschi's report had led Soult to believe that Hill's Division had embarked on board ship, would enter the mouth of the river, and might attempt a landing. With this in his mind the French commander took up a position on high ground below Oporto, overlooking the Douro. A frontal attack from the further side of a river, deep, rapid, and 300 yards broad, appeared out of the question.

Before daybreak on the 12th the British troops were in motion, and Wellesley shortly after sunrise reconnoitred the line of the river. The problem to be solved was more than formidable. Beneath him, at the bottom of some 500 feet of precipitous rock, rolled the Douro.

Ten thousand men were on the further bank to oppose his passage, and even though, in the face of them, the passage should be forced, the enemy's retreat, for all he knew, was secure, and in retreating the French might very well overwhelm Beresford.*
A high, rocky mound called the Serra, surmounted by a convent, jutted out into the river opposite Oporto, hiding from Soult the view of the country beyond it. In rear of this mound Wellesley had by 8 a.m. concentrated unobserved the Divisions of Hill and Paget, excepting the K.G.L., which, together with two squadrons of the 14th and two guns, had been despatched under Murray to Avintas, three or four miles higher up the stream. Here Murray found boats, and proceeded to cross the river, sending word of the fact to Wellesley. The latter had been compelled to halt for want of means of passage. By 10 a.m. he had received Murray's message, and at the same time Lieutenant-Colonel Waters, a Staff officer, who had crossed the river in a rowing boat, succeeded in towing three barges over from the further bank unobserved. An officer and twenty-five men of the Buffs at once embarked and occupied the Seminary, the remains of a large, isolated, and empty building on the right bank opposite the Serra, situated in a field surrounded on each side by a high wall. This edifice could hold two battalions. Its flanking walls were commanded by eighteen guns in battery on the Serra rock, which thus protected its approaches on the east and west sides. Two other barges followed unperceived, then a beating of drums showed that the alarm had been given.

* The writer has recently seen a private letter written at the time by Captain Burgh, an A.D.C. of Sir Arthur, who states that every one believed Oporto had been evacuated by the enemy, and that a party of forty men was sent across the river merely to receive the surrender of the sick and wounded left behind. Burgh was probably wrong, but nevertheless the letter is curious.

Further concealment was useless; the British troops crowded to the bank. The crash of musketry gave evidence of a keen struggle at the Seminary. Paget, who had crossed early, fell shot through the arm. Hill, whose own Brigade was leading, took command, and upheld the fight, but reinforcements could only be sent across to him in driblets. It took long to pass the main body even of his Brigade over. The enemy's attack increased in fury, and the contest became doubtful.

But at the critical moment the citizens of Oporto, who had been watching the struggle with intense excitement, grasped the situation. Unmooring the boats which lay under the right bank, they brought them, at considerable risk to themselves, across to the British side a little further down-stream. This enabled Sherbrooke to send part of his Division over from Villa Nova. The French now evacuated the lower part of the town, and at the same time Murray was seen advancing along the right bank from Avintas. The enemy thereupon abandoned the contest, and retired in confusion by the Amarante road, leaving behind him five guns and 700 sick men in the town of Oporto. Sherbrooke pressed him in rear. Hill fired into his flank as he passed the Seminary walls. The guns from the Serra spread destruction in his ranks; and had Murray attacked him in front, or even obstructed his march, it is difficult to see how the French Army could have escaped destruction. But Murray, that remarkably spiritless and inefficient officer, remained motionless, and though his two squadrons under Major Felton Harvey charged the rearguard, they could make but little impression unsupported, for the French Infantry lay down on their faces and received no injury as the troopers rode over them, then rising; the Infantry received the squadrons on their return with a heavy fire, and brought many of the 14th to the ground. Soult

IN THE PENINSULA 167

consequently extricated his troops, and Wolloeloy found himself obliged to halt for the rest of that and the following day, partly to bring his guns and baggage across the Douro, partly because the men and horses, having "marched in four days over eighty miles of most difficult country " . . . and having " engaged and defeated three different bodies of the enemy's troops," required rest; and partly because no account had been received of Beresford. On the 13th Murray, indeed, was ordered to follow the enemy in pursuit, but from his previous conduct it was unlikely that he would perform the duty with much zeal or effect.

The passage of the Douro had been effected with the trifling loss of 20 killed and 95 wounded. The French casualties are stated by Napier as 500. Fifty-eight guns were taken or found in Oporto.

Meanwhile Soult, who quickly restored order among his troops, on the 13th reached Penafiel on the Souza river. At this place he heard that Loison had, unbeknown to him, been driven in succession from his advanced positions beyond the Tamega, had even abandoned the bridge of Amarante and retired in the direction of Guimaraens. Hemmed in between the Tamega, the Douro, and the mountains which were said to be impassable, the situation of the French Army now seemed desperate and a capitulation inevitable. At the same time, as if to complete the sum of his misfortunes, the Marshal's horse fell and threw him on to some loose stones, injuring him so much that he could hardly bear to be carried even in a litter. At the critical moment fortune again smiled. A Spanish pedler pointed out a track which, ascending the right bank of the rocky Souza torrent, led over the Sierra de Catalina to Guimaraens. In spite of his bodily pain, Soult's plan of action was quickly formed. Abandoning the idea of a retreat into

Leon he resolved to march by Chaves or Montalégre into Galicia. Collecting his baggage and, by way of example, burning his own first, he destroyed the whole as well as his guns and military chest, and used the sumpter mules to carry the sick and the musket ammunition. The Spaniard led the way. Soult followed. The track was of the roughest. The rain fell in torrents. Urged on, however, by the indomitable will of their Commander, the troops scaled the mountains successfully. At Guimaraens, Soult, to his surprise, found Loison's Division and Lorge's Dragoons which had arrived from Braga. Thus by a series of most unexpected events the French Army was reunited; but hardly had one peril been overcome when another presented itself.

The road to Chaves ran *via* Braga; the absence of pursuit, however, induced the inference that Sir Arthur Wellesley was no longer following up the French but had changed his direction and was heading for Braga. It was evident that he would reach it first. A running fight accompanied possibly by disaster was to be avoided. Once more then Soult took to the mountains, having first destroyed the guns and baggage of Lorge and Loison. On the evening of the 14th he reached Carvalho, where for the first time he met Loison in person. He felt no doubt of his lieutenant's treachery, but it was no hour for recrimination, and Soult, dissembling his feelings, applauded the General for having his Division in hand and placed him in command of the advance guard where he could do no harm; for so greatly was Loison detested by the Portuguese that he would be forced to fight to save his own life. Soult himself took command of the rearguard, and having by his speed and energy gained a day's march upon the British, moved on to Salamonda.

Meanwhile Wellesley had on the 13th heard of Soult's deviation from the Amarante road, and though still

without news of Beresford he felt the change in the line
of retreat was probably due to that officer's operations.
On the 14th, Sir Arthur moved northward, uncertain
whether Soult would attempt to regain the main road
running by Valença, Tuy, and the sea-coast into Galicia,
or would try to make good his retreat by Chaves and
Montalégre. Circumstances quickly pointed to the latter
alternative, and a message was sent to Beresford to move
up the valley of the Tamega with a view to heading off
the enemy. On the 15th Wellesley was at Braga ;
Murray at Guimaraens ; Beresford near Chaves ; Silveira
between that town and Salamonda, marching on Ruivaens.
Next day, the 16th, Sir Arthur from Braga, having just
before been joined by Murray, overtook Soult's rearguard
holding a strong position at Salamonda. Attacked in
front and on the left flank, the French, demoralised
by their recent disasters, broke and fled. The consequences to their main body might have been most
disastrous, but the configuration of the ground concealed
the fugitives, whose plight was not at once evident
to their assailants. Hence the rearguard gained a
momentary respite ; rallied with all the discipline and
steadiness of veterans, and once more formed front to
their opponents.

The recovery was barely made in time. Soult, on
quitting Salamonda on the 15th, had heard that the
bridge over the Cavado at Ruivaens on the road to Chaves
had been destroyed. His sole remaining chance of escape
lay therefore in gaining Montalégre, but the prospect of
doing so was faint, for the scouts reported that even on
this road the Portuguese were engaged in breaking the
Ponte Nova bridge. A man of less tenacity of purpose
might have given way to despair. Day was drawing to a
close. The storms of wind and rain were incessant.
The soldiers, ill clad and ill fed, were ready to drop with

fatigue after climbing the rugged mountain tracks; and even should the bridge prove intact the passage of the defile would inevitably cause delay and give time for the arrival of the British. But the Marshal's spirit, triumphing over bodily pain, was still unconquered. Disdaining the proposal of those who suggested a capitulation, Soult sent for Major Dulong, an officer who had already distinguished himself in situations demanding a cool head and unflinching courage, ordered him to take 25 troopers and 100 grenadiers, surprise the guard at Ponte Nova and secure the passage of the bridge. "If you succeed," he added, "say so; but send no other report; your silence will suffice." Dulong at once set out. Favoured by the storm and the increasing darkness, he approached the bridge unobserved. A sentry was cut down without being able to give the alarm. The Ponte Nova was found to be cut, except for a narrow course of masonry a few inches wide. Along this Dulong crept with 12 of his grenadiers; reached the further side; then, falling on the enemy's picquet, surprised it asleep and killed or dispersed the whole. The rest of the grenadiers then ran up to the bridge. Some crossed, others fired their muskets and so imposed upon the Portuguese supports that they imagined the whole French army was upon them, and incontinently fled. The bridge having been won was at once put in temporary repair. At 4 o'clock on the 16th, the main body was able to begin to file across; but slowly, for it consisted of 20,000 men crowded on a narrow roadway. But an unforeseen obstacle now arose. The track beyond the bridge on which the column marched was cut out of the mountain side; on the right hand confined by the scarped wall, on the left by a steep precipice. A short distance from the Ponte Nova it was intersected by a deep gorge (forming the bed of a mountain torrent called the Miserella), and spanned by a bridge constructed on a single arch, named the Saltador, wide enough only to admit of three men abreast. Had this arch been cut the destruction of the French Army was inevitable, for it was just at this moment that Sherbrooke's Division had overtaken the rearguard and driven it from its position at Salamonda. The bridge, however, although entrenched and defended by Portuguese peasants on the further side, was still intact. The gallantry of Dulong was again conspicuous. Without hesitation he led his men to the assault. Once and again the assailants were driven back, and in organising a third attempt Dulong was himself struck down severely wounded. But the soldiers, animated by the voice and example of their leader, lifted him in their arms and with a last desperate effort carried the bridge.

Dulong had saved the Army; but the rearguard, now crossing the Ponte Nova, was decimated by the British Artillery, and, but for the approach of night, would in Wellesley's opinion have been annihilated. On the 17th the French reached Montalégre, no longer pursued except by a Staff Officer with a few troopers who picked up some stragglers. Sir Arthur had halted at Ruivaens, uncertain whether Soult would continue his retreat on Montalégre or once more cross the mountains in the attempt to reach Chaves or Monterey. On the 18th the pursuit was renewed, and the French turned to bay on the further bank of the Salas river. They were not attacked. It was not in Wellesley's power to stop their retreat, and Soult's only remaining danger lay in the chance of being headed off by Beresford. A Portuguese officer had been sent to that General with directions to accelerate his march, but the messenger loitered on the way. The order consequently arrived too late, for although the 14th Light Dragoons were promptly despatched to Ginjo,

General Franceschi repulsed their attack. Soult thus passed the critical point in safety, and on the 19th crossed the Portuguese frontier and reached Allaritz, having successfully overcome a combination of perils and difficulties such as has been the fate of few Commanders to encounter. Napier sums up the case in these words: "Soult entered Orense on the 20th, without guns, ammunition or baggage; his men, bowed down with misery and fatigue, were mostly without shoes, many without accoutrements, some without muskets. He had quitted Orense (to invade Portugal) 76 days before with 22,000 men, and 3,500 had afterwards join him at Tuy; he returned with 19,500, having lost by the sword and sickness, by assassination and capture, 6,000 good soldiers. . . .* He had entered Portugal with 58 pieces of artillery, he returned without a gun; yet his reputation as a stout and able soldier was nowise diminished."

Yet all the skill and courage of the French Marshal would have been employed in vain had Wellesley been absolutely well served by his lieutenants. The failure of Murray to strike a blow on the road to Vallonga has already been noticed; but Beresford had it also within his power to forestall the enemy both at Salamonda and Montalégre. It is, however, easier to criticise after the event than to do the right thing at the instant. Troops —particularly raw levies—also cannot be treated as machines, nor can General Officers be expected to be infallible. "I hope," says Sir Arthur in his despatch to Lord Castlereagh, "that your lordship will believe that no measure which I could take was omitted, to intercept the enemy's retreat. It is obvious, however, that if an army throws away all its cannon, equipment, and baggage, and everything that can strengthen it and enable it to act together as a body, and abandons all those who are

* 1,400 of them within the last eight days.

entitled to its protection but add to its weight and impede its progress, it must be able to march by roads through which it cannot be followed, with any prospect of being overtaken, by an army which has not made the same sacrifices. It is impossible to say too much of the exertions of the troops. The weather has been very bad indeed. Since the 13th the rain has been constant, and the roads in this difficult country almost impracticable. But they have persevered in the pursuit till the last, and have been generally on their march from daylight in the morning until dark."

Thus in disaster ended Soult's campaign so brilliantly begun five months before; and in the course of which one is at a loss whether most to admire the brilliant and chivalrous strategy of Sir John Moore, the lightning counterstroke of Napoleon, the magnificent feat of Wellesley, or the constancy of Soult himself under circumstances of unparalleled difficulty. That the last named was surprised at Oporto must always remain something of a mystery. In later years he ascribed the fact to the treachery of General Quesnel in failing to warn him until too late that the British troops were crossing the river; but it is difficult to believe that he should have found it impossible to find one responsible officer whom he could trust.

The British casualties between the 10th and 19th of May were only about 300 in number; but General Paget was forced to go home in consequence of his wound, and his loss was irreparable.

Such of the French stragglers as were not picked up by the English were terribly tortured by the peasantry, and it is no doubt of them that Wellesley in his despatch speaks when he alludes to the abandonment of those entitled to the protection of the French Army.

In other respects than that of fighting, the conduct of

the British soldiers had left much to be desired. Writing to the Secretary of State on the 31st of May, Wellesley remarks, "The army behave terribly ill. They are a rabble who cannot bear success any more than Sir John Moore's army could bear failure. I am endeavouring to tame them; but if I should not succeed I must make an official complaint of them, and send one or two corps home in disgrace. They plunder in all directions."

The process of "taming" was not delayed. The regimental officers were admonished as to the performance of their duty. General Court Martials were assembled and sentences of 1,000 lashes were awarded and inflicted. From their courage under this horrible torture the 48th Regiment gained the complimentary nickname of "The Steelbacks." Punishments of this kind to modern ideas are revolting to the last degree. Flogging was absolutely necessary to the maintenance of discipline; but fifty lashes would surely have answered the purpose equally well. People had, however, very different views in those days. Less than twenty years had elapsed since a person was burned to death in England by judicial sentence. Wellington was not a cruel man, but he was a very determined one, and he knew that a proportion of his men were unfortunately the scourings of the gaols. But the fault really lay in the habitual neglect of duty by many of the officers of those regiments which had not been trained under Sir John Moore. "The Commander of the Forces," ran a General Order dated the 29th of May, "is much concerned to be again obliged to complain of the conduct of the troops; not only have outrages been committed by whole corps, but there is no description of property of which the unfortunate inhabitants of Portugal have not been plundered by the British soldiers whom they have received into their houses or by stragglers from the different regiments of the army. . . .

IN THE PENINSULA 175

On halting days an officer of each company must visit the quarters of his men four times each day, of which one must be at 8 o'clock in the evening. On marching days an officer of each company must visit the quarters twice after the men have got into them, of which once must be at 8 p.m. An officer must also visit the quarters of the company before the soldiers march in the morning. The object of these visitings is to see that the soldiers conduct themselves regularly in their quarters; to ascertain whether there are any complaints by the landlords, and of whom; and that the men are in their quarters instead of marauding in search of plunder. . . . The Commanding Officer will report daily to the O.C. the Brigade that these visitings have been made. The officers must be quartered in the immediate neighbourhood of their companies.

"The Commander of the Forces calls the attention of the O.C. Brigades and regiments to the orders given out, and repeated, with a view to prevent the soldiers from straggling from their regiments on a march, which have hitherto been ineffectual. He desires that a report of absentees may be made after every march to the O.C. the Brigade; and the O.C. the Brigade will send this report, with a statement from what companies the men are absent, to the Commander of the Forces. . . . The circumstances which have occasioned these orders have given the Commander of the Forces the greatest concern; and he hopes, with the assistance of the officers of the army, to put an end to the disgraceful practices which have prevailed.

"The people of Portugal deserve well of the army; they have in every instance treated the soldiers well; and there never was an army so well supplied or which had so little excuse for plunder, if any excuse can in any case exist. But if the Commander of the Forces should not by these and other measures be enabled to get the better of these practices, he is determined to report to His Majesty, and send into garrison those corps who shall continue them; as he prefers a small but disciplined and well-ordered body of troops to a rabble, however numerous; and he is resolved not to be the instrument of inflicting upon the people of this country the miseries which result from the operations of such a body."

It is satisfactory to be able to say that the Guards formed an honourable exception, and throughout the war set an example of good conduct and discipline.

After evacuating Portugal Soult entered Orense on the 20th of May and occupied himself in quelling the insurrectionary movements in Galicia, and the feeble struggles of the remnant of Romana's army. At Lugo he met Ney, who roundly accused him of treachery to the Emperor. Soult indignantly denied the charge. High words arose. The two Marshals drew their swords and a duel was only stopped by the interference of their Staff. Hearing in the month of June that Wellesley was moving against Victor, Soult felt the further retention of Galicia impossible. He therefore marched to Tancora, whence he proposed, in co-operation with the 5th and 6th Corps, to move on Ciudad Rodrigo and thence on Lisbon.

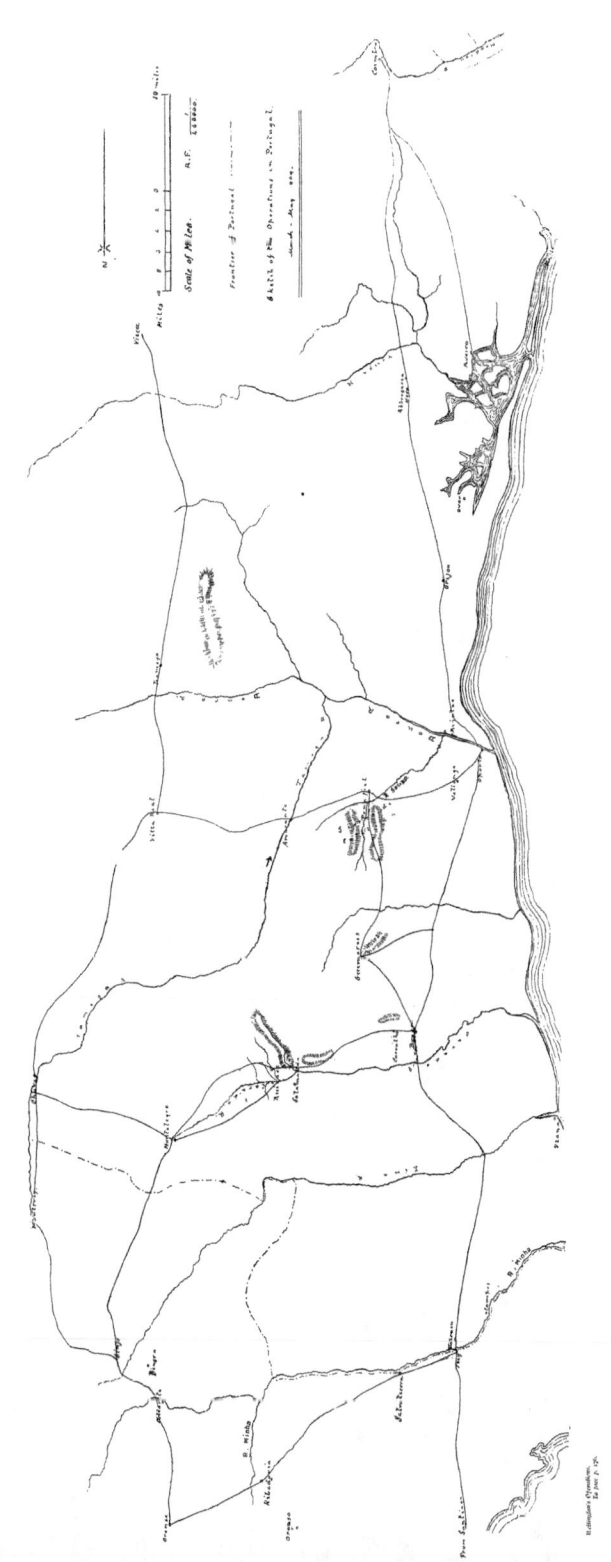

CHAPTER IX

Wellesley marches southward and takes post at Abrantes—Remarks on his troops—Observations of General Foy—Movements of the army—Wellesley advances against Victor—Battle of Talavera—Advance of Soult—Wellesley retires across the Tagus.

HARDLY had Sir Arthur Wellesley completed the expulsion of the French from Portugal, when news arrived that on the 14th of May Marshal Victor had advanced against Alcantara, had forced the bridge, and occupied the town. Sir Arthur at once put his hindmost Divisions in motion southward, and followed them a day or two later with the rest of his troops and three Brigades of Beresford's Portuguese. The alarm, however, proved groundless. Victor was half-hearted, and either the news of Soult's retreat or a very slight counter move on the part of General Mackenzie to Sobreira Formosa was enough to induce the Marshal to abandon Alcantara and retrace his steps. He took up a position at Torremocha between the Tagus and the Guadiana, where he remained inactive, daily losing men from fever. By the 8th of June Wellesley was at Abrantes on the Tagus, eager to assume the offensive, for he underestimated the strength of the French, while he overrated that of his Spanish allies. He hoped, by a sudden and unexpected descent on the Tagus, to effect the capture of the bridge at Almaraz, which would sever Victor's line of communication with Madrid; and he felt assured that, Soult having been expelled from Portugal, the advance of Cuesta's army and his own along the valley of the Tagus would infallibly cause the French to evacuate Galicia. But Cuesta, although useful in combating the presumption of Frere and the corruption of the Spanish Juntas, was an impossible man to co-operate with. His views on military matters were not less absurd than those of his compatriots, and much valuable time was lost before the British Commander could induce him to consent to a rational plan of operations. In the meantime the opportunity of cutting Victor from Madrid had been lost; for that officer, unable to discover the strength and movements of the British Army, and hearing of Soult's retreat, first made a feint of advancing (and thus induced our Engineers to blow up the bridge of Alcantara), and then, retiring across the Tagus at Almaraz on the 19th of June, took post at Plasencia. About the same time Soult appeared to Wellesley to be menacing Portugal once more from Zamorra; and, to guard against the contingency of another invasion, Beresford was sent up early in July to the north.

But the time spent at Abrantes was by no means wasted. The Army was not in a condition to take the field. Although gold had been profusely lavished by the British Government upon the Spaniards and Portuguese, Wellesley had been stinted to the last degree; and, besides the obstinacy of Cuesta, want of ready money for a time absolutely stopped his intended advance. The departmental services also were disorganised. The lack of discipline among our troops formed another subject of serious consideration. Marauding was prevalent; among the worst offenders being the convalescents recently discharged from hospital and on their way to rejoin their regiments. Nearly the whole army was inexperienced,

IN THE PENINSULA

consisting as it chiefly did of 2nd Battalions filled up with recruits drafted from the Militia. It was short of officers, and of those present many were inconceivably remiss. The Commanding Officer of an Irish regiment let his Armourer-Sergeant leave his tools behind because he did not think they would be required on active service! Of the Lieutenant-Generals detailed for the Staff of the Army, Paget had been wounded, Walham and Lord William Bentinck had not arrived, and in fact never did arrive. Payne and Sherbrooke were the only ones present, and Sherbrooke, though an excellent officer, was a hot-tempered man apt to give offence, and consequently somewhat of a thorn in Wellesley's side. The Headquarter Staff also was raw. The Adjutant-General, Sir Charles Stewart, besides being deaf, short-sighted, and deficient in loyalty to his chief, was a great deal more fond of taking every opportunity to gallop about in a Cavalry skirmish than to perfect himself in the duties of his department. From all these causes a great deal more than his proper share of the executive work fell on Sir Arthur's own shoulders. Industrious and methodical to the last degree, he gave his attention to every subject in turn. Minute regulations for the Commissariat and Transport services were drawn up. Mules and carts were purchased, although with difficulty and in insufficient quantities, for the Portuguese Government gave no assistance, and the people were reluctant to part with their property. General correspondence also occupied a large portion of the Commander-in-Chief's time. The subjects were innumerable. In a letter to the Secretary of State on the 30th of June he found himself obliged to repeat—what after sixteen years of warfare might have been known, but is even to the present day not understood by civilians—that the effective strength of a field force is very different to its strength on paper. In the present

180 WELLINGTON'S OPERATIONS

case he had nominally 35,000 men; actually, not more than 18,000 available. Among other petty annoyances came the question of Beresford's rank. That officer was Marshal in the Portuguese, and held the local rank of Lieutenant-General in the British service, thus superseding all the English Major-Generals (some of whom were his seniors in substantive rank), and in fact claiming to supersede all officers below the rank of Field-Marshal, *i.e.*, all but Wellington himself, who was Marshal-General in the Portuguese service. Great ill-feeling was thus caused. General Murray actually insisted on quitting the Army and going home in consequence; and though no great loss, his departure and the reason gave additional annoyance to Wellesley. General Tilson, who had commanded the Brigade acting in conjunction with Beresford during the recent operations, although junior to the latter, did the same; but at the last moment reconsidered his decision. It was hard on the Commander of the Forces to have to bear the burden of other people's errors; but the work of moulding his army into an efficient fighting machine made progress, slow but sure.

The state of affairs in Europe at this period gave great hopes of striking a decisive blow against the power and prestige of Napoleon. England had incited Austria to war with France. The campaign had begun inauspiciously for the French Emperor, and on the 17th of May he had been defeated at Essling by the Archduke Charles. Although the battle had not in any way been decisive, Napoleon had been forced to retire into the island of Lobau on the Danube; and cramped up in that narrow space, his position became critical. The British Government, intent on having a finger in every pie, and unable to concentrate its mind on any one object, disregarded the opportunity afforded in the Peninsula, and sent what was probably the best-staffed and best-equipped army

IN THE PENINSULA 181

that had ever left our shores to destroy the French shipping in the Scheldt and the harbour of Antwerp. The Army was 45,000 strong, and placed under the command of Lord Chatham, the selection being, it is said, the result of an intrigue on the part of one of the Ministry. Chatham was himself a Cabinet Minister, and is said to have been useful in council. But the command of an Army requires practical ability. As a General he proved quite inefficient. In consequence chiefly of his dilatoriness, the project utterly failed. It created no diversion in favour of the Austrians; it called away no portion of Napoleon's army; and was repelled by a handful of National Guards. But our soldiers died in thousands of fever on the Walcheren marshes, and the constitution of the remainder was irretrievably shattered. It would be difficult to find a parallel instance of the gratuitous destruction of an army were it not for the experience of the Crimean War, in which the Ministers of 1854 showed themselves the apt pupils of their predecessors in 1809. The failure at Walcheren was far more disgraceful than that at Buenos Ayres two years previously; but, more fortunate than Whitelock, Chatham was not tried by court-martial, still less cashiered; for by our constitutional custom a Cabinet Minister may commit any public enormity with impunity.

About the same time, a force of 12,000 men under Sir John Stuart in Sicily, which might have given effective aid in Catalonia, and which Wellesley desired should be sent thither, was allowed to embark on a ridiculous expedition against the Italian coast. It escaped loss, but in other respects ended, like that of Chatham, in a complete fiasco.

At length Sir Arthur Wellesley found himself in a position to advance. But in order to understand the general position of affairs a glance must be taken at the situation and numbers of the forces arrayed on either side.

The Spaniards were divided into three bodies, called respectively the Armies of the Left, Centre, and Right. The first of these comprised about 25,000 men, scattered chiefly throughout Galicia and the Asturias; about 6,000 being, however, assembled under the Duque del Parque, near Ciudad Rodrigo. The Army of the Right, which had been defeated on the 18th of June in an attempt on Saragossa, consisted of about 20,000 men, and occupied Catalonia, Murcia, and Valencia. The Army of the Centre, 70,000 strong, under General Cuesta, better organised and equipped than the other two, covered Andalusia: 7,000 Cavalry, 31,000 Infantry and 70 guns being under personal command of Cuesta; and 26,000 of the remainder under General Venegas in the Morena about St. Elena and Carolina.

But the Spanish armies, consisting principally of raw levies, and commanded by most incompetent Generals, were formidable only in point of numbers. There were, however, in addition, local bands of "Guerillas"—the refuse of Spanish society—which infested the whole country, harassed the French, interrupted their posts and convoys, murdered every isolated soldier that they could find—often by crucifixion or other torture—and weakened the strength of the enemy by forcing him to employ large numbers of men on escort duty.

As regards the Portuguese, great hopes were entertained, and Beresford was taking every advantage of the period of inaction to train and discipline them, but the peasantry showed extreme reluctance to enter the Army. About 15,000 were now organised, and at a later date attained a high degree of efficiency, but for the present were unreliable except when acting in conjunction with British troops.

IN THE PENINSULA

Of the French Army, the 7th Corps was engaged in repressing insurrection in Catalonia. Aragon was held by the 3rd Corps, at present commanded by Suchet. Sebastiani, with the 4th, opposed the march of Venegas on Madrid, and was in close communication with Victor. On the 30th of June, the 2nd, 5th, and 6th Corps were by Napoleon's orders formed into one army under Soult, 54,000 strong (5,300 being Cavalry), with 107 guns. Foreseeing at a distance of 1,500 miles the advance of Wellesley along the Tagus, and aware that the effect must be to ensure the evacuation of Galicia, the Emperor directed Soult to march upon Salamanca, and thence to fall on the flank and rear of the British Army. Unfortunately for the French, Ney proved insubordinate, and time was lost before his Corps could be brought into line. Mortier, too, with the 5th Corps was summoned by King Joseph to Avila, and by these mischances Napoleon's combination was marred although by no means abandoned.

All obstacles having been overcome by the end of June, Sir Arthur Wellesley was ready to advance from Abrantes. Prior to his march he issued strict orders in regard to it. The troops were always to start at daylight in order that their destination might be reached as early as possible. They were to halt for five minutes every hour and a half. Their rations were to consist of $1\frac{1}{2}$ lbs. of bread and the same amount of meat. Entrenching tools were to be carried in the proportion of 8 spades, 8 shovels, 4 picks, and 4 axes for each regiment of Cavalry; and 5 spades, 5 shovels, and 5 axes for each battalion. Personal cleanliness and inspection of necessaries were inculcated. General orders were to be issued at 10 a.m. each day, or immediately after completion of the day's march.

With the exception of the 60th and 95th Rifles who carried the Baker rifle and sword,* the British Infantry

* The 2nd Light Battalion K.G.L. was also armed with a rifle.

was armed with the "Brown Bess" musket and bayonet. The "Brown Bess," carrying spherical bullets—twelve to the pound—had an accurate range of about 100 yards only, yet proved far more efficient than the French musket of smaller bore which carried bullets weighing seventeen to the pound. In fact, throughout the war the steadiness and accuracy of the British infantry fire was a continued source of admiration and annoyance to the enemy. The infantry soldier was heavily weighted with from 50 to 60 lbs. on his back, and his uniform was ill-adapted to active service, but his powers of endurance and fighting capacity was unequalled, and as he gained experience became as good as a Frenchman in resource and knowledge of war.

The heaviest field gun was the 9-pounder, and the 6 or even 3-pounder was more common. The effective range of artillery fire did not exceed 600 or 800 yards. The devotion of the artilleryman may be judged from the fact that during the whole of Wellington's campaigns not a single gun was permanently lost. A well-informed writer in the *United Service Magazine* for May, 1902, remarks: "During the first campaigns of Sir Arthur Wellesley the Field Artillery was often without horses, and reduced to relying on teams of oxen. Their horses, when they had them, were usually those cast from the Cavalry and were still made to work in a single line of draught. There was no system for the supply of drivers, and the detachments marched or rather straggled behind the guns. By the end of the war all were regularly horsed: with eight horses in pairs, driven by men from the Driver Corps. The gunners were carried on the limbers and axletree seats. The Field Batteries, whose value was at last beginning to be recognised, could thus vie with the smartest of Horse Artillery troops. The armament of both Horse and Field Batteries was by no

IN THE PENINSULA 185

means as simple as it is now. The troops of the former were each armed with five guns (usually two 9-pounders or heavy 6-pounders and three light 6-pounders) and one 5½ inch howitzer firing a 24-pound shell. The armament of the latter (*i.e.*, the Field Battery) was somewhat less elaborate, consisting of five guns of the same nature and one 5½ inch howitzer to each Brigade. The guns used were 12, 9, 6, or 3-pounders. It was only natural that such complicated arrangements should lead to endless confusion in the allotment of ammunition and stores. . . ."
N.B.—It will be noticed that in this work the modern term "battery" is used to designate the "troop" of Horse, and "brigade" of Field Artillery.

The Cavalry soldier was dressed in a jacket so tight that he was unable to use his arms with freedom; and mounted on a horse whose short-docked tail made its life unendurable from the assaults of flies and other insects. With some exceptions, the British Cavalry was much inferior in skill and knowledge of its duties to the other arms. It had been trained for show and not for use. " We do everything so quickly," writes Tomkinson in the " Diary of a Cavalry Officer," that it is impossible men can understand what they are about. They have enough to do to sit their horse and keep in the ranks, without giving their attention to any sudden order. Before the enemy I never saw troops go beyond a trot except in charging. . . . In England I never saw, nor heard, of Cavalry taught to charge, disperse and form, which, if I only taught a regiment one thing, I think it should be that. To attempt to give men or officers any idea in England of outpost duty was considered absurd, and when they came abroad they had all this to learn. . . . On our return to English duty we continue the old system, each regiment estimating its merit by the celerity of movement. I do not think one idea has been suggested since our return from service by the experience we there gained. . . . . But we go on with the old close column and change of position."

There were, no doubt, a few good Cavalry officers, but men of the type of Somers Cocks of the 16th were rare indeed. Whether we have improved much in our Cavalry since the Peninsular War must be left to those best able to judge. With our love of field sports and hard exercise, there ought to be a Lasalle in every regiment of Cavalry. And finer material, mentally or physically, than that of which our troopers are composed it would be impossible to find.

The K.G.L. Hussars were far better trained than the British Cavalry, and studied their profession in earnest.

Barley and barley straw formed the principal forage. Even that was often scarce. The art of the horsemaster was also frequently neglected, and the loss of horses was at times enormous. The roads in the Peninsula were so bad that the forage carts could not keep up. Later on, in 1812, Colonel Scovell, a Staff officer, invented a light anvil and bellows, which could be carried on the back of a mule, and was of the greatest value.

Among the Engineer Officers were several of the highest ability, skill and resource. The secret of suspension bridges seems to have been discovered by them in the Peninsula, where the rivers frequently ran in deep rocky beds. The names of Fletcher, Squire, Sturgeon and Smith deserve more than passing mention; and there were many others hardly, if at all, inferior to them.

The Commissariat Department also produced some able men, who had to contend with innumerable difficulties. Wheeled transport was almost unknown. Baggage was carried on the backs of endless strings of mules, led exclusively by Spanish muleteers. A single Cavalry regiment required about sixty mules.

IN THE PENINSULA

The Chaplain's department did not shine. No sooner did a Chaplain arrive from England, than some paramount reason compelled him to return again. The Rev. S. Briscall, afterwards private chaplain to the Duke of Wellington at Strathfieldsaye, was a bright exception. Roman Catholics were allowed by Sir Arthur to attend the celebration of mass; but the leave was granted at the peril of the General; for, incredible as it may seem, it was contrary to the British law for soldiers to go to mass except in Ireland. They did not, however, avail themselves to any great extent of the permission. "I have not," said Wellesley, "seen any one soldier perform any one act of religious worship . . . . except making the sign of the cross to induce people to give them wine."

In view of the campaign about to be described the following observations on the armies engaged, made by the French General Foy after the end of the war, are of interest, although considered by Napier to be hardly fair to the British soldier.

FRENCH ARMY.

"A regiment usually consisted of three battalions, and possessed but one eagle, which generally accompanied the 1st Battalion. . . . Napoleon subsequently added a picked Company called 'Voltigeurs,' composed of men small in stature but active and intelligent. These Voltigeurs constituted the light infantry of the French armies, and habitually acted as skirmishers. . . . . The skirmishers harassed the enemy, escaped from his masses by their speed, and from his Artillery by their extended order. The regulations for the manœuvres of the Infantry were constantly varied by the most intelligent commanders in their practical application, to suit the requirements of modern warfare. . . . . The 'square,' which the Arabs had taught the French to adopt in

Egypt, became a fundamental formation for Infantry. The successive firing by ranks was found the most suitable to employ against Cavalry, and also from the fact that it interfered less with the use of the bayonet. . . . .

"Officers of Cavalry such as the Neys and Richepanses, were seldom found in the armies of the Republic. But at the head of the Imperial squadrons were seen Murat, Lasalle, Kellermann, Montbrun, and others who excelled in the art of regulating and directing vast 'hurricanes' of Cavalry. That decision so necessary in a commander-in-chief should also be possessed by a Cavalry leader. Above all, it is essential that he should be prodigally endowed with one precious quality which no other can replace—a quality more rare than is generally supposed—unflinching courage. With a *coup d'œil* as quick as lightning, he must combine the vigour of youth, a powerful voice, and the agility and address of a centaur.

"The French Artillery up to the Revolutionary period was considered the first in Europe. In 1792 and 1793 great numbers of cannon were employed in battle. . . . . The Horse Artillery was composed, on its first formation, of the most active artillerymen, and was afterwards recruited with the *élite* of the Grenadiers. It performed wonders, and in the campaigns in Germany, mere captains of that arm acquired the reputation of generals. Very soon the Generals would have no other artillery, since, being more mobile and more efficient, less of it was required, and the columns of the train were proportionately lightened.

"In the rear of Napoleon's Army marched a reserve which was never equalled. The Imperial Guard represented the glory of the Army and the Majesty of the Empire. Its officers and men were chosen from those whom the brave had designated as the bravest; all of them were covered with scars. Bred among dangers they had lived long in a few years; and the name of 'The Old Guard' was appropriately given to a corps whose oldest members had not reached the age of forty."

BRITISH ARMY.

"The English were looked upon by the French as sea-wolves, unskilful, perplexed, and powerless the moment they set foot on land. If their national pride appealed to the victories of Cressy, Poitiers, and Agincourt, they were reminded that the armies of Edward III. and Henry V. were composed of Normans, of the people of Poitou and of Gascons. There were, for all that, a goodly number of native Englishmen, and certainly the blows which they dealt were not the weakest. The Black Prince and Talbot were born in Albion. Nearer our own times, Marlborough and his 12,000 men were not the least formidable of the enemies of Louis XIV. The celebrated column of British Infantry at Fontenoy had suggested to a second Bossuet the image of a tower repairing its own breaches.

"Even when the *éclat* of French glory had thrown into shade both ancient and modern history, repeated instances of vigour and gallantry had been observed in the British troops employed, though under feeble commanders, in Flanders and Holland. The French soldiers returning from Egypt, talked to their comrades of the indomitable valour of the English. . . . . Their skill and intrepidity in braving the perils of the ocean have always been unrivalled. Their restless disposition and love of travelling fit them for the wandering life of a soldier; and they possess that most valuable of all qualities in the field of battle—coolness in action.

"The glory of the British army is based principally upon its excellent discipline and upon the cool and sturdy courage of the people. Indeed, we know of no other troops so well disciplined. The principal cause of their pre-eminence in this respect would, if applied to the French Army, most likely produce an exactly opposite effect. Varieties of character and condition need different means to gain the same end.

"The English non-commissioned officers are excellent, but their courage and ability are not encouraged by promotion to higher grades. They are nominated by the commanding officer of the regiment, and can be broken only by sentence of a court martial. Their authority is extensive, including the minute details of inspection, discipline, and daily instruction—duties which in other armies would not be committed to them.

"In the British Army will not be found either the strong sympathy between leaders and men, the paternal care of the captains, the simple manners of the subalterns, nor the affectionate fellow-feeling in danger and suffering which constituted the strength of the Revolutionary armies of France*; but unshaken patriotism, and tried and steady bravery, are to be met with among them everywhere. . . .

"It was thought that the English soldier had not enough intelligence and smartness to combine with the regular duty of the line the individual action of the skirmisher. When the need of a special light infantry began to be felt, the best marksmen of different corps were at first selected; but it was afterwards found advisable to make the eight battalions of the 60th, the three battalions of the 95th, and some of the foreign corps, exclusively into skirmishers. These troops are armed with the rifle. During the last war companies of these riflemen were always attached to the various

* General Foy was no doubt unaware of the system in Moore's regiments.

IN THE PENINSULA 191

brigades. The echoing sound of their horns answered the double purpose of directing their own movements and of signalling such movements of the enemy as would otherwise have escaped the notice of the general in command.

"The English, Scotch, and Irish are usually mixed together in the regiments. In proportion to its population, Ireland supplies more soldiers than the other two kingdoms. It might be supposed that the general character of the English troops would be affected by this intermingling; but the English discipline is like the bed of Procrustes—the minds as well as bodies of their fellow-subjects obey their law as that of the ruling people. Four Highland regiments—consisting of nine battalions—are, however, recruited almost exclusively from the mountains of Scotland, and their officers are selected in preference from the natives of that country. The Highlanders wear the kilt instead of small clothes; this neither harmonises with their dress nor is convenient for war, but this is of little moment in comparison with the moral advantage gained by wearing the national costume. A distinction which originates in popular feeling and custom generally imposes the performance of additional duty: there are no troops in the British service more steady in battle than the Scottish regiments.

"The infantry is the best part of the British army. It is the 'robur peditum'—the expression applied by the Romans to the 'triarii' of their legions. The English do not scale mountains or scour the plain with the suppleness and rapidity of the French; but they are more silent, more orderly, and more obedient, and consequently their fire is better directed and more destructive. Though not as callous under a heavy fire as the Russians, they close their ranks with less confusion, and preserve their original formation better. Their composition shows something of the German mechanism, combined with more activity and energy. The system of manœuvres which they have adopted since 1798 is borrowed from the Prussians. The infantry, although normally formed three deep, is more often drawn up in two ranks; but when making or receiving a charge is frequently formed four deep. Sometimes it has made offensive movements, and even charged columns, when in open order. In a retreat it stands firm, and begins its fire by volleys followed by continuous independent firing. It turns about coolly to check the enemy hanging on its rear; and while marching, it fires without separating.

"The English infantry does not hesitate to charge with the bayonet; but the commander who wishes to employ it with advantage should move it seldom and with caution, and reckon rather on its fire than on its manœuvring power.

"The pains bestowed by the English on their horses, and the superiority of their native breeds, gave at first a more favourable idea of their cavalry than has been borne out by the experience of the war. The horses are badly trained for fighting. They have narrow shoulders and a hard mouth, and know neither how to turn or halt. Docking their tails is a serious inconvenience in hot climates. The luxurious attentions lavished on them make them quite unfit to support fatigue, scarcity of food, or the exposure of the bivouac. The men are, however, excellent grooms.

"The heaviest English cavalry is far from possessing the uniformity and firm seat of the French and Austrian cuirassiers, and their light horse is still more inferior in intelligence and activity to the Hungarian hussar and the Cossack. They have no idea of the artifices of partisan warfare, and know as little how to charge *en masse*. When the fray begins you see them equally vulnerable and offensive, cutting instead of thrusting, and chopping with more fury than effect at the faces of their opponents.

"During the war in the Peninsula, the French soldiers were so much struck with the smart uniforms of the Light Dragoons, their shining helmets, and the graceful shapes of the men and horses, that they gave them the name of 'Lindors.' In 1813 this dress, which was peculiar to British troops, was exchanged for the head-dress and jacket of the German Light Cavalry. . . .

"In the mounted service it is not enough for the soldiers to be brave and the horses good. There must also be science and unity. More than once in the Peninsular War weak detachments of British Cavalry have charged French battalions through and through, but in disorder. The squadrons could not be reformed; there were no others at hand to finish the work; thus the bold stroke passed away without producing any advantage.

"The Artillery holds the first rank in the army; it is better paid, its recruits are more carefully selected, and its period of enlistment is limited to twelve years. The gunners are distinguished from other soldiers by their excellent spirit. In battle they display judicious activity, a perfect *coup d'œil* and stoical bravery. . . . Very high prices are paid for the horses employed to draw the guns, and they are consequently extremely good. The harness is as good as that used in the French carriages. No nation can rival the English in the equipments and the speed of their conveyances.

"English troops take few pieces into the field with them; the most that Lord Wellington ever had in the Peninsula barely amounted to two per thousand men. Frames, caissons, barrels, bullets, powder, and every part of the equipage are remarkable for the goodness of the materials, as well as excellent workmanship. In battles the artillery made most copious and effective use of a kind of hollow bullet called 'Shrapnell's spherical caseshot,' from the name of the inventor.

"In conclusion, it may be said that the English army surpasses other armies in discipline, and in some particulars of internal management; it proceeds slowly in the career of improvement, but it never retrogrades; and no limits can be affixed to the power of organisation to which a free and intelligent people may attain."

Spanish Army.

"A long peace, the insulated position of the country, and the lethargy of the Government, had almost extinguished the old warlike spirit of Spain. . . . The nobility had forgotten at what price their grandeur and titles had been purchased by their ancestors; arms had scarcely the dignity of a profession. There were no camps for the performance of manœuvres, none of those large garrisons in which regiments learn to know each other and to act together.

". . . Nature has endowed the Spaniard with most of the qualities required to form a good soldier. He . . . is naturally disposed to obey orders, and is capable of great devotion to an able leader. His patience is inexhaustible; he is always sober, and so frugal that he can live upon a pilchard or a bit of bread rubbed with garlic. . . . Next to the French, the Spaniards are the best for long marches and climbing mountains. The Spanish soldier is less intelligent than the French, but more so than the German or English soldier. . . . The Spanish Army was deficient in discipline; its N.C.O.'s were but little respected; one-third of the officers were taken from among them; the remaining two-thirds were filled up from the cadets.

"The Spanish infantry consisted of 39 regiments of 3 battalions each, including 4 foreign regiments. Twelve

IN THE PENINSULA 195

battalions of Light Infantry differed only from the infantry of the line in the colour of the jacket. ... In war time 42 regiments (of only one battalion apiece) formed a body of infantry, more patriotic, more brave ... than the regular infantry. ... The Cavalry of Spain amounted to 12,000 men in 24 regiments, each of 5 squadrons. ... The Spanish Cavalry was badly trained and very inferior to the Infantry.

". . . The Artillery consisted of 4 regiments of 10 companies each; out of these 40 companies 6 were Horse Artillery. Besides these, there were 64 companies of Militia gunners without officers or sergeants. There was no artillery train regularly organised. In time of war it was supplied by contracts with muleteers or by requisitions of oxen.

" In 1803, Godoy organised the Engineer corps on a similar basis to that of the artillery. It was formed on the regulations of the French service, and a School of Engineering was instituted at Alcala de Henares.

". . . The Andalusian horses, though high-mettled and docile, are lacking in the muscular power required for the shock of a heavy cavalry charge, and have not the robustness and capacity of bearing fatigue needful for the light cavalry service. The multiplication of mules has probably been the cause of the degeneracy of the Spanish horses."

During the month of June Wellesley's army—now composed exclusively of British and K.G.L. regiments, for the Portuguese hitherto attached to his Brigades had gone northward with Beresford to be trained and disciplined—had been distributed as follows :—

Fane's Cavalry Brigade	Abrantes and neighbourhood.
Cotton's ,, ,,	Thomar.
1st Regt. Light Dragoons,K.G.L.	Castello Branco.
Brigade of Guards	Punhete.

196 WELLINGTON'S OPERATIONS

Hill's Brigade	Abrantes and neighbourhood.
Stewart's Brigade	,,
A. Campbell's Brigade	,,
Sontag's ,,	,,
Cameron's ,,	Tancos.
Tilson's ,,	Castello Branco.
Langwerth's ,,	Barquina.
2nd K.G.L. ,,	Moita and Atalaya.
Mackenzie's ,,	Cartigos, Corticada and Vilha Velha.
27th, 30th and 40th Regiments	Lisbon.
Independent Garrison Company	,,

By the middle of the month the force was further organised in Divisions; but as Sir John Sherbrooke was the only Infantry Lieut.-General present, command of each other Division than the 1st was assumed temporarily by the senior officer belonging to it.

CAVALRY DIVISION.
Lieut.-General R. Payne.

			Rank and File.	
1st Brigade	Brigd.-Gen. Fane	{ 3rd Dragoon Guards	525	
		{ 4th Dragoons	545	
			—	1,070
2nd ,,	Major-Gen. Cotton	{ 14th Light Dragoons	464	
		{ 16th ,, ,,	525	
			—	989
3rd ,,	Colonel Anson	{ 23rd ,, ,,	459	
		{ 1st Light Dns. K.G.L.	451	
			—	910
	Total of rank and file in Division			2,969
	1 3-pounder Battery R.A.			

1ST INFANTRY DIVISION.
Lieut.-General Sir John Sherbrooke, K.B.

Brigade of Guards }	Brigd.-Gen. H. Campbell {	1st Bt. Coldstream	970
		1st Bt. 3rd Guards	1,019
		1 Coy. 60th Rifles	
			—— 1,989

IN THE PENINSULA

				Rank and File.	
7th Infy. Brigade	,,	Cameron	1st Bt. 40th	745	
			2nd Bt. 83rd	535	
			1st Bt. 61st	778	
					2,058
1st K.G.L. Brigade	,,	Langwerth	1st Line Bt. K.G.L.	604	
			5th ,, ,, ,,	610	
					1,214
2nd K.G.L. Brigade	,,	Lowe	2nd ,, ,, ,,	678	
			7th ,, ,, ,,	557	
			1st and 2nd Lt. Bts.	106	
					1,341

Total of rank and file in 1st Division   6,602

1 6-pounder Battery R.A.   2 6-pounder Batteries K.G.L.

2ND DIVISION.

Major-General Rowland Hill.

1st Brigade	Major-Gen. Tilson	1st Batt. The Buffs	746	
		1st Batt. 48th	807	
		2nd Batt. ,,	567	
		2nd Batt. 66th	526	
		1 Company 60th		
				2,646
6th ,,	Brigd.-Gen. R. Stewart	29th	598	
		1st Bt. Detachments	609	
				1,207

Total of rank and file in 2nd Division   3,853

3RD DIVISION.

Major-General Mackenzie (acting).

2nd Brigade	Major-Gen. Mackenzie	2nd Batt. 24th	787	
		2nd Batt. 31st	733	
		1st Batt. 45th	756	
				2,276
3rd ,,	Colonel Donkin	2nd Batt. 87th	599	
		5th Bt. 60th (5 Coys.)	552	
		1st Batt. 88th	599	
				1,750

1 Battery R.A.—6-pounders.

Total of Division   4,026

4TH DIVISION.

Brigadier-General A. Campbell (acting).

			Rank and File.	
4th Brigade		⎧ 97th	502	
		⎨ 2nd Bt.Detachments	625	
		⎩ 1 Company 60th		—— 1,127
5th "	Brigd.-Gen. A. Campbell	⎧ 2nd Bt. 7th Fusiliers	431	
		⎨ 2nd Bt. 53rd	537	
		⎩ 1 Company 60th		—— 968

1 heavy 6-pounder Battery R.A.

Total of Division   2,095

GRAND TOTAL.

Cavalry	2,969 sabres	⎫
Infantry	16,576 rank and file	⎬ 20,641
Artillery	1,011 and 30 guns	
R.E.	22 Sappers	
Royal Staff Corps	63	⎭

The gross total of all ranks and arms may be estimated at 23,200. About 9,000 additional British troops were assembling at Lisbon, but none were ready to advance before the 28th of June.

On the side of the French the numbers were as follow on the dates named. (*Vide* Napier, vol. i. app. xxx.):

In the valley of the Tagus :—

1ST ARMY CORPS.

Marshal Victor (15th July).

		Present under arms.	Total.
3 Divisions of Infantry	33 battalions	18,890	26,373
2 " Cavalry	18 squadrons	3,781	5,080
Artillery and Equipage		2,586	3,005

Total present under arms, 25,257 and 48 guns.

4TH ARMY CORPS.

General Sebastiani (10th July).

3 Divisions of Infantry	27 battalions	17,100	25,960
2 " Cavalry	25 squadrons	3,670	5,859
Artillery, &c., unknown.			

Total present under arms, 20,770 men and 30 guns.

DIVISION OF RUONNVII.

General Dessolles (15th July).

		Present under Arms.	Total.
1 Division of Infantry	10 battalions	7,681	10,254

Number of guns unknown.

King's Guards, about 5,000 men.

Grand total of troops in the valley of the Tagus, say, 58,000 men and (at least) 78 guns.

Under command of Marshal Soult :—

2ND CORPS.

Soult (15th July).

4 Divisions of Infantry	47 battalions	16,626	35,188
3 ,, Cavalry	19 squadrons	2,883	4,540
Artillery		1,081	1,620

Total present under arms, 20,590 men and 40 guns.

5TH CORPS.

Marshal Mortier (15th July).

2 Divisions of Infantry	24 battalions	15,036	19,541
1 Brigade of Cavalry	6 squadrons	896	1,491
Artillery		648	803

Total present under arms, 16,580 men and 30 guns.

6TH CORPS.

Marshal Ney (15th July).

2 Divisions of Infantry	24 battalions	13,700	17,587
1 ,, Cavalry	10 squadrons	1,446	2,092
Artillery		1,113	1,293

Total present under arms, 16,259 men and 37 guns.

Grand total of Soult's army, 53,529 men and 107 guns.

The strategical situation, so far as it was known to the British Commander, was this. Sebastiani was at Toledo with the 4th Army Corps; Victor, at Talavera de la Reyna with the 1st. The former was believed to have but 12,000 sabres and bayonets; the latter, 28,000. It was thought they might be reinforced by a few thousand men from the King's Guards and the garrison of Madrid. On the side of the allies, Wellesley with 20,000 men was at Abrantes; Cuesta with 38,000 at Almaraz. General Venegas, credited with 18,000 men—he had in reality about 25,000—was threatening Toledo from the side of La Mancha. Sir Arthur believed it would be possible, by combined action, to drive the enemy from Madrid and free all the southern provinces of Spain. But the French were operating on short interior lines; the distance between Talavera and Toledo being not much above 50 miles. The allies were on exterior lines, with divergent bases. Wellesley at Abrantes was 180 miles distant in a straight line from Almaraz, and even after his junction with Cuesta, he would still be considerably more than 100 miles from Venegas at Ciudad Real.

Unfortunately, Wellesley greatly underrated not only the numbers of the French opposed to him, but also their recuperative power, and he began his march under the conviction that Soult was at the head of only a few thousand demoralised men. The capture of the French General Franceschi gave Sir Arthur some information of what was going on in the north of Spain, and warned him that he must take measures against a possible attack on his left flank. The principal passes by which Soult could cross the Bejar mountains were those of Perales and Baños. The former was occupied by the Duque del Parque, but as an additional precaution, Beresford was directed to keep an eye on it, and a newly landed British Brigade, consisting of the 5th and 58th Regiments under General Lightburne, was placed at his disposal. General Cuesta promised to hold the pass of Baños with four battalions. In reality, however, he sent only 600 men provided with but 20 rounds of ammunition.

On the 30th of June Sir Arthur reached Castello Branco

from Abrantes. On the 8th of July he was at Coria. On the 8th his advance guard reached Plasencia, followed on the 10th by the main body. Want of supplies detained him until the 17th. The British Commander had started with very deficient means of transport, but as the Spaniards had undertaken to provide all supplies after crossing the frontier, he had seen small cause for alarm. Before he had been in Spain a week he found what little reliance could be placed on Spanish promises. There were no mules, no supplies. It might be supposed that the least Mr. Frere could have done would be to hold the Spaniards to their engagements at a time when the very subsistence of the British Army was concerned; but the British envoy was too busily engaged in interference with military and political projects to be able to attend to his proper business. Wellesley protested vigorously; and intimated clearly that unless his requirements were supplied he should go no further than the Alberche. At the same time, however, he did not fail to bestir the local authorities, and arranged with them for a supply of rations sufficient to enable him to proceed for another twelve days.

At Plasencia the army was reinforced by the 1st Battalion 61st, and the 2nd Battalion 48th Regiments, who were attached respectively to the 1st and 2nd Divisions.

Cuesta was now at Almaraz. Victor had intended to make a stand at Plasencia, but, at the order of the King, who was alarmed at the advance on Madrid of General Venegas' Corps, he had fallen back along the line of the Tagus, and on the 28th of June had taken up a position behind the Alberche. On the 18th of July the combined armies under Wellesley and Cuesta moved forward to attack him. At the same time Venegas was directed to threaten the capital from the side of Fuentes Duenas, with the view either of drawing out Sebastiani to oppose him, or of entering Madrid in the event of Sebastiani marching to join Victor. On the other side, Sir Robert Wilson, acting on Wellesley's left flank with about 4,000 irregulars, was directed to menace the capital from the west. Thus if the combination were successful, the allied armies, amounting in all to 92,000 men, would make a concentric attack upon the French forces about Madrid. Combinations of this kind by a heterogeneous force on exterior lines against good troops ably commanded, rarely attain their object, for the latter are nearly sure to throw the bulk of their force upon a fraction of that of their adversary. In the present case, apart from the fact that Joseph had concentrated 58,000 men instead of from 30,000 to 40,000 as estimated by the allies, the combination was foredoomed to failure, not only from the egregious conduct of Cuesta or the worthlessness of his troops, but actually by the treachery of the supreme Junta, which in jealousy of its Captain-General had given secret orders to Venegas not to co-operate with him.

Quitting Plasencia on the 17th of July, Sir Arthur, in pursuance of his agreement with Cuesta, crossed the Tietar at Bazagona next day and entered the valley of the Tagus, his line of march, to use Napier's expression, being "intersected by rivers with rugged banks and deep channels, whose flow is not much out of parallel with the Tagus." At the same time, Wilson on the left flank seized the passes of Arenas and San Pedro Bernado, which lead, the one on Avila, the other on Madrid; whereupon Victor, fearing that he might be cut off from the capital, established a new line of retreat upon Toledo. On the 20th the British force was at Oropesa; the Spanish at Vellada, a day's march in advance. On the 22nd, Cuesta made a ridiculous demonstration against the French outposts on the right bank of the Alberche, and would probably have met with disaster but for the timely arrival of a British force. Victor thereupon concentrated his Corps, 21,000 strong, behind the river. His position invited attack. The King was still at Madrid; Sebastiani, who had driven Venegas back to the Javalon, was still at Madrilejos, 80 miles distant. The French Marshal thus lay unsupported in presence of an enemy of three times his own strength. A defeat would entail, at any rate, the temporary loss of Madrid, with its enormous stores of supplies and the prestige attached to its occupation. Wellesley's keen eye saw the opportunity. He urged on his colleague the need of an immediate attack. Cuesta agreed. The next morning (the 23rd) the whole of the British troops were under arms at 3 a.m. No Spaniards appeared. On inquiry it was found that the whole of the Spanish Staff was in bed; and when they at last woke up, some, who were in correspondence with the enemy, persuaded their General to object to the project. It had in consequence to be abandoned. The opportunity thus lost never recurred, for in the night Victor, forewarned by traitors of high rank in Cuesta's army, drew off his troops and fell back, first to Torrijos and thence behind the Guadarama river, to secure the strategic point, Toledo, through which alone Venegas could co-operate with the Allies.

Meanwhile Marshal Soult at Salamanca had been in communication with the King; and while Cuesta was thwarting his colleague on the Alberche a combined plan of action was concerted between the French armies. Soult, with the 2nd, 5th, and 6th Corps, was directed on Plasencia, from which he was only four marches distant; and Joseph, knowing that the Marshal might be in the valley of the Tagus on the 30th, marched from Madrid at the head of Dessolle's Division and his own French guards, and on the 25th effected a junction with Victor. Next day the French were still further strengthened by the arrival of Sebastiani, who feeling no pressure from Venegas, had left 3,000 men to oppose him, if necessary, on the Tagus, and with the rest of the 4th Corps had proceeded by forced marches to join the King. Thus it had come about that in front of the Allies was a formidable army of more than 50,000 men with 90 guns, while another of equal strength was descending on their flank and rear. Wellesley was unaware of the imminence of the danger: he had received no warning either from Beresford, Del Parque, or any one else; and, although getting uneasy about Soult, trusted to the dispositions made for defending the passes over the Bejar mountains. Otherwise he would certainly have retired to Plasencia, for the supplies ordered had not come in, and his troops were in danger of perishing for want of food.

Victor's retrograde movement gave Cuesta the chance of displaying the full measure of his military talent. In spite of Sir Arthur's warning, he insisted on following up the enemy single-handed to Torrijos. The result was inevitable. Before daybreak on the 26th Latour Maubourg recrossed the Guadarama at the head of his Cavalry Division, supported by Infantry, fell upon the Spaniards, and drove them in wild panic into the angle formed by the junction of the Alberche and the Tagus. Unfortunately for the French, they ceased their pursuit just at the moment when a further advance would have caused a terrible disaster. Then, at the critical moment, the Duc d'Alberquerque turned his Division of Spanish Cavalry about, and formed front to the pursuers; and General Sherbrooke, with two Divisions despatched by Wellesley, who had foreseen the result of Cuesta's advance, appeared on the scene and interposed his troops between his fugitive allies and the enemy. But one shudders at the thought of what might have happened had the French seized the opportunity to make a resolute advance in force. It would probably have terminated the Peninsular War, for the Spaniards in wild confusion were worse than useless, and Wellesley's only alternative lay either in leaving Sherbrooke to his fate or in risking the loss of his whole army in what would almost certainly have been a futile effort to save him.

But Sir Arthur's anxieties were only beginning. It was now too late to retreat; he could not in honour abandon the Spaniards after their defeat and leave them to reap the fruits of their Commander's obstinacy. Yet even now Cuesta refused to retire across the Alberche, and it was not until the following morning (the 27th) that he at length consented to do so. By this time he realised the situation, and being thoroughly cowed, allowed Sir Arthur to command, for the time being, both armies. While Mackenzie covered the retreat Wellesley took up a defensive position six miles in rear. He posted the Spaniards with their right resting on the Tagus at Talavera de la Reyna, and their left on a mound fortified by a large redoubt astride the main road to Arzobispo. Their front extended over about 2,200 yards, being strengthened by a convent, and covered by a variety of obstacles—walls, ditches, &c.—which left them almost unassailable.

On the Spanish left the British 4th Division prolonged the line along low, level ground. Next came the 1st Division. The 2nd had been intended to occupy the extreme left of the position, with its outer flank posted on one of a chain of "round, steep hills" running parallel to the Tagus and forming the boundary of the wooded plain. Through some misunderstanding—possibly caused by Hill's temporary absence—the Division did not take up its allotted post, and the left flank of the Allies was in consequence quite unguarded. Another of these round hills, about 500 yards in front of the British line, to some extent commanded its centre, and formed a good artillery position for the enemy. To the north of this chain, and separated from it by a deep valley, was the mountain range forming the watershed of the Alberche and the Tietar. The distance between the Tagus and the "round" hills was about two and a half miles; thence to the crest-line of the "mountain range," about 1,000–1,200 yards.

The 3rd Division and the Cavalry Brigades were intended for second lines.

Excepting for the hills above mentioned, the country formed a wooded plain covered with olive and cork trees. "The front of the position, which faced about north-east, was," says Napier, "covered by a watercourse which, commencing about the centre of the line, became deep as it passed the left, and was a chasm in the valley." The ground, taken as a whole, was strong, and the Allies were superior in numbers, mustering about 57,000 men with 100 guns, against 50,000 men and 80 guns of the enemy; but the advantage was merely nominal. The only reliable troops were Wellesley's 23,000, of whom the large majority were either young soldiers or recent drafts from the Militia. By them the battle had to be maintained, lost or won.

But long before these dispositions had been completed, King Joseph, with a view to improving the advantage gained on the previous day, had put his army in motion, and at 1 p.m. had occupied the heights of Salinas on the further side of, and overlooking, the Alberche. Victor, knowing the ground, guessed the position which had been taken up by the Allies. On his advice, the 4th Corps moved against the Spaniards; the 1st against the British left, the two Corps being connected by the Cavalry Divisions.

The duty of furnishing the outposts had been entrusted

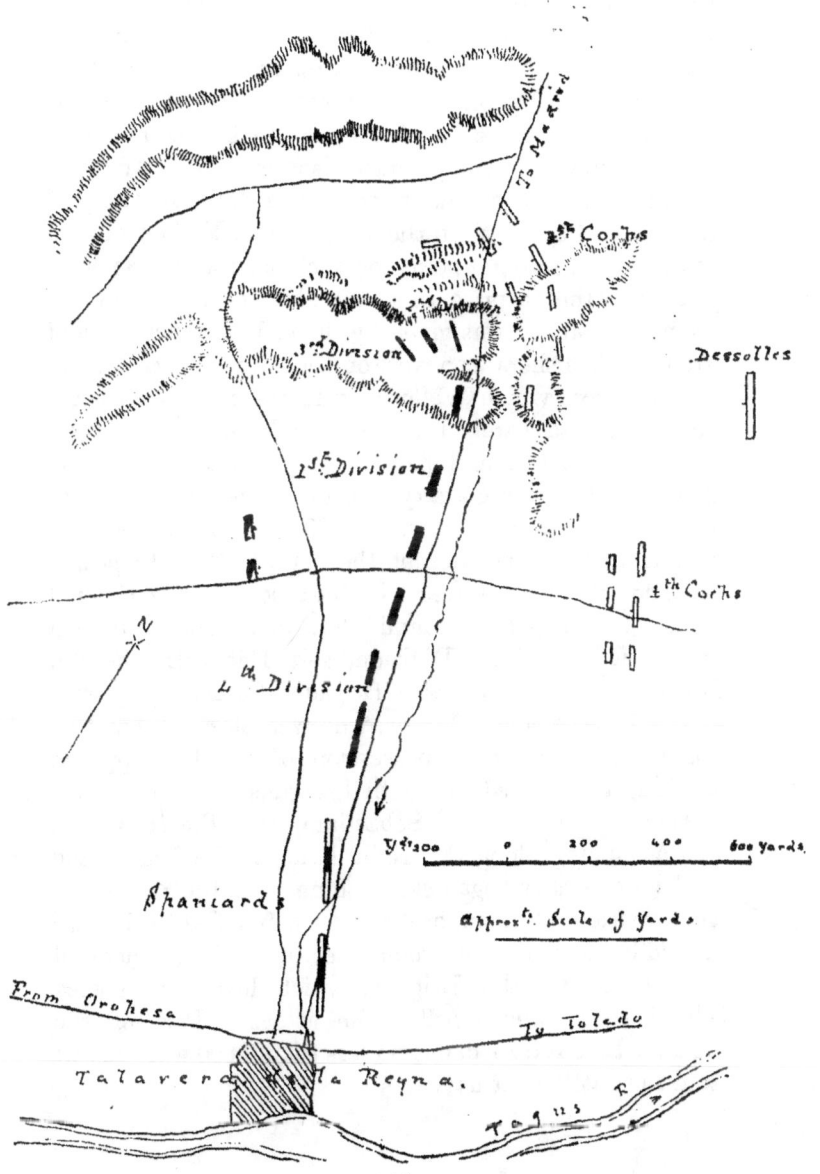

to General Mackenzie with his own Division and Anson's Brigade of Cavalry. It had been grossly neglected. In such a wooded country an efficient system of patrolling was essential. Not a single patrol seems to have been sent out. At 3 p.m. two of Victor's Divisions crossed the Alberche unperceived, fell upon Mackenzie, and in a moment threw his troops into disorder and drove them in confusion out of the wood. The 45th, in the 2nd Brigade, and the 60th in the 3rd, alone held their ground and formed a rallying-point for the remainder. So complete was the surprise that the first intimation of the enemy's approach was given by the sudden appearance of French skirmishers who were on the point of surrounding a house from which Wellesley was taking observations. Sir Arthur had barely time to jump down from the roof, mount his horse, and gallop away. The enemy was checked. Another Cavalry Brigade came up in support, and Mackenzie, with a loss of 400 men, made good his retirement to the position of the main body. He posted the 2nd Brigade in rear of Sherbrooke, while Colonel Donkin, noticing the "round" hill on the left to be still unoccupied by Hill's Division, seized it with the 3rd Brigade. The two Cavalry Brigades formed up in rear of the 1st Division. Victor, who was close at hand in pursuit, promptly took possession of the hill opposite Donkin, and opened fire with his guns.

About the same time Sebastiani, with the 4th Corps, was advancing along the right bank of the Tagus, and his Light Cavalry began skirmishing with the Spaniards. Ten thousand of them broke at once and fled to the rear in wild confusion. The remainder stood fast, supported by Cotton's Cavalry Brigade, which had been posted behind them, and repelled the attack. Part of the fugitives then returned, but no less than 6,000 were absent from the battle next day.

IN THE PENINSULA

Victor had, as we have seen, occupied the hill in front of the left of the British line. It was now getting dark and the opportunity seemed favourable for seizing the opposite height occupied by the 3rd Brigade. Ruffin's Division was ordered to the attack. Villatte supported Ruffin, while Lapisse engaged the attention of the K.G.L. Brigades forming the left of Sherbrooke's Division. The 5th and 7th Battalions K.G.L. gave way and in spite of his vigorous resistance Donkin's flank was turned, and the French crowned the hill. But at the critical moment Hill sent the 6th Brigade to reinforce the 3rd. The height was retaken and the enemy driven to the bottom. Again the French advanced; again they were driven back; and then night ended the engagement. The losses on this day had been heavy on either side. The British casualties amounted to 800; those of the French to 1,000.

At 5 a.m. next morning Victor resumed the attack with a vigorous cannonade which enfiladed the hill on our left—now occupied by the 2nd Division. Had he proved successful it might have decided the day. But instead of employing the whole of his Corps to turn the British left, Ruffin's Division and Villatte's in support were alone engaged. Hill and Wellesley were both wounded, and the former obliged to quit the field. After a desperate contest in which the French are stated by Napier to have lost upwards of 1,500 men in forty minutes, the attack was repelled and the enemy forced back to his former position. Between 7 and 10 a.m. the battle was reduced to skirmishing and artillery fire. Then all was still, and the soldiers of both armies went down in a friendly way to drink from the brook which separated the hostile lines. That the left flank was the principal object of attack and that it needed strengthening, was evident to the British Commander. Light troops of the enemy were to be seen on the mountains beyond. Sir Arthur consequently borrowed Bassecourt's Spanish Infantry Division from Cuesta and posted it in prolongation of his left upon those mountains. The low ground between this Division and Donkin was filled by the Cavalry Brigades of Fane and Anson, which were reinforced at the same time by the Cavalry Division under the Duc d'Albuquerque, who distrusting Cuesta had brought it there of his own accord, sending word at the same time to Wellesley that the Spanish Commander was betraying him. Sir Arthur took not the slightest notice of the message. Absorbed as he was in watching the movements of the enemy it is possible that he did not even hear it. At all events in later years he denied all recollection of the fact. It is however not impossible that he had provided for such a contingency as for any other that might occur in connection with such an ally as the Spaniard. But the report proved untrue.

During this interval King Joseph consulted Marshal Jourdan (his Chief of the Staff) and Victor as to engaging in a general action. Jourdan had wished to draw up the French Army during the night in the valley perpendicular to the allied front. Had the plan been carried out Joseph would have been in direct communication with Soult, and in a position to roll up the British line. It was, however, too late to do so now; and in point of fact Sir Arthur had foreseen such a movement and was prepared to change front to his left, and occupy the line of "round" hills; calling up Wilson and placing himself in communication with Venegas. Under present conditions, therefore, Jourdan counselled a retirement behind the Alberche, in order to await the results of Soult's operations on the flank and rear of the Allies. His views were undoubtedly sound, and Joseph was inclined to listen to him rather than to Victor, who felt confident in the success of a simultaneous attack upon the British

IN THE PENINSULA 211

left and centre. Just then, however, news arrived to the effect that Soult would not be able to reach Plasencia till after the 2nd of August; and Joseph, fearing that the reasons for a retirement would be misrepresented to Napoleon, decided on an immediate attack.

About 1.30 p.m. a terrific artillery fire prepared the way for a general assault. On the French left, Sebastiani, leaving Milhaud's Division of Dragoons to contain the Spaniards, threw himself upon Campbell. Lapisse in the centre attacked Sherbrooke in line of columns, while Victor once more attempted to turn the left of Hill, whose Division had by this time occupied its allotted position somewhat refused in regard to the general line. The French advanced with the utmost *élan*. The 4th Division, supported by the 2nd Brigade and two Spanish battalions, broke Sebastiani's columns with a terrible musketry fire and repelled the attack. As the enemy recoiled, ten of his guns were captured; but Campbell, declining to risk the disorder of a pursuit, maintained his original line. The 4th Corps then reformed in preparation for a new attack, but decimated once more by the deadly fire of the 4th Division and charged in flank by a Spanish regiment of Cavalry, fell back in disorder and made no further bid for victory.

Victor's attack was simultaneously opened upon the British left. This time Ruffin was ordered to make a demonstration against Bassecourt's Division. Villatte advanced against the fatal hill without support; for Victor, untaught by previous experience, once more sent a single Division to do the work of an Army Corps. Sir Arthur—who watched the battle from the top of the hill—observing the movement, directed General Payne to charge the head of the advancing columns with Anson's Cavalry Brigade supported by Fane's. It would seem that plenty of opportunity had been afforded during the last few days to reconnoitre the ground. The duty had, however, been neglected. Anson, without sending forward a single scout, put his Brigade in motion, advanced at a gallop along the valley between Hill and Bassecourt, and the next moment found himself on the edge of a deep mountain torrent. The 1st Hussars K.G.L. reined up in time. The 23rd went headlong in; but two squadrons, although in great disorder, succeeded generally in climbing the opposite bank and threw themselves upon one of Merlin's Light Cavalry Brigades, only thirty yards distant. The other Brigade came to its support; and the 23rd, naturally enough, was repulsed with the loss of half its numbers. The remainder, wheeling to the left, sought refuge under Bassecourt's Division. In its course from left to right the mountain torrent became easier; and while these two squadrons of the 23rd were thus in difficulties, the 3rd under Captain Drake, on the extreme right, encountered only a slight obstacle, crossed it with ease, found itself in the interval between two French Infantry columns, passed through them and created much confusion among the enemy's Infantry beyond. Ruffin and Villatte, on seeing the approach of Anson's Brigade, had halted. The sight of Fane's Brigade in support and of Albuquerque's Division in reserve, stopped Ruffin altogether; and though Villatte, after recovering the effect of Drake's charge, advanced, his attack upon the 2nd Division was delivered in a rather half-hearted sort of way, and repulsed without any great difficulty.

Meanwhile a desperate contest was being waged in the centre of the British line. Here Lapisse, preceded by a terrific artillery fire from the massed batteries on Victor's hill which spread destruction through Sherbrooke's ranks, had been seen to collect a large force in the olive grove opposite the Guards. In half an hour he advanced to the edge of the grove. He had now to pass an open space of from 300 to 400 yards which separated him from the British line. But the Guards, impatient at the losses which they had sustained from the artillery fire to which they were unable to reply, dashed forward from their cover, and charged in line up to and through the olive wood, driving the enemy before them. The charge proved all but fatal. The Guards had exposed both flanks to the French guns, and their front to the counter attack of the reserves. They fell back in great disorder. Cameron's Brigade came up in support but was compelled to retire by the overwhelming numbers of the enemy. The two Brigades K.G.L. also came up on the left but were stopped by the ravine, and in their turn compelled to fall back by the artillery fire. Campbell's Division, which had, as already mentioned, been restrained from following up the French, now protected the right flank of the retiring Guardsmen, but the centre of the line was completely broken and the 1st Division, carrying away part of the 3rd in support, could not be rallied until 200 yards in rear of its original position. The moment was more than critical. But Sir Arthur, watching the affray from the top of the "round" hill, had foreseen the result of the Guards' rash charge. He had no reserves. The 2nd Division was engaged with Villatte; the 4th with Sebastiani. But the former was now getting the better of its opponent, and Wellesley without hesitation ordered the 1st Battalion 48th from Stewart's Brigade to the critical point. Cotton's Cavalry Brigade was brought up in support. The 48th—"that most excellent corps," as Sir Arthur designated it in his General Order—was amply equal to the occasion; made way for the fugitives to pass through its ranks, and filling up the gap in the line, formed a rallying point for the 1st Division. Cotton's Brigade came up. The whole line advanced with loud cheers. Lapisse fell mortally wounded. His Division, assailed in front with the bayonet and torn in flank by the British guns, fell back discomfited. No further attempt was made upon the British position. The enemy had lost all cohesion and retired to his original position unmolested, for our troops were exhausted, and to have used the Spaniards—characterised by Wellesley as incapable of performing any manœuvre, however simple—for an offensive movement, would have been dangerous in the extreme. At 6 p.m. the battle was over, and then occurred one of those horrors almost too terrible for the mind to realise, for the dry grass caught fire and many of the wounded, lying helpless on the ground, perished in the flames.

Thus ended the battle of Talavera, described by Wellesley as the hardest fought action of modern times. Generals Mackenzie and Langwerth were killed, and the total of the British casualties amounted to upwards of 5,400. The Spaniards, in accordance with Sir Arthur's intention, had been but slightly engaged; but it is noteworthy that the few regiments which were actually under fire in conjunction with British troops behaved admirably. The French had lost two General Officers, 7,389 other officers and men, and 17 guns. King Joseph's Guards and the Reserve were still intact, and the British confidently expected a renewal of the attack on the 29th; but in the early morning the French retired across the Alberche and took up a position behind the river. In the course of the day, Brigadier-General Robert Crauford, who had been coming up from Lisbon by forced marches, reached the British camp with a Brigade 3,000 strong, made up of the 43rd, 52nd, and the 95th Rifles; three of the regiments trained a few years previously by Sir John Moore to such a pitch of excellence that when new to active service they were at once regarded as veterans and deemed the mainstay of the Army.

IN THE PENINSULA 215

It was a disgrace to Spain that Wellesley, three days after the battle, was forced to make an official complaint on behalf of his half-starved soldiers, who, " although they have been engaged for two days, and have defeated twice their numbers in the service of Spain, have not bread to eat. It is positively a fact that during the last seven days the British Army have not received one-third of their provisions; that at this moment there are nearly 4,000 wounded soldiers dying in the hospital of this town from want of common assistance and necessaries, which any other country in the world would have given even to its enemies; and that I can get no assistance of any description from the country." (Wellesley to J. H. Frere, July 31, 1809.)

It is now time to return to Soult. On the 30th of June that Marshal had received Napoleon's directions to take command of the 2nd, 5th, and 6th Army Corps, concentrate them and fall upon the left flank and rear of the English, who, the Emperor foresaw, would advance by the valley of the Tagus upon Madrid. Soult lost no time in communicating these instructions to the King. He did not yet know of Sir Arthur's march, and his own idea was to direct the 3rd Corps on Salamanca, besiege Ciudad Rodrigo, and by threatening Lisbon, to draw the British up to Beira. But when in a few days' time the true state of affairs was known, Soult advanced with the 2nd Corps to Salamanca, followed by Ney, although reluctantly, and with every sign of insubordination. Mortier simultaneously put his Corps in motion for Valladolid. On the 24th of July, General Foy, who had been sent to communicate with the King, returned. In pursuance of the plan arranged, Mortier was then directed on Plasencia. On the 29th, strengthened by two Divisions of Dragoons, he reached Fuente Roblo; and, hearing of Beresford's arrival at Almeida, despatched flank guards towards Rodrigo. Next day he crossed the pass of Banos without opposition, and on the 31st entered Plasencia. The 2nd Corps was only one day's march behind him. On the 3rd of August, Mortier, crossing the Tietar, reached Toril. It was now possible for him to seize the bridge of Almaraz, and by occupying the Meza D'Ibor and Mirabete mountains on the further side of the Tagus, to cut off Wellington's sole remaining line of retreat upon Portugal. Ney, however, was still north of Banos; and Soult, unaware of the actual state of affairs and of Victor's position, did not feel himself warranted in weakening his available force by detaching troops across the Tagus.

The strategical situation was now completely altered, but the imminence of his peril was unknown to Sir Arthur Wellesley. He was aware of the presence of a French force in his rear, but estimated it at only 15,000 men. News of the abandonment of the pass of Banos and the arrival of the enemy at Plasencia were brought to him only on the 2nd of August. On the 3rd he marched to Oropesa to encounter the new foe, having previously secured Cuesta's promise to remain at Talavera with a view to holding Victor in check and protecting the British wounded who crowded the town. Napier shows that the situation on this day gave an admirable instance of "the fog of war." Soult was unable to get precise information. Wellesley with 23,000 men was marching to attack 53,000; while on the other side, King Joseph, alarmed by the appearance of Wilson with his 4,000 irregulars at Escalona, had called Victor to Mustoles to make a last stand in defence of Madrid.

On the 4th Wellesley realised that he was in presence of at least 30,000 men. He had already discovered that his retreat on Almaraz had been intercepted. Just then, to his intense disgust, he descried the Spanish army approaching. For hardly had Sir Arthur quitted Talavera than Cuesta, frightened by a ridiculous tale of the King's advance, evacuated Talavera, abandoned his wounded allies to their fate, and marched off to join his colleague. It so happened that at the same moment Soult was able to get a clear view of the situation. Mortier was ordered to seize the bridge of Almaraz; the 2nd Corps was directed upon Arzobispo, Ney being then at Plasencia. The situation of the Allies was one of imminent peril—the British dying of hunger; the Spaniards worse than useless. With Soult in their front and the King in their rear—certain to advance on the first news of Cuesta's retreat—they were cooped up on their right by impassable mountains, and on their left by the Tagus. Without a moment's hesitation, and turning a deaf ear to Cuesta's protests, Sir Arthur decided on his course. The baggage and reserve artillery was instantly sent across the Tagus by the bridge of Arzobispo. The troops followed. Crauford was ordered to Almaraz to secure the bridge of boats and defend the passage of the river. The remainder of the British marched on Deleytoza to gain a new line of retreat by way of Truxillo and Merida.

Mortier had neglected to seize the bridge of Almaraz, and by the evening of the 5th Crauford had achieved the very important object of his mission. On the 6th, the 5th Corps reached Arzobispo, driving Cuesta's rearguard across the river. Ney, at Naval Moral, was close up; the 2nd Corps was at Gredo; Victor at Talavera, where he found 800 remaining of the British wounded, who had been unable to effect their escape when abandoned by Cuesta, and treated them with all the kindness to be expected of a chivalrous foe. Two thousand others, in terrible plight, had quitted the hospitals on the approach of the French and rejoined the army.

218   WELLINGTON'S OPERATIONS

Cuesta had followed Wellesley over the Tagus. On the 8th Mortier crossed the river, fell upon the Spanish rearguard and dispersed it, capturing 5 guns and 400 prisoners. Fifteen other guns, left behind by neglect, were taken next day; and the whole park would have shared the same fate had Sir Arthur not taken the matter into his own hands and hauled it up the Meza D'Ibor mountain. Victor had crossed the Tagus at Talavera on the 7th, and was urged by Soult to attack the allied position at Deleytosa, the latter promising to support him with the 2nd and 5th Corps; while Ney with the 6th Corps was to cross the river at the same time by a ford near Almaraz and attack the Mirabete mountain from that side.

Although the Allies had successfully taken up a strong position on the left bank of the Tagus, their situation was still full of peril. The country-side was covered with Spanish fugitives. Cuesta was as impracticable as ever. Everything was in disorder, and the execution of Soult's combination could have hardly failed to cause a terrible disaster. Happily, Victor was just then recalled by Joseph, and Ney did not find the ford at Almaraz. On the 11th, order was restored in the camp of the Allies. The Spaniards occupied the impregnable Meza D'Ibor. Wellesley's headquarters were at Jaraicejo, on strong ground, with his line of retreat on Merida secured so long as Crauford held the passage at Almaraz. Next day Cuesta, having had a paralytic stroke, resigned his command. The obstinate, impracticable, self-sufficient old man was succeeded by General Eguia; yet, on the whole, Cuesta was one of the least incapable of the Spanish Generals who enjoyed independent command during the war.

Soult's combination having failed, he devised a new one by which he intended to march with his three Army

IN THE PENINSULA

Corps, by the right bank of the Tagus, upon Coria, threatening Wellesley's most direct line of communication with Lisbon by Alcantara, and separating him from Beresford. Ney refused to concur. Joseph took part with Ney, and the latter was allowed to march to Valladolid. On his way he defeated Wilson and his partisans, whom he found in occupation of the pass of Banos. Wilson deserved his defeat; for he had paid but little heed to Wellesley's wishes and injunctions.

The 5th Corps was then posted at Talavera; the 2nd at Plasencia. But in the meanwhile the scene of action had been shifted to the Upper Tagus, where Venegas, with 28,000 men and 40 guns, was threatening Madrid. The 4th Corps opposed him, and it was to support Sebastiani that Victor had been recalled on the 8th from the left bank of the Tagus. In the presence of the enemy Venegas hesitated. On the 11th he met the usual fate of Spanish commanders. Attacked by Sebastiani at Almonacid, he was routed with the loss of half his army and the whole of his guns.

For some days Sir Arthur was unaware of Venegas' defeat. Meanwhile, Beresford with 14,000 men had followed Soult southward by the pass of Perales, and was now at Moraleja, expecting to be reinforced by the Brigades of Catlin Crauford and Lightburne. Under these circumstances, Wellesley, still underrating the enemy's strength, contemplated the idea of crossing the Tagus and attacking the 2nd Corps at Plasencia. But the plan had to be dropped almost as soon as formed. In spite of the renewed assurances of General Eguia, the British army was literally dying of hunger. "Half a pound of wheat in the grain," says Napier, "and twice a week a few ounces of flour, with a quarter of a pound of goat's flesh, formed the sole subsistence of men and officers." "Goats' offal sold at this time for double the usual price of the whole animal, and men and officers outbid each other for the wretched food." Privation brought on dysentery, from which hardly a man in the army was free, and the hospitals were crowded. Of the troop horses, 1,000 had died; 800 others were unfit for any work.

Under these circumstances Wellesley's course was clear. On the 20th of August he evacuated his position and retired, first to Merida, then to the neighbourhood of Badajoz, whence—to use his own expression—he could hang on the enemy's flank and prevent him crossing the Guadiana unless he came with very great forces. Beresford, leaving an outpost on the Portuguese frontier, retired to Thomar behind the Zezere. Eguia was also directed to fall back behind the Guadiana. He was then succeeded by the Duc d'Albuquerque, but the latter being out of favour with the Central Junta, was left to guard Estremadura with 12,000 men, while the rest of his army was sent to reinforce Venegas, who had halted in the Morena and now found himself in command of nearly 50,000 men.

The position taken up by Wellington was admirably chosen from the strategic point of view for its purpose of defending the south of Spain and Portugal. At the end of the year the British Commander was able to say, "The French had from the end of August not less than from 70,000 to 90,000 men disposable; they have since destroyed two armies of Spaniards which it was thought proper to expose to their attack; and yet they have not been able to advance, or to gain any solid advantage beyond that of destroying the Spaniards." . . . "The advantage of the position of Badajoz was, that the British army was centrically situated in reference to all the objects which the enemy might have in view; and at any time, by a junction with a Spanish corps on its right, or

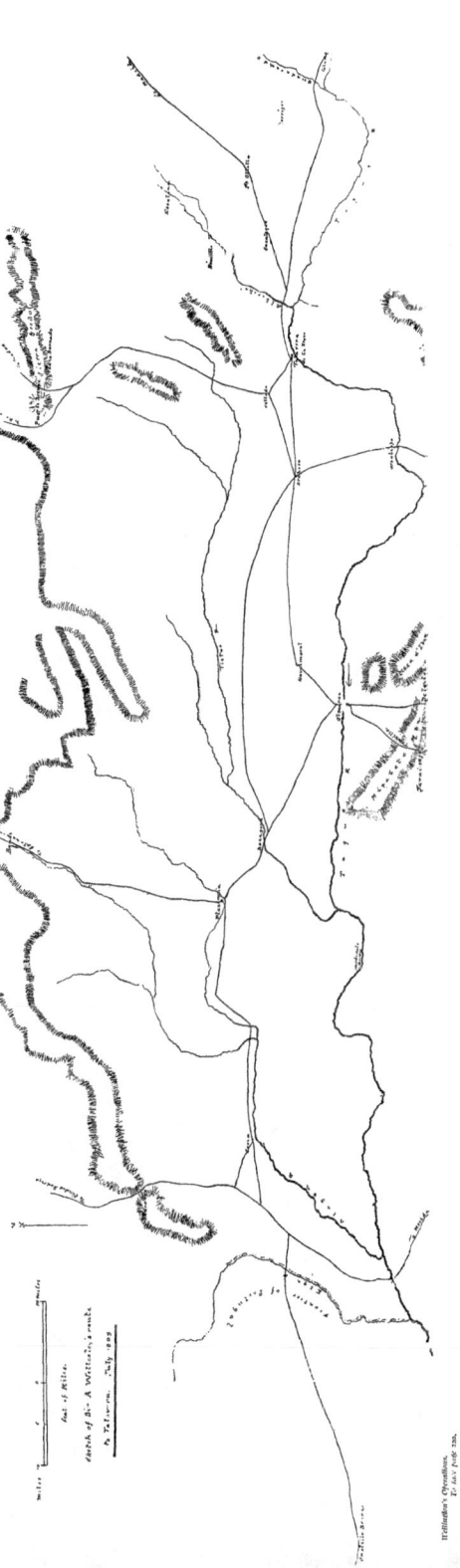

a Portuguese or Spanish corps on its left, it could prevent the enemy from undertaking anything, excepting with a much larger force than they could allot to any one object."

Speaking on the same subject, Napier remarks (bk. ix. ch. 6) : " It was the position maintained by Wellington on the frontier of Estremadura which, in the latter part of 1809, saved Andalusia from subjection. This is easy of demonstration. Joseph having rejected Soult's projects against Portugal and Ciudad Rodrigo, dared not invade Andalusia by Estremadura with the English army on his right flank ; neither could he hope to invade it by the way of La Mancha without drawing Wellington into the contest ; but Andalusia was at this period the last place where the intrusive King desired to meet a British army. He had many partisans in that province, who would necessarily be overawed if the course of the war carried Wellington beyond the Morena ; nor could the Junta in that case have refused Cadiz as a place of arms to their ally ; and then the whole force of Andalusia and Murcia would have rallied round the English army behind the Morena. Areizaga had 60,000 men,* Albuquerque 10,000 ; and it is therefore no exaggeration to assume that 100,000 could have been organised for defence. Moreover, all the Portuguese troops in the south of Portugal would have been available to aid in the protection of Estremadura. From Carolina to Madrid is only ten marches, and, posted at the former, the Allied army could have protected Lisbon as well as Seville, because a forward movement would force the French to concentrate round the Spanish capital."

Thus ended the Talavera campaign, which—without including either the wounded who escaped the French or the men crowding the hospitals—cost us 3,500 soldiers,

* ? 50,000. Areizaga succeeded Venegas.

and engendered in the British ranks a hatred of the Spaniards for which the latter were destined to pay dearly at a later date. Wellesley, having gained a bitter yet salutary experience of the fundamental difference between Spanish promises and Spanish performances, vowed that never again would he rely upon the Spaniard, and he kept his word. Prompt and resolute as he had been in escaping from one of the most perilous positions in which a commander has ever been placed, it can hardly be doubted that but for the delay caused by Ney's insubordination and Mortier's circuitous march to Salamanca, to say nothing of Joseph's flagrant error in fighting the battle of Talavera, Wellesley must have been crushed between the overwhelming masses of the enemy.

The general run of the campaign was singularly like that of Sir John Moore. In each case an advance was made into the heart of Spain with too small a force to command success; in each case reliance on Spanish assurances proved fallacious; and in each case a descent of the enemy in overwhelming numbers upon the British flank and rear necessitated a hasty retreat. Wellesley indeed gained a victory before retreating; but the battle of Talavera, although it gave confidence to the British troops, and showed them that they were the equals of those hitherto regarded as the finest soldiers in Europe, was not (and from the circumstances of the case could not be) followed by any strategical advantage; for although by his advance Wellesley had cleared the northern, as Moore had cleared the Southern provinces of the French, in neither case was a man put into the field, or even raised by those provinces, to strike a blow against the national enemy.

One may perhaps think that Sir Arthur might in the first instance have profited a little more by Sir John Moore's experience of the Spaniards; but at all events he

IN THE PENINSULA

had now so thoroughly learnt his lesson that never again during the whole course of the war did he place the slightest reliance on the Spanish people, whether military or civil. His subsequent campaigns were planned and executed entirely without reference to them. Indeed, so deeply was his mind impressed with the peril which he had so narrowly escaped that he does not seem to have ever recovered entirely from its effects, and henceforward a certain hesitancy is sometimes to be noticed in his conduct and operations foreign to his naturally bold and enterprising disposition.

Curiously enough, during the foregoing campaign both the French and the Allies were operating on exterior lines—Soult and Joseph as regards the Anglo-Spanish army; the Allies and Venegas in regard to the King. The consequence was that no decisive results were achieved, but the strategical advantage undoubtedly lay with the French. Wellesley's blow had failed. Napoleon's grasp of Spain was unshaken. Andalusia and Valencia appeared to be at the mercy of his brother; and it only remained for the Emperor to bring his victorious troops from the Danube and complete the conquest of the whole Peninsula.

Wellesley's brilliant service in expelling the French twice from Portugal, and in winning the battles of Vimeiro and Talavera, were recognised at home by his elevation to the Peerage as Baron Douro and Viscount Wellington.

CHAPTER X

Operations in Catalonia—Siege of Gerona—Its capture—Wellington rebukes the Spaniards—Battle of Ocana—Victor invests Cadiz by land—Operations in Catalonia.

DURING the summer and autumn of 1809, while the other Army Corps of the French were engaged on the Tagus, the 3rd and 7th were busy in Aragon and Catalonia. After defeating Blake at Belchite on the 18th of June, General Suchet, commanding the 3rd Corps, occupied Saragossa as his headquarters, being principally engaged in subduing the irregular bands under the guerilla chiefs who infested the neighbourhood, and in organising a system for the better government of his province. In both tasks he proved successful. By the end of the year the fortresses of Lerida and Mequimenza alone separated him from St. Cyr and the 7th Corps, which had been withdrawn behind the Llobregat. The occupation of the castle of Alcanitz, on the Guadaloupe river, afforded a base for future operations against Valencia; while the success of his civil government disarmed the hostility of the peaceable and law-abiding portion of the population.

Meanwhile St. Cyr had been engaged in the sieges of Gerona and Hostalrich, whose occupation by the Spaniards endangered the security of Barcelona. Gerona was invested on the 4th of June by the Divisions of Verdier and Lecchi, 18,000 strong. St. Cyr covered the siege on the south side with 12,000 men; while 10,000 under Duhesme—including a large proportion of sick—occupied Barcelona. On the other hand the garrison of Gerona, commanded by Mariano Alvarez, did not exceed 3,000 men. The appeals of that officer for succour were disregarded by the Central Junta, but his gallant spirit embued the garrison with heroism, and every step of the enemy was stoutly contested. On the 8th of July an assault upon the outlying fort, Montjuic, was repelled with the loss of 1,000 men; and it was not until the 11th of August that its occupants, finding the fort no longer tenable, evacuated it and retired into Gerona. The rocky nature of the ground hindered the besiegers. Eight hundred enterprising volunteers penetrated the line of investment from without and reinforced the garrison, which shortly afterwards was still further strengthened by the entry of a convoy of provisions escorted by 4,500 men. But no serious effort was made either by the Central Junta or by the Spanish regular troops under Blake to relieve the town. In October, General St. Cyr was relieved in his command by Marshal Augereau, a man in all respects vastly inferior to his predecessor. But St. Cyr, although to be classed among the very ablest of Napoleon's generals, and invariably assigned by the Emperor to posts in which the highest talent was required, was unfortunately subject to certain weaknesses which marred his military career. It also happened that his political views were strongly republican. He disliked the Emperor; but his supersession was due to want of zeal and energy, not on account of his opinions, for Napoleon was glad to make use of talent wherever he found it, and republican views were no bar to his favour, witness the case of General Mouton, afterwards Count Lobau, and, in later days, those of Carnot, Lepelletier, Lecourbe, &c.

Although St. Cyr had been designated as their future chief by the Oporto conspirators, he does not seem to have been himself privy to their proceedings. But he was a discontented man, prone to take offence at imaginary slights, and, worse still, took no proper care for the troops under his command. To compare him for the moment with another of his brothers-in-arms, St. Cyr may be justly termed an excellent officer; Lannes an excellent soldier; and the latter is the higher term of praise.

Augereau, with a reinforcement of 12,000 men, reached Gerona on the 12th of October. The siege had been turned into a blockade. The garrison was, however, by this time suffering from famine and sickness. On the 6th of December the suburbs and outworks fell into the hands of the French, and though partially recovered next day by Alvarez, it was his last effort. Exhausted nature asserted herself; Alvarez fell into delirium, and on the 10th the city surrendered. Thus after six months terminated a defence in comparison with which that of Saragossa fades into insignificance. The value of a feat of arms is not to be judged by its notoriety. One event takes the popular imagination, and is invested with a glamour which it hardly deserves. Another, of greater importance and result, is entirely overlooked. The siege of Delhi was a much greater feat of arms than the defence of Lucknow. Ladysmith will be remembered long after Pieter's Hill is forgotten.

"The fall of Gerona," observes Napier, "was a reproach to the Spanish and English Cabinets. The latter, having agents in Catalonia and such a man as Lord Collingwood to refer to, were yet so ignorant or so careless of what was essential to the success of the war as to let Gerona struggle for six months, when half the troops employed by Sir John Stuart to alarm Naples, if carried to the coast of Catalonia and landed at Palamos, would have raised the siege."

While these events were taking place on the eastern side, the Duque del Parque, in command of the Spanish Army of the Left at Ciudad Rodrigo, had concerted movements against the 6th Corps at Salamanca. He applied to Wellington for Portuguese troops; but the British Commander, satisfied that the Spaniards were in no condition to assume the offensive, pointed out that the central position of the French acquired by Napoleon's original strategy, afforded the enemy such advantages as to render him unassailable, and that the only result from Del Parque's scheme would be to expose him to defeat in front by the 6th Corps, supported by Kellermann at Valladolid, and in flank by Soult at Plasencia. "The war," he continued, "must necessarily be defensive on the part of the Allies; and Portugal at least, if not Spain, ought to avail herself of the short period which the enemy seemed disposed to leave her in tranquillity, to organise and equip and discipline her armies." "These objects could not be accomplished unless the troops were kept quiet, and yet they were very much more important to all parties than any desultory successful operations against the French about Salamanca; but any success was doubtful and certain to be temporary, because the enemy would immediately collect in numbers sufficient to crush the Allies; who must then return, having failed in their object, but with the loss of a number of men, and what was worse, time which would have been more usefully employed in preparing for a great and well-combined effort." Then, when asked to state definitely at what time the Portuguese would be in a position to cooperate with the Spaniards in Spanish territory, Wellington replied with keen irony and grave rebuke, "When there is a Spanish army with which the Portuguese can co-operate on some defined plan, which all parties will have the means and will engage to carry into execution. ... When means shall be pointed out and fixed for the subsistence of the Portuguese troops while they remain in Spain, so that they may not starve and be obliged to retire for want of food as was the case when lately in that country."

Arguments of this kind, weighty as they were, produced no sort of impression upon the Spaniards; and Del Parque, nothing daunted, proceeded to carry out his schemes unaided. The result was as expected. Advancing at the head of 30,000 men, a temporary success enabled him to occupy Salamanca; but, attacked on the 27th of November at Alba de Tormes by Kellermann, Governor of Valladolid, in conjunction with the 6th Corps—now commanded by Marchand, for Ney had returned to France—the Spanish Army was completely dispersed with the loss of 10,000 men and the whole of its artillery.

While these operations were taking place in Leon, others, showing equally little forethought, were being carried on in New Castile. The Central Junta, enraged at Wellesley's retreat into Portugal, resolved that the Spanish armies should attack Madrid single-handed. For this purpose the command of the Army of the Centre was taken from Venegas and conferred on General Areizaga. The scheme provided for the co-operation of the partidas in Aragon, and with lying effrontery Areizaga was allowed to expect the aid of the British Army, in spite of the fact that Wellesley had distinctly refused to take any part whatever in the enterprise.

Areizaga, at the head of nearly 60,000 men with 60 guns, set out from La Carolina on the 3rd of November, and, rapidly crossing the Morena, entered La Mancha. As an officer he was unknown to fame, and his principal recommendation appears to have been a remarkable

IN THE PENINSULA

consonance in brain power with that of the celebrated knight whose province he was now traversing. Of forethought and preparation we find little trace. He expected Wellington's co-operation, but had taken no steps either to form a combined plan or even communicate with him. Yet Areizaga swept through La Mancha like a whirlwind, and Joseph in alarm once more prepared to abandon his capital. Soult (who had handed over command of the 2nd Army Corps to General Heudelet and was now Chief of the Staff) with better judgment dissuaded the King, and concentrated his troops to oppose the rash assailants. The 1st Corps, supported by a Division of the 4th, was already at Mora and Yevenes 20 miles south of Toledo, on the roads leading to La Mancha. A second Division of the 4th Corps and Milhaud's Cavalry lay at Ocana on high ground 30 miles east of Toledo and 15 south of the Tagus at La Rena. Of the third Division, one Brigade garrisoned at Madrid, the other behind the Tajuna river guarded the approaches to the capital from the eastward. The 2nd Corps was at Oropesa, supported by the 5th at Talavera. Dessolles had been detached to reinforce Marchand.

So rapid was Areizaga's march that on the 6th of November the advance guard reached Consuegra, having covered more than 100 miles in four days. Regardless of the 1st Corps on his left flank, the Spanish General continued his course towards Aranjuez. On the 10th he reached Dos Barrios, near Ocana, and finding himself in presence of the enemy, paused for the first time to reflect. Over confidence was quickly succeeded by alarm. He might have crushed Sebastiani, but halted irresolutely for three days in ignorance of the numbers and position of the French, thus giving Soult time to recall the 2nd and 5th Corps from the valley of the Tagus, and Dessolles from the further side of the Guadarama mountains;

while the 1st and 4th Corps concentrated at Aranjuez. On the 14th, Areizaga having been falsely informed by the Junta of a British advance ; and truly, that Albuquerque and Del Parque had been ordered to combine their forces and co-operate with him by the line of the Tagus, resumed his march. Regardless of the fact that he was moving on exterior lines, had three rivers to cross and 100 miles to traverse, he now made a flank movement by St. Cruz with the object of approaching Madrid from the east. Part of his army was thrown across the Tagus at Villa Maurique. But then, finding himself headed off by the 1st Corps which had moved by interior lines on the other side of the river, the Spanish General recalled his Divisions and took post for battle at Santa Cruz. The 4th Corps had stood its ground at Aranjuez in the face of overwhelming numbers. The 5th was directed to reinforce it. The two wings of the French Army being now within supporting distance of one another, Victor received orders to press the Spaniards in front while the 4th and 5th Corps were directed upon their flank and rear. Advancing by the bridge over the Tagus at Aranjuez, Sebastiani, with the greater part of the Cavalry belonging to the two Corps, came upon that of the enemy on the tableland between Antiguela and Ocana. He immediately charged. The Spaniards, although in superior numbers, gave way and retired with great loss in disorder. The encounter had been unexpected by the French ; but the fact was, that Areizaga had this day retired from Santa Cruz, by Noblejas, with a view to attacking the French as they debouched from Aranjuez. On the 19th he took up a defensive position on the high land at Ocana with 7,000 Cavalry, 45,000 Infantry, and 60 guns. Before daybreak on the 20th, King Joseph, with his Guards, one of Dessolles' Brigades, and the 4th and 5th Army Corps—comprising 5,000 Cavalry, 24,000

Infantry and 60 guns—marched from Aranjuez to the attack. The Spanish left, 15,000 strong, was posted behind a ravine so steep that the troops could neither advance nor be attacked. The Centre, hampered by the same ravine, was in front of Ocana. The Right was *en l'air*, and it was against this flank that the French attacks were in consequence mainly directed. For a time the Spaniards firmly stood their ground, but some very pretty manœuvring on the part of the French—during the course of which each arm of the service in turn was beautifully supported by the other two—drove them after a three hours' fight from their position in headlong rout, with the loss of 5,000 men killed and wounded, 26,000 prisoners and 45 guns. Victor's Cavalry from Villa Tobas aided in the pursuit. The French casualties amounted only to 1,700, and Joseph was so much elated by the victory that he formed a project of making himself independent of Napoleon by force of arms. The preposterous notion was very quickly suppressed by Soult.

The battle at Ocana deserves study in detail, giving as it does an admirable illustration of the working of the three arms as well individually as in combination. It may perhaps be considered as Soult's best example of offensive action.

The victory at Ocana was not at first followed up, but on the retirement of Lord Wellington from the Guadiana, Joseph resolved to undertake the invasion of Andalusia. The 2nd Corps was left near Talavera to guard against any movement of the British Army. The 1st, 4th, 5th Corps, the Reserve and Dessolles' Division, comprising about 65,000 men, were put in motion early in 1810, and on the 18th of January the headquarters of the army were established at Santa Cruz de Mudela. The advance was continued in three columns. In the centre the 5th Corps, the Reserve, Dessolles and the reserve Artillery,

&c., approached the Sierra Morena by way of the Despena Peros pass; found it held by Areizaga with 25,000 men, the remnant of his defeated army; crowned the heights on either side of the defile, and occupied La Carolina beyond it. On the right, Victor having sent a detachment to Agudo to observe Albuquerque who was occupying Medellin with 15,000 men, crossed the Morena by way of Hinojosa. On the left, Sebastiani, penetrating with the 4th Corps by Estevan, reached Ubeda. The Central Junta, now thoroughly alarmed, sent in hot haste for Del Parque to come down from Ciudad Rodrigo and reinforce Albuquerque; but the latter, appreciating the danger of the situation, threw a garrison into Badajoz; and, marching on the 22nd for Seville, reached Carmona on the 25th. The approach of the French armies had caused a tumult in Seville; and the populace, in its indignation, had on the 24th deposed the Central Junta and entrusted the supreme power to the ancient Junta of Seville. This new authority, however, fell to pieces in three days and was replaced by the Council of Castille.

Meanwhile Sebastiani had captured first Jaen, then Grenada; and, his left flank being thus secured, Joseph entered Cordoba with the 1st and 5th Corps. Albuquerque now retired; but judging it hopeless to attempt to defend Seville, betook himself by forced marches to Cadiz, where he arrived on the 3rd of February. Seville had capitulated on the 1st; and its vast foundry and arsenal fell into the hands of the enemy. Victor, following hard on Albuquerque, reached Chiclana on the 4th, and an immediate attack vigorously pushed home might have given him possession of Cadiz. Sebastiani had already crossed the Sierra Nevada and captured Malaga; while Mortier, who had been sent against Badajoz, finding Del Parque close at hand and the fortress in a state of defence, took up his quarters at

Merida in touch with the 2nd Corps—now commanded by Mermet—which was posted at Montijo on the Guadiana.

During the month of March King Joseph returned to Madrid, leaving Marshal Soult to organise an excellent and most successful system of administration in Andalusia. "The province," says Napier (bk. x. ch. 6), "was admirably well governed. It was gradually tranquillised, the military resources were drawn forth, . . . the mines of lead at Linares were worked. . . . Privateers were fitted out, commerce " with neutral nations "in the ports of Grenada; and a secret . . . traffic carried on with Lisbon itself, demonstrated the administrative abilities of Soult." Victor blockaded Cadiz, but on a line of investment— running by Port St. Mary, Port Royal, and Chiclana, with its flanks resting on the sea at Rota and Torre Bermeja, respectively—far too large for the force at his disposal. The garrison, on the other hand, was reinforced in February by General W. Stewart with 3,000 British and 1,000 Portuguese troops, whom the Spanish Government had at last consented to admit into the city, and had a total strength of 18,000 regular soldiers, supported by the ships in the harbour. On the 24th of March, General Graham arrived and took command of the Anglo-Portuguese forces. General Blake—a Spaniard, in spite of his Irish name—was shortly afterwards appointed to command the Spanish troops. By degrees the garrison was raised to 30,000 men, of whom (very unnecessarily), 8,500 were Anglo-Portuguese, but Graham could not induce the Spaniards to attempt any enterprise, and the blockade dragged on through the summer and winter.

During this time Romana, who now commanded the Spanish troops in Estremadura, attempted to operate against the French communications with Madrid by the

valley of Guadiana, but was held in check by the 2nd
and 5th Corps, which in their turn were connected with
the 6th by the pass of Banos.

In Catalonia, Hostalrich and Lerida fell during the
month of May; but an attempt made on the town of
Valencia in March by Suchet with the 3rd Corps from
Aragon failed in the absence of a co-operating force,
which he had been led to expect from the side of
Andalusia. Suchet then returned to Saragossa; and the
failure seems to have had an important bearing on the
war, in encouraging the Spaniards to fresh resistance at
a time when Andalusia had been conquered and the cause
appeared hopeless. The incursion into Valencia had
been undertaken in opposition to the Emperor's wishes,
albeit unwittingly; for Napoleon's despatches, directing
Suchet to co-operate with Augereau and complete the
reduction of Catalonia before embarking in any further
enterprise, were intercepted by the Spaniards. Aragon
was now made into a "government" under Suchet,
independent of Joseph, and Suchet busied himself in the
administration of his province and in the suppression
of the partidas who carried on an irregular guerilla
warfare, harassed the French communications, interrupted
their posts, and necessitated the occupation of large
bodies of troops in escort duty. Useful, however, as
they were in their own way, the service of the partidas
as influencing the course of the war have been greatly
overrated. On this point it would be difficult to find
a better judge than Napier, and he discusses the case
fully (bk. ix. ch. 1). Summing up the whole question,
he observes that "the partidas of Biscay, Navarre,
Aragon, and Catalonia mustered at one time above
30,000 men accustomed to arms, and often commanded
by chiefs of undoubted courage and enterprise, yet they
never occupied half their own number of French at one

time, never absolutely defeated a single Division, never prevented any considerable enterprise, never—with the exception of the surprise at Figueras—performed any exploit seriously affecting the operations of a single *Corps d'armée.*" The French General, St. Cyr—an impartial witness and keen observer—remarks that the ferocity of the partidas " was often as dangerous to their own party as to the enemy. The atrocities committed against their own chiefs disgusted the most patriotic, abated their zeal and caused the middle class to desire peace as the only remedy of a system so replete with disorder. Numbers of distinguished men, even those who had opposed Joseph at first, began to abandon Ferdinand; and it is certain that but for the expedition to Russia that branch of the Bourbons which reigns in Spain would never have remounted the throne."

Before quitting the review of the general situation at this period it is important to draw attention to Napier's views as to " the little use made of the naval power, and the misapplication of the military strength of the Allies in the southern parts of Spain " (bk. x. ch. 5). " The British, Portuguese, and Spanish soldiers at Cadiz, were in round numbers 30,000, the British in Gibraltar 5,000, in Sicily 16,000, forming a total of more than 50,000 effective troops aided by a great navy "—having, by the way, an absolute command of the sea—" and favourably placed for harassing that immense . . . line of French operations, extending from the south of Italy to Cadiz : for even from the bottom of Calabria troops and stores were brought to Spain. Yet a Neapolitan rabble under Murat in Calabria, and from 15,000 to 20,000 French around Cadiz, were allowed to paralyse this mighty power! Minorca offered a central station, a place of arms for the troops, a spacious port for the fleet. . . . What coast siege undertaken by the 7th or 3rd Corps could have been successfully prosecuted, if the garrison had been suddenly augmented with 15,000 or 20,000 men from the ocean? After one or two successful descents, the very appearance of a ship of war would have stopped a siege and made the enemy concentrate; whereas the slight expeditions of this period were generally disconcerted by the presence of a few French companies."

CHAPTER XI

Wellington restores discipline—State of affairs in Spain—Wellington leaves the Guadiana—Posts and divisions at Abrantes, and the remainder on the Mondego—Memorandum of events in 1809.

WELLINGTON'S retreat to the Portuguese frontier was a source of great dissatisfaction in England. His operations were sharply criticised in Parliament by the Opposition and feebly defended by the Ministers, who did not comprehend their purport. Men like Colonel Tarleton, a swashbuckler of the American War, aired their views; and Lord Grey, with a magnificent assurance, which of itself should set him among the great men of Parliament, was good enough to rebuke the British Commander for his dispositions at Talavera and to favour the House of Lords with an outline of the course which he himself would have pursued in Wellington's place. The Common Council of the City of London presented a petition to the King, perverting the facts of the case with a recklessness or ignorance remarkable even among such a body and praying for an "inquiry"—in other words, a court martial upon the General who had twice expelled the French from Portugal and had repelled the attack of overwhelming numbers at Talavera. Laughable at this distance of time are the antics of these Liliputians as they stand in the pillory of history, but their incessant pin-pricks could not then fail to be deeply mortifying to the British Commander, overburdened as he already was by the cares of his army, the faint-heartedness of his friends and the exasperating folly of his Spanish allies. No wonder that his temper became irritable. One can only imagine how deeply he must have envied the lot of his opponents, strong as they were in the loyalty, the confidence, and determined support of the great French Emperor.

Dark as was the general outlook, redeeming circumstances were not entirely wanting. At the end of the year 1809 his brother, Lord Wellesley, took the place of the volatile Hookham Frere, and early in the following year Villiers was succeeded by Mr. Charles Stuart, son of the late general—a very able young man, whose services proved absolutely invaluable to Lord Wellington.

The period of rest spent on the Guadiana was no idle or useless one to the British Army or its Commander. The troops were provisioned and refitted, horses got into condition, carriages and waggons repaired. The regulations of the Army were enforced, discipline restored, and regimental officers admonished in the performance of their duties relating to interior economy. "The officers of the Army," said Wellington in a General Order, memorable and not less applicable now than then, "are much mistaken if they suppose that their duty is done when they have attended to the drill of their men and to the parade duties of their regiments; the order and regularity of the troops in camp and quarters, the subsistence and comfort of the soldiers, the general subordination and obedience of the corps, afford constant subjects for the attention of the field officers in particular, in which by their conduct, in the assistance they will give their commanding officer, they can manifest their zeal for the service, their ability and their fitness for promotion to the higher ranks, at least as much as by attention to the drill and parade discipline of the corps." Divisional route-marching—not less than 12 miles in marching order—was to be carried out twice a week, and, in fact, every means taken to weld the army into an efficient fighting machine. But in reading Wellington's Orders and Correspondence the point which impresses one most is that at this period the Staff was so inexperienced that every matter of detail had to be attended to by the Commander-in-Chief.

Wellington went down to Seville to concert measures with the Junta, but the members of the Junta concealed their plans, and the British commander came back more resolved than ever to place no dependence upon the Spaniards and—at all events for the present—to confine himself to measures for the defence of Portugal. As to the best means, or even the possibility of arranging this at all, considerable correspondence was passing between himself and the home government. On this, as on all other subjects, Wellington stated his views with admirable clearness, precision, and foresight, viewing the question from every standpoint—political, military, and financial; and though the prospect of the enormous expense necessary alarmed the Ministers, who had entered into the struggle lightly and without forethought or discernment, his views were generally approved by them; and he received a remarkably gratifying mark of appreciation from the King, who, *pace* modern writers, had a considerable fund of shrewd common sense, and whose opinion probably turned the scale. Writing through his secretary to Lord Liverpool, His Majesty "observed that the arguments and remarks which this (Wellington's) letter contains, the general style and spirit in which it is written, and the clearness with which the state of the question and of prospects in Portugal is exposed, has given H.M. a very high opinion of Lord Wellington's sense and of the resources of his mind as a soldier, and that as he appears to have weighed the whole of his situation so coolly and maturely and to have considered so fully every contingency under which he may be placed . . . His Majesty trusted that his ministers would feel with him the advantage of suffering him to proceed according to his judgment and discretion in the adherence to the principles which he has laid down, unfettered by any particular instructions which might embarrass him in the execution of his general plan of operations."

The spirit of loyalty towards his servant thus shown at a time when the latter was the most unpopular of his subjects is creditable in the highest degree to the old king, and Wellington no doubt appreciated it accordingly.

Concurrently with the exposition of his views on the general situation the British Commander was occupied in obtaining information as to the practicability of fortifying the mountains of the peninsula formed by the Tagus and the Atlantic about Torres Vedras in the neighbourhood of Lisbon, with a view to converting them into a huge entrenched camp to which he could carry his army should the French invade Portugal, and whence, as a last resource, it could embark either for England or to undertake a new line of operations based on Cadiz. The idea was not new and the details had been worked out by the French colonel, Vincent, and by Sir Charles Stuart in 1799, but Wellington intended to carry it out on a far larger scale and to make it of infinitely greater importance than had been contemplated by his predecessors. Lieut.-Colonel Fletcher, an able Engineer, was sent to examine the ground at leisure. It was quietly surveyed and

IN THE PENINSULA 241

valuable reports in detail were forwarded by that officer to Headquarters. In addition to his ordinary duties, curious as it seems, a not infrequent interchange of letters took place between Wellington and the French generals. A satisfactory feature in this correspondence was the extremely friendly tone of such communications and the confidence reposed in the British Commander by his opponents. The subjects referred to the thousand and one affairs of daily life on service—at one time the care of wounded men left in each other's hands; at another the exchange of a particular prisoner, &c., &c. And a consequence of this intercourse was that at the end of the war the general officers on either side met, not as enemies, but as old friends!

In regard to prisoners a regular scale of exchange was fixed as follows:—

British rank.	French rank.	Value in private soldiers.
General Officer Commanding	Marshal	60
General	General of Division	40
Lieutenant-General	General of Brigade	30
Major-General		20
Brigadier-General, Colonel, or Adjutant-General		15
Lieut.-Colonel or Major	Chef de Bataillon	8
Captain	Captain	6
Lieutenant	Lieutenant	4
Ensign	Sous-lieutenant	3
Non-commissioned officer	Sous-officier	2

On the 1st of November, 1809, the following was the "State" of the British Army:—

CAVALRY DIVISION.
Lieutenant-Generals Payne and Cotton.

1st Brigade.
Colonel Sir Granby Calcroft.

Regiment.	Station.	Officers.	Non-Commissioned Officers and Men.					Horses.			
			Present.	Sick.	Command.	Missing.	Total of all Ranks.	Present.	Sick.	Command.	Missing.
3rd Dragoon Guards	Merida	20	420	160	89	2	691	416	43	55	1
4th Dragoons	"	32	484	121	105	—	742	420	46	69	—
2nd Brigade. Brigadier-General Slade.											
Royal Dragoons	Belem	28	612	61	3	—	704	581	28	2	—
14th Light Dragoons	Villa Viciosa	28	498	143	51	1	721	350	73	8	—
3rd Brigade. Brigadier-General Anson.											
16th Light Dragoons	Villa Viciosa	25	556	99	51	—	731	375	72	18	3
1st Light Dragoons, K.G.L.	Valverde	25	504	85	11	8	633	400	33	5	—
Totals	...	158	3,074	669	310	11	4,222	2,542	290	157	4

Royal Artillery.

Brigadier-General Howarth, C.R.A.

Regiment.	Officers.	Non-Commissioned Officers and Men.					Horses.			
		Present.	Sick.	Command.	Missing.	Total of all Ranks.	Present.	Sick.	Command.	Missing.
R.H.A.	11	218	73	—	—	302	378	—	—	—
R.F.A.	35	652	157	364	2	1,210	576	—	—	—
H.A., King's German Legion	19	288	97	93	—	497	229	—	—	—
Totals ...	65	1,158	327	457	2	2,009	1,188*	—	—	—
Royal Engineers. ...	17	19	4	—	—	42	—	—	—	—
Waggon Train. ...	11	275	20	11	2	319	111	—	—	—

* Including 132 mules attached to the Artillery.

1st INFANTRY DIVISION.
Lieutenant-General Sir J. C. Sherbrooke, K.B.

	Regiment.	Station.	Officers.	N.C. Officers and Men.				Total of all Ranks.
				Present.	Sick.	Command.	Missing.	
Brigade of Guards. Lt.-Col. Hulse.	1st Batt. Coldstream	Badajoz	24	658	432	35	—	1,149
	1st Batt. 3rd Guards	,,	14	668	411	31	—	1,124
	1 Company 5th Batt. 60th	,,	2	47	12	2	—	63
Brigadier-General Cameron.	2nd Batt. 24th	Lobon	26	401	412	11	4	854
	2nd Batt. 42nd	,,	27	497	213	4	1	742
	1st Batt. 61st	,,	35	466	345	10	7	863
	1 Company 60th Rifles	,,	1	52	12	4	1	70
Brigadier-General Lowe.	5th Batt. K.G.L.	Talavera Real	26	426	268	13	30	763
	7th ,, ,,	,,	21	380	261	25	37	724
	2nd ,, ,,	,,	27	444	262	19	15	767
	1st ,, ,,	,,	29	437	278	9	5	758
	1st and 2nd Light Batts.	,,	7	84	47	5	2	145
	Totals	…	239	4,560	2,953	168	102	8,022

2ND DIVISION.

Lieutenant-General Rowland Hill.

Regiment		Station	Officers	Present	N.C. Officers and Men. Sick	N.C. Officers and Men. Command	N.C. Officers and Men. Missing	Total of all Ranks
	3rd Buffs	Montijo	31	679	230	24	—	964
Major-Gen. Tilson	1st Batt. 31st	,,	25	304	407	24	2	762
	2nd Batt. 48th	,,	30	482	185	16	—	713
	2nd Batt. 66th	,,	27	454	177	20	—	678
	1 Company 60th		1	51	4	2	—	64
Brigadier-General R. Stewart	1st Batt. 29th	Puebla	31	475	304	11	—	821
	1st Batt. 48th	,,	28	640	278	5	—	951
	1st Batt. 57th	,,	30	674	129	10	—	843
Brigadier-General Catlin Crauford	2nd Batt. 28th	Montijo	40	659	176	4	—	879
	2nd Batt. 34th	Torre Mayor	36	795	241	30	6	1,102
	2nd Batt. 39th	,,	38	569	214	4	—	825
Totals		...	317	5,782	2,345	150	8	8,602

3RD DIVISION.—Brigadier-General R. Crauford (temporary).

	Regiment.	Station.	Officers.	Present.	Sick.	Command.	Missing.	Total of all Ranks.
Brigadier-General R. Crauford	1st Batt. 43rd	Campo Mayor	38	892	229	7	10	1,176
	1st Batt. 52nd	,,	39	1,023	121	14	8	1,205
	1st Batt. 95th Rifles	,,	49	935	152	6	18	1,145
Colonel Donkin	1st Batt. 45th	,,	28	584	276	5	71	964
	1st Batt. 88th	,,	39	544	277	2	—	862
	5th Batt. 60th Rifles (5 Coys.)	,,	25	272	41	10	20	368
	Totals	...	218	4,240	1,096	44	122	5,720

4TH DIVISION.—Major-General Hon. G. L. Cole (temporary).

	Regiment.	Station.	Officers.	Present.	Sick.	Command.	Missing.	Total of all Ranks.
Major-General Cole	2nd Batt. 7th	Olivenza	27	491	268	16	—	802
	1st Batt. 11th	,,	37	822	145	13	—	1,017
	2nd Batt. 53rd	,,	23	468	222	9	—	722
	1st Company 60th	,,	1	41	9	2	1	76
Colonel Kemmis	3rd Batt. 27th	Badajoz	31	813	286	2	—	1,132
	1st Batt. 40th	,,	35	807	180	15	—	1,037
	97th	Olivenza	25	381	266	10	20	702
	1 Company 60th	,,	1	41	9	2	9	62
	Totals	...	181	3,882	1,390	67	30	5,550

Grand total of the British Army on the Guadiana, under Lord Wellington's immediate command:—

Officers.	Non-Commissioned Officers and Men.				Total of all Ranks.
	Present.	Sick.	Command.	Missing.	
861	16,914	6,485	1,046	267	25,523

IN THE PENINSULA

The following troops were also in Portugal:—

Regiment.	Station.	Officers.	N.C. Officers and Men.					Horses.			
			Present.	Sick.	Command.	Missing.	Total.	Present.	Sick.	Command.	Total.
Royal Staff Corps ...	Badajoz	5	41	37	12	—	95	—	—	—	—
28rd Light Dragoons ...	Villa Viciosa	22	350	49	23	133	577	223	58	2	283
Major-General ⎱ 2nd Batt. 5th	Abrantes	35	640	117	8	2	802	—	—	—	—
Lightburn ⎰ 2nd Batt. 58th	"	26	505	122	9	—	662	—	—	—	—
Major Gough, 2nd Batt. 87th	Lisbon	40	416	332	30	—	818	—	—	—	—
Major Napier, 2nd Batt. 88rd	"	28	334	467	43	8	880	—	—	—	—
Garrison Company K.G.L.	Santarem	1	23	2	5	—	31	—	—	—	—

Local rank had been granted to Generals Hill and Cotton.

The errors in the compilation of "States" had previously been so glaring—except in the case of the Guards and King's German Legion—as to call forth a severe rebuke from Lord Wellington; and, indeed, for several years afterwards he found difficulty in getting Staff-Officers to make them out correctly.

The two Battalions of Detachments had been recently sent home with a few words of commendation for their gallantry in the field, and of caution, on account of their somewhat predatory instincts.

The state of affairs existing at this period in Spain is pithily described in a private letter written about this time by Lord Wellington. "I feel that Lord Wellesley will not be able to do much with the Spaniards. Their Government is a miserable one, deficient in every quality which a Government ought to possess. Their military establishment is very defective, and they have neither General nor inferior officers of any talents, nor sufficient number of troops; and these last appear to me to be worse as soldiers than their general officers are as generals. The troops have neither arms, clothing, accoutrements, discipline, nor efficiency; there are no magazines, and no means of collecting from the country the supplies which all armies require. There is no plan of a campaign, either for carrying on the war, or for continuing the contest; and the efforts of the rulers appear to be directed in the first instance to keeping their own situations, and in the second to exciting and keeping up in the country a kind of false enthusiasm by which it is supposed that everything can be effected; and they endeavour to effect both these objects by the undertaking of little operations with little means, by the circulation of false intelligence, by the exaggeration of little successes, and the concealment of great disasters. In this consists the secret of the Government.

"As to the enthusiasm about which so much noise has been made even in our own country, I am convinced the world has entirely mistaken its effects. I believe it only creates confusion where order ought to prevail, and disobedience of orders and indiscipline among the troops . . . instead of obedience and discipline; and I fancy that upon reflection, it will be discovered that what was deemed enthusiasm among the French, which enabled them successfully to resist all Europe at the commencement of the Revolution, was force acting through the medium of popular societies and assuming the name of enthusiasm, and that force, in a different shape, has completed the conquest of Europe, and keeps the Continent in subjection. Really, when a Spaniard has cried out 'vivat,' and has put everything in confusion in his district or village, he sits down quietly and thinks he has done his duty till the first French patrol arrives, when he shows his activity by packing up his goods and running away, and there is no authority to set them or keep them right."

"When one Spanish army," says Napier (bk. viii. ch. 5), "was surprised at Arzobispo, another beaten at Almonacid, and Wilson's irregulars were dispersed at Banos, the Junta had just completed the measure of their folly by quarrelling with the British army, the only force left that could protect them. The French were therefore masters of the Peninsula, yet they terminated their operations at the very moment when they should have pursued them with redoubled activity. . . . For Napoleon was victorious in Germany, and of the British expeditions against Italy and Holland, the former had scarcely struggled into life, the latter was already corrupting in death. Joseph was assured he would receive reinforcements, none of any consequence could reach his adversaries; and in the Peninsula there was nothing to oppose him. Navarre, Biscay, Aragon, and the Castilles were subdued, Gerona closely beleaguered, and the rest of Catalonia, if not quiescent, unable at all events to succour that noble city. Valencia was inert, the Asturias still trembling, Galicia was in confusion. Romana commanding 15,000 infantry without cavalry or artillery, was then at Corunna, and dared not quit the mountains. Del Parque held Ciudad Rodrigo, but could not make head against more than a French Division; the battle of Almonacid had cleared La Mancha of troops, Estremadura and Andalusia were weak, distracted, and incapable of solid resistance. There remained only the English and Portuguese armies. . . . In this state the line of resistance may be said to have extended from the Sierra Morena to Corunna—weak from its length, weaker that the Allied corps separated by mountain rivers and vast tracts of country, and having different bases of operation, such as Lisbon, Seville, and Ciudad Rodrigo, could not act in concert except offensively; and with how little effect in that way the campaign of Talavera had proved. The French were concentrated in a narrow space, and having only Madrid to cover were advantageously situated for offensive or defensive movements. The Allied forces were for the most part imperfectly organised, and would not altogether have amounted to 90,000 fighting men. The French were above 100,000, dangerous from their discipline and experience, more dangerous that they held a central position, and their numbers were unknown to their opponents."

The defeat of Del Parque at Alba, and the retreat of Albuquerque from the Tagus—the former exposing Ciudad Rodrigo to the 6th Corps, the latter Estremadura to Joseph—determined Wellington to put into execution a plan which he had long projected, viz., to quit Badajoz, where his troops were suffering terribly from Guadiana fever—9,000 men being in hospital—and leaving one Division on the Tagus, to carry away the remainder of his army to the Mondego, with a view to providing for the more effectual defence of Portugal. He had suggested to the Junta the need of reinforcing Albuquerque with 10,000 men in order to enable that officer to maintain a position on the Meza d'Ibor; but the only reply of the Junta was to order Albuquerque to withdraw to Llerena, beyond the Guadiana. As the Spaniards thus refused to help themselves, Wellington felt that his only course lay in leaving them to their own devices and in confining himself to the primary object of his instructions, viz., the defence of Portugal.

Towards the end of December he set his troops in motion. The 2nd Division, 5,000 strong, under Hill, reinforced by a Portuguese Division of equal strength, was left at Abrantes to guard the Tagus. The remainder of the Infantry and part of the Cavalry were then transferred to the valley of the Mondego; while the rest of the Cavalry was quartered at Santarem, Punhete, &c., for purposes of forage.

Thus passed away the year 1809 which had seen so many momentous events, the balance of advantage in which rested undoubtedly with Napoleon. He had been victorious on the Tagus and on the Danube. He had overthrown Austria. He had all but conquered Spain. It only remained to expel the British from Portugal. In this the chances seemed all in his favour. He had the advantage of position, of numbers, of experience, and last but not least, the sure knowledge that the blunders and weakness of the British Government would infallibly strengthen his cause and thwart the operations of their own General.

PART III

CHAPTER XII

Problem of the defence of Portugal—Measures adopted.

THE problem of the defence of Portugal was one of considerable difficulty. Napoleon's accurate appreciation of the strategical situation had led him from the outset to select for his Army Corps a central position whence, keeping "their masses only on the principal routes, communicating by moveable columns," they "menaced all the important points without scattering their forces." The problem was further complicated by the reinforcements, forming an 8th, 9th, and Guard Corps, which were poured into the Peninsula after the conclusion of peace between France and Austria, and the expectation of the arrival of the Emperor in person, an event which, by putting an end to the jealousies of his Generals, and enabling the tangled threads to be gathered in one powerful hand, would, in all appearance, speedily complete the conquest of Spain and Portugal.

"Portugal," says Napier, "has no defensible frontier. The rivers, generally running east and west, are fordable in most places, subject to sudden rises and falls, offering but weak lines of resistance, and the Zezere excepted, present no obstacles to an enemy on the eastern frontier. The mountains afford many fine and some impregnable positions, but with the length of frontier and difficulty of lateral communications, a general defending it against superior forces would be cut off from the capital if he concentrated his troops; and if he extended them his line would be immediately broken. The possession of Lisbon constitutes the possession of Portugal south of the Douro, and an inferior army can only protect Lisbon by keeping close to it."

The length of the northern frontier of Portugal may be roughly stated at 170 miles: and it was from this side, as we have seen, that Soult had invaded it, but the direction of the rivers—the Douro, Mondego, Zezere, and Tagus—and the general circumstances of the moment, made it probable that the eastern frontier would now be the point of attack, although the particular line of invasion was uncertain. On the right bank of the Coa, the fortress of Almeida guarded the roads leading on Oporto and Lisbon, while in the Alemtejo, Elvas, supported by Campo Mayor, protected the approach to Portalègre and Abrantes. Opposite Elvas on the left bank of the bank of the Guadiana was the Spanish fortress of Badajoz, and on the more northerly line Ciudad Rodrigo, in Spanish territory twenty miles east of Almeida, formed a pendant to it. Thus whether the line of French invasion were to run by the north of Beira or by the Alemtejo, the reduction of a double line of fortresses would be an indispensable preliminary. Midway between Ciudad Rodrigo and Badajoz lay the town of Coria, astride a main road leading to Lisbon by Castello Branco. An army assembling at Coria would only be two long marches distant from one at Rodrigo, and being connected with it by the Pass of Perales, combined action would be almost ensured; but the roads leading from Castello Branco across the Sobreira Formosa were impracticable, even at their best, for any but the lightest artillery. The capture of Ciudad Rodrigo would give the invader the choice of two main roads—one by Almeida, Celorico, and the valley of the Mondego, the other by Sabugal and the valley of the Zezere—besides several which would be better described as tracks. On the other hand, an advance through the Alemtejo—after the fall of Badajoz and Elvas—would be facilitated by the fact that between June and December the Tagus is fordable as low down as Salvatierra.

The total length of the eastern frontier is about 400 miles. Presenting as it did few natural or artificial obstacles, Wellington's policy was to hold it with merely an outpost line while retaining the main body of his troops massed in central positions in rear, with the double object of being able to reinforce his outposts, or, if attacked by overwhelming numbers, to retire concentrically upon the entrenched camp covering Lisbon, whence he felt confident of being able in the last extremity to embark his army, and either return to England or renew the contest with Cadiz for his base, as circumstances might direct.

The forces at Wellington's disposal consisted nominally of about 35,000 British—in which are reckoned K.G.L.—troops, nearly the same number of Portuguese regulars, of whom 4,000 were Cavalry, and 3,500 Artillery, and 25,000 Portuguese Militia. From these numbers, however, large deductions must be made for non-effectives. There were in addition the Ordenanças—a kind of local Militia, who by degrees reached a nominal total of 300,000; but, being armed mostly with pikes and untrained, could hardly be reckoned on as effective in the general scheme of defence. The Portuguese troops of the line had however by this time greatly improved

IN THE PENINSULA 255

under Beresford's iron discipline. The Infantry was brigaded as follows :—

Regiment	Approximate Numbers	Commander	Notes
4th Regiment	1,544	Brigadier: Colonel Campbell	
10th ,,	1,449		
1st ,,	1,356		
16th ,,	1,515		
6th ,,		Brigdr.-Gen. Campbell	With the Army of Beira.
18th ,,			
11th ,,	1,535	,, ,, Coleman	
23rd ,,			
12th ,,		,, ,, Cox	At Almeida. Not clothed.
24th ,,			
9th ,,		Colonel Champlemond	
21st ,,			
3rd ,,	857		
15th ,,	1,128		
2nd ,,	1,355		
14th ,,	1,252		
13th ,,			With Gen. Hill.
20th ,,	1,300		
5th Caçadores			
7th ,,			
19th ,,			
8th ,,			Not ready to take the field. Unarmed.
22nd ,,			
5th ,,			At Elvas.
17th ,,			
1st ,,	627	Baron Eben	
2nd ,,			
4th ,,	624	Baron Leires	
6th ,,			
3rd ,,	589	Lieut.-Col. Elder	

The Portuguese Cavalry was organised in 4 Brigades, but was less advanced than the Infantry ; and both were deficient in equipment. The Artillery consisted of 8 Batteries in pretty good order.

The Militia was ill armed and equipped, but had shown improvement.

256 WELLINGTON'S OPERATIONS

As the spring wore on the numbers and efficiency increased, for Wellington insisted on reviving the ancient military organisation of Portugal. Each province had its own Militia and Ordenanças, and in April, 1810, the returns showed 412,000 available for military service. Of these, however, 77,000 were unarmed, and 219,000 furnished with pikes only. Of the remainder, 105,000 were Fusiliers, 3,700 Cavalry; but large numbers were absent, and the consequent accession of strength was rather apparent than real.

The British Army rapidly improved in health after leaving the Guadiana, but in April had still 6,000 men in hospital.

The deficiency of general officers was a source of annoyance to Wellington. "Never was an army so ill provided," wrote he to Lord Liverpool. Sir John Sherbrooke's health had broken down. In his place Wellington asked for Generals Graham, Oakes, or Sir George Provost, as being senior to General Payne; or for Lord William Bentinck, Edward Paget, or Sir Brent Spencer, in the event of Payne's recall. To command Brigades he desired Generals Dyott, Leith, Picton, Meade, Houston and Nightingall.

William Stewart and Picton were already on the way with reinforcements. Graham was sent out; but in the first instance went to Cadiz. Oakes being at Malta and Provost at Halifax were not considered available. Spencer came out a little later, but proved no great acquisition. Paget was stopped by the state of his health. Bentinck declined. Nightingall was unwell and Meade otherwise employed.

The British Army was massed in two Army Corps. One, under General Hill, consisting of the newly arrived 13th Dragoons, Slade's Cavalry Brigade, Seddon's and Madden's Portuguese Brigades, the 2nd British Infantry

Division, two Portuguese Brigades, a British and two Portuguese Batteries, occupied Portalègre, Abrantes, and Santarem with a view to resisting an attack along the line of the Tagus. The other Corps, under Wellington's personal command, comprised two Cavalry Brigades posted in the valley of the Mondego, the 1st Division (with Headquarters) at Viseu, the 3rd Division at Celorico, the 4th at Guarda, and the Light at Pinhel.

Of the Portuguese, three or four regiments were in garrison. The main body—to the number of about 17,000—was concentrated about Thomar, whence in case of retreat it could join either Hill or Wellington within two or three days.

The provinces of Minho and Tras os Montes were occupied by General Bacellar with twenty-one regiments of Militia. The lines of the Ponsul and Elga were held by a Portuguese regiment of Cavalry, ten regiments of Militia and the Lusitanian Legion. Seven regiments of Militia were in the Alemtejo and Algarves. Four regiments of the Line, aided by Militia, garrisoned the fortresses of Valenca on the Minho, Almeida, and Elvas; and those in the second line, Abrantes, Setuval, and Peniché. Twelve Militia regiments formed a reserve in Portuguese Estremadura on either bank of the Tagus. "Thus," observes Napier, "the wings of the defence were composed solely of Militia and Ordenanzas, and the whole of the regular force was in the centre."

The roads calculated to assist the advance of the invader were either destroyed or left unrepaired. Those which aided the defence were put in good order. Flying bridges were thrown across the Zezere and Tagus, and a communication established between Abrantes and Castello Branco viâ Villa Velha by a road on the left bank of the Tagus; the consequence being that should the enemy from Coria drive back the Militia on the Elga, Hill could concentrate on Castello Branco, and be joined there by Beresford from Thomar after crossing the Sobreira Formosa.

The power of the enemy to advance from the Alemtejo and crush Hill with superior numbers before Wellington could arrive from the north, made it impossible to defend the frontier. The system of defence was therefore confined to the following objects: First, to force the enemy to show his strength and advance in mass. Secondly, to gain time for the concentration of the whole Anglo-Portuguese army for the defence of the point attacked. But even in the latter case it was Wellington's intention to retire gradually upon his position at Torres Vedras, avoiding pitched battles. And in order to gain the full advantage of the situation he desired the Portuguese Government to order the people "to destroy their mills, remove their boats, break down their bridges, lay waste their fields, abandon their dwellings, and carry their property away from the line of invasion" and thus cut off from the enemy—who would be moving in large masses—all the resources of the country.

For the supply of Hill's Corps depôts were established at Belem and Abrantes; for Wellington's, at Figueras (at the mouth of the Mondego), and at Pena Cova, ten miles above Coimbra. Expense magazines were formed at Almeida, Viseu, Celorico, &c. The troops beyond the Douro were supplied from Oporto and Lamego. Lisbon was the base of operations, but as food stuffs were scarce in Portugal the country was to all intents and purposes dependent on England for its provisions.

CHAPTER XIII

Measures adopted for the defence of Portugal (*continued*)—Preparation of the Lines of Torres Vedras—Crauford commands the Light Division—Masséna—Fall of Ciudad Rodrigo—Fight on the Coa.

IT must not be supposed that the arrangements detailed in the last chapter were completed in a day. On the contrary, months were spent in gradual improvement; in drilling, arming and equipping, not only the Portuguese Militia, but even the Regular Forces, and it was not until the summer of 1810 that any degree of perfection was attained. Had the British financial assistance been judiciously applied, the position could have been considerably strengthened by equipping the population of the neighbouring Spanish provinces and thus—to use Wellington's expression—"putting the whole of Galicia and Leon in movement upon the enemy's back," but England was by this time becoming impoverished by her wastefulness; the British Commander was stinted of money, and it became doubtful whether the Portuguese Government would be able to find subsistence for the Militia, through lack of the supplies which had been promised by England but were not forthcoming.

At the end of January Wellington quitted the army for the purpose of inspecting the positions at Torres Vedras, leaving Sir John Sherbrooke in command of the left wing —or in modern parlance, "Army Corps"—occupying

Northern Beira. For Sir John's guidance he left a Memorandum stating the objects of the present position of the Army (Despatches, vol. v., Viseu, January 31, 1810). The objects were—(1) To defend the entrance of Portugal at the probable point of attack. (2) To enable it to act, if practicable, on the offensive with a view to the relief of Ciudad Rodrigo, should that fortress be attacked. (3) To invade Castille as a diversion for the Allies if such an operation could be attempted without risk. " The 3rd Division," continued the Memorandum, " at Pinhel, occupies the lower part of the Coa, and the Cavalry have posts of observation even upon the Agueda. The 4th Division has a post at the bridge of Castello Bom, at Ponte de Sequeiros, and at Rapoula de Coa, the principal passages over the Upper Coa.

" This position is perfectly secure from surprise, more particularly as General Cole has been directed to have another post of observation at Alfayetes; the Duque del Parque's army, which was in the Sierra de Gata, being ordered to cross the Tagus into Estremadura.

" It is desirable that we should not lose possession of the Coa, particularly to a small corps; but as I have no intention to maintain the possession of the Coa if the enemy should collect a large army in that quarter, General Cole and General Crauford will retire with their divisions and the hussars, &c., if they should find that the enemy has collected a large army, and cross the Mondego to Celorico.

" When the enemy shall begin to collect for this operation, General Sherbrooke will cross the Mondego by Ponte de Fiæs; the troops at Mangualde by Ponte de Palheiros, and the whole will proceed to Pinhanços, which is six leagues in rear of Celorico.

" If the enemy should continue to advance General Cole and General Crauford will retire gradually by the valley of the Mondego, as will General Sherbrooke, till the whole shall assemble at Ponte da Murcella, holding the height of Moita as an advanced post. . . . "

Wellington's visit to Torres Vedras proved satisfactory. The field fortifications were making progress under the able superintendence of Colonel Fletcher. Feeling as he did that in order to carry out his plans successfully it was essential that the works should proceed with the utmost secrecy, the British Commander never alluded to them in his correspondence; and in fact, the secret of his views and intentions in regard to them was shared only by himself and Fletcher. His absence from the army was brief. By the 18th February he was back again at Viseu watching the French, whose position daily became more and more threatening.

When the British Army had broken up its quarters on the Guadiana, and (in the month of January, 1810) had taken up its new position in the north of Beira, to General Crauford—then in command of the 3rd Division *vice* Mackenzie, killed at Talavera—was assigned the advanced post of honour. He took up the line of the Coa, with his Rifle Battalion pushed forward to the junction of the Aguedo and Douro, the enemy's outposts being on the further bank of the former river. On the 22nd of February Major-General Picton arrived, and the 3rd Division, organised afresh, was handed over to that officer; but Crauford, with his own Light Brigade and another made up of two Portuguese Light Infantry Battalions—the two Brigades forming what was henceforward called "the Light Division"—still continued in command of the outposts, the right of his line being supported by the 4th Division under Cole at Guarda—an important junction of roads—and his left by Picton at Pinhel. A regiment of K.G.L. Hussars and a battery of

R.H.A. were added to Crauford's command. The 1st Division remained in reserve about Viseu. The Cavalry Brigades were écheloned along the Tagus between Abrantes and Santarem for convenience of forage and stabling.

Lieut.-Col. J. Wilson with a few Militia battalions occupied Castello Branco and the mountains between the Tagus and the Mondego. His orders were to destroy the Estrada Nova road—thus closing a line of approach to the French—and, if attacked by overwhelming numbers, to retire (disputing every inch of ground) upon the Zezere, where he would be supported by Colonel Le Cor with the 13th Portuguese regiment and three Militia battalions.

Hill, as already mentioned, was at Abrantes with three Brigades of Cavalry and two Infantry Divisions. In the middle of February he was directed to advance with his Infantry and guns to Portalégre—a place well supplied with provisions—in order to check the enemy's movements against the Portuguese frontier south of the Tagus—movements which, from force of circumstances and the general direction of the French lines of communication, would necessarily be confined to the district between Campo Mayor and Portalégre.

The following table gives the numbers of the British troops in March, 1810 :—

CAVALRY DIVISION.
Lieutenant-General Payne.

		Effective British Rank and File.
Colonel de Grey	{ 3rd Dragoon Guards	414
	{ 4th Dragoons	443
Major-General Slade	{ Royal Dragoons	567
	{ 14th Light Dragoons	477
Brigadier-General Anson	{ 16th ,, ,,	512
	{ 1st ,, ,, K.G.L.	342
		2,755

IN THE PENINSULA 263

		Effective British Rank and File.
	1ST INFANTRY DIVISION. Lieutenant-General Sherbrooke.	
Colonel Hon. E. Stopford	{ 1st Batt. Coldstream Guards 1st Batt. 3rd Guards 1 Company 60th Rifles	537 655 47
Lord Blantyre	{ 2nd Batt. 24th 2nd Batt. 42nd 1st Batt. 61st 1 Company 60th	242 275 654 47
Brigadier-General Lowe	{ 5th Line Batt. K.G.L. 7th „ „ „ 2nd „ „ „ 1st „ „ „ 1st and 2nd Lt. Batts. K.G.L.	384 339 385 392 66
		4,023
	2ND DIVISION. Lieutenant-General R. Hill.	
Major-Gen. Hon. W. Stewart	{ "The Buffs" 2nd Batt. 31st 2nd Batt. 48th 2nd Batt. 66th 1 Company 60th	665 343 460 387 47
Major-General Houghton	{ 1st Batt. 29th 1st Batt. 48th 1st Batt. 57th 1 Company 60th	384 453 881 47
Brigdr.-Gen. Hon. W. Lumley	{ 2nd Batt. 28th 2nd Batt. 34th 2nd Batt. 39th 1 Company 60th	482 528 405 47
		5,129
	3RD DIVISION. Major-General Picton.	
Colonel Mackinnon	{ 1st Batt. 45th 1st Batt. 74th 1st Batt. 88th	550 637 527
Major-Gen. Hon. C. Colville	{ 2nd Batt. 5th 2nd Batt. 58th 5th Batt. 60th (3 companies)	508 337 141
Colonel Champlemond	{ 9th Portuguese Regiment 21st „ „	
		2,700

4TH DIVISION.

Major-General Hon. G. L. Cole.

		Effective British Rank and File.
Colonel Kemmis	3rd Batt. 27th	813
	1st Batt. 97th	344
	1st Batt. 40th	909
	1 Company 60th	47
Brigadier-General A. Campbell	2nd Batt. 7th Fusiliers	336
	1st Batt. 11th	896
	2nd Batt. 53rd	353
	1 Company 60th	47
	3rd Portuguese Regiment	
	15th ,, ,,	
		3,745

LIGHT DIVISION.

Brigadier-General R. Crauford.

Brigadier-General Drummond	1st Batt. 43rd	791
	1st Batt. 52nd	895
	1st Batt 95th Rifles	813
		2,499
Colonel Baron Eben	1st Portuguese Caçadores	
	2nd ,, ,,	
	Royal Staff Corps	39
	2nd Batt. 83rd	451
	Garrison Co. K.G.L.	21

Effective Rank and File of British Cavalry 2,755
"   "   "   " Infantry 18,607

Early in April, Colonel Peacocke, commandant at the base of operations, reported the arrival at Lisbon of the 3rd Battalion the Royals, the 1st Battalion 9th and 2nd Battalion 38th Regiments, under Major-General Leith. By the addition of a Portuguese Brigade to these troops a 5th Division was formed. Command was assumed by Leith, and the Division was posted on the

IN THE PENINSULA 265

Zezere at first behind Guarda, and later on between Thomar and Abrantes, where it formed part of Hill's Corps, and was intended to keep open the connection between that officer and Wellington, or cover the right flank and communicate with Romana as circumstances might dictate.

The Anglo-Portuguese force was thus divided into two Army Corps. The Northern, under Wellington's personal command, composed of the 1st, 3rd, 4th, and Light Divisions, as well as the Cavalry Division which had now been brought up to the valley of the Mondego; the Southern, under Hill, made up of the 2nd and 5th Divisions, the 13th Light Dragoons, a Brigade of Portuguese Cavalry, three regiments of Portuguese Infantry, and three battalions of Militia. Although separated by the Estrella mountains, the two Army Corps were connected by the new "Military Road" (which was made to run from Corticada to Espinal, whence it branched off to Coimbra or Puente de Murcella), and could thus act on interior lines in regard to an enemy's force operating by the double line of the Mondego and Tagus.

The health of the army, which had been much affected by Guadiana fever, was now fast improving. By the end of April Wellington had upwards of 30,000 British, and a still larger number of Portuguese regular troops fit for duty. Unfortunately, Sir John Sherbrooke was now compelled by ill-health to return to England, and was succeeded as second in command by Sir Brent Spencer, while a little later on General Payne was recalled and was replaced in command of the Cavalry Division by General Cotton.

A detailed account of the strategical situation will be found in "Wellington's Memorandum of Operations," Des., vol. vii. The invasion of Andalusia by King Joseph in January, 1810, was only a portion of a great movement intended to make the weight of the French arms felt throughout the Peninsula. On the eastern side of Spain the operations were foiled by circumstances, and the 1st Army Corps was checked before Cadiz. Mortier, however, as we have seen, threatened Badajoz in February with the 5th Corps, supported by the 2nd, which had advanced by the right bank of the Guadiana to Montego, and drew Hill from Abrantes to Portalégre. Ney, who had by this time returned to the 6th Corps, simultaneously menaced Ciudad Rodrigo; and Bonet, with a detached Division of the 2nd Corps, Galicia. The bulk of the 2nd Corps being at Plasencia, Wellington was thus threatened from three quarters at the same time, and liable to be attacked in detail; for, through the neglect of the Portuguese Government, the roads forming his lateral communications were then out of repair and incomplete. At the critical moment, however, Ney and Junot failed to co-operate, and the Duque del Parque, crossing the Sierra de Gata, diverted Mermet's attention. The danger then died away, and in April Wellington contemplated assuming the offensive by striking a sudden blow at the enemy's magazines at Salamanca. With this object the troops were pushed forward. Headquarters were established on the 27th at Celorico; the 3rd and 4th Divisions were at Pinhel and Guarda, while the Light Division moved to the Agueda. At the same time Hill quitted Portalégre and took post at Castello Branco to connect with Wellington. It was, however, soon found that the enemy was too strong. Astorga had been taken on the 22nd by Junot, whose Corps—the 8th—was now free to act in concert with that of Ney, the two Generals being in addition supported by the troops of Kellermann's government at Valladolid. Wellington therefore found it necessary to abandon his daring enterprise.

IN THE PENINSULA 267

Up to this period it had been expected, both at the French and British headquarters, that Napoleon would at any moment arrive in person to complete the conquest of the Peninsula. But news now arrived that the Emperor, occupied with the enforcement of the "Continental System" in Holland and Germany, had found it impossible to take the field, but had deputed Marshal Masséna, Prince of Essling, the most distinguished of all his lieutenants, to command the army detailed for the invasion of Portugal. But before he could arrive Ney and Junot had advanced in force. On the 1st of June their two Corps, with Montbrun's Reserve Cavalry—the combined force being 54,500 strong—concentrated on the Agueda, constructed two bridges, and a week later pushed a Cavalry Division across the river. On the 22nd the arrival of the heavy artillery enabled the French commanders to begin the siege of Ciudad Rodrigo in earnest. Ney invested the fortress; Junot formed a covering force along the Lower Agueda. Rivalry between the two did not further their plans, but on the 27th both were placed in a subordinate position by the arrival of Masséna, who came armed with the Emperor's authority to take command of the "Army of Portugal," composed of the 6th and 8th Army Corps, to which shortly afterwards was added the 2nd. The troops occupying the "Northern Governments" of Spain, comprising Salamanca, Valladolid, Astorga, Asturias, and Santander, and the resources of those provinces were equally placed at Masséna's disposal. With the Prince of Essling came General Fririon as Chief of the Staff, and General Eblé as C.R.A.

The strength of the Army of Portugal at this period was as follows (extracted from Napier's "Peninsular War," vol. ii., Appendix 17):—

STATE OF THE ARMY OF PORTUGAL.

April 10, 1810. Headquarters, Caceres.

	Under Arms.		Detached.		Hospital.	Prisoners.	*Effective.	Horses.	
	Men.	Horses.	Men.	Horses.	Men.	Men.	Men.	Cavalry.	Draught.
2nd Army Corps, General Reynier	18,372	4,449	1,119	132	1,628	7	21,126	3,520	1,061
6th ,, ,, Marshal Ney ...	33,759	10,159	496	110	5,086	349	39,690	7,140	3,129
8th ,, ,, General Junot...	28,045	7,070	25		5,976	99	34,145	5,312	1,758
Total of active army	80,176	21,678	1,640	242	12,690	455	94,961	15,792	5,948
Imperial Guards	17,380	3,800	174	15	733	377	18,287	2,831	984
Province of Santander	13,464	752	276		1,774		15,891	752	
,, Valladolid	4,509	124	123		859	145	5,636		124
Total under Masséna's command	115,529	26,354	2,213	257	16,056	977	134,775	19,555	7,056

* It will be noticed that in the French Army the term " effective " includes every man borne on the strength of the Corps whether present or absent.

IN THE PENINSULA

The strength of the whole of the French forces in the Peninsula on the 15th of July was:—

	Under Arms.		Detached.		Absent.		Effective.
	Men.	Horses.	Men.	Horses.	Hospital.	Prisoners.	Men.
In Spain	273,408	52,336	29,462	7,846	47,107	4,915	349,072
On the march to join...	6,121	736			636		6,757
Grand total... ...	279,524	53,072	29,462	7,846	47,743	4,915	356,729

On the approach of the enemy in force Wellington recalled sixteen Militia battalions from Braganza to the Lower Douro; and Crauford, who was lining the Agueda with his Cavalry, from Escalhon to Novas Frias, concentrated his Division at Gallegos and Espeja, having his right flank strengthened by a Spanish Division under General Carrera, who had come up from Perales. He was anxious to supply the garrison of Ciudad Rodrigo with ammunition, but for such an operation Wellington declined to quit his mountain strongholds and risk an action in the plain with an army inferior in numbers, weaker still in discipline, and weakest of all in Cavalry. As it was, Crauford's position in the plains, among woods which afforded no extended view to the front, and confronted by a vast force of Cavalry, was more than critical. Nevertheless, videttes were still pushed forward beyond the Azava, and Crauford maintained a bold front, encouraging the besieged garrison, and cleverly securing for his troops the supplies of the low lands.

General Crauford, the hero of the present operations, was a remarkable man, but one in whose character the good and bad points were so closely interwoven that he was constantly knocking down with one hand what he had laboriously and successfully built up with the other. He fed and flogged his men with equal zeal, yet in the retreat to Corunna the number of stragglers whom he lost from his Brigade was enormous, showing that he did not understand the highest form of discipline. In figure Crauford was a little fat man; in temperament, overflowing with energy, but cursed with an uncontrollable temper. "A gloomy, dissatisfied man," is Wellington's description of him. And his soured nature led him to combine with Sir Charles Stewart and other Generals to intrigue against his Commander. "At one time," says Sir Charles Napier, "all fire and intelligence, a master spirit in war; at another, as if possessed by the demon, he would rush madly from one blunder to another." His Division was in first-rate order, yet he owed more to it than it to him.

IN THE PENINSULA

Unlike many of his colleagues, however, Crauford had deeply studied his profession. He had served with the Russians against Masséna in Switzerland. He thoroughly understood the theory and practice of outpost duty, and it was partly on this account, partly on account of the excellence of his troops, that Wellington selected him for his present position; but when it came to actual fighting, Crauford was apt to lose his head. His status was rather a curious one. He was only a Colonel in the army, yet he was placed in command of a Division, in spite of the fact that several Major-Generals were only commanding Brigades—a sure proof of his reputation. He was by some years older than Wellington, and possibly a little jealous of him in consequence. Anyhow, his habit of doing a brilliant action one day, and risking his whole Division the next, must have made him a constant source of anxiety to his Commander; and to any one of less character than Moore or Wellington he would have been quite impossible as a subordinate. For obedience to orders he had little regard, in spite of the fact that through disobedience, whether intentional or not, he had lost the whole of his Brigade at Buenos Ayres in 1807.

Of the Division which Crauford commanded it is unnecessary to say more than that it has always been regarded as an ideal for the British Army; and in the Peninsula was commonly known as "*The* Division." The perfect training of the 43rd, 52nd, and 95th by Sir John Moore at Shorncliffe, had brought out the talents of a great number of their officers. These regiments were in consequence always admirably commanded, and time after time the ability of the commanding officers retrieved the errors of their present General. It was undoubtedly to Moore that these regiments owed their excellence, and it is with him and Crauford that they are chiefly associated;

but it seems to have escaped notice that it was under Wellington himself, in Denmark, that they were first brigaded together on active service.

Ciudad Rodrigo had not been expected to hold out for forty-eight hours after the arrival of the enemy's siege train. Herrasti made, however, a gallant defence, and sent repeated entreaties to Wellington for the succour which the British Commander—to his deep regret—was unable to give. General Crauford, reinforced by two squadrons of the 16th Light Dragoons, took up towards the end of June the line of the Azava river, occupying it with Cavalry and Infantry picquets from its junction with the Agueda on the left, up to Carpio on the right, with his supports posted about Gallegos, two miles in rear. A squadron of Hussars occupied Barba del Puerco, near the Douro, as a detached post. At the end of June the French Infantry advanced to the Azava. Leaving at Gallegos his three squadrons and two guns of R.H.A. in support of the outposts on that river, Crauford then retired his Infantry two miles further back to the wood of Alameda, whence his retreat across the Coa was secured either by the bridge of Almeida, or that of Castello Bom. Marching and countermarching his Division in such a way as to make the greatest possible show, the General for a time deceived the enemy as to his numbers. On the 4th of July, however, half an hour before daybreak, the picquet at Marialva was attacked and driven in so quickly by the enemy's Cavalry that friend and foe galloped into Gallegos together. With a squadron of Hussars, supported by the guns and 16th, the German Captain Kraüchenburg opposed a firm front to no less than four French regiments—in fact a Cavalry Division— and manœuvred so ably that he not only gained time for the other picquets to come in, and for Crauford to retire to the village of Alameda, but by a timely and well-

executed charge through the standing wheat as the
enemy debouched from the defile of a bridge over a
brook, drove back his advanced files in confusion—a
very pretty piece of outpost duty, giving proof of
Kraüchenburg's capacity in the higher duties of a
cavalry officer, a capacity not generally shared by his
British colleagues! The French then forded the stream
higher up, and a squadron penetrated to Alameda, where
it found Crauford drawn up in position, but being stopped
by his fire, retired to Gallegos.

Crauford then withdrew to Fort Conception, covered
by his Cavalry—now reinforced by the 14th L.D.—whose
outpost line extended along the Duas Casas river from
Fuentes d'Onoro on the right to Aldea del Bispo on the left.

Ciudad Rodrigo was now in extremis. It had been
gallantly defended. The British Army had come to the
Mondego for the express purpose of preventing its capture,
and its fall would bring a torrent of abuse from the
Spaniards upon the head of the British Commander.
Influenced by these considerations a weaker general
would probably have marched to the relief of the fortress
and, in view of the disparity of force, might have lost
half of his army to no purpose in the attempt. But
Wellington was essentially a strong man. His object
was the defence of Portugal as a whole. It was necessary therefore to subordinate everything to that end; and
although the fall of Ciudad Rodrigo would be a severe
blow, it would involve the failure of only one of his many
resources for resisting the French arms. Therefore,
although he watched keenly for any opportunity that
might enable him to strike a blow at the besieging army,
yet in the absence of such opportunity, he retained his
troops in the hill country and resolutely declined to
hazard any portion in an encounter against overwhelming
numbers in the plains.

Lord Wellington's views are clearly expressed in a letter written shortly afterwards to one of his brothers. "During the siege of Ciudad Rodrigo," he says, "the enemy having the 2nd Corps in Estremadura, from whence they could with ease have cut me from Lisbon, I was obliged to keep a corps of from 12,000 to 15,000 men in Alemtejo to watch their movements; and another body of from 3,000 to 4,000 men of the Portuguese Army, being ill disciplined and equipped, were posted in the rear of our right, as the only means of making them useful, and as a further security to that important point. We were then reduced to an army of about 32,000 men to raise the siege or relieve a place attacked by 57,000, of which 9,000 were Cavalry, and supported on their right and in their rear by the troops under Kellermann and Seras. To this add that half these troops of ours were Portuguese new troops; that we must have advanced over a plain against the enemy's superior Cavalry; and if defeated we should have had to cross the Coa in front of a victorious army, and should probably have been destroyed. I considered the relief of Ciudad Rodrigo to be so important, that I wished to undertake it notwithstanding these disadvantages, and I proposed to the Marques de la Romana that he should protect my right while I should collect the troops from the Alemtejo for the purpose; but anxious as he was that Ciudad Rodrigo should be relieved, he declared positively that he could not maintain his position if General Hill were withdrawn, as long as the 2nd Corps should remain in Estremadura. . . . Although it was most important that this place (Rodrigo) should hold out and that I knew it would not hold out a day unless they had hopes of assistance from me, I uniformly told the governor that whether I could relieve him or not must depend upon the force with which he should be attacked, and upon other circumstances."

IN THE PENINSULA 275

The reader may recall a parallel case in the late war. But the officer commanding the relief force was subjected to gross abuse for laying the situation before higher authority. On the 10th of July Ciudad Rodrigo capitulated. Although, except for an insignificant demonstration from Galicia, the Spaniards had done nothing whatever to relieve or aid Wellington in relieving the fortress, Carrera, in deep anger, separated his Division from the British Army and marched to join Romana on the Guadiana. Crauford, however, still maintained his position, and on the 11th allured a foraging party of the enemy into an ambuscade. Two hundred of the French Infantry were surrounded. Their surrender appeared inevitable. But Crauford seems at times to have had a positive genius for mishandling men under fire. Instead of displaying his nine companies of Riflemen and 52nd, he kept them concealed while he ordered his Cavalry to attack. The squadrons, cooped up behind a wall with only one narrow outlet, were necessarily slow in forming; and the French officer in command — Captain Gouache — had time to gain the crest of a hill and form square. Our Cavalry charged "in a scrambling manner." A squadron of the K.G.L. Hussars received the enemy's fire; 13 horses were killed, 13 men wounded. The remainder, opening out from the centre, passed the square on either side and, continuing their course, captured a troop of the enemy. The French Infantry being unloaded, now was the time for the supporting squadrons of the 16th to charge in their turn. But orders had been given them to prolong the left of the Hussars, and they consequently galloped past the enemy, leaving him on their right. Then a squadron of the 14th charged home, but the French having by this time had time to re-load, were perfectly steady, killed with their volley eight of the

14th, wounded ten others, repelled the remainder and made good their retreat.

The affair was a trifling one, but interesting as showing that Wellington was by no means exempt from the worries of more modern commanders. Some reflections were made by irresponsible persons upon the conduct of the 16th; whereupon Wellington wrote on the subject to Crauford, pointed out how groundless were the imputations, and then, with the dry humour of which other traces are to be found in his writings, continued, "All this would not much signify if our Staff and other officers would mind their business instead of writing news and keeping coffee-houses. But as soon as an accident happens every man who can write and who has a friend who can read, sits down to write his account of what he does not know, and his comments on what he does not understand." Then, with renewed earnestness, he points the moral as true now as then. "The consequence is that officers and whole regiments lose their reputation . . . and there is no character, however meritorious, and no action, however glorious, which can have justice done to it."

For a few days longer Crauford held his ground, but on the 21st blew up Fort Conception and fell back before the enemy's Cavalry to Almeida, but halted on the right bank of the Coa. He had admirably maintained his outpost line for three months, but in the face of 60,000 men, common prudence should have made him place the rocky stream and steep banks of the Coa between his Division and the enemy. Wellington had given him distinct orders not to fight on the right bank. Possibly Crauford did not intend to disobey, but expected to have time to make good his retreat at the last moment; but even so, to retire across a defile in presence of the enemy is a most dangerous operation; and the French are apt to strike hard and

IN THE PENINSULA 277

rapidly. More probably he was burning to show what his Division could do, for hitherto it had not been seriously engaged. Anyhow, at dawn on the 24th, after a night spent in unsheltered bivouacs amid the drenching rain of thunderstorms, Ney's Corps, 30,000 strong with 30 guns, covering the whole width of the plain, suddenly made its appearance. To this enormous force Crauford could oppose only 8 squadrons of Cavalry, 5 battalions of Infantry, and a battery R.H.A., something over 5,000 men of all ranks and 6 guns. Yet such was his overconfidence that he still delayed his retreat; and, in the face of the most elementary rules of war, determined to accept battle in front of the narrow defile of a bridge by which alone he could escape destruction. Faulty tactical dispositions added to the peril of the situation, and the inevitable outcome must have been foreseen by every soldier present expect the General. The Light Division was forced over the bridge. At the critical moment Crauford lost his head, and that his troops made good their retreat at all was due solely to the ability of the regimental officers. Even their efforts would have been in vain had it not been that Montbrun, who was not under Ney's immediate command, refused to comply with the Marshal's desire that he should advance with his Cavalry and cut the British Infantry from the bridge. Having then its line of retreat still intact, the Light Division fell back step by step, and while some crossed the bridge, others covered their passage. At one moment the bridge got choked, but a counter attack (at the instance of Captain William Napier, though he gives the credit to Major Macleod) by some companies of the 43rd, drove back the enemy and saved the situation. The rearguard then crossed the bridge. On the left bank of the Coa, posted on high rocks commanding the defile, the Division held its ground and repulsed repeated attempts of the enemy to dislodge it. Yet the peril was still imminent. The bridge of Castello Bom, seven miles up the river, afforded a passage by which Junot might co-operate with Ney by turning Crauford's right. Picton* came up, and Crauford, without actually begging for his assistance, asked if Picton proposed to bring up the 3rd Division. It is unfortunately a sort of tradition in our army that Generals of Division if left to themselves will not act in harmony. In the present case Crauford and Picton had recently had a dispute. Possibly Picton did not realise the peril of the situation. Possibly he felt that his Division, eight miles distant, could not arrive in time to be of use. At all events, without assigning any reason, he curtly replied to Crauford's question by saying he "should do no such thing," and went away. Picton's version of the incident is not known, but on the *prima facie* evidence before us he is decidedly open to censure.

At about 4 p.m. the conflict ceased. Crauford's mercurial temperament then led him from the height of over-confidence to the depth of despondency; and abandoning the Cabeça Negro mountain, a most important position to Wellington, commanding as it did the valley of the Coa, he retired during the night behind the Pinhel river.

"A fierce and obstinate combat for existence with the Light Division," is the comment of Sir Charles Napier who was present at the action, "and only Moore's regiments could with so little experience have extricated themselves from the danger, and Crauford's demon of folly was strong that day; Moore's matchless discipline was their protection—a phantom from Corunna saved them."

Sir Charles adds : 1. " He "—Crauford—" fought know-

* Picton's appearance on the scene is denied by some, but the balance of evidence seems to show that he did come.

ing he must retreat from an overwhelming force and having no object in fighting."

2. "He occupied a position a mile in front of a bridge, thus voluntarily imposing upon himself the most difficult operation in war, viz., passing a defile in face of a superior enemy and in the confusion of a retreat. The result might have been destruction. . . ."

3. "He sent no guns over to defend the passage and cover the retreat till after the troops had commenced retiring. . . ."

4. "When the passage of the bridge was made he left no men to defend it."

5. "Nothing but the excellence of his men and officers saved the Division."

Crauford's escapade gave the greatest annoyance to Wellington. "Although," says the latter in a letter to his brother, Wellesley Pole, "I shall be hanged for them, you may be very certain that not only I have had nothing to do with but had positively forbidden, the foolish affairs in which Crauford involved his outposts. . . . In respect to the last, that of the 24th, I had positively desired him not to engage in any affair on the other side of the Coa; and as soon as La Concepcion was blown up on the 21st, I had expressed my wish that he should withdraw his Infantry to the left of the river; and I repeated my injunction that he should not engage in any affair on the right of the river, in answer to a letter in which he told me he thought the Cavalry could not remain there without the Infantry. After all this he remained above two hours on his ground after the enemy appeared in his front before they attacked him, during which time he might have retired across the Coa twice over, where he would have been in a situation in which he could not have been attacked." Then, showing the proud spirit of the man which scorned to shelter itself behind a subordinate, Wellington continues: "You will say, if this be the case, why not accuse Crauford? I answer, because, if I am to be hanged for it, I cannot accuse a man who I believe has meant well, and whose error is one of judgment and not of intention; and indeed I must add that although my errors, and those of others also, are visited heavily on me, that is not the way in which any, much less a British army, can be commanded."

It is open to doubt whether Crauford's error was entirely "one of judgment and not of intention," but none the less Wellington's letter shows the principles of generosity on which he acted towards his Divisional Generals. It may be perhaps a matter of regret that this generosity did not always extend to officers of lower grade who had fallen into error.

CHAPTER XIV

Wellington's force—Correspondence thereon with the Home Government—French "Army of Portugal"—Other French forces—Fall of Almeida—Wellington retreats—Battle of Busaco—Wellington continues his retreat on Torres Vedras.

ON the 1st of August, 1810, the number of effectives in the British (and King's German Legion) portion of Wellington's army was as follows:—

NORTHERN ARMY CORPS.

Under the immediate command of Lord Wellington.

			Effective rank and file exclusive of sick.
Cavalry Division.	Lieut.-Gen. Sir Stapleton Cotton ...		3,077
1st Infantry Division.	Lieut.-Gen. Sir Brent Spencer ...		4,784
3rd „	„	Major-Gen. Picton	2,884
4th „	„	„ Cole	4,081
Light Division.	Brigdr.-Gen. Crauford		2,894
	Total (exclusive of Artillery)	...	17,220

SOUTHERN ARMY CORPS.

Lieut.-General Hill.

2nd Division.	Lieut.-Gen. Hill		5,213
5th „	Major-Gen. Leith		1,544
	Total (exclusive of Artillery)	...	6,757

Royal Artillery	2,179
Troops at Lisbon	1,344
Men " on command "	1,548
Total of effective rank and file	29,048

(Effective rank and file exclusive of sick.)

By adding one-eighth we get about 33,700 as the approximate number of effectives of all ranks. Of these something less than 21,000 were in Wellington's and something more than 6,000 in Hill's Corps. The remainder, and also about 32,000 Portuguese—with the exception of a few regiments and batteries attached to British troops, and Le Cor's Brigade at Fundao—were either in garrison or held in reserve to reinforce either wing of the English army, as occasion might demand.

The Portuguese troops were as yet by no means trained or disciplined, and reinforcements from England were urgently required. Lord Liverpool, Secretary of State for War, in a letter written on the 2nd of August, was forced to admit that " the effects of the fever contracted by our army last year in Walcheren are still of that nature that, by a late inspection, we have not at this time a *single battalion* of Infantry reported fit for service in the field with the exception of the Infantry of the Duke of Brunswick's corps."

But Wellington, with his usual acumen and clear insight, grasped the whole situation, the weakest point of which lay in the lukewarmness of the British Government. In a private letter to Lord Liverpool dated the 19th of August, he rebuked the inertness of the Ministers, urged them to renewed exertions, dwelt upon his confident hope of final success, and stated the measures which he considered indispensable, should the Government be

IN THE PENINSULA 283

really in earnest about continuing the contest. He demanded: 1. That positive orders be given to the commanding officers in Sicily and Malta to send their spare troops to the Peninsula. 2. That he himself should be responsible for the safety of Cadiz and Gibraltar, and have discretion to draw away so much of the garrison as he should think fit. 3. That as much of the Walcheren Infantry as possible should be sent to Lisbon, where in good quarters they would probably recover. 4. That stores of all kinds should be sent to the Tagus, and that he should be authorised to distribute them to the Spaniards and Portuguese at his discretion, not forgetting those on the east coast. 5. That a large fleet be kept in the Tagus.

In his reply, Lord Liverpool assured Wellington of the confidence of the Government; acquiesced in most of his demands; and promised that of the Walcheren regiments, the 4th, 50th, 71st and 92nd should proceed to Lisbon. Including the contingents from Cadiz and Sicily, Wellington would, he said, have been reinforced by nearly 14,000 men; but he hoped that when the present crisis passed away, these additional troops might, in view of the great expense of the contest, be dispensed with and sent home. Lord Liverpool meant well, and that his views were narrow in comparison with Wellington's was due probably rather to his parliamentary education and surroundings than to any personal defect.

The 7th and 23rd, which afterwards formed the famous Fusilier Brigade, were however already *en route* from Halifax, Nova Scotia; and in the middle of the month, Henry Wellesley, who had succeeded his eldest brother early in the year at Cadiz, despatched a squadron of the 13th Light Dragoons, 100 Riflemen, the 79th, 88th and 94th Regiments, to reinforce the troops in Portugal.

Looking at the other side, the French " State " of the

	Under arms.		Detached.		Hospital.	Prisoners.	Effective.	Horses.	
	Men.	Horses.	Men.	Horses.	Men.	Men.	Men.	Cavalry.	Draught.
Staff, &c.	199	222	—	—	3	—	202	222	—
2nd Corps, Gen. Reynier { Merlé, Heudelet, Marchand }	16,418	2,894	2,494	397	3,006	—	21,918	1,969	1,304
6th ,, Marshal Ney { Loison, Mermet, Marchand }	23,456	2,496	1,865	577	5,541	193	30,862	1,701	1,372
8th ,, Gen. Junot { Solignac, Clausel }	18,803	2,959	486	169	4,996	98	24,245	2,016	1,112
Reserve of Cavalry. Gen. Montbrun	4,146	4,322	1,138	831	157	31	5,441	4,907	246
Engineers, Field and Siege Artillery, Gen. Eblé... ...	2,724	2,969	206	159	409	—	3,339	—	3,128
Province of Valladolid. Gen. Serras	12,693	3,045	639	20	1,775	641	15,107	2,931	184
Provinces of Asturias and Santander. Gen. Bonet ...	12,918	—	1,394	15	1,578	107	14,885	484	—
Total under Masséna ...	91,352	18,907	8,172	2,154	17,465	1,050	115,989	14,180	7,296
9th Corps, en route, Count d'Erlon	19,144	2,436	24	—	3,147	—	22,315	2,436	—
Grand Total	110,496	21,343	8,196	2,154	20,612	1,050	138,304	16,616	7,296

IN THE PENINSULA

Army of Portugal for the 15th of August gives the figures in the table on the opposite page.

But the plans of the Emperor Napoleon embraced far more than the mere invasion of Portugal, and in order to understand the situation it is necessary to glance at the positions of the remainder of his troops in Spain.

Soult, with the 1st, 4th and 5th Corps, 72,800 strong—termed the Army of the South—occupied the country to the south and east of the Guadiana.

King Joseph with the Army of the Centre, composed of the Royal Guards, 2 Divisions of Cavalry and 2 of Infantry, amounting to 24,200 men, held Madrid and the neighbourhood.

Marshal Macdonald occupied Catalonia with the 7th Corps, 55,600 strong; General Suchet, Aragon, with the 3rd Corps of 33,000 men. Navarre was held by General Reille with a Division of the Imperial Guard and detachments, the whole amounting to 22,000 men. Caffarelli, with 6,600 men, occupied Biscay. General Dorsenne, with 10,300 men of the Imperial Guard with Cavalry attached, occupied Old Castille, holding the important points of Burges and Aranda on the main line of communications, and stretching out to Soria to keep in touch with Suchet. Detachments amounting to 6,500 men under Kellermann held Valladolid; and finally, General Bonet, with the Division 13,000 strong which, on the Emperor's arrival in 1808, had been detached from the 2nd Army Corps, was in occupation of the Asturias.

Thus, in addition to Masséna's army, a gigantic force of 241,000 men was distributed among all the provinces of Spain except Galicia in the north-west, and Murcia and Valencia on the south-east; and the grand plan of the campaign now about to begin, provided for the advance southward of Masséna on the west and of Macdonald and Suchet on the east side of the Peninsula, until they should form a junction with Soult in the south, and by so doing complete the occupation of the Peninsula.

After the fall of Ciudad Rodrigo, the line of Masséna's invasion—whether north or south of the Estrella range—was still uncertain. Reynier had come up from the Morena—whither he had marched to repel an incursion of the Spanish General Ballesteros—and, eluding Hill and Romana, while guarding his flank and rear with a detachment on the Salor, had crossed the Tagus at Alconete between the 10th and 16th of July. Hill, who was at Campo Mayor, at once making a corresponding movement, by a forced march crossed the Tagus at Vilha Velha and took up a position with 16,000 men and 18 guns at Sarzedas, in front of the Sobreira Formosa mountains. His Cavalry lined the Ponsul in advance. Leith, with 10,000 men, supported him on the Zezere. Le Cor's Brigade of Portuguese Militia at Fundao connected Hill with Belmonte—to which Slade's Heavy Cavalry Brigade had been brought up—and with Guarda. In order to prevent an enemy's corps interposing between Hill and Wellington, the Estrada Nova, the road from Belmonte to Abrantes, was broken up.

Reynier occupied Penamacor with one Division and Zarza Mayor with the other, and communication being thus established by the Pass of Perales between him and Masséna, the latter held the initiative for the approaching campaign. His delay in attacking Almeida led Wellington to think that he might after all be intending to disregard it and, in place of advancing by the valley of the Mondego, join Reynier to invade Portugal by the line of the Tagus. It was also possible that—leaving Ney to contain Wellington, and Reynier, Hill—Masséna, aided by the troops of Serras and Kellermann, which would be gradually replaced on the line of communication by the arrival of the 9th Corps, might decide to advance through the Tras os Montes upon Oporto. Napier considers this last would have been his safest course, since the capture of Oporto would have given him the good road by the sea coast to Lisbon and have enabled him to avoid the difficult and mountainous country by the Mondego.

The course of events favoured the French. In despite of Wellington's wishes, Romana, whose duty it was to hold the 5th Corps in check and whose position at Badajoz had become doubly important since Hill's retreat into Portugal, decided to take the offensive and attack Mortier in conjunction with Ballesteros. The result of the consequent battle was as usual; and the Alemtejo and Lower Tagus were laid open to Mortier. Masséna, who had only been awaiting that Marshal's co-operation, instantly attacked Almeida. The investment—formed on the 12th of August—was at first, however, so weak that Wellington revolved a project of assembling a force secretly behind the Cabeça Negro, and forcing the passage of the Coa with a view to the capture of the enemy's siege train.

Almeida, a weak fortress, was garrisoned by the 24th Portuguese regiment and two Militia battalions—in all about 4,000 men—under Brigadier-General Cox, a British officer. The enemy's fire was warmly returned, and all went well until nightfall on the 26th, when the magazine blew up with so terrible an explosion that 500 people were killed, only six houses in the town left standing, the ramparts breached and the fortress rendered untenable. Even so, Cox did not despair, but attempted to make a show of resistance and prolong negotiation. But treachery was at work among his officers. Cox was compelled to surrender, and the Portuguese regular regiment took service with the French *en masse*.

Wellington then withdrew behind the Mondego, supported by the Portuguese from Thomar, except three regiments of Cavalry, three of Infantry, two batteries of Artillery, and three battalions of Militia under Leith, who had been withdrawn into the valley of the Tagus behind the Zezere, about Torres Novas, and whose outposts watched the roads from Guarda.

Still Masséna's line of attack was doubtful: and there was the additional contingency that Reynier might recross the Tagus, and in conjunction with Mortier turn the British right of Wellington's whole line of defence. But the French Commander's hesitation arose chiefly from difficulties of supply and ignorance of the country, his information in regard to which was mostly derived from two Portuguese noblemen, the Marquises d'Alorna and de Pamplona, who had taken the side of the invader. It might have been expected that Junot would have had the country properly surveyed and reported on; but, if begun, the survey was not completed, and Masséna suffered in consequence, for the information which he got from his spies seems to have been very defective. We in England, however, have no right to criticise Junot in this matter, after the criminal fatuity shown in our neglect to survey our own colony of Natal. The want of a reliable map probably cost us hundreds of lives in the late campaign. Incredible also as it may seem, it is stated that there is at the present moment no complete survey of our Canadian frontier.

Masséna had lost invaluable time, but by the middle of September his resolution was formed to turn the defiles in rear of Celorico by way of Viseu. His three Army Corps were now suddenly concentrated: the 2nd at Guarda; the 6th and Montbrun's Cavalry at Macal de Chao; the 8th at Pinhel. Sixty-five thousand men formed his army of invasion, with 60 guns. No less than 80,000 others protected his flanks and line of communication with France by Salamanca, Valladolid and Burgos. The 5th Corps at Monasterio was threatening Estremadura; and although the facts were not then known, the Alemtejo actually lay open to the French; for Romana, advancing a second time, had been defeated on the 15th at Monasterio by Mortier and compelled to retire across the Guadiana. Local disturbances and sickness prevented Mortier following up his advantage. The Spaniards recrossed the river and the crisis died away.

The valley of the Mondego is enclosed on the right bank by the Sierra Caramula and on the left by the Sierra d'Estrella which gradually converge as the river approaches the sea, until they form a horseshoe, the toe of which on the right bank is formed by Pena Cova (a village about 36 miles distant from Viseu and 60 from Celorico); and on the left bank by the Murcella, a rugged mountain overlooking the Alva, a confluent of the Mondego. The Murcella formed a strong defensive position, a fact of which Masséna was aware. The Marshal consequently decided not to operate along the left bank of the Mondego; but what neither he nor his topographical advisers knew was that on the right bank, the Sierra de Busaco, covering the roads from Viseu, formed an equally strong position for defence. Under incorrect data, then, Masséna had resolved to distribute thirteen days' biscuit and advance in a single line along the right bank of the river in hopes of reaching Coimbra before Hill's Corps could form a junction with Wellington, hopes which seemed justified from the fact that Hill was further from Coimbra than himself.

The enemy's advance on the 15th of September drove the British outposts from Guarda, Celorico, and Trancoso. It was obvious that the invasion of Portugal had begun in earnest, and Wellington directed the two wings of his army to retire concentrically on the Alva. On the 16th

Ney, Montbrun, and Reynier crossed the Mondego, and recrossed next day to the right bank at Fornos, their advance guards being simultaneously at Mongoalde, fifteen miles lower down; while Junot's Corps moved directly upon Viseu to protect the right flank from the Portuguese Militia which, to the number of 10,000, had collected under British officers on the Douro with a view to harassing Masséna's march.

Meanwhile Wellington, covered by the Cavalry, was retiring by the left bank of the Mondego. The road, although hemmed in on the one side by the Estrella range, and on the other by the Mondego, had been put in repair; and as the river was not only fordable but well bridged, there would be no difficulty in transferring the army to the right bank if necessary, to stop the enemy's progress.

On the 18th the advance guard of the French entered Viseu. On the same day the leading Brigade of the 1st British Division reached Coimbra. Next day Captain Somers Cocks of the 16th Light Dragoons — a most enterprising and intelligent officer—retracing his steps, succeeded in reaching Celorico, where, in Napier's words, he ascertained " that Masséna, relinquishing his communications, had thrown his Cavalry, Infantry, Artillery, parcs, baggage, and hospital waggons in one mass upon the worst road in Portugal." On the 20th and 21st Wellington, who had left a rearguard on the Griz, passed the rest of his army across to the right bank of the Mondego, occupying Mortigao and Busaco; while Leith, only twelve miles in front of Hill, reached the Alva by way of Thomar and Espinhal.

The two wings had thus, to all intents and purposes, concentrated more rapidly indeed than had been expected by Wellington; for Hill (with the sound common sense which always distinguished him), having discovered the meaning of Reynier's movements on Guarda, and having heard that he had broken his bridge of boats over the Tagus, had anticipated the orders of his Commander, and had retired at once from Sarzedas to Sobreira Formosa, where on the 17th Wellington's letter reached him. On the 20th he arrived at Espinhal, 60 miles distant, and was joined by Le Cor, who with equal intelligence had brought down his Portuguese Brigade by forced marches along cross-country roads from Fundao. Had Crauford been in Hill's place he would probably have totally disregarded Wellington's instructions and have undertaken against the enemy on his own account a series of operations entailing most likely the loss of his Division and endangering the whole army. But it was characteristic of Hill, and the mark of a great mind, that he readily recognised the immense superiority of his Commander, and devoted himself to carrying out his wishes. The advancement of his own interests never seems to have entered Hill's head, and it would have taken a bold man to suggest to him any idea of intrigue against his chief. Thus a delicate and difficult combination was carried out with perfect success; and Wellington, now acting in interior lines, could look forward with far greater confidence to the result of the campaign.

Meanwhile Masséna was beginning to feel the error in his choice of a line of operations. The road had to be repaired daily in order to enable his artillery to use it. His advance guard, as already noted, entered Viseu on the 18th. Yet on the day following, his guns, ammunition column, &c., were still twenty miles distant therefrom. Montbrun's Cavalry, instead of heading the advance, was in rear of the whole column, which was crowded together in a narrow defile. Nicholas Trant, one of the British officers commanding a Portuguese Brigade of Militia, a man of ability and enterprise, moving by night from Moimenta de Beira with 2,000 of his men, preceded by a squadron and five guns, interposed between the main body of the French army and the trains and surprised the baggage column. Guns, wagons and mules jammed up in disorder, were in no condition to make resistance. The French Cavalry in rear was unable to penetrate the mass. A terrible disaster appeared inevitable; but at the critical moment the escort of Grenadiers, standing firm, poured in a destructive volley upon its assailants. The Militia fell back. The Portuguese Cavalry being unsupported, was also compelled to retire. Trant, however, renewed the attack, and summoned the column to surrender. The French commander adroitly consented to negotiate, and thus gave time for an Irish battalion in the French service, which formed part of the escort, to come up in support of the Grenadiers. Then Trant, unable to believe that Masséna could have left his guns so inadequately guarded, and fearing a trap, retired; but though the attack had failed in its primary object, eighty prisoners had been taken, and the enemy's mounted troops and artillery were so much delayed that they did not reach Viseu till the 23rd, and lost Masséna two precious days.

The British outposts now held the line of the Criz—a river which, rising in the Sierra de Caramula, finds its way into the Mondego by the left bank. The Sierra de Busaco, ten miles in rear, afforded a strong defensive position. A day's march would concentrate the army with a secure line of retreat. To fight a battle with every prospect of success, was tempting. But a tactical victory could bring Wellington no strategical advantage. Lisbon was uncovered from the south, and garrisoned only by a few newly arrived British battalions and some ill-disciplined Portuguese Militia. Whatever, therefore,

IN THE PENINSULA 293

might be the result of the battle, it would be necessary to continue the retreat at an early date; and finally Wellington decided to stand his ground merely from political motives, in order to show his own Government, which was in a state of almost abject despair, and the Portuguese Regency, which was treacherous, that he was not afraid to encounter the French in arms. Thanks to the inertness of the Portuguese authorities, the work of devastating the country in rear and thus allowing the invader no means of subsistence, had been very imperfectly carried out. If Wellington could delay Masséna only for a few more days, it would give him time for the work to be done and for the inhabitants to retire to Lisbon. Reviewing the circumstances at a later date, he considered his decision a mistake; but writing to his brother Pole Wellesley at the time, he justified his action on the ground of the strength of the Busaco position, and added that "this battle has had the best effects in inspiring confidence in the Portuguese troops, both among our croaking officers and the people of the country. It has likewise removed an erroneous impression which began to be very general that we intended to fight no more, but to retire to our ships; and it has given the Portuguese a taste for an amusement to which they were not before accustomed, and which they would not have acquired if I had not put them in a very strong position."

It was at this period when Wellington was preparing to defend his position and Masséna to attack it, that a rather important correspondence took place between the two Commanders in regard to the status of the Portuguese "Ordenanza." Masséna had declined to recognise them as soldiers, stigmatising them as *paysans sans uniforme* and as *assassins et voleurs de grand chemin*, and had given orders to shoot all who might be captured. The Portuguese troops, both regular and militia, were at this period a very ill-disciplined and unreliable body; and no doubt the Ordenanza, made up from a still lower stratum, had in many cases committed all kinds of atrocities. Wellington, however, reminding Masséna "que vous même avez augmenté la gloire de l'armée Française en commandant des soldats qui n'avaient pas d'uniforme," argued the matter on the broadest grounds, pointing out that the Ordenanza was part of the Portuguese army and subject to military law, and contending that a country invaded has the right to defend itself by every means in its power. Very much the same question arose regarding the status of the Franc Tireurs in the Franco-German War, in which case the French, with far less reason, took the view not of Masséna but of Wellington. Yet it may be doubted whether a defending army will in general gain much by the services of an ill-disciplined rabble apt to become a greater terror to its friends than its foes. In the present instance the British Commander gained a victory rather dialectical than convincing; for, uniform or no uniform, the Ordenanza cannot be placed on a par with the Revolutionary levies of 1792, and did not very effectively aid the deliverance of Portugal.

Meantime, Masséna—partly from the check to his artillery, partly from being encumbered with a mistress whom he had brought into Portugal and could now neither protect nor leave behind—was losing valuable time; which his opponent was in an equal degree utilising by getting his Divisions into position. The Light Division, with a Portuguese Brigade made up of the 1st and 16th Regiments under Pack, and the Royal Dragoons, watched the French along the line of the Criz, the bridges over which had been destroyed. The 1st Division was posted twenty miles in rear, at Mealhada on the Oporto–Coimbra road, to guard the latter town against an attack from the north which, although circuitous, would not have been impossible. The 3rd and 4th Divisions occupied Martagoa in the plain and the Sierra de Busaco behind it halfway between Crauford and Spencer. The 5th and 2nd Divisions were still on the left bank of the Mondego to guard against the contingency of the enemy crossing the river and attacking on that side.

On the 23rd of September, the French Cavalry succeeded in repairing the bridges over the Criz. Pack had already fallen back. On the 25th Masséna advanced in force, and Wellington, seeing that his opponent had resolved on an attack, occupied the Sierra de Busaco with the 3rd, 4th, and Light Divisions; called up Spencer from Mealhada, and Leith and Hill from the other side of the river. Three squadrons were retained with the army; but the mountain being impossible for Cavalry as an arm, Cottom was ordered with the bulk of it to Mealhada on the low ground, taking the place of the 1st Division which returned to the Sierra.

On the 25th, Ney brought up the 6th Corps so rapidly that Wellington, taking command of the Light Division in person, had barely time to extricate it; for Crauford, instead of proceeding direct to his allotted post, had lingered on the low ground until his retreat was well-nigh cut off. Reynier simultaneously came up on Ney's left, to the ridge opposite Busaco; and seeing that the British position was still only half occupied, and that the ground, sloping steeply down from the crest line on either side, could hold no large reserves, he desired to attack. Skirmishing took place between the French and the picquets of the 3rd Division posted at St. Antonio de Cantaro. At 8 a.m. on the 26th, Reynier wrote a letter to Ney expressing his wishes. The moment was a critical one for the British Army, neither the 1st, 2nd, or 5th Divisions being as yet in position; but although Ney agreed with Reynier, he did not feel justified in taking the responsibility of making a general attack without reference to Masséna. Masséna was, however, ten miles in rear at Martagoa. When he arrived his Corps Commanders assured him that the position could be carried by a direct attack. Unfortunately for himself the indolence which was a trait of the Marshal's character when matters were going well now showed itself. Without taking the trouble to reconnoitre the position personally, the Commander-in-Chief accepted the views of his colleagues, yet deferred the attack until the following days. He thus fell between two stools, for he lost his last chance of overwhelming the British by force of numbers and yet found no alternative to a frontal attack.

The Sierra de Busaco, a mountain eight miles in length, "abuts with its right on the Mondego, while its left is connected with the Sierra de Caramula by a rugged road impervious to the march of an army. A road along the crest afforded an easy communication from right to left; and behind the ridge on the right the ford of Pena Cova furnished a passage over the Mondego to the Alva. The face of Busaco was steep, rough, and fit for defence; the Artillery of the Allies, placed on certain salient points, could play along the front, and there was some ground on the summit suitable for a small body of Cavalry. But neither guns nor horsemen on the French side had a field, and their Infantry were to contend with every difficulty of approach and attack.

" After passing the Criz, a tableland permitted Masséna to march with a wide order of battle to Martagao; but from thence a succession of ridges led to the Sierra Busaco, which was separated from the last by a chasm so profound that the naked eye could hardly distinguish the movements of troops in the bottom, yet in parts so narrow that 12-pounders could range across" (Napier, bk. xl.

ch. 6). The weak points of the position lay in the fact that it was far too extensive to be properly occupied by the numbers of the defending army, and also that it could be turned by a road crossing the Caramula and running by the village of Boialva to Sardao and thence by the Oporto road to Coimbra. But to guard against any movement from this quarter, Lord Wellington had called up Colonel Trant and had directed him to occupy Sardao; and the great extent of the position was a source of weakness rather in theory than fact, for it could hardly be attacked except at the three points where roads leading on Coimbra crossed the ridge.

The British order of battle was as follows:—

Lieut.-General Viscount Wellington, K.B.	Commander-in-Chief.
Marshal Beresford	Commanding Portuguese Army.
Lieut.-General Sir Brent Spencer, K.B.	2nd in Command of British Troops.
Major-General Hon. C. Stewart	Adjutant-General.
Colonel George Murray	Quartermaster-General.
Brigadier-General Howarth	Commanding Royal Artillery.
Colonel Bathurst	Military Secretary.
Lieut.-Colonel Fletcher	Commanding Royal Engineers.

LEFT WING OF THE ARMY.   (Lord Wellington's Army Corps.)

Cavalry Division.
Lieut.-General Cotton.

1st Brigade.	Maj.-General Slade	{ Royal Dragoons; 14th Light Dragoons.
2nd ,,	,,	Anson	{ 16th Light Dragoons; 1st Hussars, K.G.
3rd ,,		Colonel de Grey	{ 3rd Dragoon Guards; 4th Dragoons.

1st Infantry Division.
Lieut.-General Sir B. Spencer, K.B.

Col. Hon. E. Stopford	{ 1st Batt. Coldstream Guards; 1st Batt. 3rd Guards; 1 Company 60th Rifles.

298 WELLINGTON'S OPERATIONS

Major-Gen. Cameron   24th ; 42nd ; 61st; 1 Company 60th.
Col. Hon. E. Pakenham   1st Batt. 7th ; 79th ; Royal Staff Corps.
Major-Gen. Baron Low   { 1st, 2nd, 5th and 7th Line Batts. K.G.L. ; 1st and 2nd Light Batts. K.G.L.
     2 Squadrons 4th Dragoons.
18 British or German guns (one 9-pounder, two 6-pounder Batteries).
     6 Portuguese guns (one 6-pounder Battery).

3rd Division.
Major-General Picton.

British Brigades   Col. Mackinnon   45th ; 74th ; 88th.
     Major-Gen. Lightburne   5th ; 83rd ; 3 Coms. 60th.
Portuguese ,,   Col. Champlemond   9th, 21st Portuguese Rgts.
12 Portuguese guns (one 9-pounder, one 6-pounder Battery).

4th Division.
Major-General Hon. G. L. Cole.

British Brigades   Brigdr.-Gen. A. Campbell { 2nd Batt. 7th ; 11th ; 53rd ; 1 Company 60th.
     Col. Kemmis   { 27th ; 40th ; 97th ; 1 Company 60th.
Portuguese ,,   Col. Harvey   11th, 23rd Portuguese.
     Brigdr.-Gen. W. Campbell { 6th, 18th Portuguese ; 6th Caçadores.
     6 guns R.A. (6-pounders).

Light Division.
Brigadier-General R. Crauford.

British Brigades   Col. Beckwith   { 43rd ; 4 Companies 95th ; 3rd Caçadores.
     Col. Barclay   { 52nd ; 4 Companies 95th ; 1st Caçadores.
Portuguese ,,   Brigdr.-Gen. Pack { 1st, 16th Portuguese ; 4th Caçadores.
     Brigdr.-Gen. Coleman   7th, 19th Portuguese.
2 Batteries R.H.A., one 3-pounder Portuguese Battery. Total, 18 guns.

RIGHT WING OF THE ARMY. Lieut.-General Hill's Army Corps.
Major-General Hon. H. Fane.
13th Light Dragoons.
Portuguese Brigade   Col. Le Cor.   12th, 13th Regts. ; 3 Militia Batts.
     Six 6-pounder Portuguese guns.

IN THE PENINSULA

2nd Division.

Major-General Hon. W. Stewart.

British Brigades   Lieut.-Col. Colborne { 3rd Buffs ; 2nd Batt. 48th ; 66th ; 1 Company 60th.
                 Col. Wilson   28th; 24th; 39th; 1 Coy. 60th.

Portuguese Division.

Major-General Hamilton.

Portuguese Brigades   Brigdr.-Gen. Fonseca   2nd ; 14th.
                       Lieut.-Col. Campbell   4th ; 10th.
                       Lieut.-Col. Stewart   5th Caçadores.
                       12 guns.

5th Division.

Major-General Leith.

British Brigade   Lieut.-Col. Barnes   1st ; 9th ; 38th.
Portuguese   „   Brigdr.-General Spry   3rd ; 15th ; Thomar Militia.
                Col. Baron Eben   8th ; Lusitanian Legion.
One 9-pounder and one 6-pounder Battery. 12 guns.

The gross strength of the Army was about 60,000 officers and men with 90 guns (six British and nine Portuguese Batteries). This return is taken from Sup. Des. xiii. 355. Wellington in "Memorandum of Operations," Des. vol. vii., Feb. 23, 1811, states six Portuguese Batteries only.

The Sierra de Busaco was occupied thus :—

On the extreme left, along the spur connecting it with the Sierra de Caramula, was posted the 4th Division. Next on the right came the K.G.L. Brigades of Spencer's Division, forming—together with the 19th Portuguese Regiment from Coleman's Brigade—a support for the British Brigades of the Light Division which occupied a ledge in advance of the crest line part way down the mountain side. At this point the ridge which hitherto had been running in a south-westerly direction changed its course and ran due south, forming a re-entrant angle, at the point where it was crossed by the Martagoa-Botao-

Coimbra road. This road was thus flanked by Crauford and directly defended by Pack's Brigade posted on the crest line near the Convent de Busaco, which had been loopholed and placed in a state of defence.

On Pack's right the three remaining Brigades of the 1st Division formed the centre of the line along the highest part of the ridge. Next came Lightburne's Brigade of the 3rd Division, and then the main body of it under Picton, covering the Martagoa-Coimbra road, having on its right the 8th Portuguese Regiment from Eben's Brigade, which was separated by an interval of two miles from the main body of Hill's Army Corps, of which the 5th Division, under Leith, formed the left. Then General Stewart with the 2nd Division closed a road running from Martagoa to the Pena Cove ford, and his troops extended nearly to the Mondego. On the further side of that river, the Portuguese Brigades of Le Cor and Campbell occupied the Sierra de Murcella, covering the right flank of the Army, while General Fane was on the right bank of the Alva with the 13th Light Dragoons, to "observe the movements of the enemy's Cavalry on the Mondego."

On the French side, Reynier with the 2nd Corps—formed in two columns of attack—was posted at the village of Antonio de Cantara. Three miles away on his right, the 6th Corps, under Ney, was preparing to storm the Convent, but the distance between the two Generals would necessitate their attacks being entirely independent of one another. During the small hours of the morning of the 27th, skirmishing took place at the outposts, and just before daybreak, Reynier suddenly drove in the picquets of the 3rd Division. Masséna now came up in person. He had been warned by some of his Staff that it would be better to attempt to turn the position than to assault it in a frontal attack, and on seeing the rugged

IN THE PENINSULA 301

strength of the Sierra the Marshal hesitated. Unfortunately he allowed his better judgment to be overridden by his Corps commanders, who—unaware of the fact that the main body of the Allies was concealed behind the crest-line—asserted that the position was occupied only by a rearguard; and a little before 7 a.m., the Marshal gave orders for a general attack.

It was intended that Ney and Reynier should assault the position simultaneously, but Reynier, who had already, as we have seen, driven in Picton's picquets, having rather less difficult ground to scale, began his attack before Ney was ready. Unaware of the existence of Hill's Corps, which was not only hidden but—as already stated—separated by an interval of two miles from that of Wellington, Reynier attacked the 3rd Division in the belief that he was turning the right flank of the whole British line. His 1st Division, although assailed in flank by the three headquarter companies of the 60th, climbed the rocks with incredible hardihood, and—sheltered by the very steepness of the mountain-face—reached the summit with little loss, drove back Eben's Portuguese, penetrated into the gap between the 3rd and 5th Divisions, and took up a position athwart the ridge, fronting south. Reynier's 2nd Division, following close behind, wheeled to the right, and some of the skirmishers actually began to descend the reverse slope of the mountain. The British line was thus cut in two, and the arrival of a French reserve might have decided the day. Picton had, however, no idea of resigning the contest. Forming front to his right with Mackinnon's Brigade, he made a vigorous counter attack upon the enemy's 2nd Division, which had already ensconced itself in a strong position among the rocks. The brunt of the assault fell on the 45th and 88th. Aided by two guns posted by Wellington in person on the enemy's flank, the gallant regiments after a desperate struggle drove the French in confusion down the mountain-side.

Meanwhile General Leith, seeing no enemy in front of his position, and noticing Picton's need, was bringing the 5th Division (in pursuance of Wellington's orders to his Generals to give each other mutual support) along the ridge to his colleague's assistance. Barnes's Brigade led. His left battalion was stopped by a precipice; but the 9th Regiment succeeded in deploying, then, without returning the enemy's fire, charged Reynier's first Division with the bayonet and drove it from the crest. No pursuit was attempted, but the musketry fire decimated the French as they retreated in confusion down the precipitous mountain-side. Leith's remaining Brigade came up in support of Barnes. Hill in person was rapidly approaching from the right, and the danger in this quarter was at an end.

In the course of this attack the French had lost General Graindorge, and their other casualties were terribly heavy. Reynier seems indeed to have ordered the Brigades of Foy and Sarrut to renew the attack, but the attempt must have been of a half-hearted nature, and little else than long-range firing took place.

On the French right, Ney met with no better fortune. Impeded to a greater extent than Reynier by the difficulties of the ground, it was not until after 8 a.m. that he was able to advance in force to the assault. By a grievous error the interval had not been used to prepare the attack with artillery fire. Loison's Division, headed by Simon's Brigade, advanced against Crauford's front, while Marchand manœuvred to turn his right flank. A few skirmishers only of the Light Division were to be seen dotted here and there among the fir-woods. Undeterred by the shrapnel fire of Ross's R.H.A. battery, cleverly posted among the rocks, Simon briskly ascended the

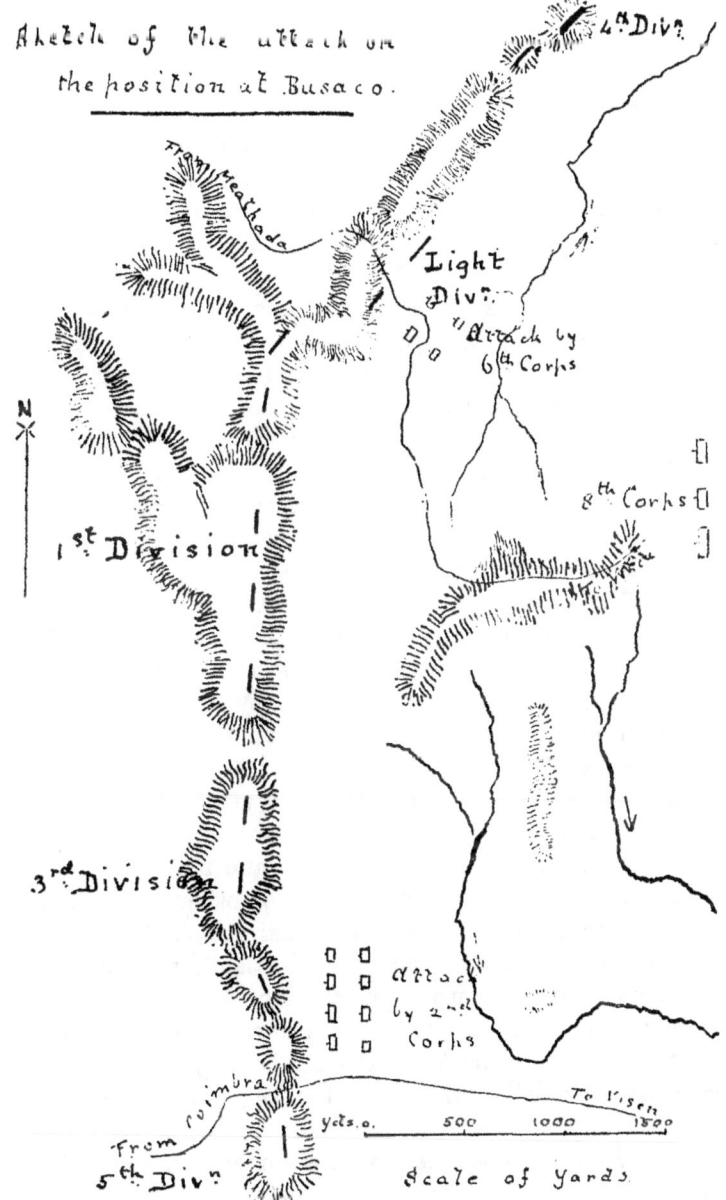

height. But as he reached the rocky basin in which the Division lay hidden, a terrible surprise awaited him. Crauford in a loud voice suddenly called the 43rd and 52nd to their feet, and ordered them to charge the enemy who, undeployed, was still advancing in column of sections. With heroic fortitude the foremost of the Frenchmen met the charge. A British soldier fell to the fire of every man of the leading section. But nothing could withstand that victorious attack. Assailed at once in front and on both flanks, raked by three murderous volleys at five yards' distance, the remnant of the French column recoiled, gave way, and fled in disorder down the slopes. Meanwhile Marchand, with his Division in extended order, had made good his footing and threatened the summit of the ridge. Pack's Brigade, however, held him in front, and Loison's failure exposed his right flank to Ross's guns. Isolated as he was, and unsupported by the 3rd Division in reserve, Marchard then found himself obliged to abandon the attempt and to retire across the ravine. A worse combined attack never was made. The 8th Corps, held in reserve in rear of Ney, was not brought into action at all, and 25,000 men had been hurled upon a mountain position held by nearly 60,000.

Skirmishing continued during the afternoon, but the French made no further bid for victory, and the loss of five Generals and 5,000 other officers and men convinced Masséna—as it has perhaps convinced other Generals in more modern actions—that the frontal attack of a strong position by a series of unconnected assaults without preliminary reconnaissance, against an unshaken enemy in superior numbers, cannot be undertaken with impunity.

On the side of the Allies Colonel Barclay of the 52nd, who commanded a Brigade of the Light Division, died soon afterwards of wounds received. Otherwise only 200 were killed and 1,050 others were wounded or missing, the losses being as nearly as possible evenly divided between the British and Portuguese; but the British casualties would have been insignificant except for those of the 88th, which suffered to the extent of 16 officers and 268 men. The losses of the French were enormous, and are probably under-estimated at 5,000 men *hors de combat*. General Graindorge was among the killed; Generals Merlé, Maucune, Foy, and Simon were wounded. The last named remained a prisoner in our hands. He had been wounded in the face by shrapnel, but the bullets were extricated so easily, and hurt him so little, that Wellington lost all faith in that species of shell for the future.

The Allied Army was now full of confidence; and to the Portuguese, who had for the first time been tested in a general action and had done well, the experience was invaluable.

On the day after the battle Masséna's Staff found a mountain road from Mortagao to Boyalva and Sardao, which turned the left of the British position. During the afternoon of the same day—the 28th—the French, headed by the 8th Corps and Montbrun's Cavalry, were set in motion. Colonel Trant, who had been ordered to Boyalva to stop such a movement, had been delayed by the folly of the Portuguese General Bacellar, and though he was at Sardao with 1,500 exhausted men, he was quickly driven behind the Vouga. Masséna's turning movement executed within ten miles of an enemy in position, was a violation of the rules of war, and his peril was increased by the confusion of his army—inextricably mixed up with guns, horses, and waggons on a narrow mountain road. Perhaps he knew that the Portuguese troops were not as yet sufficiently disciplined to be mobile; if so, he was justified, for Wellington did not venture to attack, but on seeing the direction of his march gave orders for an immediate retirement upon Lisbon.

Within an hour the army was in motion. Hill's Corps, crossing the Mondego, retreated by the military road upon Espinhal and Thomar; Wellington's, covered by the Light Division, by Mealhada upon Coimbra. Crauford, however, halted on the right bank of the Mondego. The 1st Division that day reached a point between Fornos and that river. The 4th Division was north of Fornos; the 3rd at Eiras; the 5th at Dianterne; the Light at Botao; and the Cavalry at Mealhada. On the 30th Masséna was at Mealhada, and a rapid movement by his right might have enabled him to ford the Mondego below Coimbra and intercept Wellington in his retreat on Leira; for Crauford was still on the right bank of the river, and the British Cavalry Brigades, which took the duties of the rearguard when the Light Division had disentangled itself from the mountains and had debouched on to the level country, were posted at Fornos, four miles north of Coimbra on the Oporto road. They were extremely badly handled. The country was thickly enclosed. The regiments were in consequence confined to a single road, along which they retired in great confusion, hard pressed by the enemy's Cavalry under General St. Croix.

Had Wellington intercepted the French during their turning movement in the defile of Boyalva, and simultaneously attacked them in rear, it seems probable that he would have inflicted a terrible disaster upon the enemy crowded together in a narrow mountain path. He judged it better to leave them alone, but by doing so lost much of the advantage gained by his victory. Wellington's proclamation to the Portuguese exhorting them to destroy all food supplies, to carry off their goods and retire to Lisbon, had been disregarded; and though he had renewed his entreaties at Busaco, the time had been hardly long enough to allow the wretched in-

IN THE PENINSULA 307

habitants, now thoroughly frightened, to carry his wishes into effect. The consequence was that although the Commissariat stores had been removed to Figueras—whence they were sent by ship to Lisbon—the roads along which the British troops were retiring were choked with an innumerable mass of refugees of all classes, mixed up with mules and carts on which they were trying to carry away some remnant of their little property. The scene was heart-breaking; but the position of the British Army perilous in the extreme. Happily no serious attack was made, but Wellington's care and forethought were for the most part thrown away. The bridges were not broken, and much of the food supply was not destroyed. Thus it happened that on the advance of the French they found abundance; and but for their wastefulness, Wellington's plans might have altogether failed.

On October 1st the Allied Headquarters were at Redinha, 16 miles south of Coimbra; next day at Leira, 27 miles further on. Some plundering took place, but was promptly checked. Two Dragoons were hanged, and discipline was thus restored. The British Brigade of Leith's Division, which had most recently arrived from England, seems to have been the worst offender. On the 4th the rearguard halted at the Rio de Nanda, with picquets at Pombal. On the 5th, the enemy's Cavalry came on in force, and some very pretty skirmishing took place between the opposing squadrons, supported by their Horse Artillery. The French, in greatly superior numbers—36 squadrons against 10—although repeatedly checked, were not to be denied. The British Cavalry consequently retired; and being attacked in flank and rear was in some danger at the defile near Rio de Nanda, but extricated itself eventually with little loss. On the same day the main body of Wellington's Corps evacuated Leira, and retired in two columns; one, covered by two Brigades of Cavalry, viâ Batalha and Rio Mayor; the other by Alcobaça and Obidos (along the road which he had traversed just before the battle of Vimeiro in 1808), with De Grey's Heavy Brigade as its rearguard. Masséna followed the first-named.

But although Masséna had succeeded in gaining the Coimbra road, his position was still full of peril. He was cut off from his base, and about 33,000 of the Portuguese Militia, under Silveira, Trant, and others, threatened him from the north of Beira. Prudence dictated the establishment of a new base at Oporto, as well as the employment of the 9th Corps in dispersing the Militia and securing the line of communications between Oporto and Almeida. But Masséna contented himself with filling up Coimbra with his sick and wounded, 5,000 in number; and, leaving these defenceless people with a most inadequate guard, marched in pursuit of Wellington.

Retribution quickly followed this neglect. It has already been noticed that Colonel Trant, unable from the exhaustion of his men to stop Masséna's flank march upon Sardao, had fallen back behind the Vouga. When the French had well committed themselves to their march on Lisbon, Trant returned to Mealhada. Soon after daybreak on the 7th he surprised a French outpost at Fornos, eight miles distant. Then following up his advantage with his Cavalry, he seized the bridge over the Mondego at Coimbra by a *coup de main;* and, having thus cut off the garrison from the main body, entered the town with his Infantry and captured the whole of the invalids. A daring enterprise, showing the value of irregular troops when properly handled; and by contrast, the feebleness of the efforts of the guerilla bands in Spain.

CHAPTER XV

Occupation of the Lines of Torres Vedras.

THE British retirement steadily continued. On October 8th, Cotton—with the Brigades of Slade and Anson, which formed the rearguard of the column retreating by the more easterly route—reached Alcoentre at the end of a short day's march, in pouring rain. Whether on this account it was supposed that the enemy would make no aggressive movement, does not appear. At all events, in the teeth of reports sent in by the officer on picquet, Cotton and the Brigadiers quartered themselves in the village; and not only were the guns of the R.H.A. Battery left in the street unprotected, but the drivers were allowed to take the harness to pieces and clean it, while the Cavalry Brigades, passing through the village, bivouacked on the south side. The consequences might have been expected. At 2 p.m. the enemy, coming on in force, suddenly drove in the picquet squadron. The guns were in imminent peril. The drivers hitched on the horses anyhow. One howitzer was actually abandoned. But at the critical moment, Captain Somers Cocks of the 16th, whose squadron was first for duty, mounted the first men that he could get hold of, reinforced the picquet squadron, charged the advancing enemy along the narrow street and, driving him out of the town, covered the retirement of the guns and Cavalry Division to Quinta de Toro. The situation was saved, but the Generals should have been broken for their unpardonable carelessness. However, if Wellington had made a practice of trying by court-martial every general officer who deserved punishment for incompetence or disobedience of orders, he would have had but few left; and it is only fair to say that a good many profited by their experience and did eventually improve.

While these rearguard skirmishes were taking place, the lines of Torres Vedras were being occupied by the main body of the army. These famous lines " consisted," says Napier (bk. xi. ch. 8), quoting from Colonel J. T. Jones, R.E., " of three distinct ranges of defence.

"The first, extending from Alhandra on the Tagus to the mouth of the Zizandre on the sea-coast, was, following the inflections of the hills, 29 miles long.

"The second, traced at a distance, varying from 6 to 10 miles, in rear of the first, stretched from Quintella on the Tagus to the mouth of the St. Lorenza, being 24 miles in length.

"The third, intended to cover a forced embarkation, extended from Passo d'Arcos on the Tagus, to the tower of Junquera on the coast. Here an outward line, constructed on an opening of 3,000 yards, enclosed an entrenched camp, the latter being designed to cover an embarkation with fewer troops if such an operation should be delayed by bad weather. This second camp enclosed Fort St. Julian, whose high ramparts and deep ditches defied an escalade, and were armed to enable a rearguard to resist any force. From Passo d'Arcos to the nearest part of the second line was 24 miles; from the first line it was two marches, but the principal routes led through Lisbon, where means to retard the enemy were prepared.

IN THE PENINSULA

"Of these stupendous lines, the second, whether for strength or importance, was the principal; the others were appendages, the third a mere place of refuge. The first line was originally designed as an advanced work, to stem the primary violence of the enemy, and enable the army to take up its ground on the second line without hurry or pressure; but while Masséna remained on the frontier, it acquired strength, which was now so much augmented by the rain that Wellington resolved to abide the attack there permanently.

"It offered five distinct positions, which shall be described from right to left.

"1. From Alhandra to the head of the valley of Calandrix. This portion, five miles long, was a continuous and lofty ridge defended by thirteen redoubts, and for two miles rendered inaccessible by a scarp 15 to 20 feet high. It was guarded by Hill's Corps, and flanked from the Tagus by a flotilla of gunboats manned with British seamen.

"2. From the head of the vale of Calandrix to the Pé de Monte. This portion, also of five miles, presented two salient mountains forming the valley of Aruda, that town being exactly in the mouth of the pass. Only three feeble redoubts, incapable of stopping an enemy, were constructed here, and the defence was entrusted to the Light Division.

"3. The Monte Agraça. This lofty mountain overtopped the adjacent country, and from its summit the whole of the first line could be seen. The right was separated from the Aruda position by a deep ravine which led to nothing; the left overlooked the village and valley of Zibreira; the centre overhung the town of Sobral. The summit was crowned by an immense redoubt armed with 25 guns, round which three smaller works, containing 19 guns, were clustered. The garrisons, amounting to

2,000 men, were supplied by Pack's Brigade; and on the reverse slope, which might be about four miles in length, Leith was posted in reserve.

"4. From the valley of Zibreira to Torres Vedras. This portion, seven miles long, was at first without works, because it was only when the rains had set in that the resolution to defend the first line permanently was adopted. But the ground, rough and well defined, having a valley in front, deep and watered by the Zizandre, now a considerable river, presented a fine field of battle. Here Spencer and Cole, reinforced with a 6th Division, formed of troops recently come from England and Cadiz, were stationed under the immediate command of Wellington, whose quarters were fixed at Pero Negro, just under the lofty Secora rock, on which a telegraph was erected to communicate with every part of the line.

"5. From the heights of Torres Vedras to the mouth of the Zizandre. The right flank of this portion and a pass in front of the town of Torres Vedras were secured by a great redoubt, mounting forty guns, and by smaller forts judiciously planted so as to command all the approaches. From these works to the sea a range of moderate heights was crowned with minor redoubts; but the chief defence there, after the rains had set in, was to be found in the Zizandre, unfordable and overflowing so as to form an impassable marsh. Such were the defences of the first line, strong, but at several points defective; and there was a paved road, running parallel to the foot of the hills through Torres Vedras, Runa, Sobral, and Arnda to Alhandra, which gave the enemy an advantage.

"The second and most formidable line shall now be described from left to right.

"1. From the mouth of the St. Lourença to Mafra.

In this distance of seven miles there was a range of hills, naturally steep, artificially scarped, covered by a deep and in many parts impracticable ravine. The salient points were secured by forts which flanked and commanded the few accessible points; but as the line was extensive, a secondary post was fortified a few miles in rear, to secure a road leading from Ereceira to Cintra.

"2. The Tapada or Royal Park of Mafra. Here there was some open but strong ground which, with the pass of Mafra, was defended by a system of fourteen redoubts, constructed with great labour and care, well considered with respect to the natural features, and in some degree connected with the secondary post spoken of above: the Sierra de Chypre, covered with redoubts, was in front and obstructed all approaches to Mafra itself.

"3. From the Tapada to the pass of Bucellas. In this space of ten or twelve miles, forming the middle of the second line, the country is choked by the Monte Chique, the head of which is in the centre of and overtops all the other mountain masses. A road conducted along a chain of hills, high and salient though less bold than any other part of the line, connected Mafra with the Cabeça, and was secured by a number of forts. The country in front was extremely difficult, and behind was a parallel and stronger ridge which could only be approached with artillery by the connecting road in front; but to reach that, the Sierra de Chypre on the left, or the defile of the Cabeça on the right, must have been carried. Now the latter was covered by a cluster of redoubts constructed on some inferior rocky heads in advance; they commanded all the approaches, and from their artificial and natural strength were nearly impregnable . . .

"4. From Bucellas to the low ground about the Tagus. The defile of Bucellas, narrow and rugged, was defended by redoubts on each side, and a ridge, or rather collection of impassable rocks, called the Sierra de Serbes, stretched to the right of it for two miles without a break, and then died away by a succession of ridges into the low ground on the bank of the Tagus. These declivities and the flat bank of the river offered an accessible opening, two and a half miles wide. It was laboriously defended indeed by redoubts, watercuts, retrenchments, and carefully connected with the heights of Alhandra; yet it was the weakest part of the line, and dangerous from its proximity to the valleys of Calandrix and Aruda.

"Five roads practicable for guns pierced the first line of defence : two at Torres Vedras, two at Sobral, one at Alhandra; but as two of these united again at the Cabeça, there were only four points of passage through the second line, that is to say, at Mafra, Monte Chique, Bucellas, and Quintella in the flat ground. Hence the aim and scope of all the works were to bar those roads and strengthen the favourable fighting positions between them, without impeding the movements of the army; the loss of the first line therefore would not have been injurious, save in reputation, because the retreat was secure upon the second and stronger line: moreover the guns of the first line were all of inferior calibre, mounted on common truck carriages, immovable and useless to the enemy. The Allies' movements were quite unfettered by the works, but those of the French Army were impeded and cramped by the Monte Junta, which, rising opposite to the centre of the first line, sent out a spur called the Sierra de Baragueda in a slanting direction towards the Torres Vedras mountain, and only separated from it by the pass of Runa, which was commanded by heavy redoubts. Masséna was therefore to dispose his army on one or the other side of the Baragueda, which could not be easily passed; nor could a movement over it be hidden from the Allies on the Monte Agraça, who from thence

IN THE PENINSULA

could pour down simultaneously on the head and tail of the passing columns with the utmost rapidity, because convenient roads had been previously prepared, and telegraphs established for the transmission of orders."

The total number of forts was 150, armed with 600 guns. During the previous year Admiral Berkeley, who commanded the British Squadron at the mouth of the Tagus, had reported that the troops could be embarked on board the fleet even should the heights of Almada, on the left bank of the river, be in the enemy's hands. He now admitted that he had been mistaken, and thus jeopardised Wellington's whole scheme by his erroneous calculation. Happily there was no immediate danger of an attack on that side, but works were begun there without loss of time.

The lines were entered without hindrance or incident, except that General Crauford, by an unnecessary delay at Alemquer (in defiance of his instructions), once more placed the whole army in imminent danger. Gunboats on the Tagus flanked the position, and on the left bank Fane's Cavalry Brigade patrolled the country, watching the enemy's movements up to the mouth of the Zezere and destroying his boats.

The following was the distribution of the Allied Army on the 10th of October :—

Unit.	Station.
3rd Division	Torres Vedras.
Brigdr.-Gen. Campbell's Portuguese Brigade	
,, ,, Coleman's ,, ,,	
Colonel de Grey's Cavalry Brigade	Ramalhal, in front of Torres Vedras.
5th Division	Enxara dos Cavalleiros.
6th ,,	Ribaldeira.
4th ,,	Duas Portas.
1st ,,	Sobral.

Unit.	Station.
14th Light Dragoons	In front of Sobral, towards Abregada.
Brigdr.-Gen. Pack's Portuguese Brigade	In front of Sobral, towards Alemquer.
Light Division	Arruda.
Cacadores of Light Division	Matos and Carvalhal, behind Arruda.
2nd Division	Alhandra.
Major-Gen. Hamilton's Portuguese Division	Villa Franca.
Le Cor's Portuguese Brigade	Alverca.
Major-General Fane's Cavalry	Loures.
3 Squadron's of ditto	On outpost duty in front of Gen. Hamilton.
Sir S. Cotton with Cavalry Brigade	S. Antonio do Tajal, *en route* for Mafra.
Headquarters	Santa Quintina, near Sobral.

On the 24th of October Wellington received the further support of 6,000 Spaniards under Romana, who had been persuaded to cross the Tagus and occupy Enxara de los Cavalleiros.

On arriving opposite the lines, Masséna was positively astounded. Not only was he unaware of the fortifications, but so greatly had the French topographical department neglected its work that the existence of the mountains was unknown. The Marshal, however, quickly observed that the line occupied by the Allied Army was too much extended to be strong throughout, and that the defenders were terribly hampered by the crowds of Portuguese refugees who entered the lines with them. He therefore determined to make an immediate attack upon an obviously vulnerable point at Arruda. Ney and Reynier, however, refused point blank to carry out his orders, and Masséna gave way. He never got another chance, for Crauford quickly made his post impregnable.

To cover his disappointment the French Commander

flattered himself that he was besieging Lisbon, but it would in some respects be more correct to say that he was himself besieged. Shut in as he already was on three sides, by the sea, the Allies, and the Tagus, even in rear he had little freedom of action ; for the town of Obidos having been garrisoned by Wellington, and the Militia being active on the Mondego, his line of communications became extremely narrow, and his convoys were liable to surprise and capture. Although by occupying the islands in the Tagus, and by scouring the country in the neighbourhood of Santarem and Thomar (where Wellington's orders in regard to devastating the country had been neglected), he got plenty of provisions, his position was actually in danger, for Wellington had a force sufficient to hold Reynier in check on the right and to overwhelm the head of Junot's Corps at Sobral on the right before that General could hope to get assistance from Ney at Otta, fourteen miles distant.

The British Commander, however, after carefully weighing the pros and cons, decided that it would not be long before he would ensure the enemy's retreat without the risk and bloodshed of a battle. Writing to Lord Liverpool on the 27th of October, 1810, he observes : " I am not quite certain that I ought not to attack the French, particularly as they have detached Loison either to look for provisions or to open the road for their retreat; but I think the sure game, and that in which I am likely to lose fewest men, the most consistent with my instructions and the intentions of the King's Government ; and I therefore prefer to wait the attack. Besides, although I have the advantage of numbers, the enemy are in a very good position, which I could not turn with any large force, without laying open my own rear, and the road to the sea." And on another occasion : " I have little doubt of final success, but I have fought a sufficient number of battles to know that the result of any is not certain even with the best arrangements."

At this period also, political, not less than military, matters were engaging Lord Wellington's attention. More than 40,000 refugees from Beira were crowding the banks of the Tagus in his rear. Corn had to be got at any price. The Portuguese Government was partly inert, partly treacherous, and the question of feeding these unfortunate people devolved upon the British Commander and his very able civil colleague, Mr. Stuart. They traded in corn, importing largely from America and elsewhere with great success. Yet in spite of their efforts and the soup kitchens organised by regimental officers, thousands died of hunger. Early in October Stuart took his seat on the Board of Regency, and thenceforward exercised a measure of control. He did much to suppress the intrigues of the other regents, and eventually was given sole control of the British subsidies. Wellington and Admiral Berkeley were also members of the Regency, but do not seem to have attended the meetings of the Council.

Despondency prevailed among the British General Officers, notably Spencer and Charles Stewart, whose letters gave evidence of incapacity to appreciate Lord Wellington's vast designs, and want of loyalty towards their chief. These letters, and many communications, written or verbal, by other officers, were the more dangerous that they coincided with those of the party in power; for the latter, overwhelmed with the timidity habitual to Conservatives, and tormented by a strong opposition (in those days it was, at any rate, the strength and not the weakness of the opposition which hindered the good intentions of the Ministers), felt but little confidence in the ability of Wellington, whose characteristics were

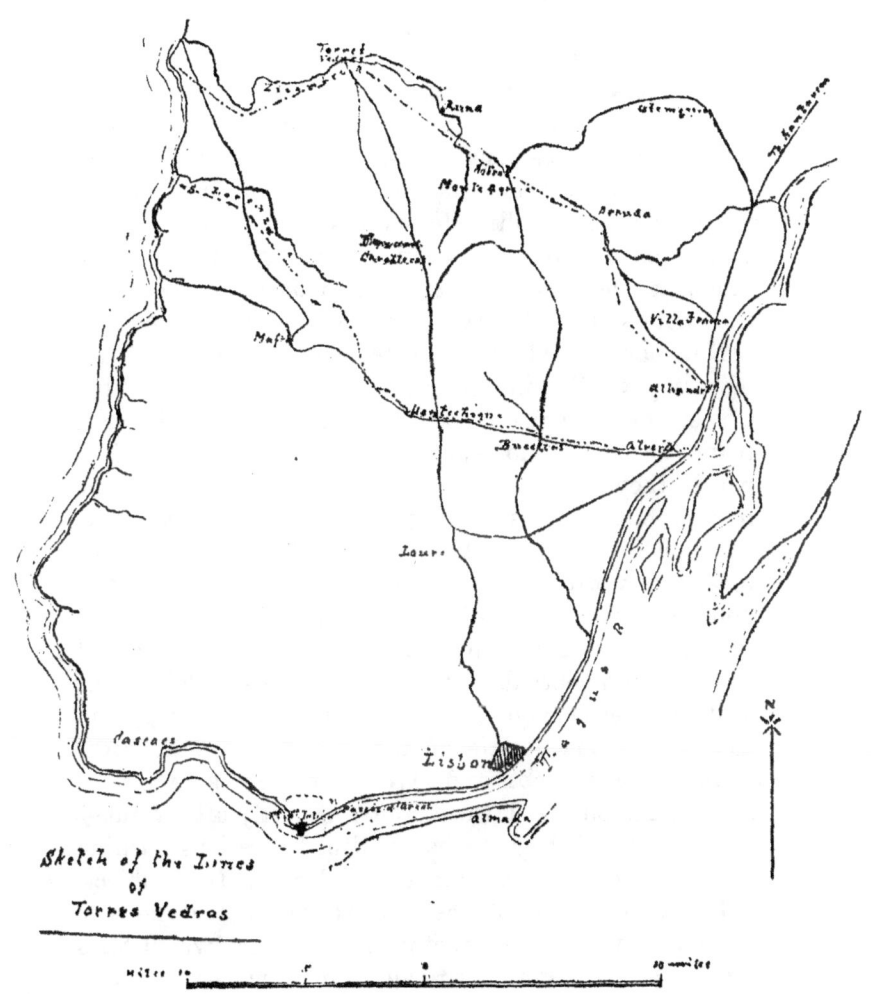

so exactly the opposite to their own, to stem the tide of French invasion and make good the defence of Portugal. Indeed they were inclined to regard him as a person of weak intellect for entertaining such hopes.

In writing to Lord Liverpool, the British Commander quietly and dispassionately gave the reasons for the course which he was pursuing, and for the hopes which he entertained of ultimate success. He paid no regard to the feelings of despondency expressed by his subordinates; but their letters recoiled on themselves, and the writers thenceforward forfeited his confidence.

Newspapers and the private correspondence of his officers gave Wellington an infinity of trouble. Staff Officers—who ought to have known better—would write to newspapers at home, giving details of movements of which they had been confidentially informed; and the newspapers, ready as at the present day to publish anything and everything without reserve, became Napoleon's most trustworthy source of intelligence. In his correspondence we constantly find the Emperor basing instructions to his lieutenants upon information gleaned from English journals. "We are the most indefatigable writers of letters and news that exist in the world; and the fashion and spirit of the times give encouragement to this," observed Wellington, in a letter to Mr. Stuart on the 17th of June. Shortly afterwards—on the 10th of August—he published a serious warning to his officers in a General Order on the subject. " The Commander of the Forces will not make any inquiry to discover the writer of the letters which have occasioned this unnecessary alarm in a quarter in which it was most desirable it should not be created. He has frequently lamented the ignorance which has appeared in the opinions communicated in letters written from the Army, and the indiscretion with which those letters are published. It is impossible that many officers of the Army can have a knowledge of facts to enable them to form opinions of the probable events of the campaign; but their opinions, however erroneous, must, when published, have mischievous effects.

"The communication of that of which all officers have a knowledge, viz., the numbers and disposition of the different divisions of the Army and of its magazines, is still more mischievous than the communication of opinions, as must be obvious to those who reflect that the Army has been for months in the same position; and it is a fact come to the knowledge of the Commander of the Forces that the plans of the enemy have been founded on information of this description extracted from the English newspapers, which information must have been obtained through private letters from officers of the Army.

"Although the difficulties inseparable from the situation of every army engaged in operations in the field, particularly in those of a defensive nature, are much aggravated by communications of this description, the Commander of the Forces only requests that the officers will, for the sake of their own reputations, avoid giving opinions upon which they cannot have a knowledge to enable them to form any; and that if they choose to communicate facts to their correspondents, regarding the positions of the Army, its numbers, formation of its magazines, preparations for breaking bridges, &c., they will urge their correspondents not to publish their letters in the newspapers until it shall be certain that the publication of the intelligence will not be injurious to the Army or to the public service."

Such a grave yet gentle rebuke could not fail to have an effect so far as the officers were concerned, but the chief value of the liberty of the press, in the eyes of

some persons, is the power of publishing any twaddle, however dangerous and ill-advised. Writing to his brother Henry, in November, Wellington remarks :—
" I think much mischief is done in England, not only to me personally, but to the character of the Army and of the country, by foolish observations upon what passes here, in all the newspapers. But in England we are accustomed to read these calumnies, and to read this nonsense, which it is to be hoped makes no real impression, particularly as the same newspaper generally contradicts the first statement, or argues against the first reasoning, in the course of a short time after it has been inserted." History repeats itself. Take the question of the Army at the present day, on which every journal is ready to give its opinion with the utmost assurance; and it will be found that hardly one does not express views diametrically opposed to those which it entertained a few years ago and which the cycle of time will no doubt lead it to express again at no distant date.

By this time the health of the Army had much improved. The number of men actually in hospital was under 4,000. But another cause of anxiety soon arose in the frequent cases of desertion to the enemy. Between April and December, 10,000 of the Portuguese regular troops deserted, and two-thirds of the Militia were absent without leave—probably in order to get food, for they were terribly neglected by their government. But the crime of desertion was not confined exclusively to the Portuguese. Writing on the 12th of November to the Secretary of State, Wellington remarks : " Your lordship will be concerned to observe the continued and, I am concerned to add, increasing desertion of British soldiers to the enemy, a crime which, till within the last few years, was almost unknown in the Army. It is difficult to account for the prevalence of this crime, particularly in this army lately. The British soldiers see the deserters from the enemy coming into their lines daily, all with a story of the unparalleled distresses which their army are suffering, and of the loss of all hope in the result of their enterprise; at the same time that they know and feel that they are suffering no hardship or distress; ... and having every prospect of success.

"The deserters from the British regiments are principally Irishmen; and I attribute the prevalence of the crime very much to the bad description of the men in all the regiments which are drafted from the Irish Militia; and also to the singular habits which many soldiers had acquired, and had communicated to others, in the retreat of the army through the north of Spain in the winter of 1808–9; and *in their subsequent service in the French army*, and in their wandering back again into Portugal." *

It would, however, seem probable that part at least of these desertions were due to the inhuman sentences of courts martial; for the number of lashes inflicted on account of comparatively small offences appears nowadays absolutely incredible. However, there was no dallying with the crime. "Although the Commander of the Forces laments the fate of the unfortunate soldiers who have committed this crime, he is determined that they shall feel the consequences of it during their lives, and that they shall never return to their friends or their homes. He accordingly requests that the Commanding Officers of regiments from which

---

* The italics are our own. The phrase seems curious. Does it mean that after Moore's embarkation, the British stragglers taken prisoners had no objection to fighting on the side of the French against the Spaniards? Or does it merely refer to the period when, as prisoners of war, they marched about with the French Army?

any soldier has deserted to the enemy, will as soon as possible send to the Adjutant-General's office a description of his person, together with an account when he was enlisted with the regiment, where born, to what parish he belongs, in order that the friends of these soldiers may be made acquainted with the crime which they have committed, may be prepared to consider them lost for ever, and may deliver them up to justice in case they should ever return to their native country."

The old difficulty in regard to General Officers also reappeared, and indeed continued till the end of the war. In the first place, shockingly bad appointments were made to the Staff. Thus, in a letter to the Military Secretary at the Horse Guards in August, Wellington observes: "I have received your letter announcing the appointment of ——, ——, and —— to this army. The first I have generally understood to be a madman; I believe it is your opinion that the second is not very wise; the third will, I believe, be a useful man.... There are some in this army whom it is disreputable and quite unsafe to keep.... Really when I reflect upon the characters and attainments of some of the General Officers of this army, and consider that these are the persons on whom I am to rely to lead columns against the French Generals, and who are to carry my instructions into execution, I tremble; and, as Lord Chesterfield said of the Generals of his day, 'I only hope that when the enemy reads the list of their names he trembles as I do.'"

But it was not only the quality of his Generals but the amount of leave of absence which they required which was a source of annoyance to Wellington. Generals Nightingall, Houston and Howard indeed came out in January, 1811, but more than double that number had gone home. Once more the British Commander gave

IN THE PENINSULA

vent to his feelings to the Military Secretary. "I am much annoyed by the General and other Officers of the Army going home. They come to me to ask leave of absence, under pretext of business, which they say it is important to them to transact; and indeed I go so far as to make them declare that it is paramount to every other consideration in life. At the same time, I know that many of them have no business, and that there is no business which cannot be transacted by power of attorney. But how is leave to be refused upon such an application?

"I shall be very much obliged to you, however, if you will tell any General Officer who may come out in future, to settle all his business before he comes out, for that he will get no leave to come home.

"The inconvenience of their going is terrible, and the detail it throws upon me greater than I can well manage; for I am first to instruct one, then a second, and afterwards, upon his return, the first again, upon every duty. At this moment we have seven General Officers gone or going home; and, excepting myself, there is not one in the country who came out with the Army, except General Alexander Campbell, who was all last winter in England."

CHAPTER XVI

Masséna retires—Takes up a position about Santarem.

THE pressure on Masséna's rear, and the exhaustion of the supplies in the immediate neighbourhood of his lines, soon began to tell upon him. His position became untenable, and when the morning mists on the 15th of November had cleared away, the British outposts found no enemy in their front. The plans of the French Commander were, however, still uncertain. He might intend to cross the Tagus, or be merely preparing a new line of advance on Torres Vedras by the western side of the Monte Junto. Hence at first Hill and Crauford, on the Villa Franca and Alemquer roads, alone followed him up. But next day it became obvious that Masséna had no such intention. There seemed every reason to believe that he was making a general retreat; and Wellington, having brought the 1st Division to Cartaxo, and the 4th, 5th, and 6th to Alemquer, was preparing to attack him, when the Marshal suddenly halted and took up a new position of great strength. His left, formed by Reynier's Corps, resting on the Tagus, occupied ground in front of Santarem, almost impregnable and covered by the Rio Mayor. On Reynier's right—but at a distance of twelve miles in a straight line, and nineteen by road—Junot took post on hilly ground about Permes; while the

Cavalry prolonged the line as far as Ourem and Leiria. The 6th Corps, at Thomar, formed a reserve to the whole. In this position the French not only secured great resources of corn and cattle, but communicated by Ourem and Leiria with Coimbra, and, having built bridges over the Zezere, opened up new communications with Spain; one, through Castello Branco; the other, by the Estrada Nova and Belmonte. At the same time, observes Napier, he also preserved the power of resuming offensive operations, whether by a passage of the Tagus on his left, or by turning the Monte Junto on his right.

The distance in a straight line from Santarem to Ourem is 28 miles; to Leiria, 37. Reynier's isolated position seemed at first to invite attack; and reconnaissances were made with a view to ascertaining its strength. It was, however, found that the position was only to be approached by a narrow causeway, for heavy rains had flooded the Rio Mayor and made a turning movement impossible; and after a few days, abattis and entrenchments made all chance of successful attack hopeless.

To penetrate Masséna's line between Santarem and Alcanhede might still have been possible; but, although at this time Wellington had nominally 70,000 men under his command as against 50,000 of the enemy, 12,000 of his men were wanted on the left bank of the Tagus by Lisbon to guard against a possible attack from the side of the Alemtejo; 10,000 would be required to hold Reynier in check; and thus, with an army composed of men belonging to three—or, indeed, including the K.G.L., four—different nations, and not very superior in numbers, Wellington would have to conduct a delicate operation in country "almost impassable from the recent rains" against an enemy acting on interior lines, and fight a hazardous battle, the loss of which would in all probability entail the abandonment of Portugal. "The enemy," he said, "can be relieved from the difficulties of their situation only by the occurrence of some misfortune to the Allied Army; and I shall forward their views by placing the fate of the campaign on the result of a general action on ground chosen by them instead of on that chosen by me.

"I therefore propose to continue the operations of the light detachments on the flanks and rear of the enemy's army, and to confine them as much as possible, but to engage in no serious affair in this part of the country on ground on which the result can be at all doubtful."

On the other hand, the fact that he did not attack was a great relief to the French, whose numbers were often diminished—Marbot says to the extent of 30 per cent.—by the parties detached to gather supplies from the neighbouring country, and who consequently dreaded an attack in force.

There can, however, be no doubt that Wellington was justified by the event. His situation rapidly improved. Even as early as the 13th of December he observes, in a letter to his brother at Cadiz, that there was no longer a prospect of the British Army being under the necessity of embarking.

Masséna had also no inclination to resume the offensive. He was expecting the speedy arrival of the 9th Army Corps, as well as convoys from Castille, whose progress he could aid either by the line of the Mondego or of Belmonte. His army covered two distinct lines of retreat, and was at the same time in a position to communicate with a force from the side of Andalusia in the event of Soult advancing to co-operate with him. He had—at all events for the time being—plenty of food from the plains of Golegao, and was often helped by the capture of convoys nominally intended for the British Army, but which —apparently by the treachery of highly-placed Portuguese officials—were allowed to get within his reach. Time seemed to be as much in favour of Masséna as of Wellington. If Soult were to advance through the Alemtejo the direction of his march would compel the Allies to fall back to the lines of Torres Vedras, and—as the works on the left bank of the Tagus were still incomplete—might entail the abandonment of Portugal by the British Army. The sufferings of the people—so great that 40,000 persons are said to have died in the neighbourhood of Lisbon during this winter—might induce the Portuguese to side against the English and look to the French as their protectors. Of the Portuguese Regency also several members were treacherous and ready to use their influence in the same direction. Finally, reinforcements were at hand, for on the 22nd of December the 9th Army Corps, under command of General Drouet, Count d'Erlon, was on the Coa. But Masséna's hopes of substantial aid therefrom proved fallacious. The Marshal ordered D'Erlon to join him at once; but the latter, leaving a Division under Claparède on the frontier, brought up only the second, under Conroux, consisting of but 6,000 men. Even then he was independent of Masséna, since—odd as it seems—he had not been placed under the Marshal's orders.

Thus passed away the year 1810, the events of which are summarised in the Memorandum by Lord Wellington, *vide* page 299. In spite of certain checks and disappointments, its general course had been highly favourable to the French, who might now flatter themselves that one more effort should expel the British from Portugal, and that, once expelled, their Government would be in no mood to re-attempt the liberation of the Peninsula.

WELLINGTON'S OPERATIONS

The close of the year ultimately proved to indicate the high-water mark of the tide of Gallic invasion. Thenceforward, slowly and intermittently, yet very surely, the tide began to ebb until at length it had receded behind the Pyrenean mountains.

IN THE PENINSULA 331

CHAPTER XVII

Soult advances in order to co-operate with Masséna—Captures Olivenza—Defeats Mendizabel on the Gebora—Masséna's difficulties—Retreats—Pursued by Wellington—Sufferings of both armies—Fall of Badajoz—Masséna continues his retreat.

TO enable one to judge of the stupendous efforts made by Napoleon for the subjugation of Spain and Portugal the following report of a confidential agent sent to Irun, &c., aided by the register of a resident of that place—(Query: The cobbler mentioned by Napier?)—is of interest.

The first appearance of the French troops in Spain was made on the 19th of October, 1807, and up to the end of the year 1810 there had entered as in the table on the following page. The figures, exceeding half a million of men besides 15,000 drivers, &c., include 53,000 French troops who had returned to France since 1807, but, as will be noticed, do not include the reinforcements which entered Spain from time to time by the Eastern Pyrenees.

	Infantry.	Cavalry.	Forges and Ammunition Carts.	Cannon.	Mortars.	Howitzers.
1807	47,500	7,120	100	94	18	55
1808	209,300	36,200	1,800	196		
1809						
January	11,210	1,892	136	8		
February	3,270	3,170	6	350		
March	4,300	—	28	—		
April	7,200	200	7	40		
May	1,560	—	28	—		
June	850	—	50	—		
July	600	80				
August	1,380	—	30	—		
September	1,500	—	20	—		
October	96	—	—	—		
November	3,280	80	—	—		
December	8,940	1,700	—	36		
Total in 1809	44,950	4,302		434		
1810						
January	26,500	10,150	590	10	4	
February	18,150	5,670	453	16	6	
March	18,036	2,290	645	16	6	
April	6,414	854	325	—		
May	5,090	1,500	82	—		
June	9,790	640	188	27		
July	7,140	50	32			
August	9,800	2,240	278	12		
September	2,990	500	275	—		
October	7,550	1,500	97	8		
November	11,750	—	92	—		
December	1,300	340	152	7		
Total in 1810	124,510	25,734	3,209	96	16	
1811						
Jan'ry 28th	600	180				
Grand Total	426,860	73,536	5,414	820	34	55

IN THE PENINSULA

On the other hand, up to the 22nd of February, 1811, 48,228 Spanish, British, and Portuguese prisoners had entered France by the pass of Irun.

At the opening of the year a new factor began to influence the strategical situation. Signs of menace appeared from the side of Andalusia. Marshal Soult had hitherto been engaged in operations against Cadiz. Although an advance on Lisbon in combination with Masséna had from the outset formed a principal part of his instructions, he felt it necessary as a preliminary to make himself master of the fortresses of Olivenza and Badajoz, and applied for the Emperor's permission to his plan. Wellington's vigilance prevented Soult receiving intelligence of Masséna. The Emperor's orders were intercepted by guerillas. It was not till towards the end of December that instructions had reached him to move through the Alemtejo to aid Masséna.

Of the Army of the South, the 1st Corps was occupied in the blockade of Cadiz. The 4th was engaged in putting down insurrection in the direction of Murcia. The 5th, commanded by Mortier, was alone available. Expecting to be opposed by Mendizabel and Ballesteros, who occupied Estremadura and would harass his communications with Seville, Soult decided to avail himself of the Emperor's permission to capture the frontier fortresses as a preliminary. Napier, who is perhaps unduly biassed in Soult's favour, seems to concur in this decision. The French General Thiébault, who was decidedly prejudiced against the Marshal, considers, on the contrary, that he should have ignored the fortresses, the garrisons for which would absorb a considerable portion of his comparatively weak force, and should have marched with every available man of the 5th Corps upon Santarem. It is to be noticed that had he done this Soult would have been easily in time to carry out the share of the combination assigned him by Masséna and Napoleon, and that in accordance with the Emperor's new arrangements he would have opened another line of communication with Madrid by the valley of the Tagus, and would have been supported by the Army of the Centre. From Merida to Niza *viâ* Valencia d'Alcantara is about 100 miles; from Niza to the mouth of the Tagus about 50 miles. Soult should have been opposite Punhete by the 20th of January, when he would have taken Beresford in flank.

On the 2nd of January, 1811, a force, made up of 4,000 Cavalry, 16,000 Infantry, and 54 guns, under Soult's personal command, was concentrated at Seville. On the 5th it entered Zafra. Next day the advance guard seized the bridge of Merida over the Guadiana, which, in despite of Wellington's urgent advice, had been left intact. Lord Wellington's annoyance was extreme. He had been the first to detect and warn the Spanish Generals of the approaching storm. Yet all in vain. "I think," wrote he, "the conduct of the Spaniards upon this occasion beats everything they have ever done before. If they had only delayed Mortier for a few days upon the Guadiana I believe really that the people in my front must have gone; and be it remembered that 400 French Infantry held the bridge and post of Merida for a month in the summer of 1808 against Cuesta's whole army! So much for the Spaniards. We shall now see whether, having brought upon us nearly the whole French army, *boasting* will relieve Cadiz."

A Brigade of La Houssaye's Cavalry, belonging to the Army of the Centre, protected Soult's flank in his march on Olivenza by guarding the line of the Tagus from Arzobispo to Alcantara. On the 11th Olivenza was invested. Ballesteros had been called away to the Condado de Niebla on the 21st of December, the very day on which Soult had marched from Cadiz. The French had therefore to reckon only with Mendizabel. One Division of this officer's force, however, garrisoned Olivenza, and the remainder, which was in the neighbourhood of Badajoz, was kept at a distance by Soult's Dragoons.

The enemy's approach in Estremadura, at a time when the fortifications of Almada were far from complete, could not fail to give Wellington considerable anxiety. It was also intensely annoying to him that Mendizabel should have immured 4,500 of his best men in Olivenza, "a place without artillery, ammunition, or provisions, under circumstances in which it was impossible, if they should be attacked, that they could be relieved." The British Commander advised the reoccupation of the right bank of the Guadiana and the destruction of the bridges of Merida and Medellin; the preparation of an entrenched camp on the heights between Badajoz and Campo Mayor for Romana's army; the return of Ballesteros; and fourthly, that the boats for a bridge at Badajoz should be sent to Elvas to enable Romana, if occasion offered, to attack the enemy on the left bank of the Guadiana. "All these measures," said Wellington, in conclusion, "are very simple and practicable if they are immediately commenced in earnest; but if this plan, or some other of this description, is not adopted at an early period, and it forms part of the enemy's plan to blockade Badajoz . . . he will succeed in obtaining possession of the place, which has no chance of being preserved, unless Masséna should be obliged to withdraw from his position in Portugal."

For the Spaniards to act promptly was impossible. On the 23rd Olivenza surrendered, and its garrison became prisoners of war.

On the 28th Ballesteros was attacked at Castillejo by a

Division under Gazan, and driven across the Guadiana into the Algarves with the loss of 3,000 men.

On the day previous Soult had invested Badajoz. Mendizabel had been strongly advised by Wellington, and ordered by Romana, to take up a strong position in rear of the watersmeet of the Gebora and Guadiana, and there to await the arrival of the outlying detachments which, to the number of 8,000 or 10,000 men, were fast approaching. So posted, Wellington believed it would be impossible for Soult either to invest or even interfere with the communications of the place. Unfortunately the sudden death of Romana removed all check on Mendizabel. He promptly shut himself up in Badajoz—which, although a siege had been expected for the last twelvemonth, was destitute of provisions—with 6,000 men, and was immediately surrounded by the French Army. Fortune, however, favoured him. The severity of the weather necessitated the recall over the river of the French Cavalry which had been investing the western side of the fortress. Mendizabel then concentrated at Elvas the troops formerly under Romana, now commanded by Virues, and the Brigade under Carlos D'Espana; but instead of profiting by the opportunity and taking up the position recommended by Wellington, he again occupied Badajoz. On the 8th of February he attempted to raise the siege by a vigorous sortie, but, being repelled, retired behind the Guadiana, taking up a position on the heights of San Christoval, but without entrenching it. Here, in spite of the protection of the Gebora river and the Fort, he was surprised on the morning of the 19th and driven off in headlong rout with the loss of 900 men killed, 8,000 captured, and the whole of his artillery. Truly had Wellington observed " with troops of any other nation success is certain, but no calculation can be made of any operations in which Spanish troops are engaged." In this affair the French

IN THE PENINSULA

casualties, as stated in Soult's despatch, amounted only to 26 killed and 171 wounded.

The siege was then resumed. Fortunately, the civil population had fled, leaving plenty of stores and provisions for the 9,000 men composing the garrison. The French had lost nearly 2,000 men since they had left Seville; the season was against them and food scarce. Rapid progress was not to be expected.

On the other hand, the annihilation of Mendizabel's army was a serious blow to Lord Wellington, whose position became for the moment rather critical. The works guarding the left bank of the Tagus at Almada were, as already stated, incomplete. Everything therefore now depended on the defence of Badajoz. On Soult's approach the detachment on the left bank of the Tagus had been reinforced. General Hill had gone to England sick, and the command was given to Beresford, who had under him five regiments of Cavalry, the 2nd and Hamilton's Portuguese Division of Infantry, making up about 16,000 men and 18 guns, without reckoning a Spanish Brigade under Don Carlos D'Espana, whose misconduct made it a hindrance rather than an aid.

Wellington had been only awaiting the arrival of reinforcements from England to detach this force against Soult, but the defeat of the Spaniards on the Gebora put an end to the scheme. The only remaining resource was an attack upon Masséna, and Wellington planned a tactical combination on a large scale. Beresford was to cross the Tagus at Abrantes and fall on the enemy's rear; while of the troops on the right bank two Divisions were to contain Reynier at Santarem, and the remainder, operating by Rio Mayor and Tremes, force back Masséna's centre and right, and then drive Reynier into the river. But in the absence of the reinforcements, which were delayed by contrary winds, the plan had to be abandoned;

and when, at a later date, he was able to inspect the enemy's position, Wellington was glad that he had not attempted it.

He was well aware (1) that, although Masséna was holding on to his position with all the tenacity which had characterised his defence of Genoa ten years earlier, the resources of the country which had so far supplied his opponent were exhausted; (2) that an important convoy under General Gardanne had failed to reach him; and (3) that no long time would elapse before he would be compelled by famine to retreat. But matters were even more favourable to the Allies than Wellington was aware of. It was only by systematic torture of the starving peasantry that the French were able to induce them to part with their scanty stores, and the spirit of insubordination in the French camp had spread to such an extent as of itself to render Masséna's position almost untenable.

On the 5th of February General Foy, who had been sent to make a personal report to the Emperor, returned with a small reinforcement. The instructions which he brought were to the effect that the Emperor considered it of the first importance to hold on to Santarem, construct bridge-heads on both banks of the Tagus, harass the Allies, and appropriate the resources of the left bank. In the event of a retirement becoming inevitable, the army was to take post behind the Mondego, for Foy had been unable to convince the Emperor that in the country beyond that river the army could not subsist. Napoleon quite approved of Masséna's plan either to starve out Lisbon or force the British to embark, and thus strengthen the hands of the Opposition in England. To this end he had decided (1) to amalgamate the 3rd, 4th, 5th, 6th and 7th Governments, comprising the Spanish provinces between the boundaries of France and

IN THE PENINSULA 339

Portugal, under the command of Marshal Bessières, with the title of "The Army of the North," which was to assist and act as a reserve to the Army of Portugal; (2) that the 9th Army Corps should shortly be placed under command of Masséna; (3) that Soult should forthwith march with the 5th Corps on Santarem to enable Masséna to act on both sides of the Tagus and appropriate the resources of the Alemtejo, while the Army of the Centre should open a new line of communication by way of Madrid and the Tagus. Finally, reinforcements were to be despatched as soon as practicable.

Had everything been carried out as the Emperor desired, the result of the campaign might have been very different; but day after day passed, and the only sign of Soult to the Army of Portugal was the booming of the guns of Badajoz, showing that the fortress still held out. Ney, Reynier, and Drouet declared they would remain no longer. All through the month of February Masséna held his colleagues at bay. March, however, still brought no tidings of Soult, but, on the contrary, it did bring news of the arrival of Wellington's reinforcements. The Marshal then gave way. On the night of the 5th he broke up his camp. His first idea seems to have been to cross the Tagus at the mouth of the Zezere and march to join Soult before Badajoz. But the vigilance of Beresford prevented him getting any further information; while Wellington, acting on interior lines, had collected so many boats on the Tagus that he could have thrown his troops over from the right to the left bank much more quickly than his adversary, and, in co-operation with the Portuguese Militia from the Ponçul, could have opposed him with a greatly superior force. These considerations determined Masséna to retire upon the Mondego, where he hoped to seize Oporto and be joined by the remaining Division of the 9th Corps under

General Claparède—at present occupying Guarda as a post on the line of communications—and by other troops. With his effective force raised from 50,000 to 70,000 men he would then be enabled to advance once more against Lisbon in co-operation with Soult and a connecting force on the Zezere, in accordance with the instructions given by Napoleon in 1809.

In his despatch to the Chief of the General Staff, Marshal Berthier, dated March 6th, Masséna explains his position. After relating his preparations for crossing the Tagus and the reasons which led him at last to consider the operation too hazardous, he goes on: " Such was the position when General Foy arrived on the 5th of February, bringing your despatch of the 22nd of December. In accordance with the tenour of it, together with the verbal message from His Majesty brought by General Foy, I reckoned on the prompt co-operation of the 5th Corps which, you said, was to be brought to the left bank of the Tagus at Villa Flor. Having received no direct orders to effect the passage of this river, and seeing nothing to make me think His Majesty considered it essential for me to do so, I determined to suspend this operation, and not uselessly to expose the army to attack and all the contingent hazards, at a time when I could hope to gain the same advantages by the arrival of the 5th Corps. General Foy having, on the 27th of January, despatched a courier to the Duke of Dalmatia (Soult) to say that the Army of Portugal was prepared to cross the Tagus, but that the co-operation of his army as directed by His Majesty was absolutely essential, it seemed that a strong detachment ought to be on the point of reaching the river. Thus I had to await the arrival of the 5th Corps at Villa Flor to give me precise information as to the resources of the Alemtejo, and bring heavy guns which we badly want but could not carry across the mountains of Beira.

"My hopes have not been realised. Although my information gave me assurance that a French Corps was in the higher Alemtejo, I was unable to gather, either by frequent reconnaissances or by spies or by the enemy's movements that this Corps was near the Tagus. For some time salvoes of artillery were heard in the direction of Badajoz; but the cessation of these sounds for more than three weeks prove that the siege is either raised or the place taken; that consequently I cannot expect any co-operation, and that the upshot is that, instead of the Army of Portugal being assisted by that of the South, the former has, on the contrary, served to protect and cover the operations on the Guadiana.

"The month of February was spent in improving and completing our means of passage and our works. During the whole time I continually harassed the enemy with demonstrations, frequent reconnaissances, expeditions on the Tagus and its islands, and operations against the peasantry collected about Pombal, Espinal, Castello Branco, &c., in which we always gained the advantage and procured provisions. We made it our business to move in the direction of Villa Flor, Montalvao, or even higher up the Tagus in order to get news of the 5th Corps, and our demonstrations along the river were redoubled with a view to prevent the enemy detaching towards Badajoz. . . . Whilst we were working incessantly at Punhete and other parts of the line the enemy was busily strengthening his defences. He concentrated the whole Corps of Hill and Beresford between Punhete and Chamusca; and by means of the works which he had thrown up opposite Santarem he has been able to throw a part of Picton's Division across to the left bank of the Tagus in the direction of Alpiaca and Almeirim. By means of signals all these troops can concentrate in a few hours upon any threatened point. Thus the passage of the Tagus, already very difficult on account of the steep banks, its width, the swiftness of its current . . . has become hazardous in the extreme, since with inferior numbers we should have to carry entrenchments well manned, or establish a bridge under the enemy's fire in order to attack his line afterwards. . . . If the passage of the Tagus does not succeed, in addition to the loss and moral effect the army loses its line of operations on Coimbra, it is thrown back upon Spain, with no other line of retreat than a sterile and terrible country, with roads leading over rocks, precipices and torrents where it must expect to lose part of its artillery, and be reduced to abandoning its sick, wounded, and stragglers. . . . In consequence of General Foy's report of His Majesty's intentions to spin out the war and conduct it on a sound system while continuing to hold the enemy in check, I have had, my Lord, to decide a new question,—Is it better to carry the whole army into the Alemtejo or into the district between Pombal and Coimbra?

"My opinion is that in throwing ourselves into the Alemtejo, and leaving a river like the Tagus between ourselves and the enemy—without the power of keeping our bridging equipment, which in default of horses cannot be carried—the Allied Army would no longer be held in check; but that under cover of this barrier and of the entrenchments of Setuval and Almeida, Lord Wellington would place the English into cantonments to recruit them, at the same time sending detachments of Portuguese and Militia to contain the 9th Corps, to hinder its progress beyond the frontier, and to strengthen and re-organise the northern provinces of Portugal. Moreover the recent destruction of food stuffs by the English, and the unhealthy state of the Lower Alemtejo, would soon compel our army to ascend the river in the direction of Portalégre, or to throw itself upon the Guadiana, districts

IN THE PENINSULA 343

intended, probably, some day or other for the 5th Corps. The army, which is in want of many things, would be still more remote from the supplies which General Foy tells me have been accumulated at Ciudad Rodrigo and Almeida, and from its true lines of operation and communication; and it would, in addition, be left a long time out of reach of letters from France. In fine, my Lord, the reasons for which I had projected a passage into the Alemtejo no longer exist, for the Army of the South seems destined to besiege fortresses.

"I think, on the other hand, that I recognise all the advantages of, and an entire conformity with the intentions of His Majesty, in the change of position which the army is about to effect by pivoting on Pombal with a view to forming front between the Zezere and the sea. It will face the enemy, and will have neither earthworks nor Tagus to cross. It will be in a position to act incessantly against his outposts, his detachments, his weak points, should the enemy unexpectedly approach us: a contingency incredible by reason of the devastation of the country, the dearth of provisions, and his studied inactivity. Were the English remaining near Lisbon, I should continue to act by detachments on the Zezere and Tagus; and by means either of the bridge of Pedrogão or some other which I should build, the left bank of the former river would be supported. When the army is a little re-organised and has had reinforcements and ammunition, it will still be in a position to take up a post in advance, should His Majesty desire it; and if, when the Tagus is low, His Majesty should think well to push our posts beyond the river, the army would find supplies in the Alemtejo for some months after the harvest.

"I hope to find subsistence on the Mondego for 50 or 60 days; which will give time for the organisation of the supplies which can be passed through Spain. By placing a Division of the 9th Corps at Trancoso and Guarda, another towards Pinhanços on the Mondego and about Viseu, a double line of communications with France and Spain will be solidly and systematically established. This Army Corps will hold the approaches from the head of the Zezere valley, will keep an eye on the enemy's parties who may be able to menace Elja, and will for some time find provisions in the fertile valleys of La Cova de Beira. In short, if the 5th Corps occupies the frontier of the Alemtejo, or besieges fortresses, the enemy will find himself disturbed on both sides of the Tagus, and compelled either to divide his force or to abandon one bank entirely; then, by means of a separate corps—which it would be necessary to post in any case at Alcantara—the Armies of the South and of Portugal would be enabled to act in concert and the latter would still be in a position to cover and protect the communications of the former.

"To sum up. The hazard connected with the passage of the Tagus at the present moment; the failure of the 5th Corps to co-operate—an assistance which I was led three months ago to expect; the impossibility of occupying both banks, and the fact of the position of the enemy beyond the Tagus being less menacing than on the right bank; the change of the situation in the Alemtejo owing to its devastation by the English and by the operations of the Army of the South; all these considerations lead me to the opinion that it is more in conformity with General Foy's report of His Majesty's intentions and policy and with the interests of the Army, to march upon Pombal, take up a position there and maintain the troops as long as possible on the banks of the Mondego. This is the step which I am about to take, for it is impossible to stay any longer in our present positions. The Army has borne all that it is physically possible to bear. By dint of industry, care, and self-denial, it has subsisted for six months in a country where it could not be expected to subsist a fortnight: a country, the devastation of which by the enemy was prevented solely by the rapidity of our marches. At the present time, the district which we occupy, and its environs within a radius of five or six marches, are totally exhausted. The few remaining inhabitants are reduced to live on roots, acorns, and herbs. The fatigue parties no longer find, even at a distance, the Indian corn which for a long time past has formed the food of the officer as well as of the private soldier. Meat is exhausted; straw entirely consumed; and the horses have been on green food for more than a month, at a time of year when the grass is extremely short. Thus it happens every day that a certain number are lost by the Cavalry and Artillery. The men's clothing is in a very bad state, and it has become so difficult to repair or replace shoes, that many have foot-gear made out of fresh skins. The weather daily deteriorates the cartridges and reserve of biscuit. Ammunition is scarce. Gun carriages are much diminished by daily wear and tear. The transport waggons—of which we never had too many—are necessarily much reduced. . . .

"High praise is due to the Army for its perseverance and devotion. Its hardships have been increased by the rains which have fallen during the last few months; and I should not have exacted such sacrifices had I not to some extent anticipated His Majesty's intentions and been of opinion that as this campaign could not be terminated by one brilliant stroke, it must—more particularly in view of the political crisis in England—resolve itself into a contest of tenacity against the English Army and the whole of Portugal. My bridging equipment and the works at Punhete have favoured my dispositions not a little. They have been worth another

Army Corps to me by retaining in front of them a considerable detachment of the enemy, . . . and these demonstrations, by holding the enemy to the Tagus, have greatly helped the operations of the Duke of Dalmatia.

" On the 6th of March the Army will execute its movement for the change of position. . . . The 2nd and 8th Corps will take post the next day upon the heights of Golegao and Torres Novas. The artillery will appear to prepare a passage of the river at Punhete, . . . and for two days the enemy will be in uncertainty as to our object. . . . Leiria is the pivot of the movement and the centre of resistance. I shall concentrate there, under command of the Duke of Elchingen (Ney), the 1st Division of the 9th Corps, two Divisions of the 6th, and the Cavalry of the Army. On the third day, before the enemy has had time to unravel my intentions, the Army will be in line from Leiria to Thomar, and will be put in motion; the 2nd Corps from Thomar in the direction of Espinhal; the 3rd Division of the 6th Corps from Chao de Macans upon Anciao; the 8th Corps from the same village upon Pombal and Redhinha; the 6th and 9th Corps will form the rearguard from Leiria upon Pombal. The Army will halt in its new positions, will effect the passage of the Mondego, and the 9th Corps will march upon Celorico. In consequence of these dispositions the enemy will be unable to operate against the various columns of the Army, and will remain in a state of indecision until the completion of the change of position. . . ."

Wellington was by this time well aware of Masséna's intention to retreat. He decided to follow him up with five Divisions and to send the 2nd and 4th, under Beresford, to relieve Badajoz. The British Commander was, however, terribly handicapped by the want of General Officers, for although Generals Houston, Nightingall and

IN THE PENINSULA

Howard had joined the Army, no less than seven, viz., Cotton, Hill, Leith, Fane, Anson, Tilson and Robert Crauford—the last named in despite of a personal appeal made to him by Wellington—had all gone home; and though some, such as Hill, had done so purely on account of their health, others would seem to have asked for leave on less pressing grounds. The consequence was that makeshifts had to be contrived, and that in the operations about to begin Wellington declared that he was obliged to be General of Cavalry, of the advance guard, and the leader of two or three columns, sometimes on the same day. He felt their desertion bitterly. "I did everything in my power," said he in a letter to Lord Liverpool, "to prevail upon them not to go, but in vain; and I acknowledge that it has given me satisfaction to find that they have been roughly handled in the newspapers."

In his retreat, Masséna showed himself worthy of his reputation. Having destroyed his spare ammunition, unhorsed guns and superfluous stores, and having sent his sick to Thomar, he made a feint with the 2nd Corps on the Zezere; then, suddenly concentrating his Cavalry and the 6th Corps at Leiria, threatened the lines of Terres Vedras from the west side of the Monte Junta. Wellington—as Masséna had foretold—hesitated to advance without more definite knowledge; and the French Marshal, having gained a start of four days, then withdrew the 2nd Corps and Loison's Division of the 6th by the Espinhal road and rapidly concentrated the 8th Corps, the two remaining Divisions of the 6th and that of the 9th in front of Pombal on the Soure.

The strategical situation of the opposing armies was not unlike that after the passage of the Douro in 1809; the Zezere taking the place of the Tamega. But in the present case, Wellington had no desire to hem the enemy in. On the contrary, his fear was lest the measures which he had taken should have made this retreat too difficult.

The following extract of a letter from Colonel Jenkinson, R.A., dated 21st of March, and quoted at length in Sup. Des. vii. p. 85, gives an account of Wellington's preliminary movements: "Lord Wellington had long held out, contrary to the opinion of every person in the army, that he did not entertain the slightest doubt of the enemy being compelled to retire for want of provisions, and daily made a most minute reconnaissance of their position; and on the 5th was persuaded that if retreat was not their object, some important movement was intended.

"Before daybreak on the 6th Lord Wellington received a letter from a person he had been in the habit of corresponding with at Santarem, stating that the enemy had retired, and he immediately put his army in motion in three columns: the left on the great Coimbra road, the centre by Santarem and Thomar to Pombal, and the right upon the road from Santarem through Golegao, Atalaya, and Thomar to Espinal, calculating on their being compelled to take the road by the Ponte de Murcella.

"The first day the Cavalry, Ross's troop (R.H.A.) and Light Division reached Pernes, the 1st and 4th Divisions of Infantry were posted near Golegao, the 6th Division* and other troops at Santarem, and the 3rd and 5th Divisions one march on the great Coimbra road; and a British Brigade of Infantry crossed the Tagus to observe whether any column of the French passed the Zezere; and having found it to be otherwise, and that they had destroyed all their boats on that river, they crossed the Tagus and joined their Corps.

* A 6th Division had been recently organised, and new arrivals enabled Wellington to form a 7th Division shortly afterwards.

"The 8th, the Cavalry and Light Division pushed on to Caceres and came up with the rearguard of the enemy's column upon that road, and which was harassed for some hours by the former and two of Ross's guns, which so alarmed them that they blew up four ammunition waggons and halted a *corps d'armée* at the junction of the Caceres and high road in order to keep us in check.

"The position they selected was well calculated to prevent our small force from effecting anything against them, and we were therefore compelled to halt until such a reinforcement should arrive as would enable us to remove them from it. . . ."

On the 10th, Nightingall's Brigade of the 1st Division was following Reynier. The 3rd and 5th Divisions were at Leiria. In view of the French concentration the 4th Division had been recalled on its march to Badajoz; and, together with the 1st, 6th, and Light Divisions, Pack's Portuguese Brigade and the Cavalry—commanded in Sir Stapleton's absence by General Slade—was advancing by way of Thomar. On the approach of Wellington, Masséna retired through the town of Pombal, covered by his rearguard under Ney. Next morning—the 11th— his picquets were driven in by the Light Division and followed up through the town, now in flames. Ney, however, took up a strong position on the heights beyond, and though during the course of the day outflanked by the British troops coming down the Soure river, made good his retreat at dusk.

On the day following, the British advance guard, consisting of the Cavalry and Light Division under Sir William Erskine, found him eight miles further on, in occupation of the wooded tableland in front of the village of Redinha, with his right posted on the heights overlooking the Soure and his left on the Redinha stream. Ney showed a bold front, and Wellington, after a preliminary skirmish, thinking the Marshal had a much larger force than the 5,000 or 6,000 men actually present, felt it prudent to deploy 30,000 men. An hour was thus lost. Then the attack was launched. "Figure to yourself," writes Jenkinson, "14,000 men with their colours unfurled, advancing in line, and supported by solid columns of Infantry and Cavalry on their flanks, and a second line in rear of the centre. The advance of the whole army in line, which was formed as if by magic . . . was majestic beyond description. . . ." The Light Division on the left advanced rapidly against the enemy's right; the 4th Division against his centre, while Picton's "fighting 3rd Division" had enveloped and threatened to roll up his left and cut him from the village of Redinha. But Ney had taken advantage of Wellington's deliberation to withdraw his troops behind the river, and his position was now held merely by a line of skirmishers. Covered by the smoke of a volley these at once disappeared over a bridge which had not previously been visible to Picton, and immediately placed the burning village of Redinha between themselves and their pursuers. Although Picton's light troops—of which the 60th were the nucleus—dashing forward crossed the Redinha river by a ford close to the bridge almost simultaneously with the French, the ford was too narrow to admit of Colville's Brigade joining them at once, and below the bridge the river was unfordable. Otherwise Ney would have been in a parlous condition, for his line of retreat on the further bank ran parallel to the river down stream and close to it; but being directly away from the 3rd Division, the latter found the direction of their attack useless and failed to intercept the French. Ney consequently making good his retreat, escaped; yet with so little to spare that he retired twelve miles before taking up another defensive position at Condeixa.

The intention of Masséna having been to retire behind the Mondego at Coimbra, he had on the 10th directed Ney to send a Brigade to seize that town. The order was disregarded, and as time was pressing, the French Commander next day sent Montbrun there with a Cavalry Division. Wellington's object, on the other hand, was to press his opponent so closely in his retreat as to drive him out of Portugal without stopping. But believing it impossible to hold the line of the Mondego he had given the Portuguese General Bacellar, who commanded the Militia on the right bank, orders to secure Oporto; and had directed Colonels Trant and Wilson to retire when pressed from the Vouga and Mondego in succession, taking care to secure all boats and break up all roads in their retreat. But Trant was a singularly bold and enterprising officer. Although he had destroyed an arch of the Coimbra bridge, the fords of the Mondego were passable and the greater part of his force had, by Bacellar's orders, already retired on the Vouga. Noticing, however, that the Mondego again showed signs of flood, and encouraged by the sound of Wellington's guns approaching, he resolved with his 300 remaining Militiamen to hold the river against the French Cavalry, whose scouts were already fording it a league higher up. Strangely to say his boldness was crowned with success. An advanced party having been repulsed, Montbrun—the man who under the eye of the Emperor had achieved the dazzling exploit of forcing the Somosierra pass with a charge of Cavalry—now allowed himself to be overawed by a handful of raw Militiamen, made no further attempt to force the passage, and lost Masséna the key of his retreat! Such is human nature!

The Commander-in-Chief, weakly accepting Montbrun's report without an attempt to verify it; and influenced by a rumour of the parallel advance of the British 2nd Division along the Zezere, instantly changed his line of retreat; and abandoning all idea of holding the country beyond the Mondego, directed his troops to turn eastward at an acute angle, and march on Puente de Murcella. Ney, who had barricaded the road leading on Condeixa from the south, was ordered to cover the movement; but the sudden change of direction exposed the whole flank. Wellington, detecting the alteration of plan, instantly deduced therefrom that Trant was still holding Coimbra, and directed Picton to move to his right by mountain paths towards the only road now available for the enemy's retirement.

Ney, at Condeixa, finding himself in imminent danger of being cut off, abandoned the town and followed the retreating columns. He could hardly have done otherwise; but neglected to report his movement to the Commander-in-Chief, and Masséna, who was outside Fuente Coberta—a village about five miles east of Condeixa—where the Divisions of Clausel and Loison had been posted to guard the right flank of the retiring army, was, about 3 p.m., surprised by the sudden appearance of Picton's Division, and as nearly as possible captured. It was indeed with difficulty that the Marshal after nightfall succeeded in regaining the French lines; and the unhappy lady who shared his fortunes, mounted on a horse which again and again fell down over the boulders which strewed the mountain paths, had a bitter experience, although gallantly borne, of the hardships of warfare.

Communication was immediately established by Wellington with Coimbra. During the night the outlying Divisions of the French army regained the main body, and in the morning (14th) Erskine, advancing in a thick mist, without the most ordinary military precautions, found himself involved in a frontal attack upon the 6th and 8th Corps posted at Cazal Nova on the "almost

IN THE PENINSULA

inaccessible hills leading in succession to the strong pass of Miranda de Corvo." In order to enable the guns and baggage to pass the defile at Miranda, it was absolutely essential for Ney to gain time. Wellington's intention had as usual been to turn the French out of their position by menacing their flanks. By Erskine's folly the combination was spoilt. The Light Division, although deployed in one thin line, was unable to show a front equal to that of the enemy; and even though protected by the stone walls on the mountain side, had as much as it could do to hold its ground. It was relieved by Picton, who not only sent the 60th to prolong its line to the right, but with Ross's battery and the remainder of his Division turned the enemy's left. The 1st, 5th, and 6th Divisions then came up in support of the centre; and Cole, appearing on Picton's outer flank, still further enveloped the French left. "General Picton's advance to turn their left was so rapid, and the attack of the Light Division on their right so furious, that they were obliged to abandon the hill with precipitation, the effect of which was beautiful; for their guns which were at one moment playing on the face of the hill which presented itself to us, were by Picton's Division and Ross's guns getting so completely round their flank, suddenly withdrawn and opened almost to their rear, which was followed by the rapid retreat of their Infantry, and the no less rapid advance of ours and our Artillery, which soon gained the height and played with the finest effect upon them while retiring in the utmost disorder." (Letter of Col. Jenkinson, R.A., Sup. Des. vii. p. 87.) Ney then retired to Miranda de Corvo, contesting every available position on the way. A hundred of his men were taken and many killed or wounded, but he inflicted a loss of 130, and, having held on till sunset, gained his object in enabling Masséna to pass his troops, baggage, and guns through the defile of Miranda. Only fourteen ammunition waggons and two hundred mules were abandoned.

Cole, with the 4th Division and the Heavy Cavalry Brigade, then moved by order to Penella, where they joined Nightingall and crossed the Essa. The movement dislodged Reynier, who rejoined Masséna from Espinhal; and the French Commander-in-Chief, fearing to have his left enveloped in the morning, retired by night across the Ceira. But finding his army now crowded into a narrow defile between the mountains and the Mondego, he destroyed much of his impedimenta, took up a strong position behind the river and directed Ney to gain time for the main body by disputing the passage, but not to risk a general action.

"The result of these operations," wrote Wellington to Lord Liverpool on the 14th, "has been that we have saved Coimbra and Upper Beira from the enemy's ravages: we have opened the communication with the northern provinces: and we have obliged the enemy to take for their retreat the road by Ponte de Murcella, on which they must be annoyed by the Militia acting in security upon their flank, while the Allied Army will press upon their rear.

"The whole country, however, affords many advantageous positions to a retreating army, of which the enemy have shown that they know how to avail themselves. They are retreating from the country, as they entered it, in one solid mass, covering their rear on every march by the operations of either one or two *corps d'armée* in the strong positions which the country affords, which *corps d'armée* are closely supported by the main body. Before they quitted their position they destroyed a part of their cannon and ammunition, and they have since blown up whatever the horses were unable to draw away.

They have no provisions, excepting what they plunder on the spot, or having plundered, what the soldiers carry on their backs, and live cattle.

"I am concerned to be obliged to add to this account, that their conduct throughout this retreat has been marked by a barbarity seldom equalled, and never surpassed. Even in the towns of Torres Novas, Thomar, and Pernes, in which the headquarters of some of the corps had been for four months, and in which the inhabitants had been invited by promises of good treatment to remain, they were plundered, and many of their houses destroyed on the night the enemy withdrew from their position, and they have since burnt every town and village through which they have passed; . . . there is not an inhabitant of the country of any class or description, who has had any dealing with the French army, who has not had reason to repent of it and to complain of them. This is the mode in which the promises have been performed, and the assurances have been fulfilled, which were held out in the proclamation of the French Commander-in-Chief, in which he told the inhabitants of Portugal that he was not come to make war upon them, but with a powerful army of 110,000 men to drive the English into the sea.

"It is to be hoped that the example of what has occurred in this country will teach the people of this and of other nations what value they ought to place on such promises and assurances; and that there is no security for life, or for anything which makes life valuable, excepting in decided resistance to the enemy."

Before daybreak on this—the 14th—Wellington had the extreme mortification of hearing that Badajoz had fallen on the 11th. He had had favourable accounts of the garrison, but unfortunately in a sortie on the 2nd, the

Governor, Menacho, had been killed; and although Wellington had told his successor, General Imas, that Masséna was in full retreat and that Beresford was on his way to relieve the garrison, Imas with his garrison of 9,000 men, not only surrendered forthwith (to a force of only 13,000), but handed Wellington's confidential letter over to Soult.

But for one or two petty fortresses such as Elvas, and Campo Mayor, and Beresford's force, the road to Lisbon now lay open to Soult. Cole was therefore directed to join Beresford *viâ* Thomar with the 4th Division. Nightingall was then ordered to feel his way alone from Espinhal, and if unopposed, to march thence by the north bank of the Essa upon Miranda, and there to come in touch with the main body of Wellington's army.

Disregarding Masséna's orders to retire across the river, Ney retained on the near bank of the Ceira Lamotte's Brigade of Cavalry and two Divisions of Infantry with guns, occupying strong ground with his centre resting on the village of Foz de Aruce. At 4 p.m. on the 15th Wellington came up. Rapidly grasping the situation, he employed his usual tactics, holding the enemy's right and centre with the Light Division, and turning his left with the 3rd. Picton's men at once drove that part of the enemy opposed to them on to the bridge in confusion. An accidental shell from a French battery falling among its own Infantry led the latter to believe itself surrounded, and completed the rout. Lamotte's Cavalry had just been withdrawn across the river. Attempting to return in support of the Infantry, it encountered the fugitives on the narrow bridge. A terrible scene of confusion ensued, and many men also who tried to cross the river by the ford were drowned in the flood. French authorities state that the remainder of the Divisions of Mermet and Ferey stood fast and repelled the British by

IN THE PENINSULA

a counter-attack. In his despatch Massóna said that but for want of provisions he had the opportunity of crossing with the 2nd and 8th Corps and of inflicting a signal defeat on the British. But his account bears the mark of being highly coloured for the Emperor's perusal. The 37th French Regiment lost its eagle in the bed of the Ceira, and Ney retired at the earliest opportunity across the river. The French estimated the British losses at 1,200; the official returns state 70 only, killed and wounded. The enemy admitted a loss of 200. Under the circumstances, Napier's statement of 500—of whom half were drowned—would seem to be more probably correct. In retreating, Ney blew up the bridge, fording the river himself with a rearguard.

On the 16th the Allied Army halted. "The destruction of the bridge at Foz d'Aruce, the fatigue which the troops have undergone for several days, and the want of supplies," observed Wellington in a letter to Lord Liverpool, "have induced me to halt the army this day. Marshal Sir William Beresford and I had repeatedly urged the Governours of the Kingdom to adopt measures to supply the troops with regularity and to keep up the establishments while the army was in cantonment on the Rio Mayor river, which representations were not attended to; and when the army was to move forward, the Portuguese troops had no provisions, nor any means of conveying any to them. They were to move through a country ravaged and exhausted by the enemy; and it is literally true that General Pack's Brigade and Colonel Ashworth's had nothing to eat for four days, although constantly marching or engaged with the enemy.

"I am obliged to direct the British Commissary General to supply the Portuguese troops or to see them perish for want; and the consequence is, that the supplies intended for the British troops are exhausted, and we must wait till more come up, which I hope will be this day."

Nor did the evil end here. " Three of General Pack's Brigade died of famine yesterday on their march, and above 150 horses have fallen out from weakness, many of whom must have died from the same cause. . . . The mules of the artillery are unable to draw the guns, for want of food, for any length of time; the baggage mules of the army are nearly all dead of famine, and the drivers have been neither paid nor fed.

" This is the state of the Army at the commencement of the campaign. . . . I have this day told General Pack and Colonel Ashworth that if they cannot procure food for their troops with the Army they must go to Coimbra, or elsewhere, where they can, for I cannot bear to see and hear of brave soldiers dying for want of care." (Wellington to Mr. Charles Stuart, March 18, 1811.)

On the 17th of March the allied army crossed the Ceira, from which Ney had withdrawn the previous night to join Masséna, who had crossed the Alva by the Puente de Murcella, and had taken up a strong position on the further bank, with the intention of halting for some days. He was, however, now hemmed in between the Alva, which ran parallel to his line of retreat, and the Mondego. Wellington quickly detected the weak point. Holding the enemy in front with Anson's and Pack's Brigades, together with the Light Division supported by the 6th; throwing forward Hawker's Cavalry Brigade, the 3rd, 1st, and 5th Divisions with Ashworth's Brigade, in échelon over the Sierra de Guiteria, along the left bank of the Alva, he very soon rendered Masséna's position at Puente de Murcella untenable. The enemy retired for eight miles, and then halting, offered battle on the Sierra de Moita. Picton, Leith, and Spencer thereupon concentrated at Arganil, threatening his line of retreat.

IN THE PENINSULA 359

Trant and Wilson were on the right bank of the Mondego, on a line parallel to that of the French. The Light and 6th Divisions, crossing the Ceira at Foz d'Aruce, approached from the front. Outflanked and fearing to be intercepted at the defiles leading to Celorico, Masséna had no alternative but to resume his retreat. Destroying baggage and ammunition, and leaving his outlying parties to their fate, the French Commander retired in some haste. The Cavalry Brigades of Anson and Hawker followed in pursuit through Pinhanços, supported by the 3rd, 6th, and Light Divisions; while Trant and Wilson closed in at Fornos and Silveira took post at Trancoso; but although a more open country had now been reached, and opportunities for successful Cavalry action seem to have occurred, Slade was not a great cavalry leader, and the chances were lost. On the 21st of March Masséna reached Celorico with the 6th and 8th Corps, while Reynier with the 2nd occupied Guarda.

Thus ended the retreat, for Wellington had left half of his army at Moita to receive the provisions which were being forwarded from Oporto.

CHAPTER XVIII

Fight at Sabugal—Masséna evacuates Portugal—Wellington's cares.

ALTHOUGH Masséna had been driven back to the frontier of Portugal, his resourceful mind was by no means exhausted, and he had every intention of resuming the offensive. The Marshal lost no time in planning new combinations. He resolved to leave all his sick at Almeida, and to transfer his effective army by way of Sabugal and Pena Macor on to the Elga, a confluent of the Tagus, whence he would be in a position to open up communication with King Joseph as well as Soult. The design bears the impress of a powerful mind; for, as Napier observes: " A close and concentric direction would thus have been given to the armies of the South, the Centre and of Portugal, and a powerful demonstration against Lisbon would have brought Wellington back to the Tagus. The conquests of the campaign, namely Ciudad Rodrigo, Almeida, Badajoz, and Olivenza, would have been preserved, and Bessières could have protected Castille and menaced the frontier of Portugal." But the insubordination of his Army Corps commanders, which had hampered Masséna so long, now rose to positive mutiny. Ney refused to obey orders. Masséna thereupon superseded him in the command of the 6th Corps, and handed it to Loison as the senior Divisional General. But the delay had thwarted the Prince of Essling's plan.

IN THE PENINSULA 361

Its execution was perforce postponed, and the Prince was obliged to content himself with the occupation of Guarda by the 6th Corps, of Belmonte by the 2nd, and the eastern valleys of the Estrella by the 8th and Cavalry, in the hope of establishing communication with Soult, and of holding Guarda for eight days, pending the revictualling of Almeida, which had provisions remaining for only ten days.

By the 28th of March, however, Wellington had again brought the whole of his army to the upper Mondego, and next day he made a concentric attack on the "nearly impregnable" position of Guarda. Picton cleverly placed his Division within a quarter of a mile of the enemy's left flank and rear. His troops were, however, a little too quick for the rest of the army, and for a time seemed in danger of being overwhelmed. Fortunately he was not attacked, and upon the approach of the Light and 6th Divisions from the other side, the French abandoned the mountain without firing a shot, retiring, with the exception of their rearguard, in the greatest confusion *viâ* Sabugal across the Coa. General Slade was sent in pursuit. Had he been a Lasalle or a Kellermann, the retreating army might have been materially damaged, and Reynier, at Belmonte, cut off; but, as it was, nothing of importance was done.

On the 1st of April Wellington reached the Coa, behind a bend of which Masséna had posted his army. The 2nd Corps occupied Sabugal, which formed the apex of a nearly equilateral triangle whose sides were about ten miles long, and whose other angles were formed by Alfayetes and Rovinhas, the headquarters of the 8th and 6th Corps respectively. The 9th Corps, now formally attached to the Army of Portugal, guarded the line of communication with Almeida.

The following dispositions were thereupon made by

Wellington to attack Reynier:—The Cavalry Division was ordered to join Erskine's troops at daybreak on the 3rd and cross the upper Coa with a view to enveloping the enemy's left and intercepting his line of retreat on Alfayetes. The Light Division, and the 3rd Division, on the left of the Light, were ordered to cross the river by fords 2,000 and 3,000 yards respectively below the Cavalry. As soon as the movement of these troops should begin to produce an effect, the 5th Division and guns were to force the bridge of Sabugal and attack the right centre of the French. The 1st and 7th Divisions were to be in support, while the 6th was to remain at Rampula opposite the 6th Corps. The objects of the combination were to isolate Reynier and destroy his Army Corps before the 6th and 8th could come to his aid. But Sir William Erskine was not the person to be entrusted with the most difficult task in an operation of this kind; and, in addition, a variety of misadventures occurred. The morning proved misty, and the various units failed to reach their starting points in proper time. An officious Staff Officer ordered Colonel Beckwith, who commanded a Brigade of the Light Division, to attack at once, although the flanking movements were obviously incomplete, and of Beckwith's Brigade only a part was at hand. Crossing the river in obedience to this peremptory command, Beckwith, instead of being able to pass round the French flank, found himself in immediate contact with their left. "The attack," says Napier, "was thus untimely, partial, dangerous, and on the wrong point; for Reynier's whole Corps was in front, and Beckwith, having only one bayonet battalion and four companies of riflemen, was assailing 12,000 Infantry supported by Cavalry and Artillery." The Brigade reached the top of the hill overlooking Reynier's camp, and thus happily secured a good defensive position, being

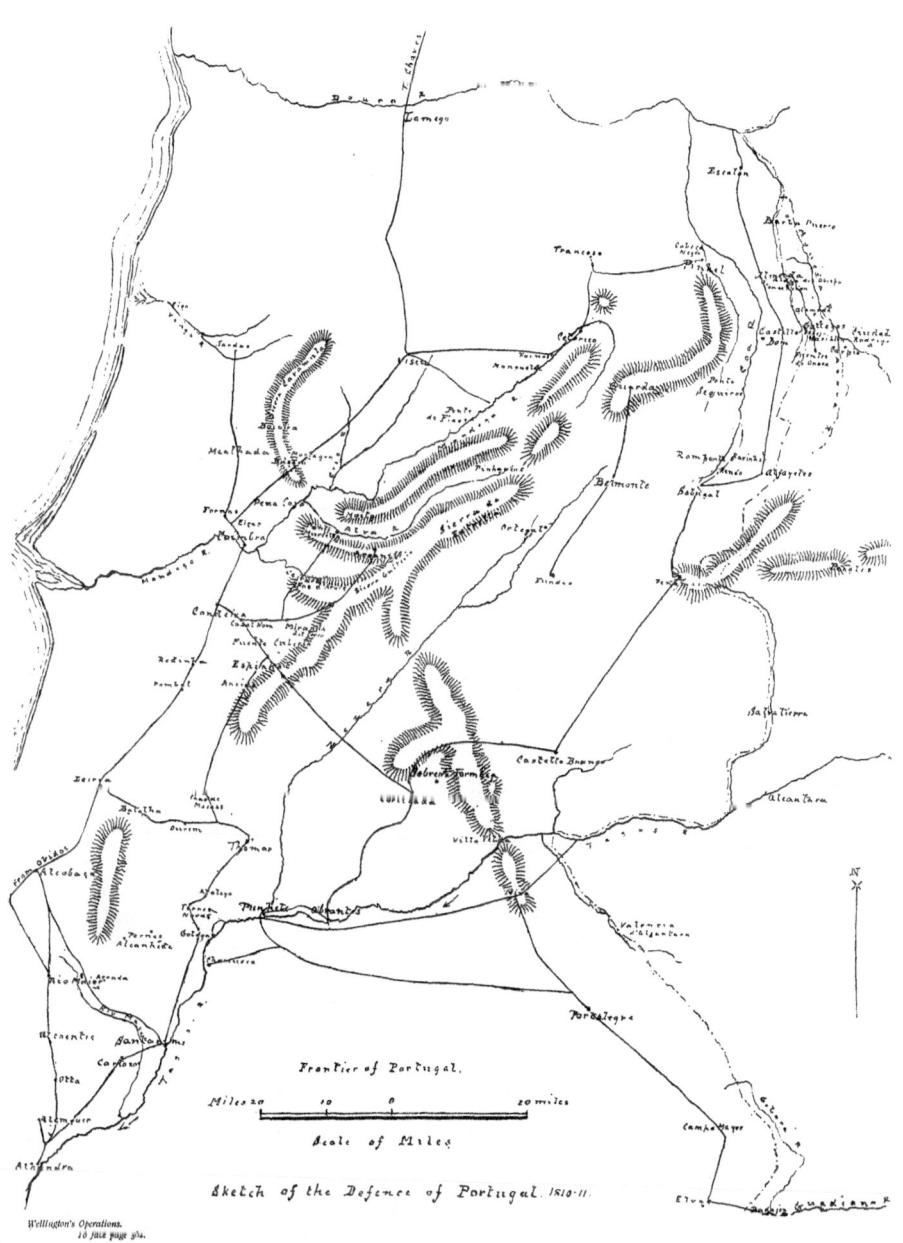

IN THE PENINSULA

covered by a wood and having a clear field of fire to its front. The mist and rain, which had led them into the midst of the French, now favoured our troops by concealing their numerical weakness. Three companies of Caçadores came up, and, in spite of fierce counter attacks again and again repeated, Beckwith, by dint of hard fighting, not only held his ground, but captured one of two French howitzers which had been firing grape at point blank range. The 1st Brigade of the Light Division, under Colonel Drummond, and two guns R.H.A. of Bull's Battery now came up to Beckwith's assistance, and the unequal fight continued with varying fortune.

Reynier, resolved to end the affair, then massed a Division 6,000 strong against the left flank of the British, and in the face of such overwhelming numbers it seemed impossible for the gallant Light Division to hold its ground much longer. But at the critical moment the approach of the 3rd and 5th Divisions, headed by Colonel Williams of the 60th with his Light Battalion, decided the contest. Although the 6th Corps, attracted by the firing, was coming up, and now within three miles of the field of battle, Reynier, threatened on both flanks by the converging columns and by the Cavalry, fell back to Rendo, and thence in conjunction with Loison to Alfayetes. The British loss amounted only to 20 killed and 147 wounded, of whom 73 belonged to the 43rd; but that of the enemy to 1,800, of whom 300 were prisoners.

The action, as Wellington remarked in his despatch, was one of the most glorious in which British troops had ever been engaged. Its result was the abandonment of Portugal by Masséna, who forthwith crossed the frontier at Ciudad Rodrigo; but, had not the combination been spoilt, Reynier's whole Corps should have been destroyed or captured. Writing on the following day to Beresford, Wellington observes : " These combinations for engagements do not answer unless one is on the spot to direct every trifling movement. I was on a hill on the left of the Coa, immediately above the town, till the 3rd and 5th Divisions crossed, whence I could see every movement on both sides, and could communicate with ease with everybody; but that was not enough."

Perhaps Wellington himself was something to blame for the comparative failure. To entrust a delicate manœuvre to men such as Slade and Erskine was to court failure. General Officers were, it is true, very scarce. Seven, as already noted, were absent. Of those remaining, Picton was the best. During the pursuit of Masséna the 3rd Division had worked splendidly. Its light troops, under Williams, were inferior to none in the army; and Picton, although rough in manner, and consequently not much liked by Wellington, was a man of undoubted ability, and far more likely than Erskine to attain success in such a case as this.

On the morning of the fight at Sabugal, Wellington sustained a severe loss in the capture of Colonel Waters, an officer of the Headquarter Staff, by a patrol of the enemy. The story of Waters' adventures and marvellous escape a few days later is told with variations by Napier and Gronow; but, though it need not be repeated here, Waters was such a remarkable man as to deserve a passing mention. Gronow* says of him: "Without using the word in an offensive sense, he was the most admirable spy that was ever attached to an army. One would almost have thought that the Spanish war was entered upon and carried on in order to display his remarkable qualities. He could assume the character of Spaniards of every degree and station, so as to deceive the most acute of those whom he delighted to imitate. . . . But what rendered him more efficient than all was his won-

* " Reminiscences," vol. i. pp. 14–18.

IN THE PENINSULA 365

derful power of observation and accurate description, which made the information he gave so reliable and valuable to the Duke of Wellington. Nothing escaped him. When amidst a group of persons he would minutely watch the movement, attitude and expression of every individual that composed it; in the scenery by which he was surrounded he would carefully mark every object: not a tree, not a bush, not a large stone escaped his observation; and it was said that in a cottage he noted every piece of crockery on the shelf, every domestic utensil, and even the number of knives and forks that were being got ready for use at dinner.

"His acquaintance with the Spanish language was marvellous: from the finest works of Calderon to the ballads in the *patois* of every province he could quote, to the infinite delight of those with whom he associated. He could assume every character that he pleased: he could be the Castilian, haughty and reserved; the Asturian, stupid and plodding; the Andalusian, laughing and merry. . . . Nor was he incapable of passing off, when occasion required, for a Frenchman; but as he spoke with a strong German accent, he called himself an Alsatian; . . . and as there is a strong feeling of fellowship . . . amongst all those who are born in the departments of France bordering on the Rhine . . . he always found friends and supporters in every regiment in the French service."

After Waterloo he acted as Adjutant-General to Wellington's Army; but of his many accomplishments that which was probably the most appreciated among his comrades in the Peninsula was his ability in hunting Lord Wellington's pack of foxhounds!

With the exception of Almeida, which was blockaded, Portugal had now been evacuated, and to all intents and purposes for the last time, by the French. Napier points out that Wellington had effected what to others appeared incredibly rash and useless to attempt. Yet it has pleased certain French writers to stigmatise him as a person without life or energy, and devoid of every military quality except excessive caution, not realising how greatly such criticism recoils upon their own countrymen.

"Masséna," says Napier (bk. xii. ch. 5), "entered Portugal with 65,000 men, and his reinforcements at Santarem were about 10,000; he repassed the frontier with 45,000; the invasion therefore cost him 30,000 men, of which 14,000 might have fallen by the sword or been taken. Not more than 6,000 were lost during the retreat." The campaign proves the truth of Soult's judgment on Masséna given in later days: "Excellent in great danger; negligent and of no goodness out of danger." His advance into Portugal, when every prospect was bright, was marked by grievous errors. His line of advance upon a single road—and that the worst in Portugal; his dilatory yet unprepared attack upon the Busaco mountain can hardly be accounted for except by a combination of carelessness and overweening confidence. His irresolution in not making an immediate attack upon the lines of Torres on his arrival may have been decisive of the whole campaign, for in view of the confusion prevalent at the moment within the lines, which were thronged with disorganised multitudes of refugees, it is impossible to say that the French might not have succeeded in forcing both the outer and second lines of earthworks, with the result that Wellington would have been compelled to retire—not improbably in disorder—upon the inner line, with no alternative but to embark as best he might. That Masséna did not make the attack is no doubt due to his recent terrible repulse at Busaco. He is often spoken of as an old man. He had had, it is true, a hard and adventurous life, but at the time of taking command of the Army of Portugal was only fifty-two. Yet he seems to have lost all power of keeping his Corps Commanders in order. To be sure, Ney—the very counterpart, by the way, of Crauford—was a terrible man to have as a subordinate. He had equally been a thorn in the side of Soult two years previously; and Napoleon himself was destined in 1815 to find what an impossible man he was to deal with; but Reynier, Montbrun, and Junot were allowed to behave almost as badly as Ney.

It is to be deeply regretted that the French retreat was stained, to use Wellington's expression, "by a barbarity seldom equalled, never surpassed." But looked at purely from the military point of view, the generalship was worthy of Masséna's highest reputation. To the military student the operations—the moves and counter-moves as on a chess-board—of the rival Commanders, each a past-master in the art of war, cannot fail to be of the utmost interest. Wellington was never tired of doing his great opponent justice, and considered him by far the ablest of Napoleon's lieutenants. "He was always just where I did not want him to be." In after days Masséna, without a shade of rancour, sought out Wellington at Paris, and showed the greatest pleasure in making his personal acquaintance. "What a terrible time you gave me," said he, laughing. "You turned every hair on my head grey!"

Masséna's despatches to the Emperor convey the impression that, taking the campaign as a whole, he was not quite satisfied with himself, and that he was aware that Napoleon would not be quite satisfied with him. Such indeed proved to be the case. The object with which he had been sent into Portugal was to ensure its evacuation by the British Army. No one was better informed than the Emperor as to the state of politics in England. He thoroughly appreciated the cowardice of the British Government and its lack of confidence in the ability of its General. He knew that it was pitifully weak in Parliament, that it was anxious to withdraw its troops from the Peninsula, and that in the event of its defeat, which was more than probable, the Opposition on assuming the reins of government would at once do so.

In regard to matters of detail the Emperor was equally well informed. He regularly received the English newspapers, which published Wellington's despatches, giving every detail of the works at Torres Vedras, their garrisons, and the number of their guns. Disgraceful as it was on the part of the newspapers to publish such information, the manner in which it was communicated to the Press was still more disgraceful; for it was derived from letters written in some cases directly to the newspapers by officers of high rank in Wellington's Army, the Adjutant-General being, it is said, one of the principal offenders.

Being thus aware of the exact state of our affairs both at home and abroad, the Emperor knew that the question of the British occupation of Portugal hung on a thread, and was determined not to lose the golden opportunity of driving Wellington into the sea. He had never ceased to urge Masséna and Soult to redoubled efforts to that end, making perhaps hardly enough allowance for the physical obstacles to be encountered, and not realising the indomitable energy and tenacity of the British Commander. Thus his disappointment at Masséna's failure was proportionate to his sense of the opportunity lost, for which Masséna's hardihood at Santarem and the brilliant conduct of his retreat could by no means atone.

To Wellington the campaign had been a succession of

triumphs moral and physical; and one is at a loss whether to admire most the stern, terrible resolution which converted the country into a desert rather than let it afford supplies to the enemy; the foresight which provided for the vast entrenchments which formed an impregnable citadel at Torres Vedras; the courage whereby he upheld the drooping spirits of weak-kneed Conservative politicians at home and exhorted those in Portugal to their duty; or the unfailing skill with which, during the retirement of the French, he turned their flanks, menaced their line of retreat, and by ability in manœuvre forced them out of a series of the most formidable mountain positions. Between the 16th of March and the 2nd of April inclusive, the British loss amounted to only 1 man killed and 9 wounded.

More no doubt he could have done, particularly in the earlier stages of the retreat, and on more than one occasion a vigorous attack might have led to the destruction of the enemy; but the losses of his own army would have been great, and he was restrained by political considerations, for in the event of a reverse the British Government would infallibly have evacuated the Peninsula. Let it also be remembered that within a fortnight of the commencement of the retreat Wellington's manœuvring had demoralised the enemy to such an extent that Masséna dared not make head against him; that the French Commander evacuated the terrible position at Guarda without firing a shot, and, after the partial action at Sabugal, abandoned all hope of retaining hold on Portugal.

Yet during this notable campaign the purely military part of his work was among the lightest of Wellington's cares. He was incessantly engaged in a voluminous correspondence: at one moment to urge the Portuguese Regency to ensure the execution of its own orders, or to save its own soldiers from dying of hunger; at another to revive the drooping spirits of the Ministers in England and spur them to continued effort. His sorely needed reinforcements he was unable to get before March—the Walcheren fiasco had in fact played such havoc with our Army that there were no regiments available at home—but he pointed out the fallacies contained in their statements as to the expense of the war, encouraged them by showing that his views had proved correct in the past and might not unreasonably be expected to continue to prove correct in the future, and concluded a despatch to Lord Liverpool on March 23rd with these weighty words : " My opinion has been that it was the interest of Great Britain to employ in Portugal the largest Army that could be spared from other services. . . . I should be sorry if Government should think themselves under the necessity of withdrawing from this country on account of the expense of the contest. From what I have seen of the objects of the French Government, and the sacrifices they make to accomplish them, I have no doubt that if the British Army were for any reason to withdraw from the Peninsula, and the French Government were relieved from the pressure of all military operations on the Continent, they would incur all risks to land an Army in His Majesty's dominions. This indeed would commence an expensive contest ; then would His Majesty's subjects discover what are the miseries of war, of which, by the blessing of God, they have hitherto had no knowledge ; and the cultivation, the beauty, and prosperity of the country, and the virtue and happiness of its inhabitants would be destroyed, whatever might be the result of the military operations. God forbid that I should be a witness, much less an actor in the scene. . . ."

Supported at home only by his brother, Lord Wellesley,

and in the Peninsula only by his brother Henry and Charles Stuart, the envoys at Cadiz and Lisbon respectively, mistrusted by the Government in England; plotted against by the Government in Portugal; deserted even by his General Officers, Wellington stands out a figure of heroic mould, towering above the Liliputians around him, and tearing himself from the meshes of the net with which they were continually striving to encircle him. "Unus homo nobis cunctando restituit rem. Noenum rumores ponebat ante salutem." One man single-handed restored the balance by his patient tenacity, for the great ultimate object, not temporary dash, was his aim. Portugal was saved not by, but in spite of, her own and the British Governments.

CHAPTER XIX

Affairs in the South—Battle of Barossa—Fall of Campo Mayor—Recaptured by Beresford, who then advances to the Guadiana—Crosses the river.

WHEN Soult left Cadiz to co-operate with Masséna, the 1st and 4th Army Corps remained in occupation of Andalusia, the former under Victor continuing the blockade of Cadiz, the latter, commanded by Sebastiani, acting partly as a covering force, partly to keep order in the centre and east of the province. On the 15th of February the strength of the 1st Corps was about 23,500 officers and men, of whom 20,572, with 1,386 horses, were actually present under arms. The 4th Corps comprised 19,143 officers and men, of whom 16,703 with 4,007 horses were present under arms. A reinforcement of 5,200 men from the Northern Government was on the march to join the 1st; and one of 6,000 to join the 4th Corps.

As soon as Soult had marched away, General Graham, who commanded the British troops within the Isla de Leon, determined to embark a force, land it at Tarifa, and, by approaching the French from the rear, to compel them to raise the blockade. The idea was for Ballesteros to menace Seville simultaneously, while Sebastiani was to be held in check by the partidas. The project was in the first instance spoilt by bad weather, but not abandoned; and towards the end of February, 1811, not less than 600

Cavalry and 10,000 Infantry, of which rather more than one-third were British, were embarked for the purpose. The force landed at Algesiras, and was joined on the 23rd at Tarifa by the 28th from Gibraltar and a Light Battalion, under command of Lieutenant-Colonel Browne of that regiment, made up of the Light and Grenadier companies of the 9th, 28th, and 82nd.

The purely British part of the force was now composed as follows :—

Lieutenant-General Graham, Commanding.
Lieutenant-Colonel Macdonald   Deputy Adjutant-General.
   ,,   ,,   Hon. C. Cathcart   ,,   Quartermaster-General.

Corps.	Officer Commanding.	Rank and File.	Guns.
2 Squadrons 2nd Hussars K.G.L.	Major Busche	180	
Royal Artillery	Major Duncan		10
Royal Engineers	Captain Birch	47	
Brigade of Guards	Brigdr.-Gen. Dilkes	1,221	
2nd Batt. 1st Guards. Detachment Coldstream and 3rd Guards.			
Infantry Brigade	Colonel Wheatley	1,764	
1st Batt. 28th, 2nd Batt. 67th, 2nd Batt. 87th, and 2 Companies 20th Portuguese.			
Flank Battalion	Lieut.-Col. Barnard	594	
Detachment 3rd Batt. 95th Rifles and 2 Companies 47th.			
Flank Battalion	Lieut.-Col. Browne	475	
2 Companies 2nd Batt. 9th, 2 Companies 28th, 2 Companies 2nd Batt. 82nd.			
1 Company Royal Staff Corps	Lieutenant Read	33	

Total of Rank and File   4,294

After making allowance for officers, N.C.O's., R.A., &c., the Division may be reckoned at 5,000 officers and men with 10 guns.

With a view to ensuring unity of purpose, Graham—contrary to Wellington's instructions—ceded command of the British contingent to the Spanish Commander-in-Chief, General La Pena, who landed on the 27th.

Under Soult's government Andalusia had been remarkably tranquil, and many Spaniards, who (having taken the oath of allegiance to King Joseph) were termed "Juramentados," served with the French army. The landing of the allied force, however, served to light up the spirit of insurrection, while Ballesteros advancing from Fregenal, menaced Seville. The French troops thereupon concentrated : Sebastiani at Estipona ; other forces at Seville, Cordova, and Ecija. Victor occupied the lines in front of the Isla at Cadiz with a force composed partly of regular troops, partly of Juramentados. Medina was held by four battalions under General Cassagne, and the Marshal retained the remainder of the 1st Army Corps under his own personal command, its strength being as follows :—

			Officers and Men.
1st Division. General Ruffin	9th Regiment (2 Batts.)		1,108
	24th ,,		680
	96th ,,	(2 Batts.)	1,349
2nd Division. General Leval	45th ,,		464
	8th ,,	(2 Batts.)	1,439
	54th ,,		1,143
	Battalion d'Élite		439
	1st Dragoons		222
	Artillery		238
3rd Division. General Villatte	27th Regiment (2 Batts.)		1,601
	94th ,,		945
	95th ,,	(2 Batts.)	1,042
	2nd Dragoons		165
		Total	10,735

(These figures represent the number of men under arms and available for service. They are taken from a "State" made out a few days after the battle of Barossa, and include those killed and wounded in the battle. The numbers must consequently be taken only as approximate, but should be very nearly correct.)

On the 2nd of March, Villatte was despatched with his Division and the 2nd Dragoons against a Spanish force which had emerged from the Isla and crossed the Santi Petri. On the 4th he was directed to attack the head of any column approaching from the sea-shore. With the 1st Dragoons and the 1st and 2nd Divisions Victor took post at Chiclana with the intention of attacking the main body of the Allies on the march.

The distance from Tarifa to Chiclana was between 50 and 60 miles. On the 1st of March the Allied Army started along the road to Medina. Two Spanish Divisions, commanded respectively by General Lardizarbal and the Prince of Anglona, formed the advance guard and centre. Graham, reinforced with the Spanish Walloon and Ciudad Real Guards, was in reserve. The Spanish and K.G.L. Cavalry were brigaded together under General Whittingham, a British officer in the Spanish service; but each nation retained its own artillery.

Next day the Convent of Casa Vieja, commanding the line of march, was taken; and by the arrival of the Spanish Brigadier-General Béguines, the Allied Army was raised to a total strength of 800 Cavalry, 12,000 Infantry, and 24 guns.

Shortly after leaving Casa Vieja, the Spanish Commander, La Pena, heard rumours that Medina was strongly occupied. Without verifying the report, he at once retraced his steps, returned to Casa Vieja, and thence took the road—at right angles to that hitherto pursued—leading in a north-easterly direction to Vejer, and by so doing virtually abandoned the object of the enterprise. The march on the 3rd was extremely harassing. The road passed over a causeway now submerged by the waters of a lake in flood. The men marched through water up to their waists. After fifteen hours Vejar was at length reached. At 3 p.m. on the 4th, the march was resumed. The men had had no time to dry their clothing and equipment, and with a view to bringing them into action in good fettle, Graham had begged La Pena to make short marches. But the Spaniard seemed to think it necessary to show his superiority by thwarting his colleague on every point; and it was not until 8 a.m. next morning that, after a sixteen hours' march and a skirmish, in which the advance guard of Spanish Cavalry was routed by a French squadron, the wearied and straggling army debouched on to the plain of Chiclana.

La Pena's pusillanimous conduct at Casa Vieja had shaken the confidence of his allies and led to bad results. Writing from Tarifa on the 27th of February, he had informed General Zayas at Cadiz that Medina would be in his hands on the 2nd of March, and that he would be close to the Isla de Leon on the evening of the 3rd. Zayas, without ascertaining whether La Pena had been able to keep his word, threw a pontoon bridge across the Santi Petri, close to its mouth, on the night of the 3rd. Next day La Pena, as we have seen, was not at hand, but at night the bridge was attacked by four companies of the French and partly broken. The Spaniards lost hundreds of men, and had the attack been made in greater force the Isla would have fallen into the enemy's hands. The position of La Pena and Graham, with Sebastiani on their rear and Victor on their front and flank, would in such a case have been perilous in the extreme. As it was, the attack was eventually repelled, although with difficulty and the assistance of the British 10-inch howitzers from the Isla.

On reaching the plain of Chiclana, La Pena, without waiting to communicate with Zayas, despatched Lardizabal to the mouth of the Santi Petri. After a sharp encounter with Villatte, Lardizabal and Zayas joined hands and occupied the left bank of the Santi Petri,

IN THE PENINSULA

covering the mended bridge; while Villatte retired behind the Molina de Almanza.

The Allied Army had entered the plain of Chiclana at a point "close to a low mountain ridge called the Cerro de Puerco, or Boar's neck, from its curving shape bristling with pine-trees, and from the number of those animals always to be found there. This ridge, distant from the point of Santi Petri about four miles, gradually descends for a mile and a half to the Chiclana plain. On its north side the plain is broken by ravines, pits, and broken ground; a large pine forest hems it in on all sides at unequal distances. Situated midway between the hill and Santi Petri point, close to the western point of Cerro de Puerco, stands La Torre, or the Tower of Barossa. The eastern point of this ridge looks upon the space between Chiclana and the Santi Petri; whilst its western boundary looks down upon the boat road leading from Vejer to Bermeja and the Isla de Leon, passing within less than half a mile of the tower above mentioned" ("A Boy in the Peninsula," p. 182).

La Pena, having now apparently no other idea than to get into the Isla, advised Graham to follow Lardizabel; but Graham, appreciating the importance of the Cerro de Puerco, and knowing that the enemy must be close at hand, declined to comply with the order unless the Spanish Commander would undertake to hold the Cerro in force with a rearguard. La Pena gave the necessary promise, and Graham, leaving only Browne's flank battalion on the Cerro to guard the baggage, marched down at noon towards Bermeja.

Up to this point no sign had been given of the French, who were concealed by the pine wood, nor had the patrols brought in any intelligence. But Victor had been keenly watching the Allies, and seeing them now dispersed between Santi Petri, Bermeja, the Cerro and the Vejer road, seized the opportunity to attack. His immediate force consisted of 7,000 men and 14 guns, and he momentarily expected the arrival of Cassagne's Brigade, which he had called up from Medina.

La Pena, without acquainting Graham, had withdrawn the Prince of Anglona's Division by the road skirting the sea in the direction of Santi Petri. On the Cerro, under command of Whittingham remained the Cavalry Brigade, five Spanish battalions, four guns, and Browne's battalion. Hardly was Graham out of sight when a disorderly movement of the Spaniards on his right warned Browne of the approach of the French Cavalry, which was outflanking the Allies with a view to seizing the road to Vejer. Whittingham, without further ado, quitted the position, abandoning the four guns, and leaving Browne to bear the whole brunt of the threatened attack. The French Cavalry now wheeled directly towards the British rearguard, and, opening out, displayed guns and a large force of Infantry close behind. With less than 500 men it was impossible to make head against the whole French Army, and Browne therefore withdrew his little force slowly and steadfastly, following Graham in the direction of Bermeja, while the baggage made the best of its way, but in considerable disorder, down to the sea coast.*

At this moment General Graham was warned by Staff Officers of Victor's approach. Turning his Division about he met Browne, and instantly ordered that officer to retake the Cerro de Puerco, supporting him in person. Browne and his battalion obeyed with alacrity. Leval on the enemy's right, and Ruffin on his left with eight guns, were already in possession of the hill, and received Browne with so deadly a volley that 11 officers and

* It is only fair to say that Whittingham, in his report to La Pena, stated that the English battalion retired first. The balance of evidence would, however, seem to be to the contrary.

nearly 200 men fell. Fifty more fell at a second volley. Most of the remainder then took what cover they could find, and in a few minutes only one officer and a dozen men were left standing. But support was already at hand. Duncan, arriving with his ten guns, unlimbered, and opened a terrific fire upon Leval's column. The Brigade of Guards, although in the utmost disorder on account of the pine woods, came up on Browne's right " with astonishing celerity and steadiness " under a *feu d'enfer;* and forming some sort of a line, pressed gallantly on to attack Ruffin and a Brigade under General Rousseau composed of the Grenadier companies of the various regiments. The remnant of Browne's battalion then actually charged and captured a howitzer.

The scene presented to Graham on emerging on to the plateau was not encouraging. The enemy crowned the heights. Leval pressed on his left. The Spanish battalions and the baggage were in full flight to the sea coast. But Graham—" that daring old man," as Napoleon was wont to term him—never hesitated for an instant. Hemmed in between Victor and the sea, his choice lay only between victory or destruction, and he resolutely maintained the attack. Wheatley on the British left, preceded by Andrew Barnard's riflemen and Portuguese, assailed Leval, who pressed forward to meet him. A desperate charge of the 87th overthrew the 8th French Regiment, which lost its eagle but not its honour, for at the end of the day no less than 726 of its officers and men had fallen. The 28th coming up, turned Leval's right, and the French column, struck in front and flank, fell back, pursued by Wheatley's victorious Brigade ; and although the battalions forming the French reserve came up to the aid of their comrades, they were unable to stem the retreat.

Meanwhile, on the British right, Dilkes, with the Guards and some companies of the 67th, who in the confusion had attached themselves to him, gained the top of the Cerro de Puerco. But Ruffin and Rousseau resolutely maintained their position, and the opposing lines fought at ten yards' distance. Victory hung in the balance. It almost seemed as though the Homeric contests were being renewed. Victor on the one side, Graham on the other, were conspicuous in the front, cheering on their men. But the terrific struggle was too hot to last, and Graham's loud shout "Charge!" was answered by a British cheer and a rush, and the next moment the enemy's troops were hurled down the steep slopes of the ridge. In their retreat they came in contact with Leval's men, and in spite of their terrible losses both Divisions re-formed and gallantly attempted to renew the contest.

The fire, however, of Duncan's guns quickly put an end to the attempt. Béguines brought up the Spanish regiments of Guards in support of Dilkes; and as the enemy resumed his retreat Colonel Frederick Ponsonby, a Staff Officer, bringing up the two squadrons 2nd Hussars K.G.L. from Whittingham's Brigade, charged and re-charged through the French Dragoons, who were covering the retirement of their Infantry, and was only checked by Rousseau's grenadiers thrown into squares. Had Whittingham brought up the remainder of his Brigade to support Ponsonby great results might have followed, but Whittingham was chained by the advance of an imaginary column of French Infantry, and showed himself as inert and spiritless as the Spanish Commander-in-Chief. In after years he pleaded the strict orders of La Pena in excuse. He gave no such reason in his official report at the time.

The British troops, exhausted by their long march and

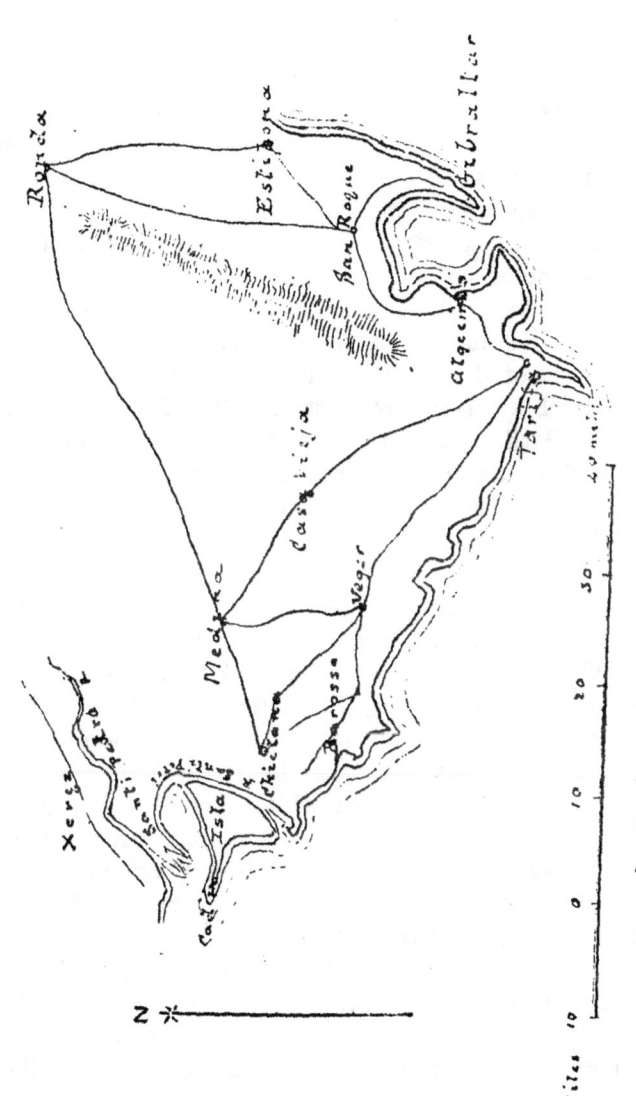

want of food, were unable to follow the enemy in pursuit, and Victor drew off his men unmolested, although in great disorder, upon Chiclana. Two hours later he was joined by Cassagne. The fight had lasted for only an hour and a half, but it would be difficult to instance a modern battle in which the carnage was as great. Of the 12,000 men engaged on both sides, no less than 3,300 were struck down. The British loss, 1,242 out of 5,000, amounted to 25 per cent.; that of the French to 2,061, or 30 per cent. of their strength. The heaviest casualties occurred in Browne's flank battalion, which lost two-thirds of its numbers, and in the 8th French Regiment, which lost rather more than half. The French Chief of the Staff, General Bellegarde, was killed; Generals Ruffin and Rousseau were mortally wounded. Six guns were taken by the victors, and Graham in his despatch claims 400 prisoners, but these would seem to be wounded men already included among the French casualties. The Eagle of the 8th Regiment was one of five taken actually in battle during the Peninsular campaigns. The others were captured at Salamanca and Vittoria, one of them also by the 87th.

From want of transport the wounded were left on the field all night. Among them was General Rousseau. He had left in camp a white poodle. The dog, finding that his master did not return, set off in search of him. During the night he found him lying on the ground, licked his hand, and succeeded in drawing the attention of the fatigue parties who were engaged in gathering the wounded. The General died a few hours afterwards, but the poodle refused to leave his master's body, and followed it to the grave. General Graham then took care of the dog, and sent it home to Perthshire, where it lived for many years.

While the action at Barossa was in progress Lardiza

IN THE PENINSULA 383

bal, as already stated, aided by 4,000 men under Zayas, vigorously attacked Villatte and forced him behind the Molinos de Almanza. The fighting was sharp, and Villatte lost 300 men. Anglona's Division seems, however, to have taken no part in the contest; neither did La Pena bring it up in support of the hardly pressed British. The Spanish Commander, in fact, left his allies absolutely to their fate, nor did any Spanish troops join in the fight, the nearest approach to any action being the passive *rôle* played by the Cavalry and Béguine's Brigade, which interposed between the Guards and the sea, thus to some extent securing the right flank, and advanced about the time that the firing ceased. "Had the whole body of the Spanish Cavalry," wrote Graham indignantly, a few days afterwards, to Henry Wellesley, "had the whole body of the Spanish Cavalry, with the Horse Artillery, been rapidly sent by the sea beach to form in the plain and to envelop the enemy's left; had the greatest part of the Infantry been marched through the pine wood in our rear, to turn his right, what success might have been expected from such decisive movements? The enemy must have either retired instantly, and without occasioning any serious loss to the British Division, or he would have exposed himself to absolute destruction, his Cavalry greatly outnumbered, his Artillery lost, his columns mixed and in confusion; a general dispersion would have been the inevitable consequence of a close pursuit; our wearied men would have found spirits to go on, and would have done so trusting to find refreshments and repose at Chiclana. This moment was lost. Within a quarter of an hour's ride of the scene of action the General (La Pena) remained ignorant of what was passing, and nothing was done!"

After the battle considerable alarm prevailed in the French camp, and by the admissions of Generals

Legentil and Garbé, an attack at daybreak next morning would have had very serious results, and was dreaded accordingly. But the Spaniards were immovable, and in view of the manner in which he had been treated, Graham resumed the independent command of his own troops and marched them across the Santri Petri into the Isla. The only action taken on the 6th was that of Admiral Keats, who landed seamen and marines, and destroyed several of the French works on the north side of the bay, whereupon Victor retired from Chiclana, and concentrated behind the San Pedro river; but the Spaniards made no effort to follow up the blow, and Victor two days afterwards returned to Chiclana.

Thus ended an enterprise well conceived, and which, if equally well carried out, should have effected its purpose of raising the blockade of Cadiz. But, as Wellington had long ago found to his cost, any plan involving co-operation with a Spanish force was certain to fail. The diversion of Ballesteros proved a fiasco, and, but for the enemy's blunders, Graham might easily have been involved in disaster. Napoleon put his finger on the blot of Soult's combination. That officer, on quitting Seville, should have placed Sebastiani and Godinot under Victor's orders. (Napoleon to Berthier, March 29-30, 1811.) As it turned out, Sebastiani at Estipona was about eighty miles from the scene of action, opposed only by a few irregular bands. Had he marched towards the Allies as soon as he heard of the British landing at Algesiras he might well have been at Conil on the evening of the 4th, and have come up to Barossa next morning in time to co-operate in Victor's attack. In that case it is difficult to see how the British force could have escaped destruction.

On hearing at Badajoz of the battle of Barossa, Soult waited only to receive the surrender of the fortress, and

IN THE PENINSULA 385

then, appreciating the critical nature of the situation, hastened southward to Victor's assistance with a few battalions of the 1st Army Corps.

Marshal Mortier, with the 5th Corps, then besieged, and on the 21st of March captured, Campo Mayor after a gallant resistance on the part of the Portuguese garrison, only 200 strong. The place was, however, retaken on the 25th by Beresford (whose force had been organised and despatched by Wellington with so much secrecy that his appearance brought Mortier the first news of his approach), and Latour Maubourg's Cavalry were driven into Badajoz in confusion by the 13th Light Dragoons.

Beresford's force consisted of the 13th L. Dg., De Grey's British (3rd Dragoon Guards and 4th Dragoons) and Madden's Portuguese, Cavalry Brigades; the 2nd and 4th Divisions under William Stewart and Lowry Cole; Hamilton's Portuguese Division and three batteries; amounting in all to about 25,000 officers and men of all arms, with 18 guns. Beresford's instructions were to cross the Guadiana at Jerumenha, invest Badajoz before the breaches in the ramparts could be repaired, and, if possible, capture it and Olivenza. Mortier, having thrown 3,000 men into Badajoz and 400 into Olivenza, had barely 10,000 men left for active operations, and had Beresford, without losing a moment, marched along the right bank of the Guadiana, crossed the river at Merida and driven back the 5th Corps, the fall of Badajoz would, in Napier's opinion, have been inevitable. But Beresford was not the man to carry out a brilliant operation of this kind. After three weeks of incessant marching his men were fatigued and shoeless. He found it difficult to bridge the Guadiana at Jerumenha, and he put his troops into quarters about Elvas pending an opportunity of effecting the passage. The delay gave General Phillipon, the Governor of Badajoz, time to repair the fortifications and re-victual the garrison.

There were many difficulties in the way of making a bridge over the Guadiana, and it was not until the night of the 6th-7th of April that the Army crossed and took up a position on the left bank, undisturbed by Latour Maubourg, who with a Brigade of Cavalry, an Infantry Division, and four guns came up too late to oppose the passage, and was allowed to retire unmolested. Beresford then advanced to Albuera; Mendizabel, with the 5th Spanish Army, reoccupied Valencia and Albuquerque; and Ballesteros, Fregenal. Blake was placed by Castanos, Captain-General of Estremadura, under command of Beresford.

Olivenza surrendered to the Allies on the 14th. Beresford marched on Zafra to drive Latour Maubourg over the Morena and cut off the Brigade of General Maransin. In a skirmish with a Brigade of the enemy's Cavalry the 13th Light Dragoons, a fine dashing regiment, once more distinguished themselves by overthrowing their opponents and pursuing them for six miles, inflicting a loss of 250 men.

On the 21st, Wellington arrived in person. In the belief that Masséna was exhausted, he had been contemplating the project of advancing with the bulk of his army to raise the siege of Cadiz, leaving only a retaining force in Beira. But on the 24th, letters from Sir Brent Spencer, whom he had left temporarily in command on the Coa, brought news of a fresh advance on the part of Masséna, and Wellington at once hastened back to the north.

PART IV

CHAPTER XX

Difficulties of the rival commanders—Advance of Masséna—Battle of Fuentes d'Onoro—Retreat of the French—Escape of Brennier from Almeida—Masséna superseded by Marmont.

WHEN, in the beginning of April, 1811, after the fight at Sabugal, Masséna evacuated Portugal, he retired to Salamanca and went into quarters between that town and Ciudad Rodrigo to rest and refit his army. During the last few months circumstances had arisen which materially affected his position. The Emperor, not anticipating the contingency of a retreat from Portugal, had, as we have seen, with a view to relieving Masséna of a part of his work, given command of the "Northern Governments" up to the frontier of Portugal to Marshal Bessières, whose force consisted of 70,000 men. But although the intention of Napoleon had been that Bessières should do all in his power to aid Masséna, the latter, on re-entering Spain, found himself not the less shorn of much of his former power and dependent upon Bessières for even such an essential as the revictualling of Ciudad Rodrigo. Almeida, on the other hand, being within Portuguese territory, was included in Masséna's sphere of command, but as he was unable to supply it without Bessières's permission, the case was not materially altered. In order, therefore, to enable Masséna to resume the offensive, the loyal co-operation of Bessières was a *sine quâ non*. But the latter, whether imbued with jealousy of his colleague—a vice which has been notoriously and disgracefully prevalent in more recent campaigns waged by other nations than the French—or with inertness arising from his openly expressed dislike of the war, made every possible pretext to evade the orders of the Emperor (officially conveyed to him) to aid Masséna with 15,000 men. Again and again did Masséna write in the nicest and most friendly terms, appealing to his colleague's patriotism in view of the urgent need for the immediate relief of Almeida, whose resources, it was known, were rapidly becoming exhausted. Bessières still hung back, but Masséna, hearing that Lord Wellington had gone down to Badajoz, determined to make the effort in his absence and prior to the removal of the 9th Army Corps, which he could only count on for a short time longer, since Napoleon, foreseeing that Wellington would wish to concentrate his troops for the relief of Cadiz, had assigned this Corps to the Army of the South.

Towards the end of April Masséna advanced from Salamanca and on the 26th concentrated at Ciudad Rodrigo. As Bessières had brought no supplies, he was dependent for subsistence on the fortress which he had twice provisioned. The practice of marauding had been strictly forbidden as soon as the French army had retired from Portugal into Spain.

Meanwhile the British commander had as many difficulties to contend with as his opponent. An intercepted letter from Berthier to Masséna spoke of a combined effort designed by the Emperor by which the British would be driven back into Lisbon by the armies of

Portugal and the south. "We have," the letter went on, "the most perfect information from the English, and much better than that in your possession. The Emperor reads the London newspapers and a great number of letters written by 'the Opposition' daily, some of which blame Lord Wellington and speak in detail of your operations. England trembles for its army in Spain, and Lord Wellington has always had the greatest dread of your operations. For the English even a partly successful battle on a large scale . . . would, on account of the loss of life incurred, be equivalent to a defeat."

By the end of April Wellington had greatly broadened his lines of communication by utilising the Douro and Mondego so far as they were navigable and establishing subsidiary bases between Lamego and Ruiva. Expense magazines were organised at Celorico, whence the supplies were conveyed to the army viâ Castello Bom on mules. It was intended to form a depôt also at Abrantes on the Tagus, the third great artery of Portugal, and to supply thence magazines at Castello Branco and Guarda, but the land transport over the Estrella mountains was so difficult that it was impossible to make use of this line to any great extent.

The sudden floods to which both the Coa and Agueda were liable forbade Wellington to undertake the blockade of Ciudad Rodrigo in addition to that of Almeida. The army under his command had been much reduced. He had no money and was actually compelled in consequence to disband all the Portuguese Militia just at the time that it was beginning to become a serviceable force; and so grossly had the Portuguese Government neglected its own soldiers that, although Wellington had taken upon himself the burden of feeding three-fourths, many of the remainder died of hunger. A large proportion of the others were in hospital, and at the end of March, out of a nominal strength of 17,000 Portuguese Infantry, only 8,493 were fit for duty. The Cavalry was no better. Horses had died of famine in scores. After the battle of Fuentes d'Onoro (5th of May) Barbacena's Brigade was reduced to less than a single squadron. "Everything else is the same," continues Wellington to Charles Stuart, May 9, 1811. "The sick and wounded are taken care of by our medical officers; the artillery has no mules, and the guns must be sent away; they have no ammunition, and we are at this moment picking up the French ammunition in our camps to make up again with powder and materials furnished by us! It is because the departments at Lisbon do not care to find means to forward the reserves; and then, in order not to lose a battle, the British Commissary-General must find means of transport for the musket as well as the gun ammunition of the Portuguese Army, which means of transport ought to be used to bring up food for the horses and soldiers of the army.

"All this falls upon me. I am involved in a most serious situation, and it is quite impossible for me to allow matters to go on as they are."

In addition to his other innumerable vexations, Wellington was being pressed from home in regard to the expense of the war. It is perfectly true that incredibly large sums had been showered indiscrimately upon the Governments, whether local or central, of Spain and Portugal, but Wellington had no difficulty in showing that the actual cost of the British Army in Portugal was not enormously greater than if it had been in England. As to his projects for the future, he pointed out that he must be guided by circumstances, which varied almost every day. King Joseph had resigned his crown and was in France. His bodyguard of 20,000 men was therefore available for active operations, and would probably join the Army of the South in Andalusia. It might, therefore, be Lord Wellington's best course to transfer the bulk of his army to Badajoz and, as Napoleon had anticipated, undertake direct operations for the relief of Cadiz. On the other hand, as an alternative, which he seems to have preferred, he might, after taking Almeida and Ciudad Rodrigo, advance into the heart of Spain, separate the Army of the South from that of the North, open communication with Valencia and the British Army in Sicily, and establish a new base on the Mediterranean. "This great design," says Napier, "would relieve Cadiz as effectually as the other and, successfully executed, would have surpassed Marlborough's march to Blenheim."

All plans of offensive operations would, however, be destroyed, either by the arrival of fresh reinforcements for the French or by the recall to England of part of the British Army. In view of the probability of war between France and Russia, the former contingency appeared rather remote; the latter depended solely upon the caprice of the Ministry; but, as a middle course, and one that would in some degree reduce the expenses, Wellington proposed to send home for recruiting purposes the officers and N.C.O.'s. of four Companies of his seven weakest regiments, retaining only six Companies of each in the field. (In those days there were ten service companies per battalion.) He also suggested other economies.

During Wellington's absence in the south, Sir Brent Spencer had been engaged in the blockade of Almeida. The main body of his army was on the Coa. The Light Division occupied Espeja and Gallegos, with their picquets on the Azava; while the outpost line was continued as far as the Upper Azava by a Cavalry Brigade.

On the 27th of April the Advance Guard of Masséna

came into contact with the British outposts. Wellington, arriving next day, concentrated the Army on the Duas Casas river. On the 2nd of May, Masséna, having been joined only that morning by Bessières—who arrived, however, with but Wathier's Cavalry Brigade and one of the Guard, total strength 1,500 men, 6 guns and 30 gun teams—advanced in force, whereupon the British outposts retired across the Duas Casas.

The line now occupied by Wellington with about 36,000 of all arms and 42 guns, ran due north and south for about 8 miles along a tableland forming the watershed of the Duas Casas and Turones from Fort Conception on the left to the high ground behind the village of Fuentes d'Onoro—name of good augury—on the right. The front of the position was protected by the former river, "flowing in a deep ravine," fordable in several places and bridged opposite Alameda and Fuentes d'Onoro. On the right the tableland died away in a wooded plain.

Almeida was blockaded by the 2nd Regiment and Pack's Portuguese Brigade. If Masséna were to march through Alameda directly on the fortress, he would expose his flank to the attack of a concentrated army. Hence the blockade was only lightly covered.

On high ground, with its left Brigade a mile and a half south of Conception, in advance of the road running thence along the plateau to Nava de Aver, was posted the 5th Division, now commanded by Sir W. Erskine; for Craufurd having just rejoined the Army had resumed command of the Light Division. On the same road, opposite Alameda and more than a mile distant from Erskine's right, the 6th Division was drawn up. Next to the 6th, but at an interval of two miles, were the two Cavalry Brigades—also under their old Commander, Stapleton Cotton—and the 3rd and 1st Divisions supported respectively by the 7th and Light, about a mile west of the village of Fuentes d'Onoro. Five miles still further to the right, an isolated hill at Nava de Aver was occupied by the Spanish Chief, Don Julian Sanchez, with his Guerilla horsemen. Headquarters were at Villa Formosa immediately in rear of the 1st Division.

The line of retreat ran in rear of the right of the line, through Freneda and Aldea de Ribeira upon Sabugal and the valley of the Zezere; abandoning the line of the Mandego in favour of the more direct route to Lisbon, for the distance from Guarda to Santarem by the Estrada Nova was 34 leagues, or about 130 miles; by Coimbra, 47 leagues or 180 miles.

On the afternoon of the 3rd the enemy was seen approaching the position held by the Allied troops. He had nearly 4,000 Cavalry as against 1,000 under Wellington; but only 36 guns against 42, and his Infantry was inferior in numbers. The total strength of his force was stated by Masséna at 35,000, and could hardly have exceeded 40,000 men. The 6th Corps and Montbrun's Cavalry appeared on the road from Espeja, directing their march on the village of Fuentes d'Onoro. The 2nd Corps and Solignac's Division of the 8th—for Clausel's had been left to guard the line of communication—were coming up by two roads from Gallegos, upon Alameda. The 9th Corps formed the general Reserve. (Masséna to Berthier, May 7th.) As the weight of the attack appeared to threaten the British left, the Light Division, which had been connecting the 1st with the 6th, moved to support the latter.

The attack was however in reality made on the other side. Loison with the 6th Corps assailed the village of Fuentes d'Onoro, which was defended by Colonel Williams with the 60th and the Light Companies of the 3rd Division, supported by the 83rd and three Light Infantry

Battalions from the 1st Division. The houses skirting the stream were captured, but on the higher ground with a chapel as a reduit, a desperate fight was maintained against overwhelming numbers. Williams fell dangerously wounded, and the result of the contest seemed doubtful; but at the critical moment, Wellington successively reinforced the defenders with three battalions from the 1st and 3rd Divisions, which, in a bayonet charge, drove the assailants back over the rivulet. This isolated attack which had been made without orders from the Commander-in-Chief, cost the Allies about 260 men, and the enemy—according to Marbot—600; the casualties of the French having been greatly augmented by their close columns of attack, and by the fact of the Hanoverian Regiment in their service—which wore a red uniform—being fired into alike by friend and foe. The combat had ceased before 6 p.m.

The next day passed without renewal of the action, but a change was made in the disposition of the Allied Army. In view of the fact that by seizing the hill at Nava de Aver—at present occupied by Julian Sanchez' guerillas—Masséna would be in a position to mass his army upon Wellington's right flank and enfilade his line, the British Commander moved the 7th Division under General Houston to the right; posting two battalions in the village and woods of Pozo Velho, and prolonging the line to the right in the direction of Nava de Aver. The Light Division on the morning of the 5th took up the ground vacated by the 7th Division. The whole line thus watched or occupied extended over 12 miles from Fort Conception on the left to Nava de Aver on the right; for Wellington had to provide for two distinct and indeed divergent objects—one, the blockade of Almeida; the other, his line of retreat, which, as noticed, ran in rear of his right by Freneda and Aldea de Ribiera upon

Sabugal and the valley of the Zezero a shorter communication, as we have seen, with Lisbon than that by the Mondego, and one facilitating a junction with Beresford in the Alemteja. Of the two objects, the line of retreat was by far the more important. Consequently, he had posted four Divisions in the right half of the position, leaving only the 5th and 6th to hold Reynier in check should that officer make an attempt to relieve Almeida.

But though the direction of the French advance on the 3rd had seemed to foreshadow an attack upon the British left, a reconnaissance on the following day quickly showed Masséna the vulnerable point of his antagonist. By massing his main body at Nava de Aver, he might fairly hope to overwhelm Wellington by force of numbers, and not only relieve Almeida but drive the Allies past their line of retreat into the *cul de sac* formed by the junction of the Coa, the Douro and the Agueda.

By daybreak on the 5th, the 1st and 2nd Divisions of the 6th Corps had been drawn up opposite Pozo Velho, supported by Solignac's Division of the 8th which had been brought thither from Alameda. On the left of this body was massed the whole of the Cavalry under Montbrun. The 3rd Division of the 6th Corps, with the 9th Corps in reserve—forming the centre of the French line—occupied the valley of the Duas Casas at Fuentes d'Onoro and the lower houses of the village, in readiness to attack the remainder on the higher ground. Masséna's right wing was formed by the 2nd Corps, one Division of which was posted at Alameda, and the other half way between that village and Fuentes d'Onoro, with orders to make demonstrations and co-operate with the left in the event of success attending the main attack.

The Duas Casas takes its rise in marshy ground below Nava de Aver. Having bridged the marsh with fascines, at dawn on the 5th a company of Light Infantry belonging to the 8th Corps surprised Julian Sanchez and his guerillas asleep; killed thirty of them and put the rest to flight. The good faith of Sanchez is open to question. He had undoubtedly been tampered with, as Thiébault openly states. Anyhow, he did not halt until he had placed the Turones between himself and his assailants, and by so doing had laid bare the whole of Wellington's right flank. The two battalions of the 7th Division which held Pozo Velho were driven out, and the masses of Montbrun's Cavalry, supported by four batteries of Artillery and four Divisions of Infantry, were thrown across the marsh upon Wellington's right flank and rear. Masséna, almost without firing a shot, had thus early gained an enormous strategical advantage. He was overpoweringly strong at the crucial point. He already commanded the British line of retreat; and it only remained to drive the attack home, roll up Wellington's line of battle and hurl him into the Douro.

But Wellington was always at his best when in a tight place; and in fighting a losing battle, unequalled. Promptly moving the 1st and 3rd Divisions to their right to make head against the 6th Corps, he despatched the Light Division at the same time in support of the 7th, and the Cavalry—whose two Brigades mustered only 1,000 Sabres—to guard its outer flank.

Montbrun quickly drove in the Cavalry videttes, and in so doing cut off Captain Norman Ramsay, who was on outpost duty, with two guns of Bull's Battery, R.H.A. But Ramsay, with great presence of mind, limbered up and with the assistance of a Squadron of the 14th, charged through the enemy's ranks and regained his own lines in safety. A Cavalry *melée* then took place. The British Squadrons, out-numbered and over-matched, got the worst of it; and Montbrun, pursuing his advantage,

IN THE PENINSULA 397

charged down upon the 7th Division, cut up the 85th Regiment, and was only checked by the fire of the Chasseurs Britanniques—a foreign regiment (composed chiefly of French prisoners of war) attached to Houston's Division—which had been strongly posted behind a stone wall.

The Light Division, which had had a little more time than the 7th to prepare for Montbrun, held its own and formed a rallying point for Cotton's beaten Cavalry.

It was now obvious that a crushing disaster was in store for the Allies, unless their line could be contracted and a position taken up on a new front. Orders were consequently sent to Houston to fall back behind the Turones and take up a position fronting south, on the crest line of the hills which extended for two miles between that rivulet and the village of Frenada. His retirement was covered by the Light Division, while the 1st and 3rd occupied in an irregular line the high ground from the Turones to Fuentes d'Onoro. The completion of the change of front depended entirely upon the conduct of the Light Division. The moment was more than critical; for the Squadrons of Montbrun's Cavalry, between 2,000 and 3,000 strong, covered its front and flanks, threatening every moment to overwhelm the squares into which its battalions had been thrown, whilst its retrograde movement was hampered by the crowd of baggage mules, led horses, and non-combatants who had assembled in the plain behind Nava d'Aver, as being remote from danger and nearest the line indicated for retreat. Napier observes that if the 6th Corps had resolutely advanced in support of the Cavalry, while the 9th was attacking Fuentes d'Onoro; and if Montbrun had made a general charge, "the loose crowds of non-combatants and broken troops would have been violently dashed against the 1st Division, to intercept its fire and break its ranks, and the battle would have been lost." As it was, some of the battalions of the 1st Division which had not completed their change of position, were knocked about by the Cavalry, and Colonel Hill of the Guards and some men were captured. But Loison and Montbrun had been quarrelling all the morning, and failed to give mutual support; while Bessières most disgracefully refused Montbrun the help of the Cavalry of the Guard. Consequently, no real attack was made, and the slender squares of the Light Division, retiring as steadily as if on a mere field day, reached their goal in safety and formed up in rear of the 1st Division, which they connected with the 7th by a chain of skirmishers in extended order.

On Wellington's new line, running perpendicular to the valleys of the Duas Casas and Turones, the enemy opened a heavy artillery fire. French writers believe that a vigorous cavalry charge would even then have pierced the line; but Bessières once more refused to allow the co-operation of the Brigade of the Guard; and the British guns on their side opening a terrific fire, Montbrun was compelled to retire out of range. Except for an attempt on the part of some French Infantry to penetrate between the 1st and 7th Divisions by the bed of the Turones, no further attack was made on this side.

Meanwhile the village of Fuentes d'Onoro had been vigorously attacked by Ferey's Division of the 6th and Claparède's of the 9th Corps. Happily the assault—it would seem through Loison's perversity—had not been delivered until the crisis of the action on the British right had passed away. As it was, the main portion of the village was captured. But Wellington, relieved on the right, was able to send successive reinforcements to the defenders, who, after desperate fighting, continued to hold on to a few of the houses on the high ground; and, with the aid of a heavy artillery fire, repelled all attempts to dislodge them.

Observing that Wellington had concentrated his forces, and that nothing was to be gained from an attack upon the British right, Masséna determined to change his tactics and make use of Reynier's Corps (which so far had been hardly engaged at all) to pierce Wellington's left and penetrate directly to Almeida. In order to do this it would however be necessary to support the 2nd with the bulk of the other Corps; but just then General Eblé, the Commander of the Artillery, reported that he had in reserve only four cartridges per man. Including those in their pouches, only thirty rounds per man were available —a quantity utterly inadequate to overcome the stubborn resistance to be expected. Masséna consequently ordered every available waggon to be sent to Ciudad Rodrigo for a further supply; but was met with the reply that they had been already despatched there to bring up the next day's bread. He then applied to Bessières for the waggons belonging to the Guard, but on the ground that the teams were tired, Bessières declined to lend them till the following day. One can easily believe that, as Marbot says, Masséna thereupon lost his temper and that a violent scene ensued between the two Marshals. Bessières deserved to be shot for his disloyalty.

The combat in Fuentes d'Onoro ceased at nightfall. In the two days' fighting, the British loss amounted to 235 killed, 1,234 wounded, and 317 missing. That of the French was probably rather greater. Wellington employed the next day in entrenching his position; and when, in the evening, Masséna's waggons had returned from Ciudad Rodrigo with the ammunition, the British line was too formidable to be attacked.

The crisis had passed away, but Napier, speaking of

the retirement of the Light Division as it covered that of the 7th, observes that "there was not during the whole war a more perilous hour." Wellington's dispositions were in the first place undoubtedly faulty; and indeed, writing to the Secretary of State a few days after the action, he admits that in taking up such an extended position, he had in view two objects incompatible with each other, and says that on finding this to be the case, he abandoned the less important (namely, the communication across the Coa by Sabugal) in order to maintain the blockade of Almeida. But Napier informs us that Wellington was not prepared to risk much for the blockade; and if in reality he considered the communications with Sabugal of so little importance, it seems strange that he had arranged his line of retreat and sent all his baggage in that direction, remaining himself to fight a battle with a deep river behind him, spanned only by a single bridge at Castello Bom. The paragraph in the despatch looks like an afterthought to account for the retreat of his right wing.

Masséna showed that he knew how to take advantage of the false movements of his adversary; and, but for the disloyalty of every one of his lieutenants, might well have inflicted a terrible disaster. So well did the French Commander dispose his troops that Wellington was convinced that he had been outnumbered in the fight by three to one. But, at the critical hour, the coolness with which the latter changed his front, and the consummate skill of the Light Division, saved the day.

On the 8th the French Army retired over the Duas Casas, and on the 10th over the Agueda: the 6th and 8th Corps at Ciudad Rodrigo, the 2nd at Barba de Puerco. Wellington did not dare to follow them up. But the fate of Almeida and its garrison appeared to be sealed. Three French soldiers, however, gallantly volun-

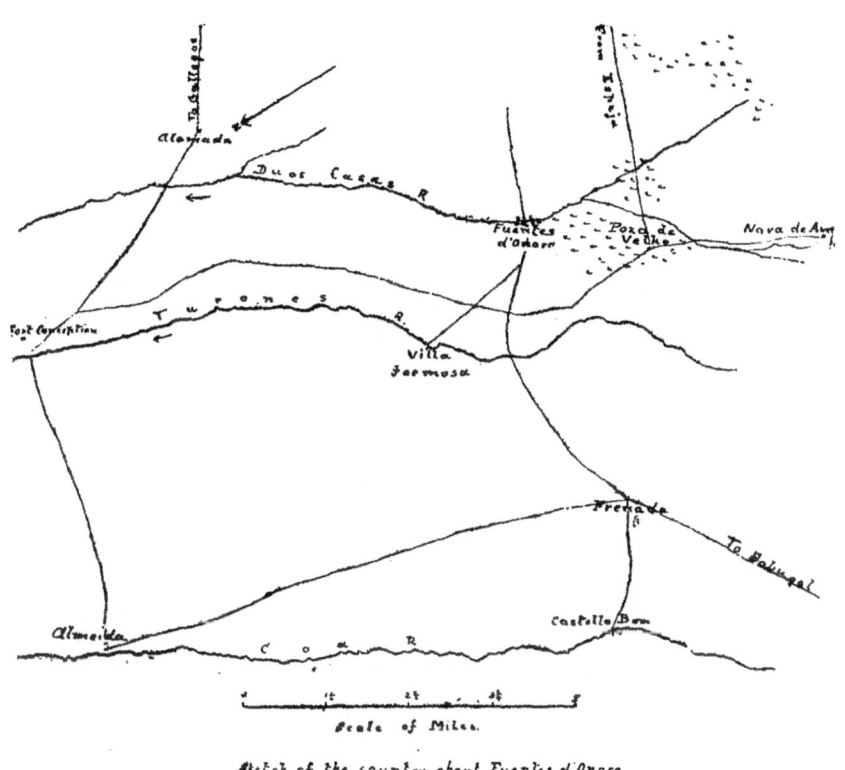

Sketch of the country about Fuentes d'Onoro.

[To face p. 400.

IN THE PENINSULA

teered to take a message to General Brennier, the Commandant, instructing him to destroy the guns and fortifications and evacuate the place. Two of the messengers were detected in plain clothes and shot. The third, in uniform, crawling up the deep gorge of the Duas Casas as far as Conception, succeeded in his mission. In anticipation of such orders Brennier had already made his preparations.

Wellington, half expecting the General to make an attempt to break out, sent word to him that to blow up a fortress and retire was contrary to the law of nations, and that if he did so every man captured would be shot. At the same time his Lordship directed General Campbell to resume the blockade with the 6th Division, and Sir W. Erskine to send the 4th Regiment from Val de Mula, opposite Fort Conception, to Barba de Puerco, a distance of about 12 miles. Erskine delayed to carry out the orders. At midnight on the 10th Brennier exploded his mines, broke out and reached Barba de Puerco, where he was received by General Heudelet and a Division of the 2nd Corps. He did not, however, get away scathless. General Pack, on hearing the explosion, realised what was happening. With ten private soldiers he followed up Brennier's column of 1,500 men, firing muskets to attract the notice of all the troops in the neighbourhood. On reaching the village of Barba de Puerco, a few of the Royal Dragoons appeared, and by skirmishing with the French, cut off some and slightly delayed the rest. The 4th and 36th Regiments were now at hand. The men of the former, throwing off their knapsacks, closed upon the column just as it was descending the gorge of the river. The ground beneath gave way, and many men, both English and French, were hurled into the abyss. Many others of the enemy were killed by our fire. Three hundred prisoners were taken; the remainder of the French column crossed in safety, but Colonel Cochrane, rashly following them over the bridge with the 36th in the excitement of the moment, was repelled by Heudelet with some loss.

Wellington was furious. He characterised the escape of the garrison as "the most disgraceful military event that has yet occurred to us." He censured severely, and with reason, Colonel Cochrane. He seems to have had an inkling as to the reason that the 4th had not occupied Barba de Puerco; but it was a rule with Wellington to shield—at all events, in public—the General Officers on his Staff and to reserve his censure for the regimental officers, however little they may have been to blame. The Colonel of the 4th was so much hurt by his Chief's strictures that he shot himself.

But allowance must be made for the British Commander. For three years he had waged war, not only against the French, but against his own and the Portuguese Government as well. During all that period his mind had been on the rack. It is hardly therefore a matter for surprise if his nature became seared as with a hot iron, and that, having once formed an opinion, whether right or wrong, nothing would induce him to change it. Thus it happened than on occasions his firmness degenerated into obstinacy, and instances like the present one account for the feeling with which he was regarded by his troops. He had their unlimited confidence and respect, but never their affection. To the private soldier he was "That long-nosed b—— that licks the French." It is probable indeed that at times he must have been regarded both by officers and men as a fiend in human form. Success was absolutely essential to his position. Had he met with reverses it is impossible to say that he could have induced his troops to make any such renewed efforts as were made by Buller's

IN THE PENINSULA 403

Army after Colenso and Spion Kop. But it would be unfair to pursue the comparison too far; for the charm which Sir Redvers, throughout his life, has had for the soldiers under his command, although not adorned like that of Napoleon by grace of manner, is in its way not less remarkable than and indeed only paralleled by that of the French Emperor.

The escape of Brennier was the last ray which lit up the career of Wellington's great adversary, Masséna. On the 7th of May the latter was joined by Marshal Marmont—a young man of thirty-seven, excellent in the theory of war, and a former A.D.C. to the Emperor—who took command of the 6th Corps. Four days later Marmont produced a commission superseding Masséna and conferring on himself the command of the Army of Portugal. The reason for Masséna's supersession is not quite clear. To say, as is said by many writers, that Napoleon never forgave failure is to deny pretty nearly every act in the Emperor's life. It is quite true that he had pointed out the error made in attacking the position at Busaco; but, in general, and so late as the 11th of April, he had appreciated the Marshal's difficulties and approved of his plans. Yet on the 20th he appointed Marmont to the command. What, in the interval between the 11th and 20th, caused him to take this step does not appear. Possibly it was only then that he realised the way in which the Corps Commanders were setting their chief at defiance; and thought that a younger and more active man was required to enforce discipline.

Masséna's supersession must have been a bitter blow to him. Like others in more recent times, he had done admirably under the most trying circumstances. He had earned what is probably the best test of ability, viz., the unstinted admiration of his opponent, and yet for his talent, patriotism, and fortitude, his only reward was disgrace. It was not long before time brought its revenge, and France anxiously sought again the services of her most distinguished Marshal.

Bessières deservedly received a stinging reprimand from Napoleon. "The Emperor sees that you have been useless to the Army of Portugal. . . . Why all this reluctance to concentrate and employ your troops in presence of our implacable foes, the English? The Emperor hopes you will retrieve the enormous blunders that you have made. You have about 50,000 men under your command. What a splendid opportunity to concentrate them at once to support the Prince of Essling and crush the English!"

Marmont assumed command with an air of "cocksureness," and within three days wrote to tell Berthier that he was convinced that the present unfortunate position of the army was due to the unwillingness of Masséna to give battle either during his retreat or his operations around Almeida although he had several opportunities of fighting such a battle, which "he would have certainly won," and by so doing have altered the whole face of the campaign.

The irony of fate destined Marmont at a very early date to show hesitation in attack, under circumstances far more favourable than his predecessor had enjoyed; and also to learn by bitter experience that a battle with British soldiers commanded by Wellington was by no means *évidemment gagnée.*

The reflections of Marbot, who was one of Masséna's Aides-de-Camp during this campaign, are worth notice. "I ought," he says, "to point out the chief causes of the reverses sustained by the French (in the Peninsula), in spite of the fact that our troops nowhere showed more zeal, more patience—above all, more valour. . . . King

Joseph's lack of military capacity prevented any concentration of command, and complete anarchy reigned among the marshals and the various corps commanders, each confining himself to the defence of the provinces occupied by his troops, and refusing any aid to his colleagues who governed the neighbouring districts. The most peremptory orders from the Emperor were unable to produce any co-operation, there was no obedience, and each asserted that he himself needed all the resources at his disposal. Thus St. Cyr was nearly crushed in Catalonia without the support of a single battalion from Suchet, who was governing Aragon and Valencia; Soult was left alone in Oporto, while Victor refused to obey the order to join him. Soult, in his turn, allowed Masséna to wait for him for six months in vain at the gates of Lisbon; finally Masséna could not obtain help from Bessières to beat the English before Almeida. . . .

"But, in my opinion, the principal cause of our reverses, though one which has never been pointed out by any soldier who has written on the Peninsular War, was the immense superiority of the English Infantry in accurate shooting, a superiority which arises from their frequent exercise at the targets, and in a great measure also from the formation in two ranks. I know that a great many French officers deny that this latter cause is a true one, but experience has shown that soldiers confined between the first and third rank nearly always fire in the air, and that the third rank cannot take aim at an enemy who is hidden from them by the two ranks in front. It is asserted that two ranks do not offer sufficient strength to resist Cavalry, but the English Infantry can in a moment form four deep to receive a charge, and our squadrons were never able to catch it in two ranks, though as soon as it has to fire it quickly resumes this formation."

CHAPTER XXI

Beresford besieges Badajoz—Battle of Albuera—Hill relieves Beresford.

HARDLY had Masséna retired from Fuentes d'Onoro than news came from Beresford of the advance of Soult in force upon Badajoz. Marmont had withdrawn his army to the neighbourhood of Salamanca. Wellington at once took action. Leaving the Cavalry, the 1st, 5th, 6th, and Light Divisions on the Azava, he despatched the 7th Division on the 13th of May, and the 3rd on the 14th *en route* for Badajoz; but being detained by the Almeida transaction, was unfortunately unable to follow in person before the 15th.

Before quitting Beresford in April, Wellington decided not to undertake the siege of Badajoz until Castanos, as Captain General, had consented to the following arrangements: Blake and Ballesteros to take post at Xerez Cavalheros and Burgillo; Mendizabel at Llerena to watch the passes of the Morena; Castanos himself to occupy Merida. Beresford, in second line, to cover the siege. Albuera, as a central position, to be the point of concentration for battle.

These arrangements having been assented to, the 2nd Division with 6 field guns, commanded by William Stewart, on the 5th of May invested Badajoz on the left bank of the Guadiana. The 4th and a Spanish Division covered the investing force. The Cavalry with Ross's troop R.H.A. was posted near Zafra. On the 8th, a Brigade of the 2nd Division, with a Portuguese battalion and four light Spanish guns, occupied the right bank of the river and invested the fort of San Christoval.

"This," says Napier, "was the first serious siege undertaken by the British in the Peninsula; and, to the discredit of the English Government, no army was ever worse provided for such an enterprise. The engineer officers were zealous . . . yet the ablest of them trembled at their destitution in all things necessary to real service. Without a corps of sappers and miners; without a private soldier who knew how to carry on an approach under fire, they were compelled to attack fortresses commanded by the most warlike, practised and scientific troops of the age: and the best officers and the finest soldiers sacrificed themselves in a lamentable manner to compensate for the negligence and incapacity of a government, *always ready to plunge the nation into war without the slightest care of what was necessary to obtain success.*" (The words in italics show how apt a pupil was the Government in 1899 of its predecessor in 1811.) "The sieges carried on by the British in Spain were a succession of butcheries, because the commonest materials and means necessary for their art were denied to the engineers."

Beresford's delay, on his first arrival, had given the French Commandant time to repair the works. By the 10th the Allies had lost 700 men and had erected only one small battery. On the 12th the approach of a French army forced Beresford to raise the siege.

On hearing of the siege of Badajoz, Soult had lost no time in marching to its relief. The force available for the purpose was, however, small. The nominal strength of the Army of the South, after deducting 1,000 men in hospital, amounted to nearly 66,000 officers and men; but more than 20,000 were required for the blockade of Cadiz, and after detaching an adequate number to hold in check the insurgents of Murcia and the garrisons of Tarifa, Algeciras, and Gibraltar, there were left for the Marshal only 2 Divisions of Cavalry, 4 Brigades of Infantry and 30 guns drawn from the 1st, 4th, and 5th Army Corps. In the event of being joined by the 9th Corps and by a Division from the Army of the Centre he hoped to raise his numbers to 35,000 men and 40 guns.

Having quitted Seville on the 10th of May, Soult reached Villa Franca on the 14th. In accordance with previous arrangement, Beresford on the morning of the 15th took post at Albuera. He drew up his Infantry on a ridge nearly three miles in length, fronting due east; its centre commanding the village and stream of Albuera at a distance of about 900 yards. Hamilton's Portuguese Division was on the left, its outer flank guarded by Colonel Otway with a Brigade of Portuguese Cavalry. The 2nd Division was posted in the centre to protect the line of retreat upon Valverde. The right of the position on the strongest ground was left for the Spaniards, but so dilatory was Blake that he did not arrive with his advance guard before 11 p.m., and was not in position before 3 a.m. on the 16th. A Brigade consisting of two Light Battalions K.G.L. under Baron Charles Alten, which had been despatched by Wellington from Celorico early in April, occupied the village of Albuera. " The ascent from the river was easy, and the ground practicable for Cavalry and Artillery." The 4th Division was still in front of Badajoz, but Cole had orders to bring up Kemmis' Brigade (which was before San Christoval) over the Guadiana by a ford above the fortress, and to hold his other two Brigades in readiness to march at the shortest notice.

The position thus occupied, although strong in itself, was oblique to the line of the enemy's advance; and not only were the Spaniards on the right exposed to the attack of Soult's entire force, but the high, wooded ground beyond the Albuera stream, 2,000 yards only from the right front of the ground indicated for the Spaniards, was left unoccupied. Had Beresford held these wooded heights with his centre, and the high ground beyond them with his left, while changing the front of the Spaniards to the south-east, he would equally have secured his line of retreat and would not have lent his right flank to the advancing French.

But the fact is that the circumstances did not justify Beresford in accepting battle at all. Victory would merely enable him to resume the investment of Badajoz. Defeat would mar the whole of Wellington's combinations, would force the Commander-in-Chief to give up the ground that he had so hardly won, and to retire again within the lines of Torres Vedras; would, in short, imperil the whole defence of Portugal. Wellington had written on the 12th to notify the departure of the 3rd and 7th Divisions, and actually arrived in person at Elvas on the 19th. The junction of the two Divisions with Beresford's force would enable the offensive to be resumed. A voluntary retirement across the Guadiana would therefore be only temporary; but a forced retreat over a single bridge after an unsuccessful action would mean ruin; and Beresford's mode of occupying the position at Albuera did, in fact, expose the only line of retreat.

At three p.m. on the 15th, the French Cavalry coming up established itself on the wooded heights beyond the stream. Beresford thereupon called up Cole from Badajoz, and Madden with his Brigade of Portuguese Cavalry from Talavera Real. Madden did not get the order, but Cole arrived with two Brigades at 9 a.m. on the 16th, just as the battle began, and was posted in rear of the 2nd Division. His 3rd Brigade, under Kemmis, had failed to ford the Guadiana, and was marching up by the bridge of Jerumenha. The main body of the Allied Cavalry was commanded by General Lumley, and drawn up in rear of the centre. In point of numbers the advantage rested with the Allies, for Beresford had under his command, according to our English computation, over 2,000 Cavalry, 30,000 Infantry, and 38 guns, in reality about 38,000 officers and men of all arms, including 15,000 Spaniards. But of these the British Infantry counted less than 8,000 of all ranks. The Portuguese and Germans might indeed be expected to give loyal support; but the whole course of the war had shown the Spanish troops to be worse than useless, and their Commander, General Blake, was out of temper at being placed under Beresford.

Soult, who had been joined by Dessolle's Reserve Division from the Army of the Centre, the headquarters of which were at Madrid, did not fail to notice the defective manner in which the Albuera position had been occupied, and realised that an attack in overwhelming force upon the right flank of the Allies would inevitably roll it up, and drive it from the ridge and over the line of retreat to Valverde. Taking advantage, therefore, of the hill already mentioned between the Feria and Albuera streams, he massed behind it, unnoticed by Beresford, the whole of Latour Maubourg's Cavalry, the 5th Corps—now commanded by Girard—and all his guns but ten. The Brigade of Godinot, supported by the remaining ten guns and two Brigades of Light Cavalry, with Werlé's Infantry Brigade in reserve, was directed to attack the bridge and village of Albuera.

At 9 a.m. on the 16th, Godinot's guns opened the

battle. With his Infantry he made an attempt to force the passage of the Albuera stream; but his columns, torn by the Portuguese artillery under Major Dickson, made no progress; and though a Lancer Brigade forded the river on his left, it was driven back again by the British Cavalry. The attack indeed at this early stage was intended as little more than a feint, and Werlé, in pursuance of Soult's plan of action, marched to join the 5th Corps on the French left. Beresford, observing the movement, withdrew the Portuguese Division forming his left wing, sent one Brigade to support Alten at the bridge of Albuera, and held the rest in readiness as a general reserve. The 2nd Division was directed to reinforce Blake. The Cavalry Division, the R.H.A., and the 4th Division were to support the 2nd. The Marshal then sent word to Blake to change front to the right, and repel the attack of 5th Corps which was now obviously impending. To obey the orders of an Englishman—a Rubio, a despised heretic—was more than Blake's Irish-Castilian blood would allow him to do. He refused to change his front, and Beresford was forced to come up and give the executive words of command in person. The delay was almost fatal. Before the movement could be completed the French were upon them. The two Brigades under Girard had been reinforced by Werlé. Latour Maubourg had been joined by the greater part of the Light Cavalry. Thus, "half an hour had sufficed to render Beresford's position nearly desperate. Two-thirds of the French were in compact order of battle, perpendicular to his front, and his army, composed of different nations, was making a disorderly change of front." To do them justice the Spaniards were ready to fight, but unable to manoeuvre. Struck in front by the enemy's fire, and outflanked by Latour Maubourg's Cavalry, they fell back in confusion. Soult, pursuing his

advantage, brought up his reserves of Infantry and
Artillery. The moment was critical, but General Stewart
was now at hand with the 2nd Division. Conscious of
the appalling danger, that officer, disregarding the wish of
the Brigadier, Colborne, to deploy, pushed his foremost
Brigade (consisting of the Buffs, 2nd Battalion 48th,
66th, and 31st) up the hill, past the Spanish right, in
column of companies. The result was that which
happened to the 58th at Lang's Nek seventy years afterwards. Encountered on the top by a heavy fire, the
Brigade, while attempting to deploy, broke into a charge.
But at this moment the French Division of Light Cavalry,
covered by the heavy mist and rain, appeared suddenly
from the enemy's left, took the Brigade in flank and rear,
overwhelmed the Buffs and 66th, and captured six guns.
The fury of the charge was partly spent by the time it
reached the 31st on the left. That regiment, which was
still in column, forming square most gallantly held its
ground; then, the mist clearing away, General Lumley
rapidly brought up four squadrons, and taking the French
Cavalry in the disorder of its charge, cut down many and
dispersed the remainder.

General Houghton now brought up his—the 3rd—
Brigade, consisting of the 29th, 57th, and 1st Battalion
48th, properly deployed and in good order, although the
regiments were harassed in their advance by a mass of
broken Spaniards falling to the rear. The 2nd Brigade,
under Colonel Abercrombie, of the 28th, also came into
action on the left of the 3rd, and part of the Spanish
Infantry advanced once more. Ably supported by the
Artillery under Julius Hartmann, the Allies held their
own, yet only with great difficulty, and, had the enemy
deployed in time, must have been overwhelmed by his
fire. It was too late for the French to do so now under
the terrific fire of the British line, but the desperate con-

IN THE PENINSULA 413

test continued with unabated force, and not less than two-thirds of our troops had fallen. Then Soult succeeded in outflanking the British right. Our ammunition failed, and Beresford, despairing of success, sent orders to General Alten to evacuate the village of Albuera, and take up such a position as would enable him to cover the retirement of the main body by the road to Valverde.

Happily Colonel Hardinge, a staff officer, appreciating the crisis, had on his own initiative ridden to ask General Cole to reinforce the fighting line with the 4th Division, and had directed the remaining Brigade of the 2nd Division, under Colonel Abercrombie, to attack the French right. He now told Beresford what he had done; and the Marshal, countermanding the orders given to Alten, directed that officer to retake the village of Albuera.

Lumley's Cavalry Division had been holding Latour Maubourg in check. The interval between it and Stewart was now filled by the Portuguese and British Fusilier Brigade, composing what was present of the 4th Division. While Cole advanced diagonally towards the left flank of the enemy's Infantry, and recovered five of the six guns lost, Abercrombie's Brigade of the 2nd Division, made up of the 28th, 24th, and 39th, wheeling inwards attacked the right. The remnant of the Brigades of Colborne and Houghton, which had been giving way, was now supported on either flank, and the decisive result of this manœuvre can only be given in Napier's incomparable words: " Such a gallant line, issuing from the midst of the smoke and rapidly separating itself from the confused and broken multitude, startled the enemy's masses, which were increasing and pressing onwards as to an assured victory; they wavered, hesitated, and then vomiting forth a storm of fire, hastily endeavoured to enlarge their front, while a fearful discharge of grape from all their artillery whistled through the British ranks. Myers (commanding the Fusilier Brigade) was killed, Cole and the three Colonels, Ellis, Blakeney, and Hawkshaw, fell wounded, and the Fusilier Battalions, struck by the iron tempest, reeled and staggered like sinking ships; but suddenly and sternly recovering, they closed on their terrible enemies, and then was seen with what a strength and majesty the British soldier fights. In vain did Soult with voice and gesture animate his Frenchmen, in vain did the hardiest veterans break from the crowded columns and sacrifice their lives to gain time for the mass to open out on such a fair field; in vain did the mass itself bear up, and fiercely striving, fire indiscriminately upon friends and foes, while the horsemen hovering on the flank threatened to charge the advancing line. Nothing could stop that astonishing infantry. No sudden burst of undisciplined valour, no nervous enthusiasm weakened the stability of their order, their flashing eyes were bent on the dark columns in their front, their measured tread shook the ground, their dreadful volleys swept away the head of every formation, their deafening shouts overpowered the dissonant cries that broke from all parts of the tumultuous crowd, as slowly and with a horrid carnage it was pushed by the incessant vigour of the attack to the farthest edge of the hill.* In vain did the French reserves mix with the struggling multitude to sustain the fight, their efforts only increased the irremediable confusion, and the mighty mass, breaking off like a loosened cliff, went headlong down the steep; the rain flowed after in streams discoloured with blood, and eighteen hundred unwounded men, the remnant of six thousand unconquerable British soldiers, stood triumphant on the fatal hill."

* A remarkable testimony to the superiority of the line over the column formation.

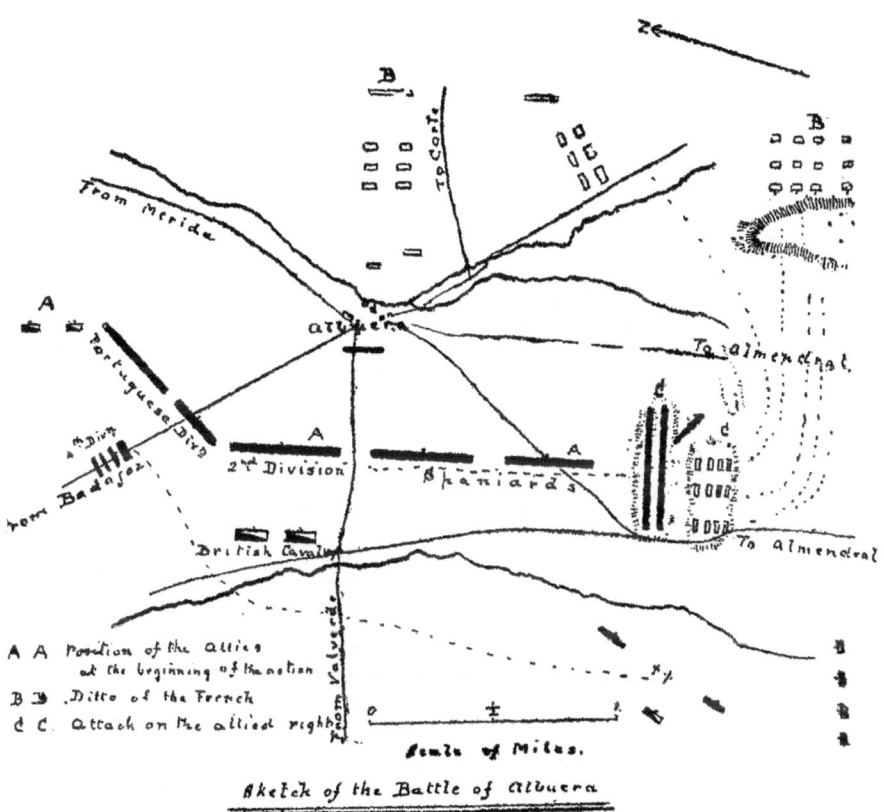

[To face p. 414.

During the advance of the 4th Division, Latour Maubourg slowly retired, followed by Lumley. Alten retook the village of Albuera. He was now supported by that part of the Spanish force which at the outset had formed Blake's first line, and had hitherto not been engaged. The Portuguese under Hamilton and Collins —10,000 strong—were brought up to reinforce Cole, but so rapid was that officer's advance, that they never came into action, although they sustained loss from the enemy's artillery fire which covered the retirement of his Infantry with unabated vigour. The superiority of the French in Cavalry, and the exhaustion of the British Infantry, forbade any attempt at pursuit. The battle was virtually over at 1 p.m., although the cannonade at the bridge of Albuera continued for two hours longer. Soult halted among the woods on the further side of the Albuera stream, and Beresford formed a new line with his right, 2,000 yards beyond the ground previously taken up, in occupation of the heights forming the scene of the recent contest, which heights, as Wellington observed, "ought never for a moment to have been in possession of the enemy."

The losses had been terrific. On both sides lay lines of the corpses of men who had fallen in their ranks. Beresford's official return gave 984 officers and men killed, 2,993 wounded, and 570 missing, the greater part of whom shortly reappeared. The Spaniards had lost in addition about 2,000 men. The total loss of the Allied Army may consequently be reckoned at something over 6,000 men, of whom some 3,600 were British. Among the General Officers, Houghton, Collins and Sir W. Myers were killed; Cole and Colborne wounded. In Houghton's Brigade, every Field Officer was *hors de combat*, and command was taken by a Captain who, curiously enough, was a French *émigré*. The 29th

Regiment belonging to this Brigade had hardly 100 officers and men remaining. The 57th lost 400 out of 570 bayonets. In the Fusilier Brigade, the 1st Battalion of the 7th had lost 66 killed and 285 wounded; the 2nd Battalion, 48 killed and 294 wounded. The 23rd had 76 killed and 257 wounded. One company was brought out of action by a corporal. It was found necessary to amalgamate the two battalions of the 7th and the 48th; and so heavy were the losses in Colborne's Brigade that the Buffs, 29th, 31st, 57th, and 66th had to be formed into one provisional battalion. Five weeks after the battle these five regiments could muster only 813 bayonets between them. A howitzer and the colours of the three regiments which in 1809 had formed Hill's Brigade were taken by the enemy.

The loss of the French was ascertained to exceed 7,000. The effect of the fire of the Brigades of Abercrombie and Myers into the flanks of Soult's crowded columns must have been terrific. Five French Generals were killed or wounded: among the former was Werlé; among the latter, Maransin.

The Spanish Commander refused to lend aid to our wounded, and so few of our own men were left to perform the most ordinary duties that those injured had to be left lying where they were for hours, or indeed, days. On the 20th—four days after the action—an eye-witness saw the chapel at Albuera full of the French wounded. Many, with limbs amputated, were lying on the hard stones without even straw.

Thus ended the Battle of Albuera, of which Wellington in a private letter quaintly remarked : " They "—the Allies—" were never determined to fight it; they did not occupy the ground as they ought; they were ready to run away at every moment from the time it commenced till the French retired; and if it had not been for me who am now suffering from the loss and disorganisation occasioned by that battle, they would have written a whining report upon it, which would have driven the people in England mad."

Beresford's errors were glaring. He occupied the ground in such a way "as to render defeat almost certain; his Infantry were not in hand, his inferiority in guns and Cavalry was not compensated by entrenchments. He had superior numbers of Infantry on a position which was contracted to three miles; yet ten thousand never fired a shot, and three times the day was lost and won, the Allies being always fewest in number at the decisive point." "It was the astounding valour of their troops in offence, the astonishing firmness of Houghton * in defence, that saved the day." (Napier, bk. xii. ch. 7.)

The night after the battle passed in terrible gloom. So large a proportion of the British had been wounded that the survivors were unable to remove the injured; and Blake refused to help the men who had shed their blood in such profusion for his worthless self and country! It is no wonder that the British troops had the utmost dislike for their so-called allies.

The feeling, it is only fair to say, was cordially reciprocated. The Spaniards regarded the English and French respectively very much in the way that Liberal Unionists of the present day regard their Conservative allies and Liberal opponents. Circumstances compelled them to act with the English; but they did so unwillingly and in a spirit of arrogant contempt. Their leanings were towards the French, with whom they would gladly have been re-united; and they were lost in self-admiration for

---

* Houghton's merits seem to have been hitherto unappreciated. He was looked on as an indolent man. But when the supreme moment came, he rose to the occasion.

allowing sentiments of patriotism to outweigh their feelings of repulsion towards their present ally.

The night after the battle passed, as already noted, in gloom. Beresford, suffering no doubt from the reaction after the strain and excitement, was in the depths of despair. He wrote to Wellington, anticipating a renewal of the action in the morning, and a defeat which he was determined not to survive.

The Marshal's fears proved happily groundless. Kemmis's Brigade of the 4th Division came up in the morning, and during the 17th the armies remained in their respective positions. At nightfall, however, Soult sent away his wounded and retreated early on the 18th by Los Santos to Llerena. At daybreak on the 19th Hamilton's Portuguese Division resumed the investment of Badajoz on the left bank of the Guadiana. Wellington arrived in person on the same day. The 3rd and 7th Divisions came up on the 25th and completed the investment on the right bank.

At Wellington's instance, Beresford took up a position at Almendralejos; but the pressing needs of the Portuguese Army urgently required his presence at Lisbon, for out of 40,000 regular troops whom he had organised, more than half had deserted or died of hunger; and General Hill, who happily returned from England at the opportune moment, relieved Beresford and resumed his old command.

www.ingramcontent.com/pod-product-compliance
Lightning Source LLC
Chambersburg PA
CBHW061924220426
43662CB00012B/1800